Learning
Dreamweaver CS4

Ramesh Bangia
B.Sc., Dip. Comp. Sc.
Formerly: Managing Editor, Software Today
Formerly: Incharge Computer Centre, Hindustan Copper Ltd., New Delhi

KHANNA BOOK PUBLISHING CO. PVT. LTD.

Learning Dreamweaver CS 4 — Ramesh Bangia

Published by
Khanna Book Publishing Co. (P) Ltd.

Regd. Office:
1694-95 Nai Sarak, 1st Floor
Delhi - 110 006 (India)
Tel. 011-23283211, 23256658
Telefax: 011-23256658
Website: www.khannaedu.com
E-mail: contact@khannaedu.com

ISBN 978-93-80016-38-2

First Edition 2010

Printed in India by Seth Printers, Noida (U.P.)

Preface

Learning of a software is both easy and difficult. It depends upto what level you are planning to learn. If you are learning only for the working use, then it is very easy. But, when you try to go deep into it, then you realise how difficult it is to master it.

Dreamweaver CS 4 is such a vast subject that it will take a lot of time to understand it fully. This book has been written in mind to make you aware of the options available in the software and how they can be used. It is like telling the child about the steps and stairs. You are the one who is to climb the stair. This book will just guide you how to use the stairs.

I am indeed debited to my publishers Khanna Book Publishing Co. Pvt. Ltd., for their suggestions and encouragement given in producing this book.

I would like to thank my family specially my wife Sadhna, kids Mayank and Samarth, for without their criticism this book would not have seen the day.

Suggestions for improvement of the book are indeed welcome.

Ramesh Bangia

Contents

1 Introduction to Dreamweaver CS4

Introduction

Dreamweaver is a HTML tool which not only helps you create Web sites but also allows you to author and edit HTML files. You can in fact use it for creating multimedia applications too.

If you are not new to Dreamweaver and have worked with the earlier versions. I give here the new features of the latest version CS4 of the software.

What's new in Dreamweaver CS4

Dreamweaver CS4 includes various new features that improve usability and help you to build pages whether you're working in the design or the coding environment. Dreamweaver CS4 provides support for best practices and industry standards, including support for advanced CSS use, XML and RSS feeds, and accessibility requirements.

Following is a list of top new features for Adobe® Dreamweaver® CS4.

Live view

Dreamweaver CS4 lets you design your web pages under real-world browser conditions with new Live view, while still retaining direct access to the code. Changes to the code are immediately reflected in the rendered display.

Code hinting for Ajax and JavaScript frameworks

You can now write JavaScript more quickly and accurately with improved support for JavaScript core objects and primitive data types. You can also put the extended coding functionality of Dreamweaver to work by incorporating popular JavaScript frameworks including jQuery, Prototype, and Adobe Spry.

Related Files and Code Navigator

Dreamweaver CS4 lets you efficiently manage the various files that make up today's web pages. Click any related file to see both its source in Code view and the parent page in Design view. The new Code Navigator feature shows you all the code sources that affect your current selection, such as CSS (Cascading Style Sheets) rules, server-side includes, external JavaScript functions, Dreamweaver templates, iFrame source files, and more.

InContext Editing

You can enable end users to make simple edits to their web pages without help from you or additional software. As a Dreamweaver designer, you can limit changes to specific pages, distinct regions, and even custom formatting options quickly and easily.

CSS best practices

The Dreamweaver CS4 Property inspector lets you create new CSS rules, and provides clear, simple explanations of where each property fits in the cascade of styles.

HTML data sets

You can integrate the power of dynamic data in your web pages without the learning curve of mastering databases or XML (Extensible Markup Language) coding. Spry Data Sets recognize content in a simple HTML table as an interactive data source.

Adobe Photoshop Smart Objects

Insert any Adobe® Photoshop PSD (Photoshop Data File) document in Dreamweaver to create an image Smart Object. Smart Objects are tightly linked to the source file. Make any changes to the source image and update your image in Dreamweaver without opening Photoshop.

Subversion integration

Dreamweaver CS4 integrates Subversion® software, an open source versioning control system, for a more robust check-in/check-out experience. Update your site and check in modifications directly from within Dreamweaver.

New user interface

Work faster and smarter across Adobe Creative Suite® 4 components with a shared user interface design. Toggle quickly from one work environment to another with the workspace switcher.

Deprecated features

The following features have been deprecated for Dreamweaver CS4:

- Timelines
- Web services
- Layout mode
- Site Map view
- Java Bean support
- Adobe® Flash elements (Image Viewer)
- Adobe® Flash text and Adobe® Flash buttons
- ASP.NET and JSP server behaviors and recordsets

Let us now start working with the software. But, before that we must start it.

Starting Dreamweaver

As you would do with any other Windows based software, you start Dreamweaver, from the Start button. Since Dreamweaver is part of Adobe family, you will get it under the name of Adobe Dreamweaver CS4, as shown next.

On starting you will get a blank slate of the software, which is shown on the next page. Various items of the screen are marked.

These are explained here.

Insert bar	It is a floating panel. It contains buttons for inserting Web page elements, such as images, tables, forms, and hyperlinks.
Document window	It is the main area of working.
Document toolbar	The main toolbar of the page.
Panel group	Various panels can be displayed here for working.
Status bar	It shows the status of the page.
Property inspector	Various properties of the page are shown here.

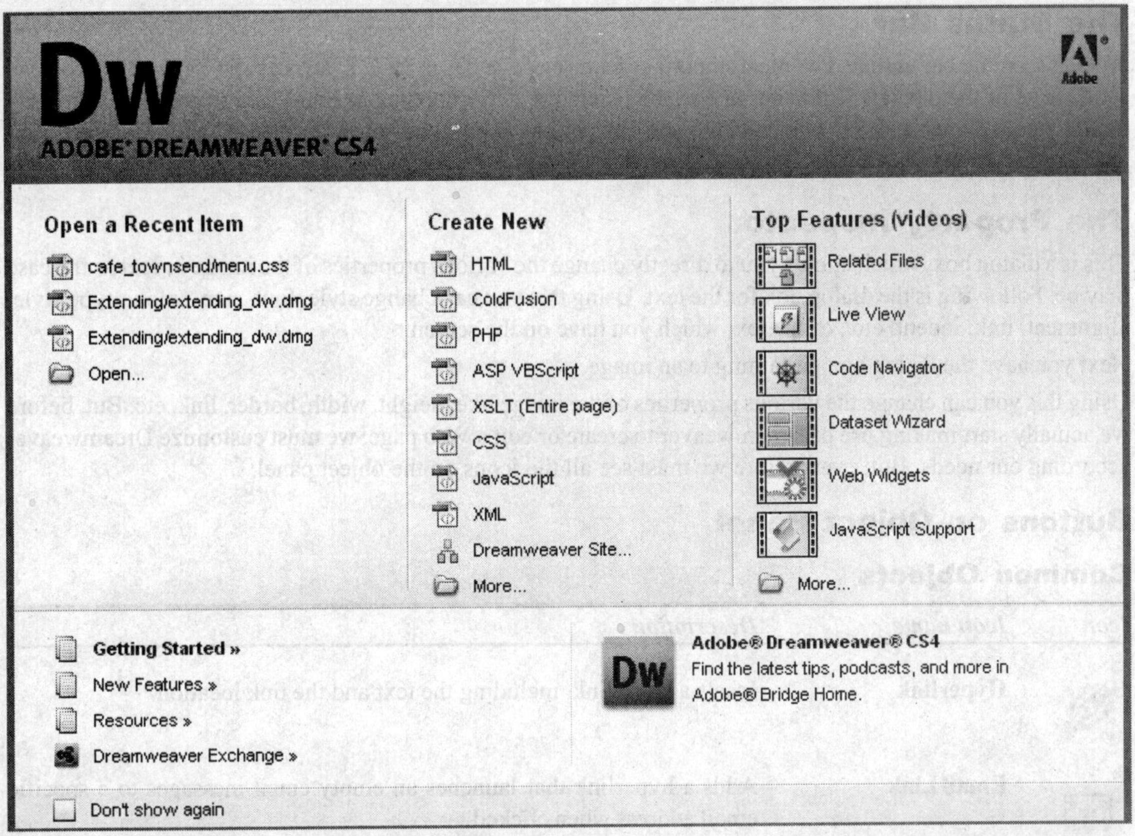
Dw
ADOBE® DREAMWEAVER® CS4
Adobe
Open a Recent Item
cafe_townsend/menu.css
Extending/extending_dw.dmg
Extending/extending_dw.dmg
Open...
Create New
HTML
ColdFusion
PHP
ASP VBScript
XSLT (Entire page)
CSS
JavaScript
XML
Dreamweaver Site...
More...
Top Features (videos)
Related Files
Live View
Code Navigator
Dataset Wizard
Web Widgets
JavaScript Support
More...
Getting Started »
New Features »
Resources »
Dreamweaver Exchange »
Adobe® Dreamweaver® CS4
Find the latest tips, podcasts, and more in
Adobe® Bridge Home.
Don't show again

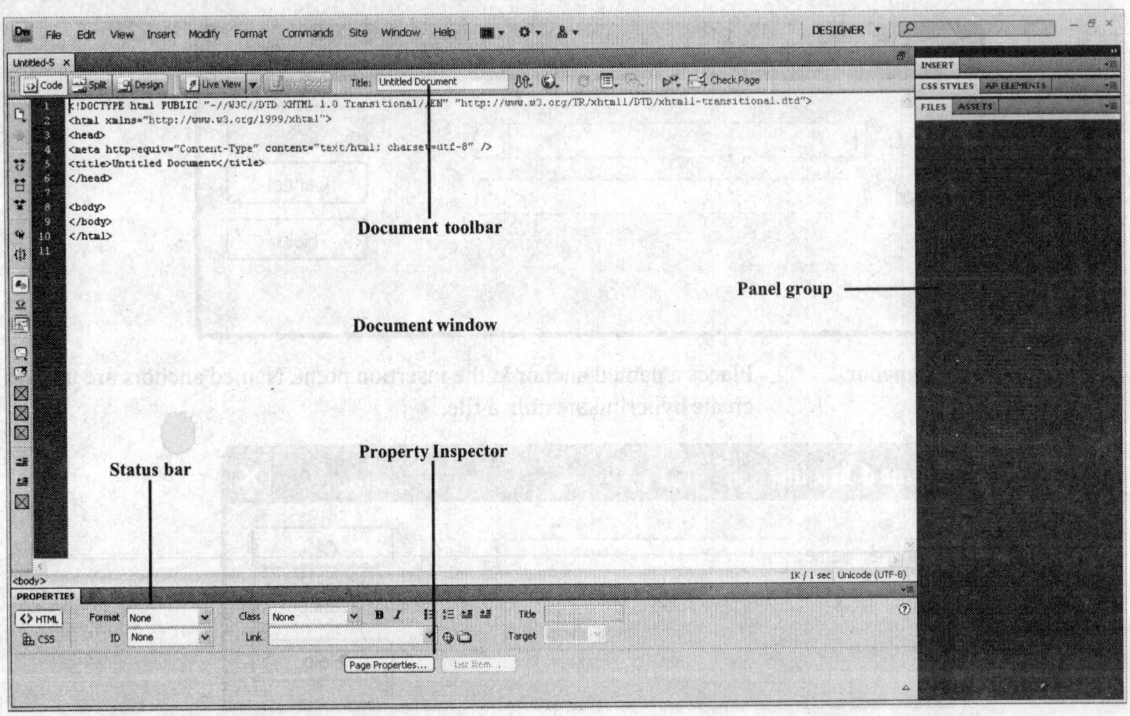
File Edit View Insert Modify Format Commands Site Window Help
DESIGNER
Code Split Design Live View
Title: Untitled Document
Check Page
INSERT
CSS STYLES AP ELEMENTS
FILES ASSETS
Document toolbar
Panel group
Document window
Property Inspector
Status bar
PROPERTIES
HTML
CSS
Format None
ID None
Class None
Link
Title
Target
Page Properties...
List Item...
1K / 1 sec Unicode (UTF-8)

The Status Bar

We had seen the bar earlier. The most important feature of the bar is the display size. Before stating you can set the size of the display. If it is not one of the listed one, you can click at Edit Sizes to go to the edit sizes dialog box and choose the one needed by you. This dialog box is shown on the next page.

The next items shows the down load statistics.

The Property Inspector

This is a dialog box, which allows you to directly change the various properties of the image or text as the case may be. Following is the dialog box for the text. Using this you can change style, font, size, colour, type style, alignment, link, indent, etc., of the text which you have on the screen.

Next you have the dialog box pertaining to an image.

Using this you can change the various properties of the image like, height, width, border, link, etc. But, before we actually start making use of Dreamweaver to create or edit a Web page, we must customize Dreamweaver according our needs. But, even before we must see all the icons on the object panel.

Buttons on Object Panel

Common Objects

Icon	*Icon name*	*Description*
	**Hyperlink**	Insets a hyperlink, including the text and the link location.
	**Email Link**	Adds a hyperlink that launches an empty email messages to a specific email address when clicked.

Icon	*Icon name*	*Description*
	**Named Anchor**	Places a named anchor at the insertion point. Named anchors are used to create hyperlinks within a file.

Horizontal Rule Creates a horizontal rule at the insertion point.

Table Creates a table at the insertion point.

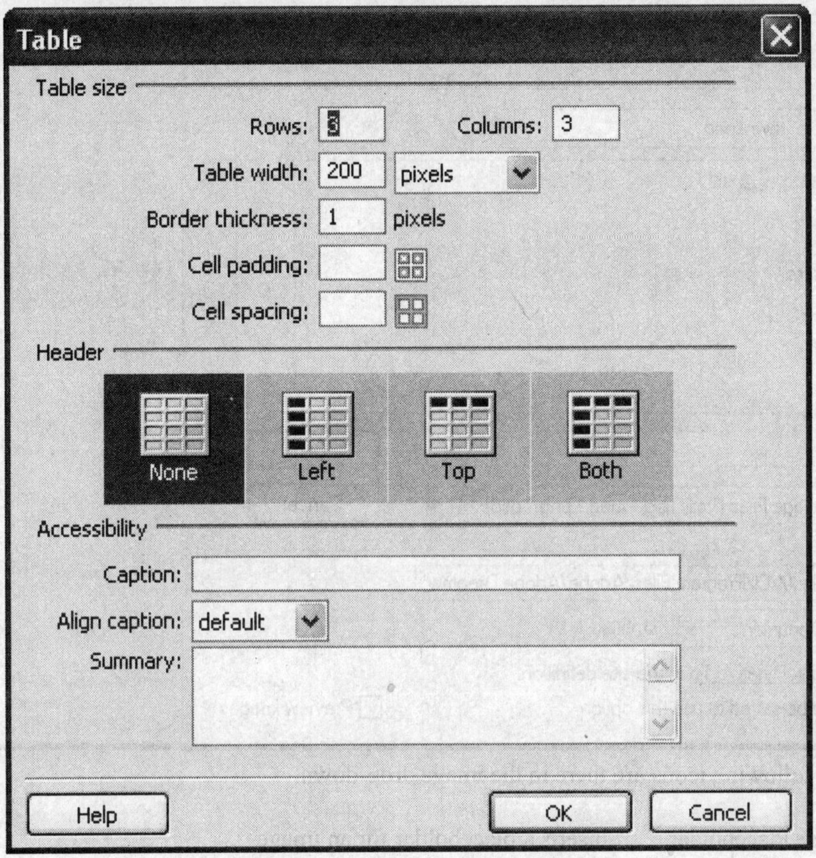

Insert Div tag You can use div tags to create CSS layout blocks and position them in your document. This is especially useful if you have an existing CSS style sheet with positioning styles attached to your document. Dreamweaver enables you to quickly insert a div tag and apply existing styles to it.

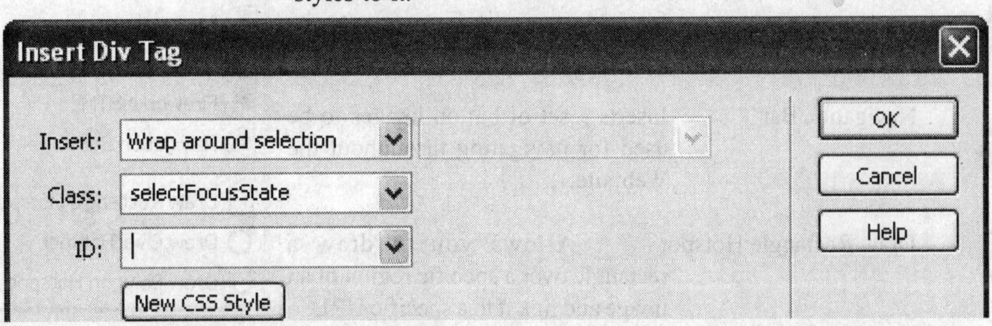

Images Places an image at the insetion point.

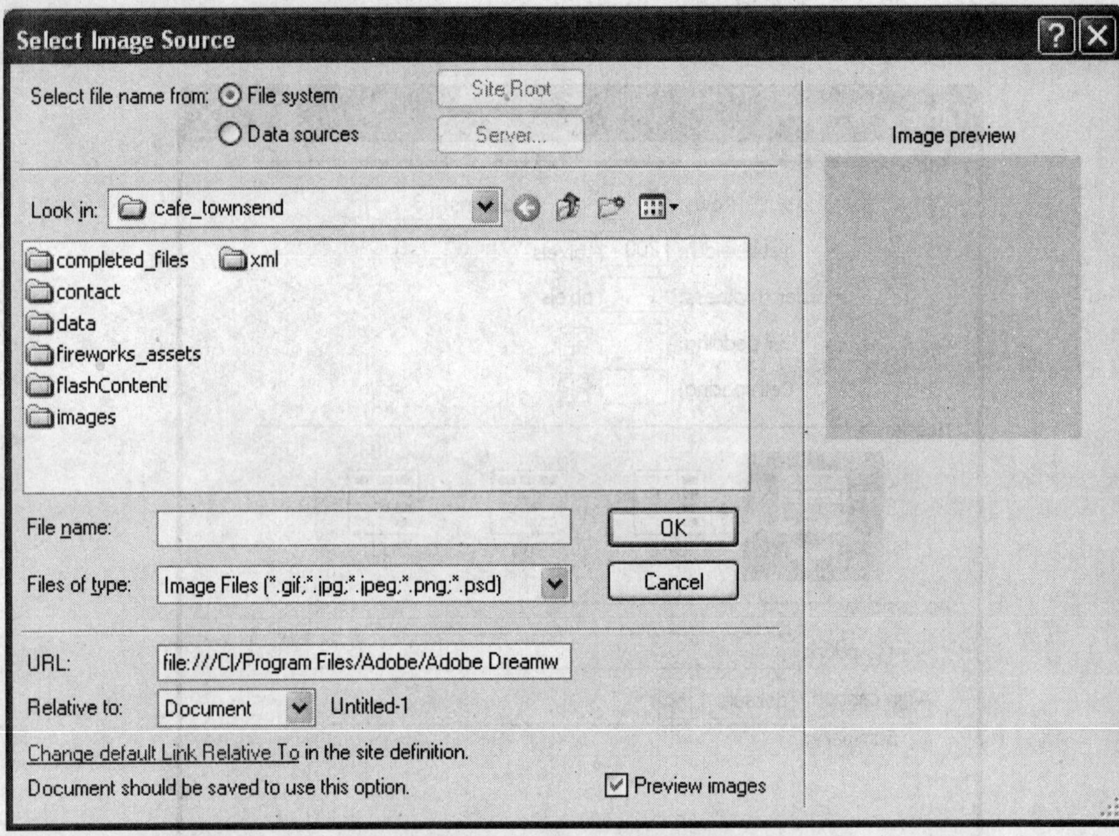

The following icons are there in the image drop-down.

- Image Placeholder — Inserts a placeholder for an image.

- Rollover Image — Prompts you for two images: the regular image and the image that appears when the user puts his or her cursor over the image.

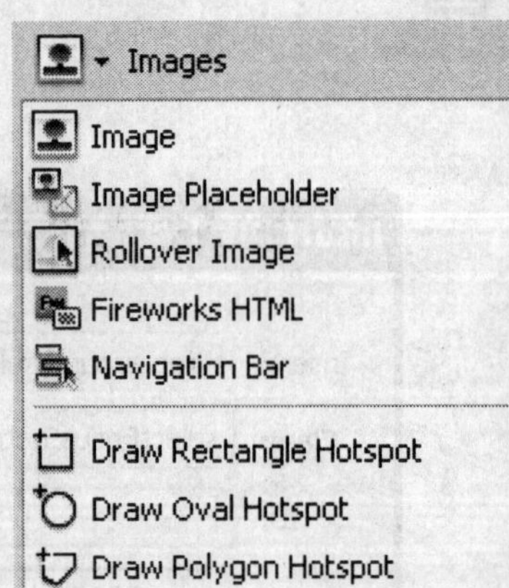

Fireworks HTML — Places HTML that has been exported from Macromedia Fireworks at the insetion point.

Navigation Bar — Inserts a set of button images to be used for navigating throughout the Web site.

Draw Rectangle Hotspot — Allows you to draw a rectangle over a specific region of an image and link it to a specific URL.

Draw Oval Hotspot	Allows you to draw a circle over a specific region of an image and link it to a specific URL.
Draw Polygon Hotspot	Allows you to draw a polygon over a specific region of an image and link it to a specific URL.

Media

It has the following options

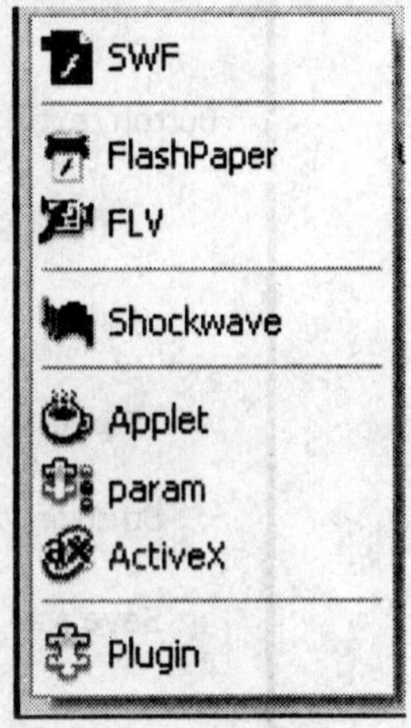

SWF	Places a flash movie at the insertion point.
Flash Paper	Places one of the available prefabricated Macromedia Paper at the insertion point.
FLV	Places an editable Flash video at the insertion point and creates a Flash file.
Shockwave	Places a Shockwave movie (a Macromedia Director movie prepared for the Web) at the insertion point.
Applet	Places a Java applet at the insertion point.
Param	Inserts a tag that enables you to enter parameters and their values to pass to an applet or an ActiveX control.
ActiveX	Places an ActiveX control at the insertion point.
Plugin	Places any file requiring a browser plug-in at the insertion point.
Date	Inserts the current date at the insetion point.
Server-side Include	A server-side include is a file that the server incorporates into your document when a browser requests your document from the server.
Comment	Inserts a comment at the insertion point.

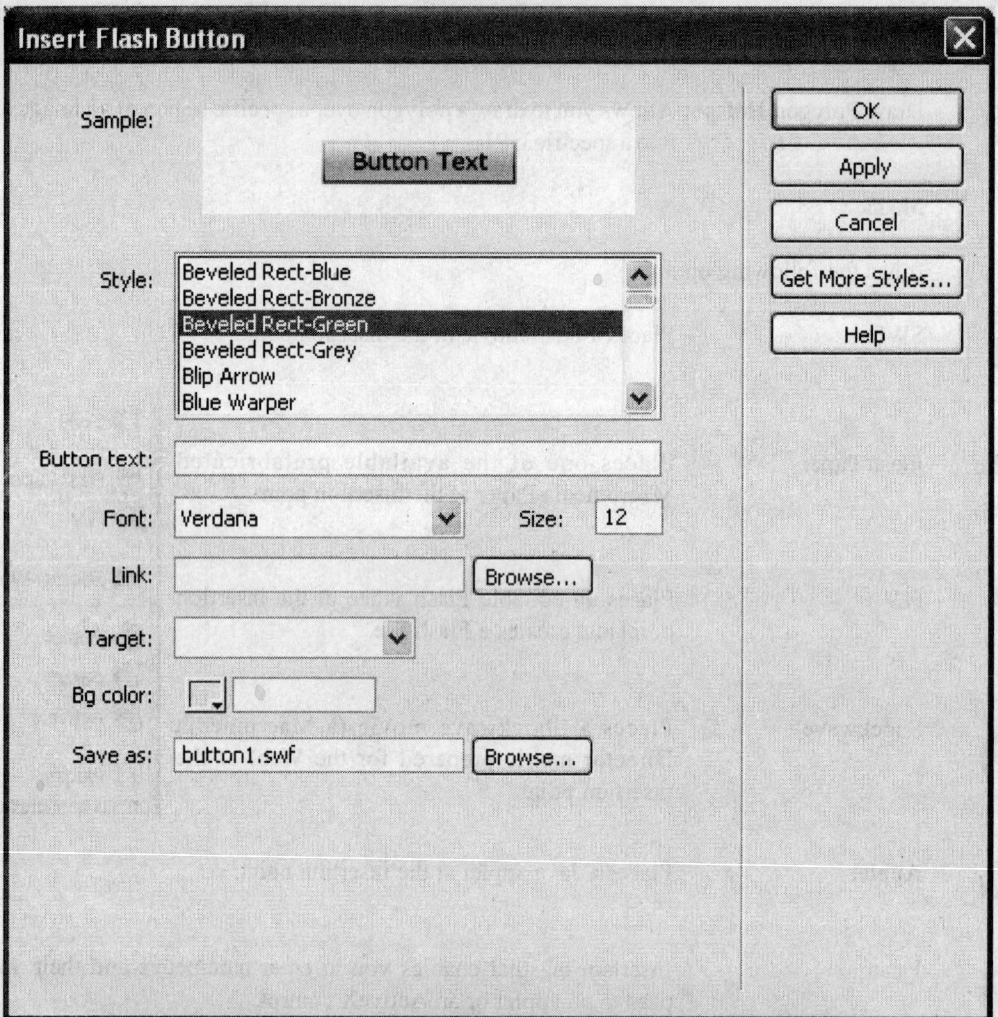
Insert Flash Button
Sample:
Button Text
Style:
Beveled Rect-Blue
Beveled Rect-Bronze
Beveled Rect-Green
Beveled Rect-Grey
Blip Arrow
Blue Warper
Button text:
Font:
Verdana
Size:
12
Link:
Browse...
Target:
Bg color:
Save as:
button1.swf
Browse...
OK
Apply
Cancel
Get More Styles...
Help

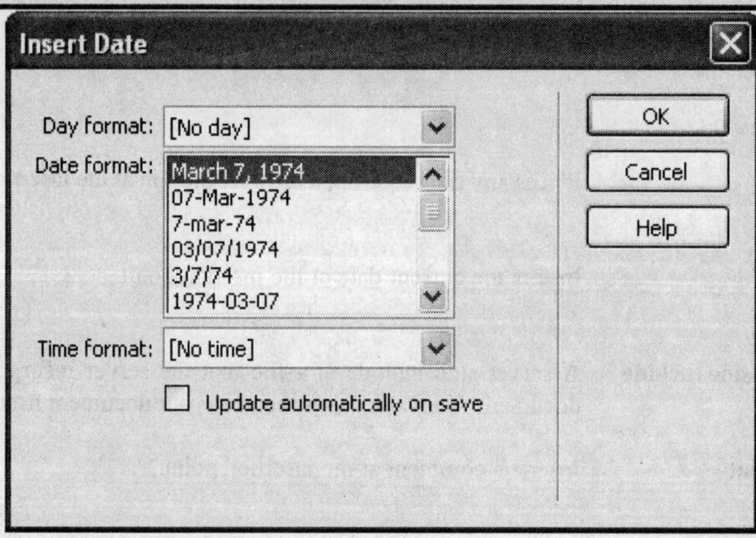
Insert Date
Day format:
[No day]
Date format:
March 7, 1974
07-Mar-1974
7-mar-74
03/07/1974
3/7/74
1974-03-07
Time format:
[No time]
Update automatically on save
OK
Cancel
Help

Head

It has the following options.

Meta — Creates a Meta tag on Dreamweaver page.

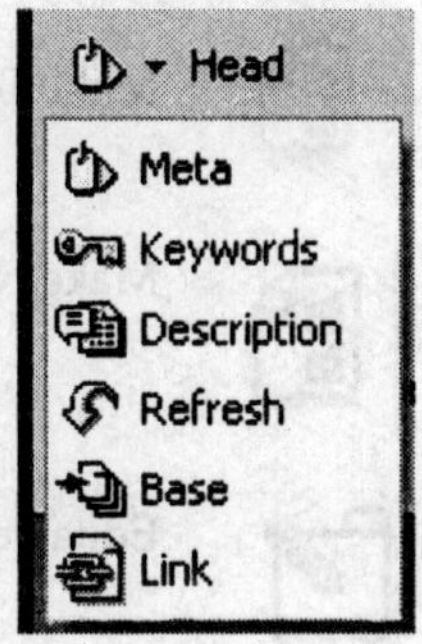

Keywords — Allows you to insert keywords from the other languages.

Description — Allows you to insert description.

Refresh — This will refresh the Dreamweaver page.

Base — Sets the base element.

Link — **Adds a editable optional region to a template.**

Script

It has the following options.

Script — Allows you to add Script.

No Script — Allows you to add tag from noscript.

Templates

It has the following options.

Make Template — Creates a Dreamweaver template from the current Web page.

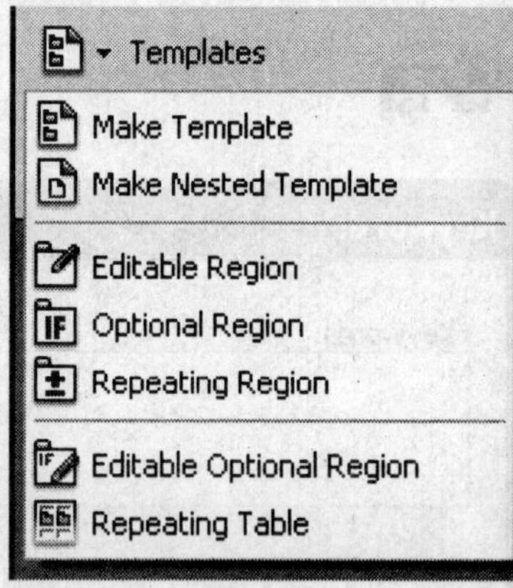

Make Nested Template — Creates a nested Dreamweaver template from the current template.

Editable Region — Adds an editable region to a template.

Optional Region — Adds an optional region to a template; this region can be set to enter show or hide.

Repeating Region — Adds a repeating region to a template.

Editable Optional Resion — Adds a editable optional region to a template.

Repeating Table — Adds a repeating table to a template and defines which cells can be edited.

Tag Chooser — Enables you to choose a tag to insert from a hierarchical menu of all available tags.

Layout Category

Standard Mode — Turns on Dreamweaver's Standard mode, at the same time turning off either Expanded Tables mode or Layout mode.

Expanded Tables Mode — Turns on Dreamweaver's Expanded Tables mode, temporarily adding cell padding and borders to all tables.

Insert Div Tag — Adda a <div> tag, the tag that Dreamweaver uses to create layers.

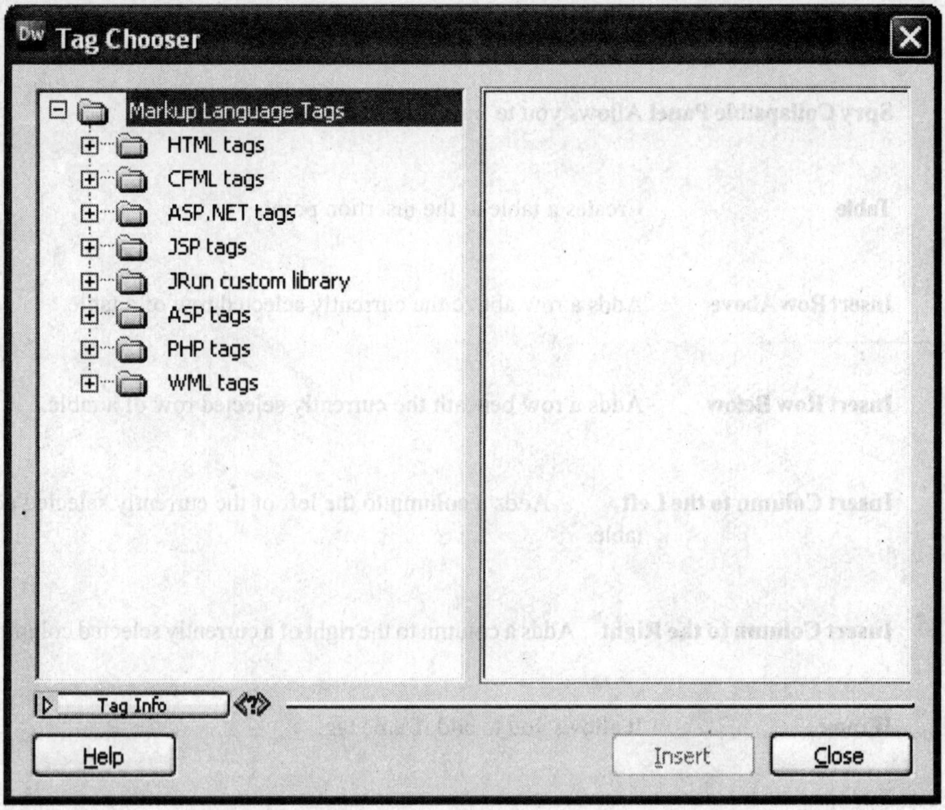

Draw AP Div Add an AP Div element tag.

Spry Menu Bar Allows you to insert spry menu bar.

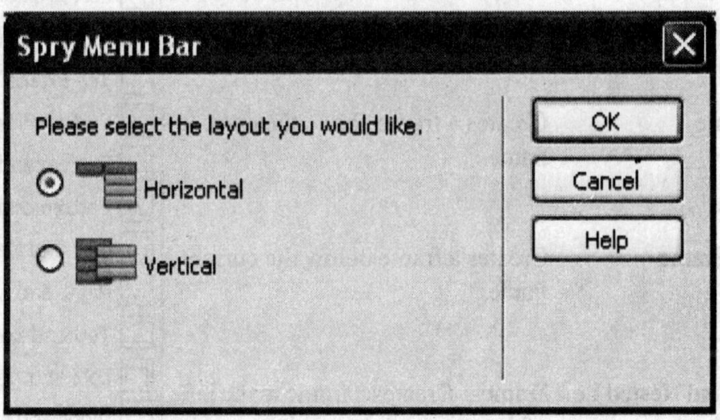

Spry Tabbed Panels Allows you to insert spry tabbed panels.

Spry Accordin Allows you to insert spry accordin.

Spry Collapsible Panel Allows you to insert spry collapsible panel .

Table Creates a table at the insertion point.

Insert Row Above Adds a row above the currently selected row of a table.

Insert Row Below Adds a row beneath the currently selected row of a table.

Insert Column to the Left Adds a column to the left of the currently selected column in a table.

Insert Column to the Right Adds a column to the right of a currently selected column in a table.

IFrame It allows you to add iframe tag.

Frame It has various options as shown next.

Left Frame Creates a frame to the left of the current frame.

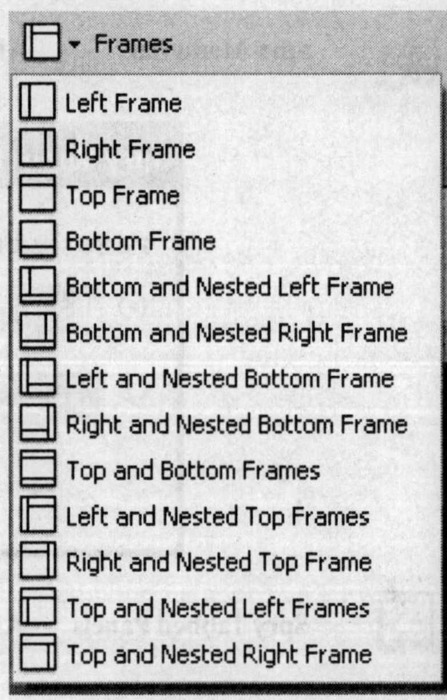

Right Frame Creates a frame to the right of the current fame.

Top Frame Creates a frame above the current frame.

Bottom Frame Creates a frame below the current frame.

Bottom and Nested Left Frame Creates a frame to the left of the current frame and then adds a frame below.

Bottom and Nested Right Frame   Creates a frame to the right of the current frame and then adds a frame below.

Left and Nested Bottom Frame   Creates a frame below the current frame and then adds a frame to the left.

Right and Nested Bottom Frame   Creates a frame below the current frame and then adds a frame to the right.

Top and Bottom Frames   Creates a frame below the current frame and then adds a frame above.

Left and Nested Top Frame   Creates a frame above the current frame and then adds a frame to the left.

Right and Nested Top Frame   Creates a frame above the current frame and then adds a frame to the right.

Top and Nested Left Frame   Creates a frame to the left of the current frame and then adds a frame above.

Top and Nested Right Frame   Creates a frame to the right of the current frame and then adds a frame above.

Forms Category

Form   Places a form at the insertion point.

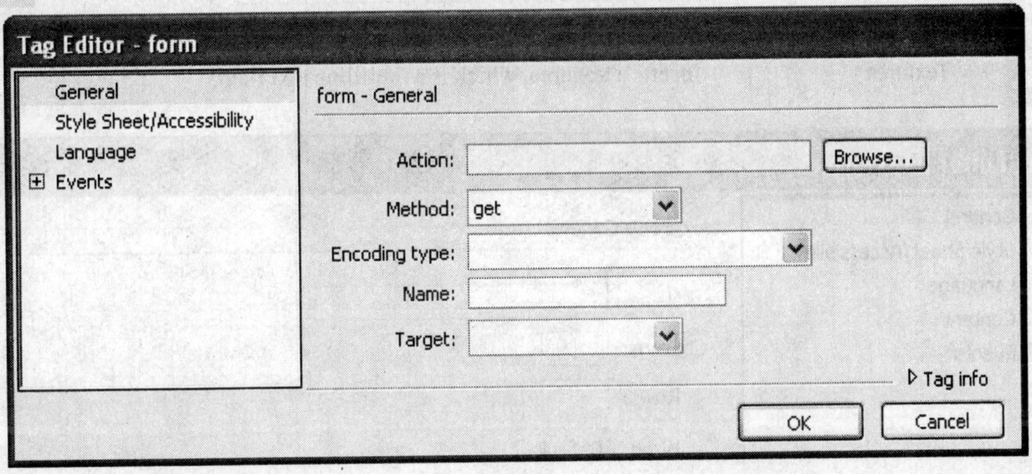

Text Field Inserts a text field into a form.

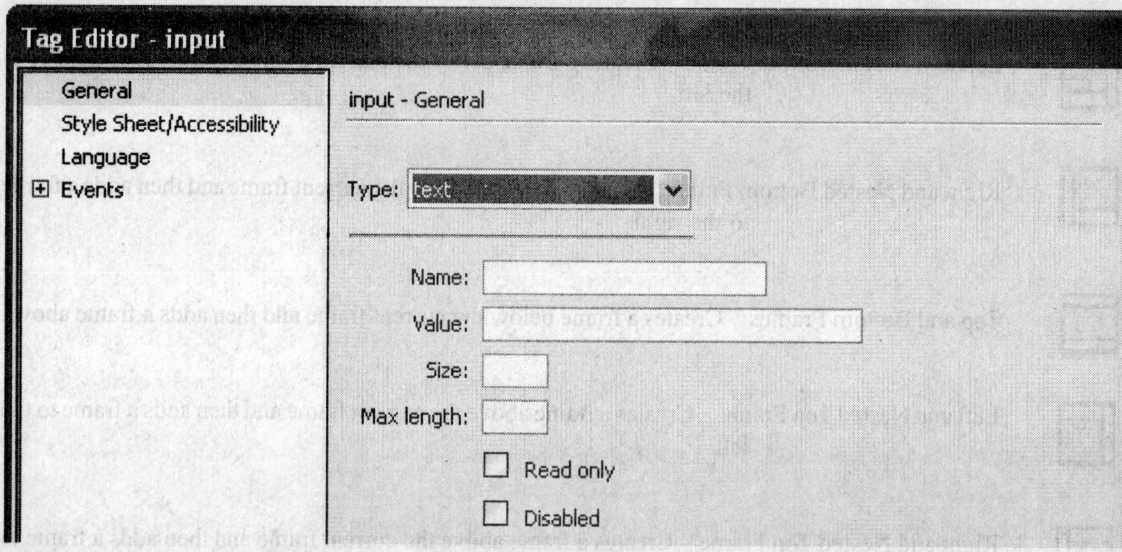

Hidden Field Inserts a hidden field

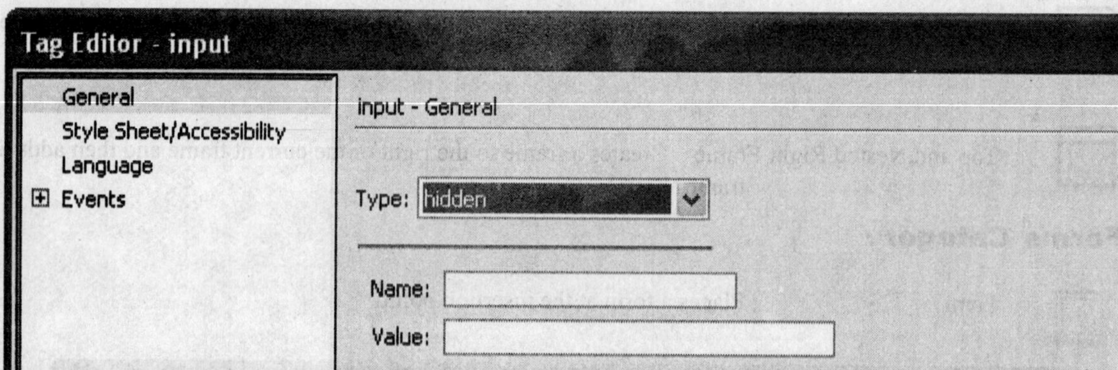

Textarea Inserts a textarea, which is a multiline text field.

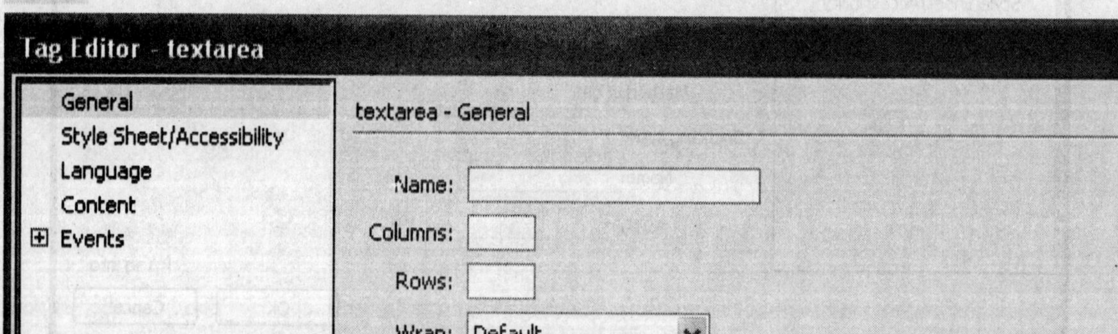

Check Box — Inserts a check box.

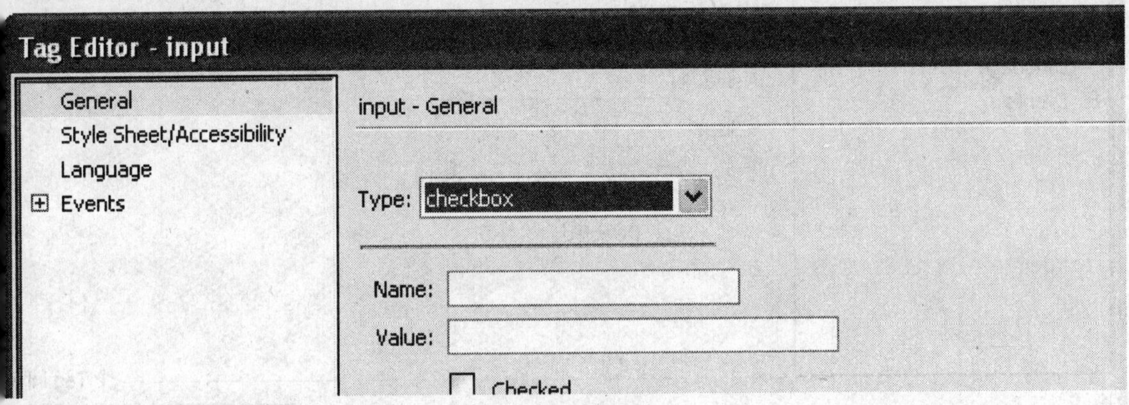

Radio Button — Inserts a radio button into a form.

Radio Group — Inserts a group of related radio buttons.

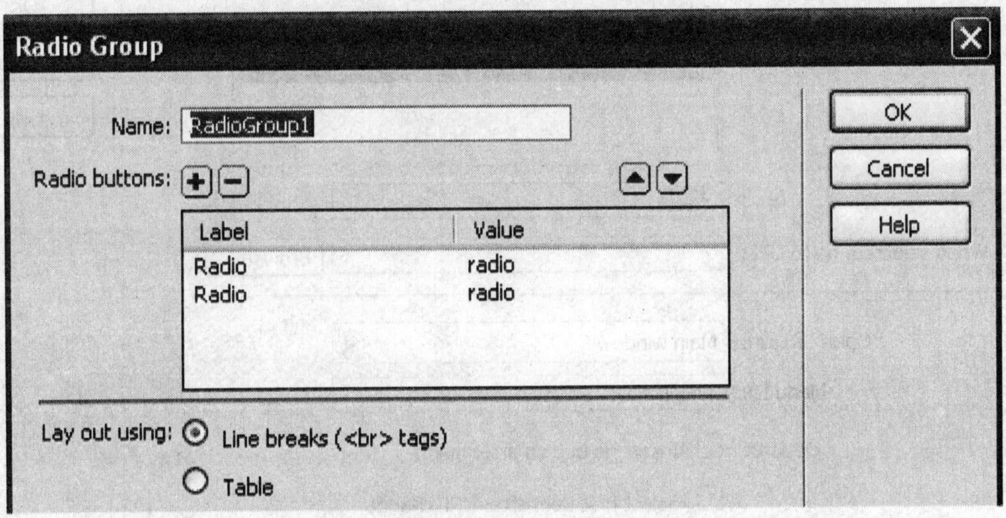

List/Menu — Inserts a list or a drop-down menu into a form.

Jump Menu — Creates a jump menu that allows users to select a Web site from a menu and go to that site.

Image Field — Inserts an image field, enabling an image to act as a button, into a form.

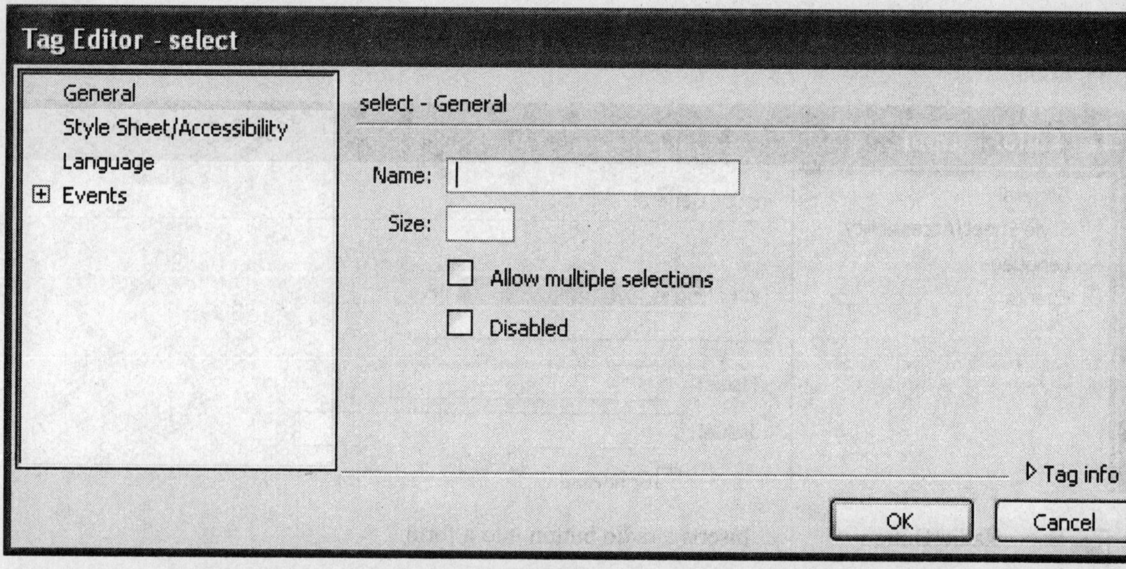

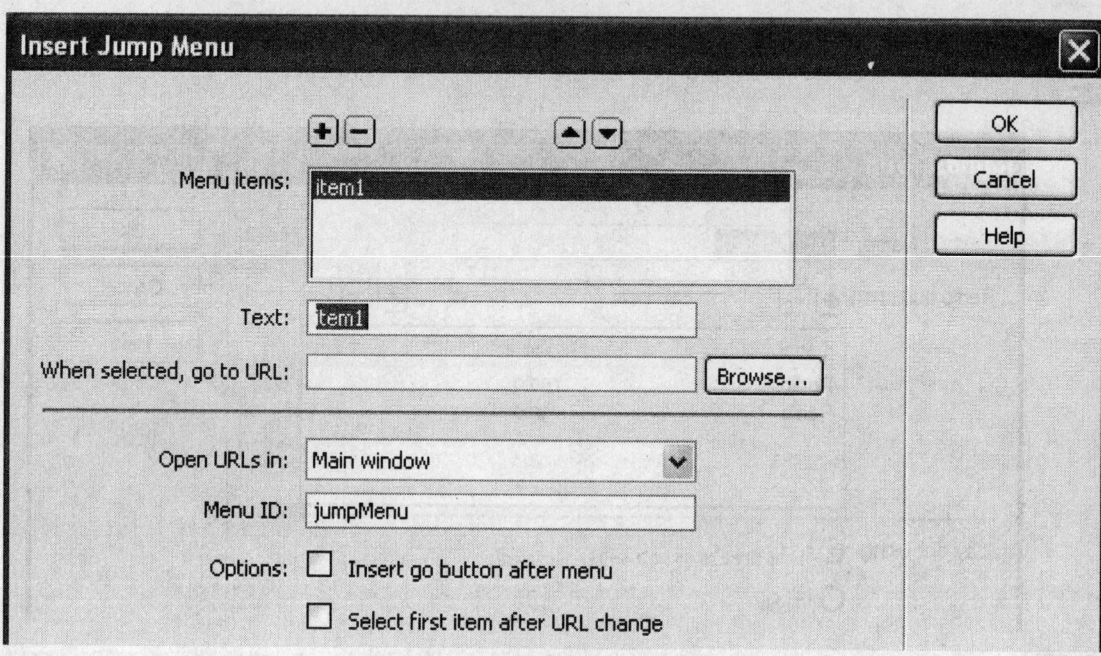

	File Field	Inserts a file field, enabling the user to upload a file, into a form.
	Button	Inserts a button, into a form.
	Label	Assigns a label to a form element, enabling browsers for people with visual impairments to access extra information about the form elements nested within the label.

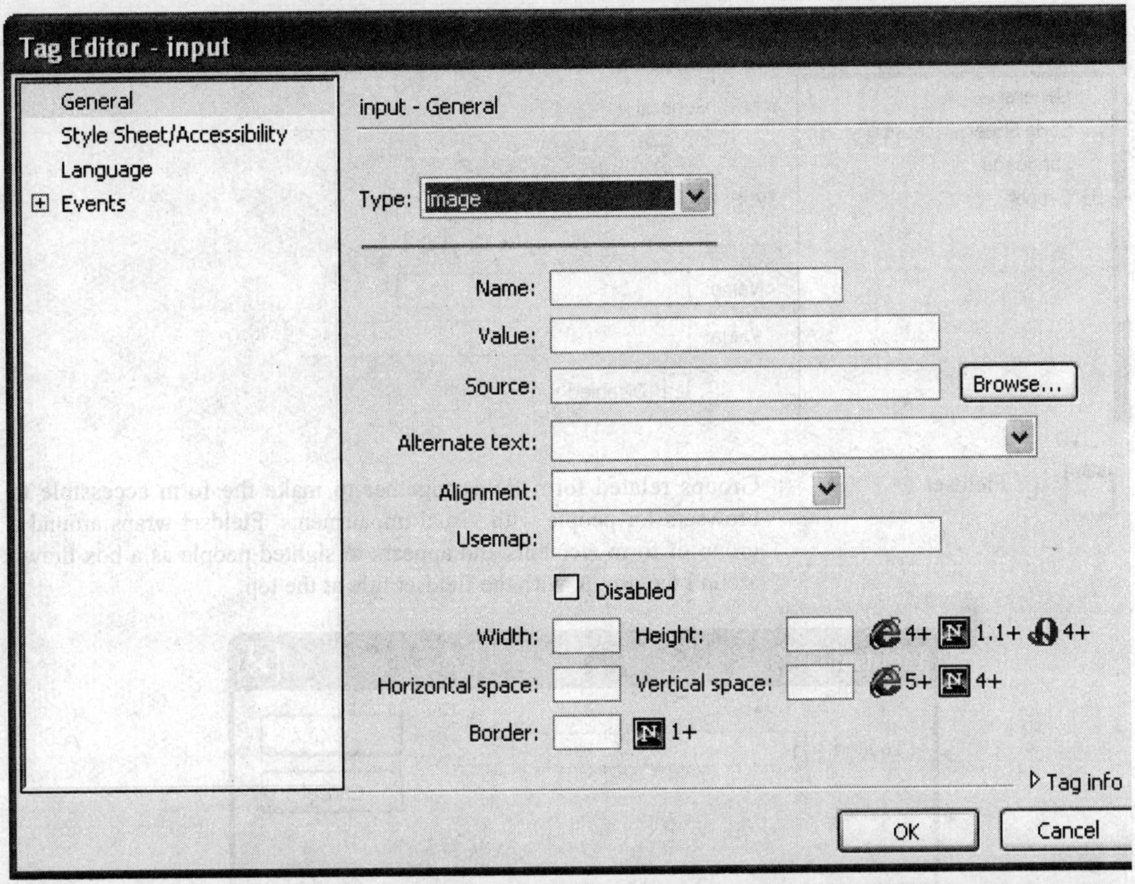
Tag Editor - input
General
Style Sheet/Accessibility
Language
Events
input - General
Type: image
Name:
Value:
Source:
Browse...
Alternate text:
Alignment:
Usemap:
Disabled
Width:
Height:
4+
1.1+
4+
Horizontal space:
Vertical space:
5+
4+
Border:
1+
Tag info
OK
Cancel

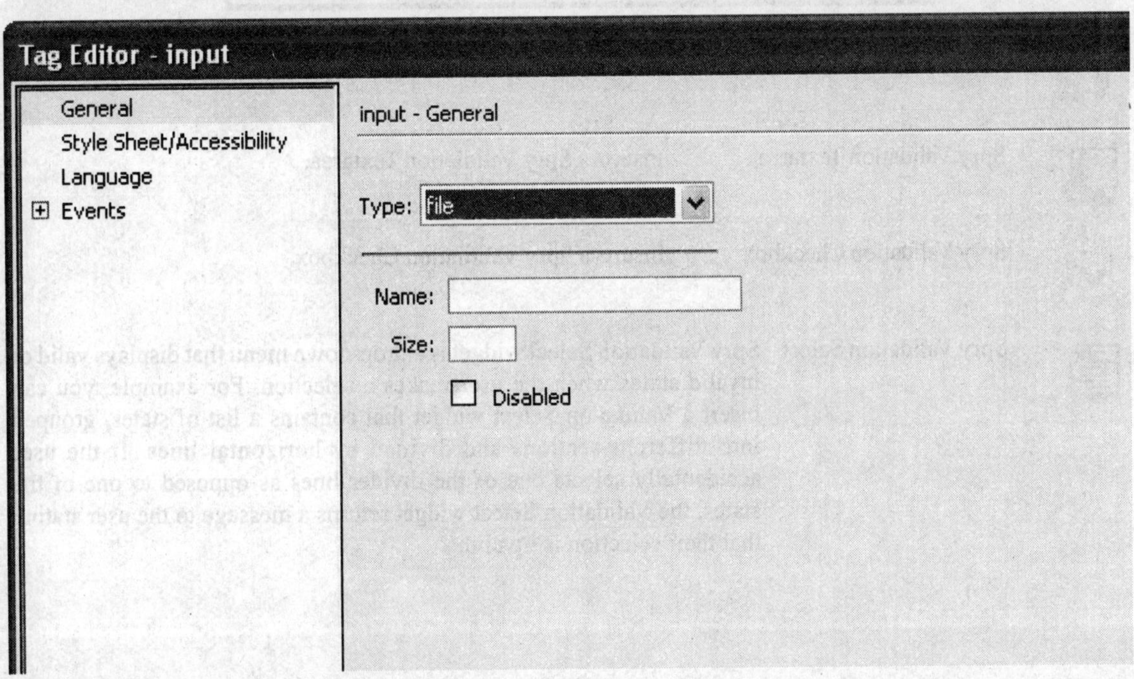
Tag Editor - input
General
Style Sheet/Accessibility
Language
Events
input - General
Type: file
Name:
Size:
Disabled

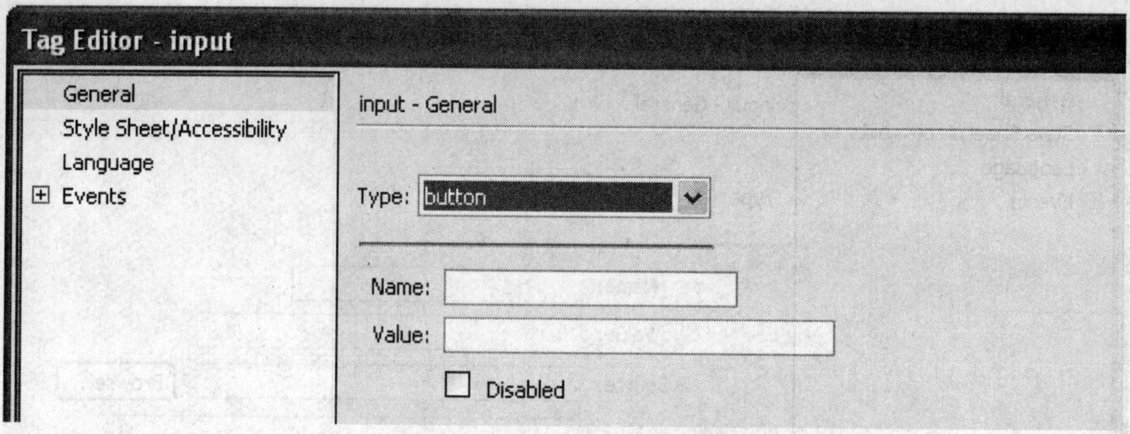

Fieldset — Groups related form fields together to make the form accessible to browsers for people with visual impairments. Fieldset wraps around a group of form elements and appears to sighted people as a box drawn around the group, with the fieldset title at the top.

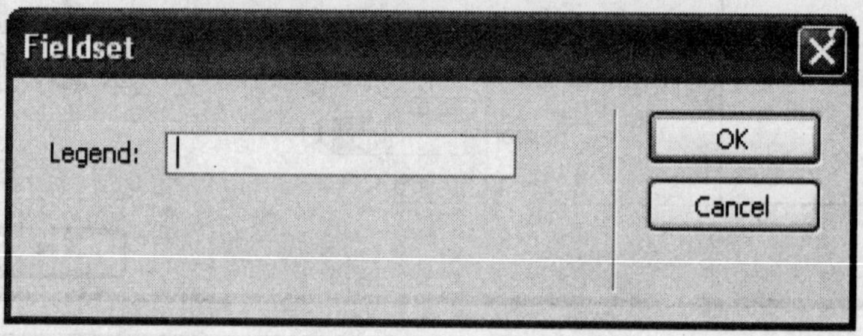

Spry Validation Text Field — Inserts a Spry Validiation Text Field.

Spry Validation Textarea — Inserts a Spry Validiation Textarea.

Spry Validation Checkbox — Inserts a Spry Validiation Checkbox.

Spry Validation Select — Spry Validation Select widget is a drop-down menu that displays valid or invalid states when the user makes a selection. For example, you can insert a Validation Select widget that contains a list of states, grouped into different sections and divided by horizontal lines. If the user accidentally selects one of the divider lines as opposed to one of the states, the Validation Select widget returns a message to the user stating that their selection is invalid.

Data Category

Import Tabular Data	You can import and format tabular data and import text from Microsoft Word HTML documents.

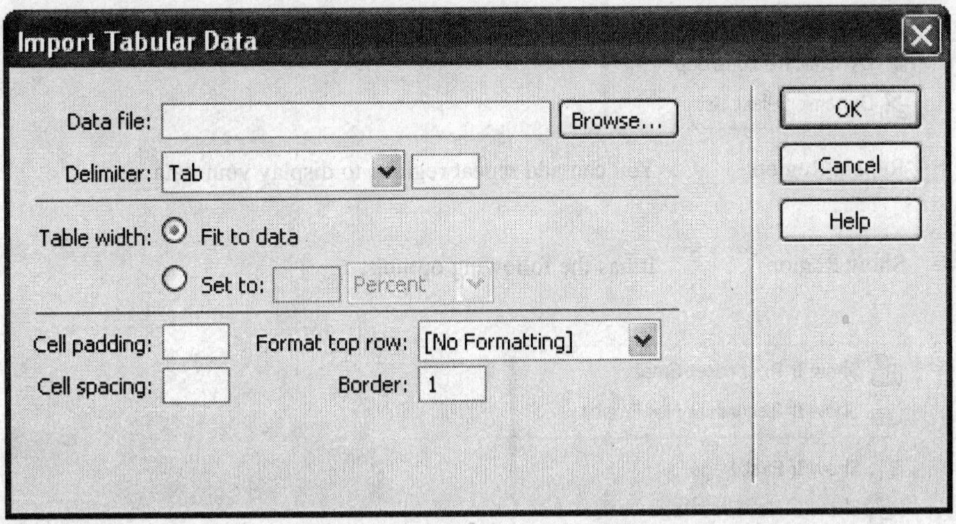

Spry XML Data Set	With the Spry framework, you can insert data objects to allow users to interact with a page quickly and dynamically from a browser window.
Spry Region	With this you can add a Spry Region.
Spry Repeat	You can repeat the spry data.
Spry Repeat List	You can insert the spry repeat list.
Spry Table	You can insert the spry table.
Recordset	You can start a recordset from here.
Stored Procedure	Recall a stored procedure.
Dynamic Data	Inserts dynamic data, a list of which is shown next.

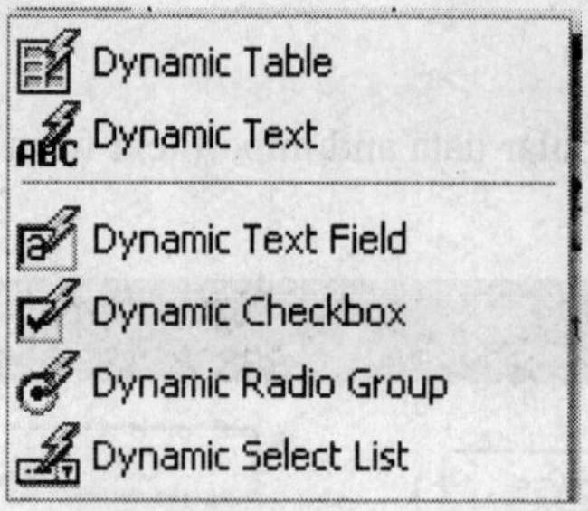

 Repeat Region — You can add repeat regions to display your data.

 Show Region — It has the following options.

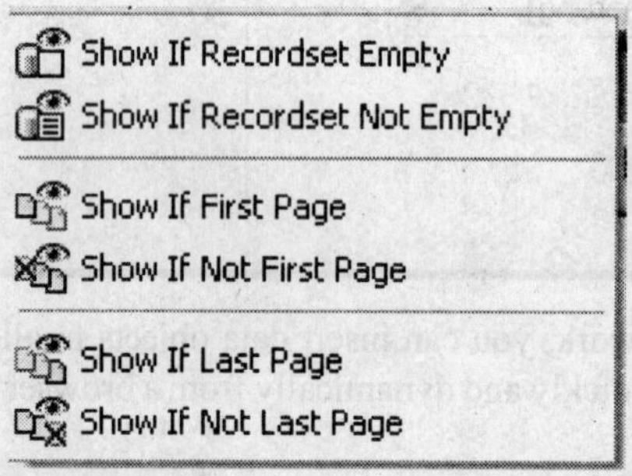

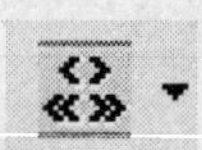 Recordset Paging — Record the set from one page to another. It has the following options.

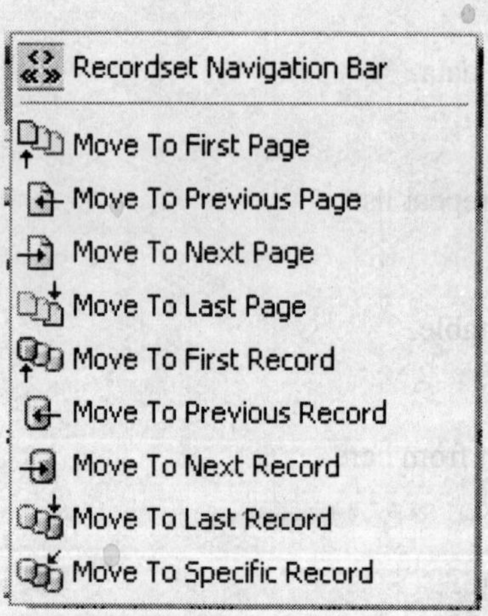

 Go To Detail Page — You are transferred to the detail page. It has the following options too.

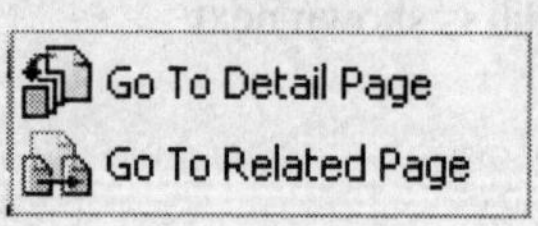

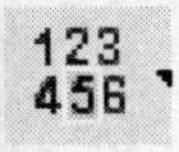

Display Record Count Displays the record count. It has the following options too.

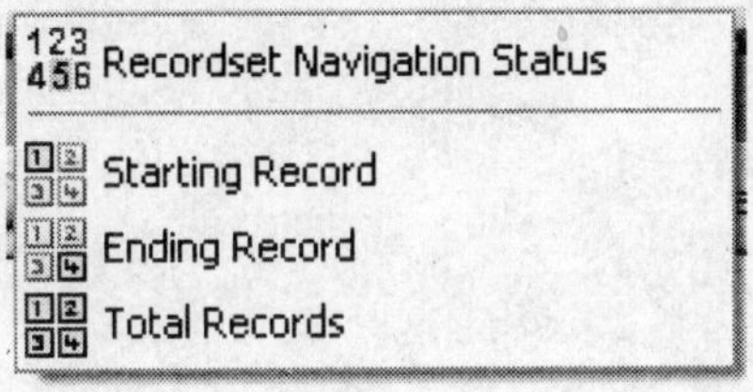

Master Detail Page Set Shows the details of the masster page.

Insert Record Inserts a new record. It has the following options too.

Update Record Updates the existing record.

Delete Record Deletes an existing record.

User Authentication Shows the users details with the following options.

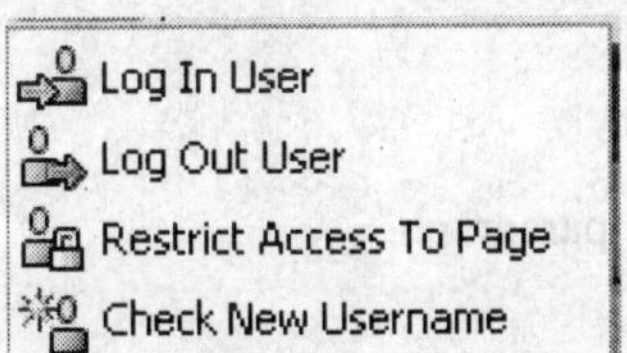

XSL Transformation Inserts an XSL Transformation.

Spry Category

This list if not explained here since all of these appear in the various categories.

Spry XML Data Set

Spry Region

Spry Repeat

Spry Repeat List
Spry Table
Spry Validation Text Field
Spry Validation Select
Spry Validation Checkbox
Spry Validation Textarea
Spry Menubar
Spry Tabbed Panels
Spry Accordion
Spry Collapsible Panels

Text Category

Name	Description
Bold	Makes the selected text bold by using the b tag. This tag has been dropped from recent versions of HTML. The approved tag for bold text is the strong tag.
Italic	Makes the selected text italic. This tag has been dropped from recent versions of HTML. The approved tag for italic is the emphasis of tag.
Strong	Makes the selected text bold by using the approved strong tag.
Emphasis	Makes the selected text italic by using the approved emphasis tag.
Paragraph	Makes the selected text into a paragraph.
Block Quote	Makes the selected text into a block quote, indented from the right and the left by using the blockquote tag.
Preformatted Text	Creates a grid of four evenly spaced frames. The current Document window stays in the largest, lower-right frame.
Heading 1	Makes the selected text a heading size 1 (largest) by using the h1 tag.
Heading 2	Makes the selected text a heading size 2 by using the h2 tag.

Icon	Option	Description
h3	Heading 3	Makes the selected text a heading size 3 by using the h3 tag.
ul	Unordered List	Makes the selected text into an unordered (bulleted) list.
ol	Ordered List	Makes the selected text into an ordered (numbered) list.
li	List Item	Makes the selected text into a list item (by using the li tag), a single item in an ordered or unordered list.
dl	Definition List	Creates a definition list. A definition list consists of definition terms and definition descriptions.
dt	Definition Term	Creates a definition term within a definition list.
dd	Definition Description	Creates a definition description within a definition list.
abbr.	Abbrevation	Wraps the abbr tag around text, adding a full-text definition to an abbreviation. This aids search engines in indexing a Web page property.
W3C	Acronym	Wraps the acronym tag around text, adding a full-text definition to an acronym. This aids search engines in indexing a Web page properly.

The following options appear under Break icon.

Icon	Option	Description
BR	Line Break	Places a line break, the br tag, at the insertion point.
	Non-Breaking Space	Inserts a special character ( ) that creates a space. The non-breaking space character also prevents a line break from occurring between two words.
“	Left Quote	Inserts the special character for a left quote.
”	Right Quote	Inserts the special character for a right quote.
—	Em-dash	Inserts the special character for an em dash (—).
£	Pound	Inserts the special character for the pound currency symbol.
€	Euro	Inserts the special character for the euro currency symbol.

¥	Yen	Inserts the special character for the yen currency symbol.
©	Copyright	Inserts the special character for the copyright symbol.
®	Registered Trademark	Inserts the special character for the registered trademark symbol.
TM	Trademark	Inserts the special character for trademark symbol.
¢¶ ½	Other Characters	Opens a menu that displays many additional special characters.

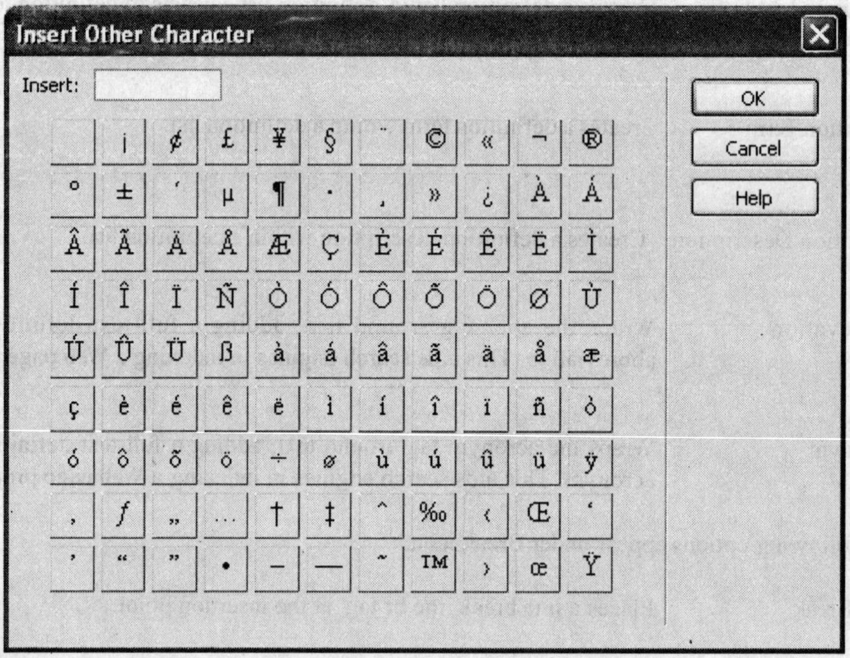

Customizing Dreamweaver

Everyone has its own style of working. So before starting to work with the software, it is better to see what options you can set to make the working easier. For this we have the options of customizing the software using the options in Set Preference which is available under the Edit menu. Here and on the next pages, you will see the various screens of the preferences, you can set. If you do not desire to do any changes at this stage, you can keep in mind the options available here and can use them later too.

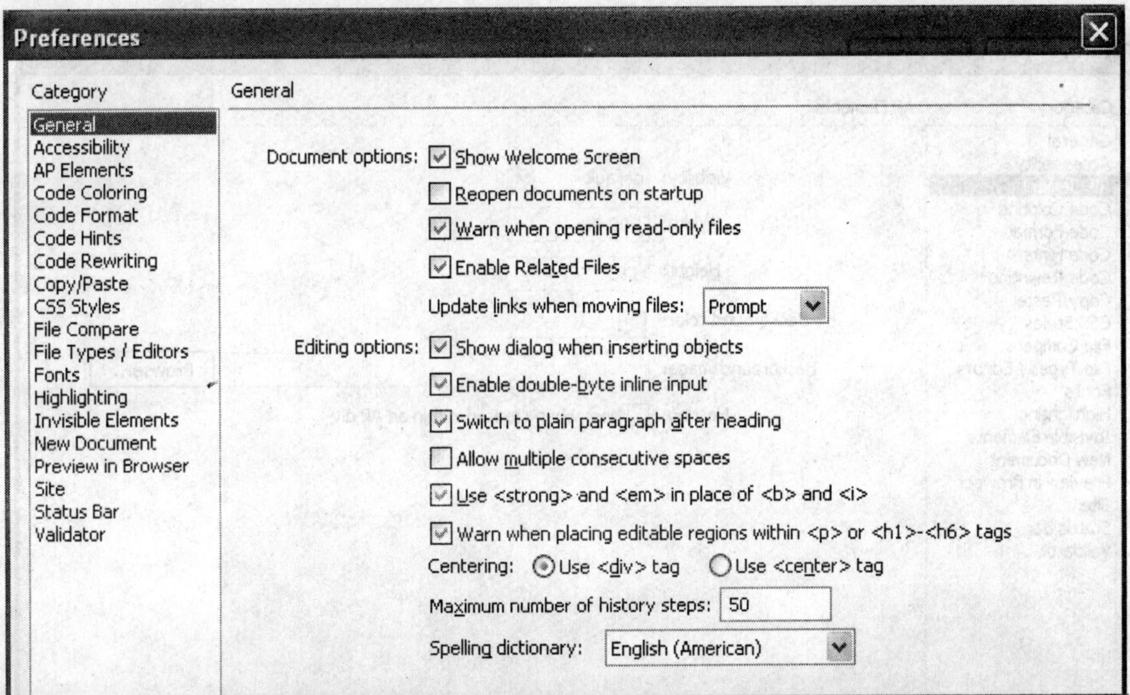
Preferences
Category
General
Accessibility
AP Elements
Code Coloring
Code Format
Code Hints
Code Rewriting
Copy/Paste
CSS Styles
File Compare
File Types / Editors
Fonts
Highlighting
Invisible Elements
New Document
Preview in Browser
Site
Status Bar
Validator
General
Document options: Show Welcome Screen
Reopen documents on startup
Warn when opening read-only files
Enable Related Files
Update links when moving files: Prompt
Editing options: Show dialog when inserting objects
Enable double-byte inline input
Switch to plain paragraph after heading
Allow multiple consecutive spaces
Use <strong> and <em> in place of <b> and <i>
Warn when placing editable regions within <p> or <h1>-<h6> tags
Centering: Use <div> tag Use <center> tag
Maximum number of history steps: 50
Spelling dictionary: English (American)

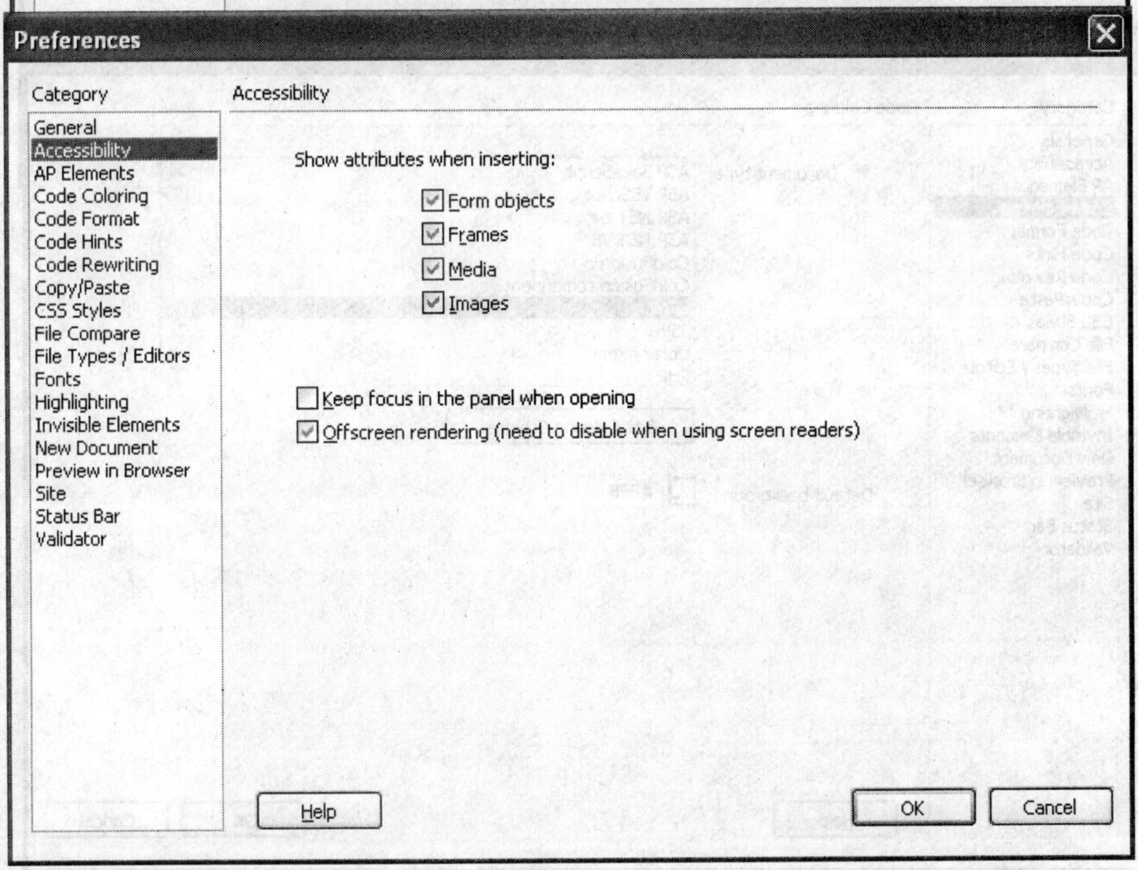
Preferences
Category
General
Accessibility
AP Elements
Code Coloring
Code Format
Code Hints
Code Rewriting
Copy/Paste
CSS Styles
File Compare
File Types / Editors
Fonts
Highlighting
Invisible Elements
New Document
Preview in Browser
Site
Status Bar
Validator
Accessibility
Show attributes when inserting:
Form objects
Frames
Media
Images
Keep focus in the panel when opening
Offscreen rendering (need to disable when using screen readers)
Help
OK
Cancel

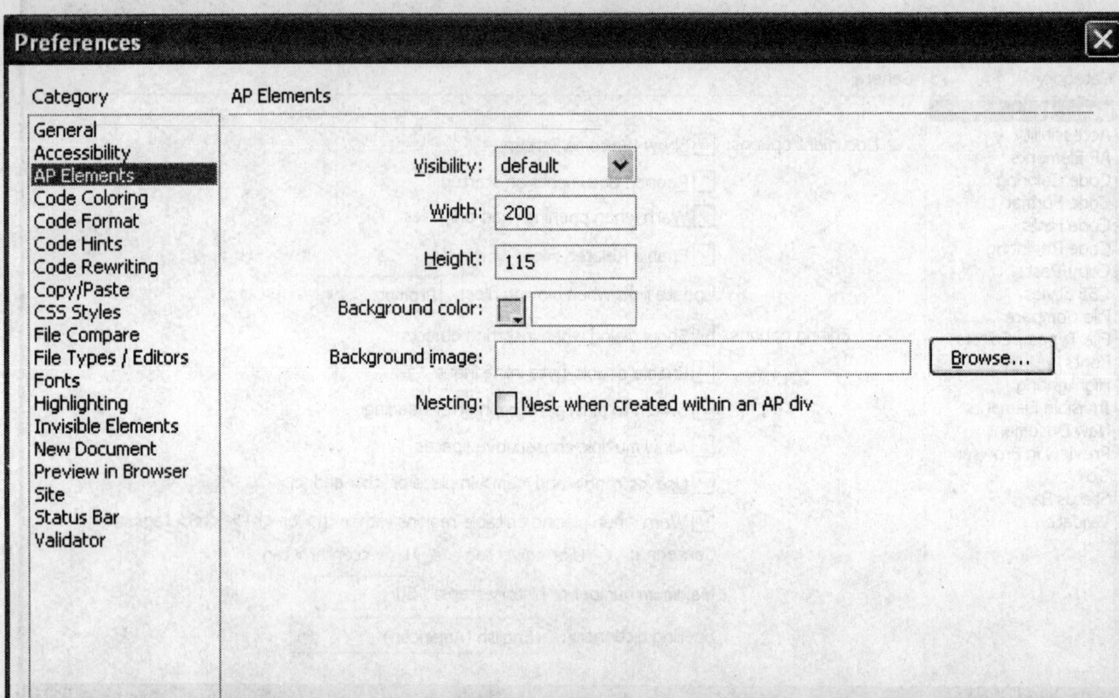
Preferences
Category
AP Elements
General
Accessibility
AP Elements
Code Coloring
Code Format
Code Hints
Code Rewriting
Copy/Paste
CSS Styles
File Compare
File Types / Editors
Fonts
Highlighting
Invisible Elements
New Document
Preview in Browser
Site
Status Bar
Validator
Visibility: default
Width: 200
Height: 115
Background color:
Background image:
Browse...
Nesting: Nest when created within an AP div

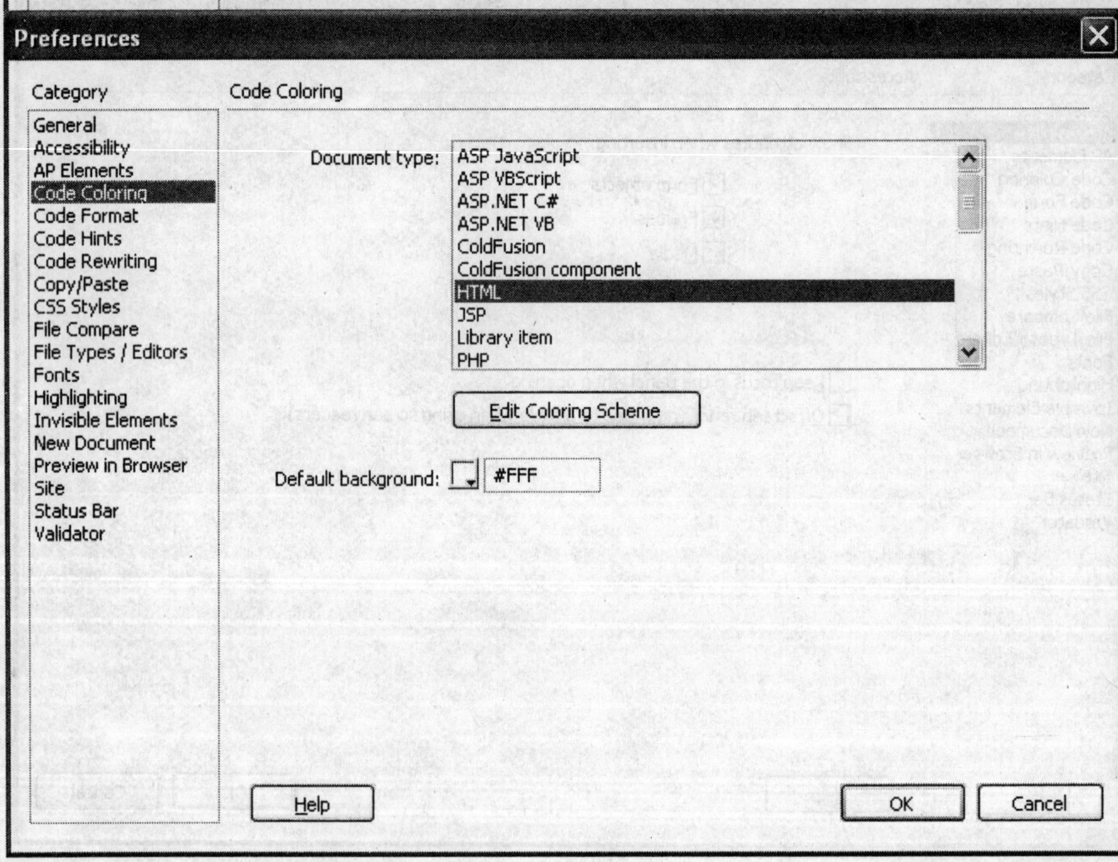
Preferences
Category
Code Coloring
General
Accessibility
AP Elements
Code Coloring
Code Format
Code Hints
Code Rewriting
Copy/Paste
CSS Styles
File Compare
File Types / Editors
Fonts
Highlighting
Invisible Elements
New Document
Preview in Browser
Site
Status Bar
Validator
Document type:
ASP JavaScript
ASP VBScript
ASP.NET C#
ASP.NET VB
ColdFusion
ColdFusion component
HTML
JSP
Library item
PHP
Edit Coloring Scheme
Default background: #FFF
Help
OK
Cancel

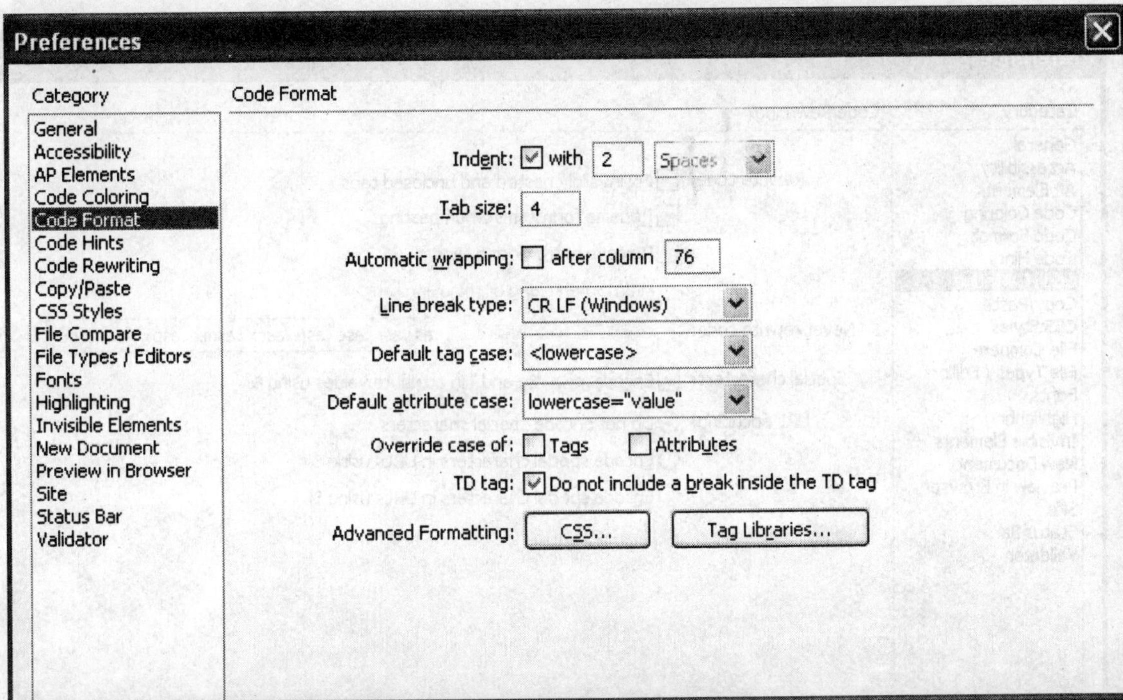
Preferences
Category
Code Format
General
Accessibility
AP Elements
Code Coloring
Code Format
Code Hints
Code Rewriting
Copy/Paste
CSS Styles
File Compare
File Types / Editors
Fonts
Highlighting
Invisible Elements
New Document
Preview in Browser
Site
Status Bar
Validator
Indent: with 2 Spaces
Tab size: 4
Automatic wrapping: after column 76
Line break type: CR LF (Windows)
Default tag case: <lowercase>
Default attribute case: lowercase="value"
Override case of: Tags Attributes
TD tag: Do not include a break inside the TD tag
Advanced Formatting: CSS... Tag Libraries...

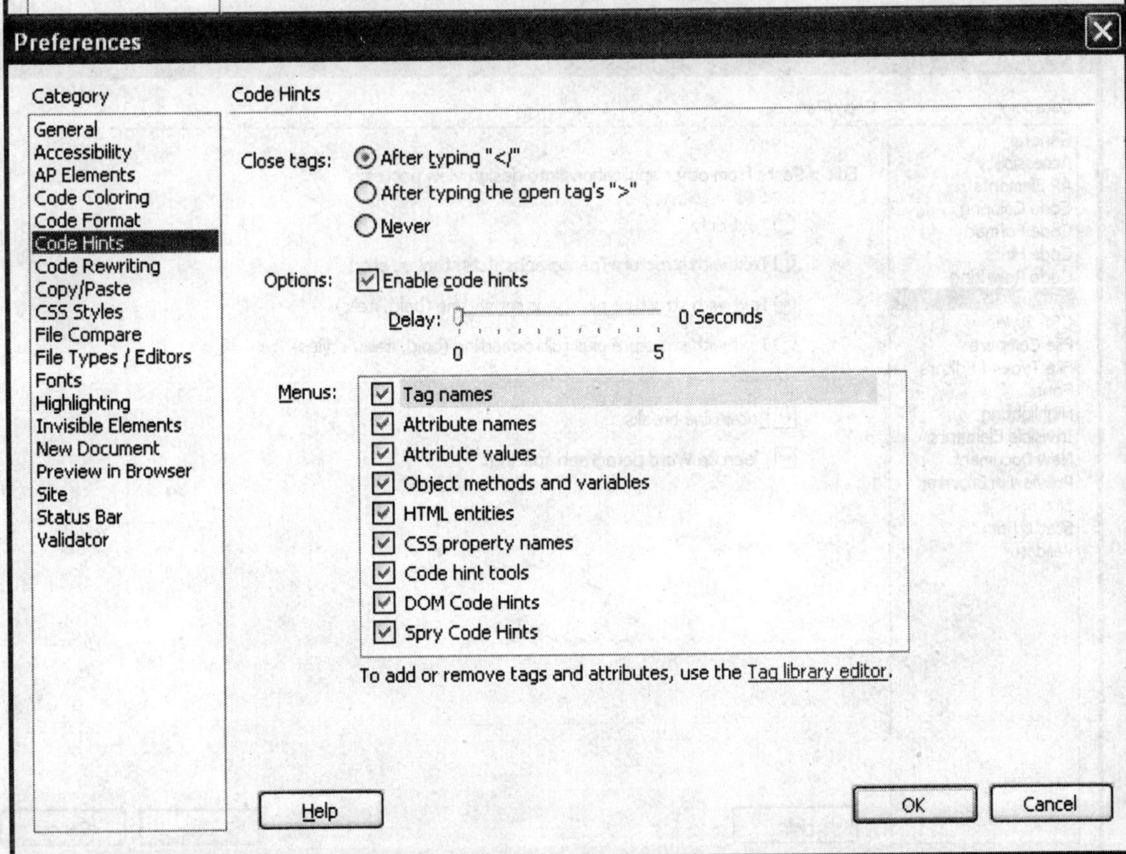
Preferences
Category
Code Hints
General
Accessibility
AP Elements
Code Coloring
Code Format
Code Hints
Code Rewriting
Copy/Paste
CSS Styles
File Compare
File Types / Editors
Fonts
Highlighting
Invisible Elements
New Document
Preview in Browser
Site
Status Bar
Validator
Close tags: After typing "</"
After typing the open tag's ">"
Never
Options: Enable code hints
Delay: 0 Seconds
0
5
Menus: Tag names
Attribute names
Attribute values
Object methods and variables
HTML entities
CSS property names
Code hint tools
DOM Code Hints
Spry Code Hints
To add or remove tags and attributes, use the Tag library editor.
Help
OK
Cancel

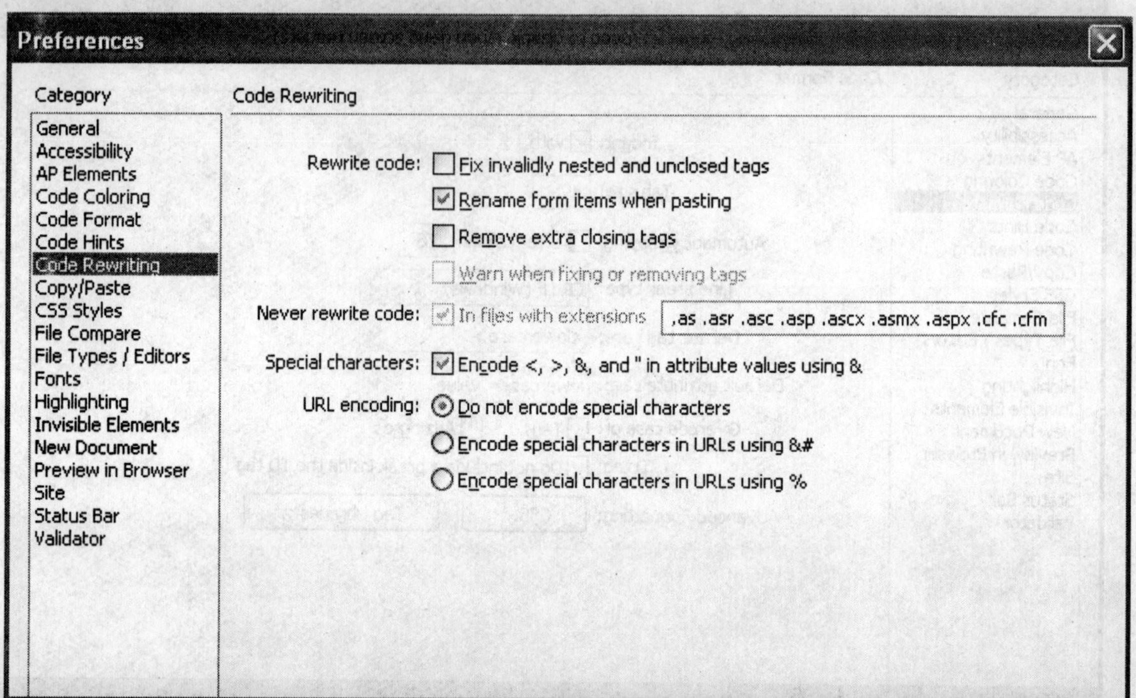
Preferences
Category
General
Accessibility
AP Elements
Code Coloring
Code Format
Code Hints
Code Rewriting
Copy/Paste
CSS Styles
File Compare
File Types / Editors
Fonts
Highlighting
Invisible Elements
New Document
Preview in Browser
Site
Status Bar
Validator
Code Rewriting
Rewrite code: Fix invalidly nested and unclosed tags
Rename form items when pasting
Remove extra closing tags
Warn when fixing or removing tags
Never rewrite code: In files with extensions .as .asr .asc .asp .ascx .asmx .aspx .cfc .cfm
Special characters: Encode <, >, &, and " in attribute values using &
URL encoding: Do not encode special characters
Encode special characters in URLs using &#
Encode special characters in URLs using %

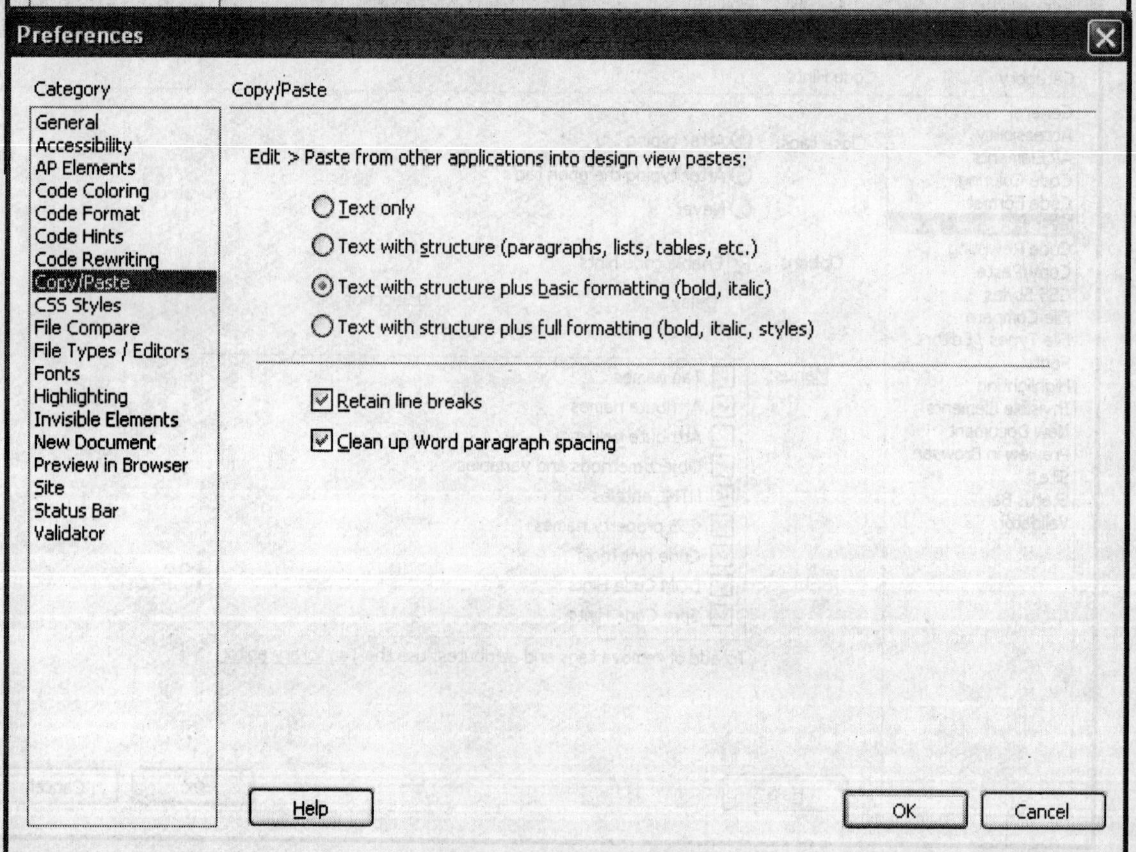
Preferences
Category
General
Accessibility
AP Elements
Code Coloring
Code Format
Code Hints
Code Rewriting
Copy/Paste
CSS Styles
File Compare
File Types / Editors
Fonts
Highlighting
Invisible Elements
New Document
Preview in Browser
Site
Status Bar
Validator
Copy/Paste
Edit > Paste from other applications into design view pastes:
Text only
Text with structure (paragraphs, lists, tables, etc.)
Text with structure plus basic formatting (bold, italic)
Text with structure plus full formatting (bold, italic, styles)
Retain line breaks
Clean up Word paragraph spacing
Help
OK
Cancel

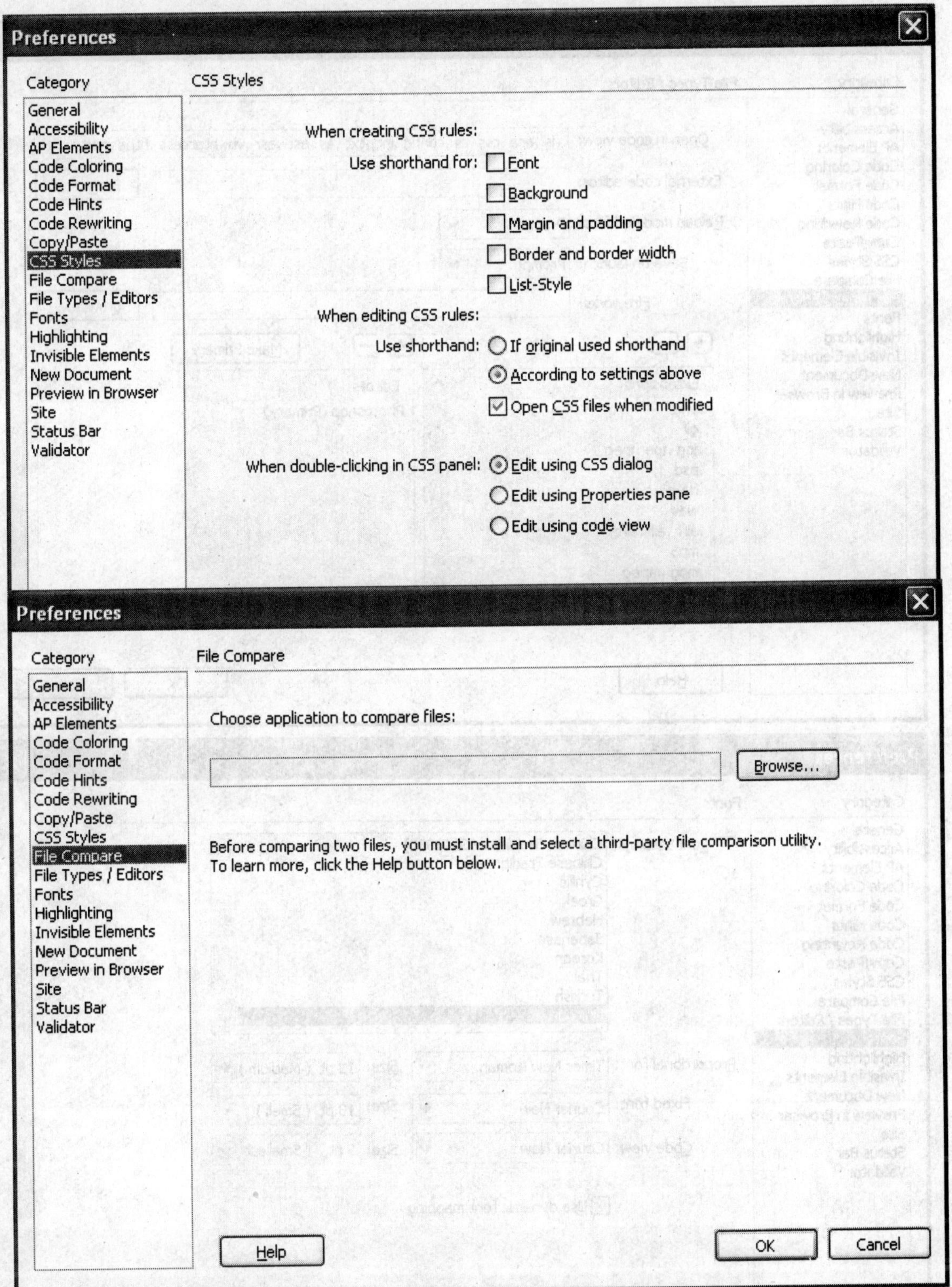
Preferences
Category
General
Accessibility
AP Elements
Code Coloring
Code Format
Code Hints
Code Rewriting
Copy/Paste
CSS Styles
File Compare
File Types / Editors
Fonts
Highlighting
Invisible Elements
New Document
Preview in Browser
Site
Status Bar
Validator
CSS Styles
When creating CSS rules:
Use shorthand for:
Font
Background
Margin and padding
Border and border width
List-Style
When editing CSS rules:
Use shorthand:
If original used shorthand
According to settings above
Open CSS files when modified
When double-clicking in CSS panel:
Edit using CSS dialog
Edit using Properties pane
Edit using code view
Preferences
Category
General
Accessibility
AP Elements
Code Coloring
Code Format
Code Hints
Code Rewriting
Copy/Paste
CSS Styles
File Compare
File Types / Editors
Fonts
Highlighting
Invisible Elements
New Document
Preview in Browser
Site
Status Bar
Validator
File Compare
Choose application to compare files:
Browse...
Before comparing two files, you must install and select a third-party file comparison utility.
To learn more, click the Help button below.
Help
OK
Cancel

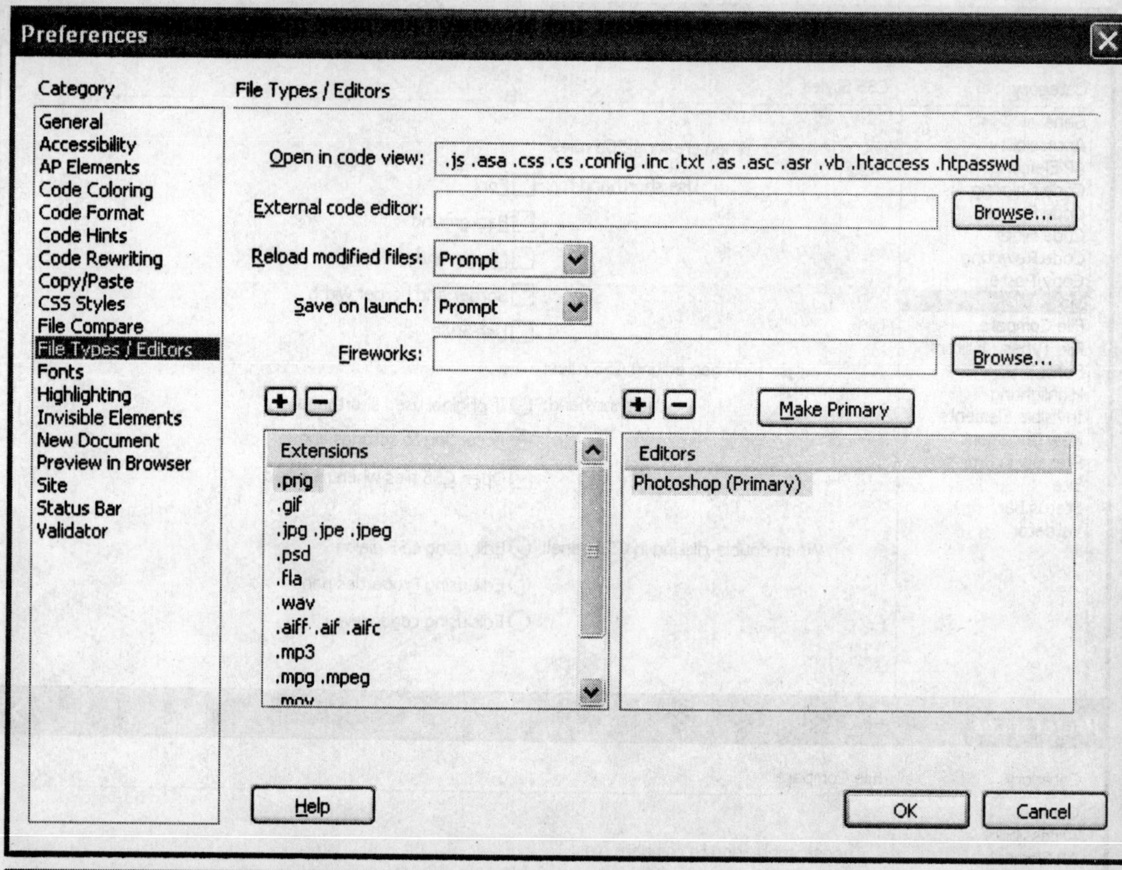
Preferences
Category
General
Accessibility
AP Elements
Code Coloring
Code Format
Code Hints
Code Rewriting
Copy/Paste
CSS Styles
File Compare
File Types / Editors
Fonts
Highlighting
Invisible Elements
New Document
Preview in Browser
Site
Status Bar
Validator
File Types / Editors
Open in code view: .js .asa .css .cs .config .inc .txt .as .asc .asr .vb .htaccess .htpasswd
External code editor:
Browse...
Reload modified files: Prompt
Save on launch: Prompt
Fireworks:
Browse...
Make Primary
Extensions
.png
.gif
.jpg .jpe .jpeg
.psd
.fla
.wav
.aiff .aif .aifc
.mp3
.mpg .mpeg
Editors
Photoshop (Primary)
Help
OK
Cancel

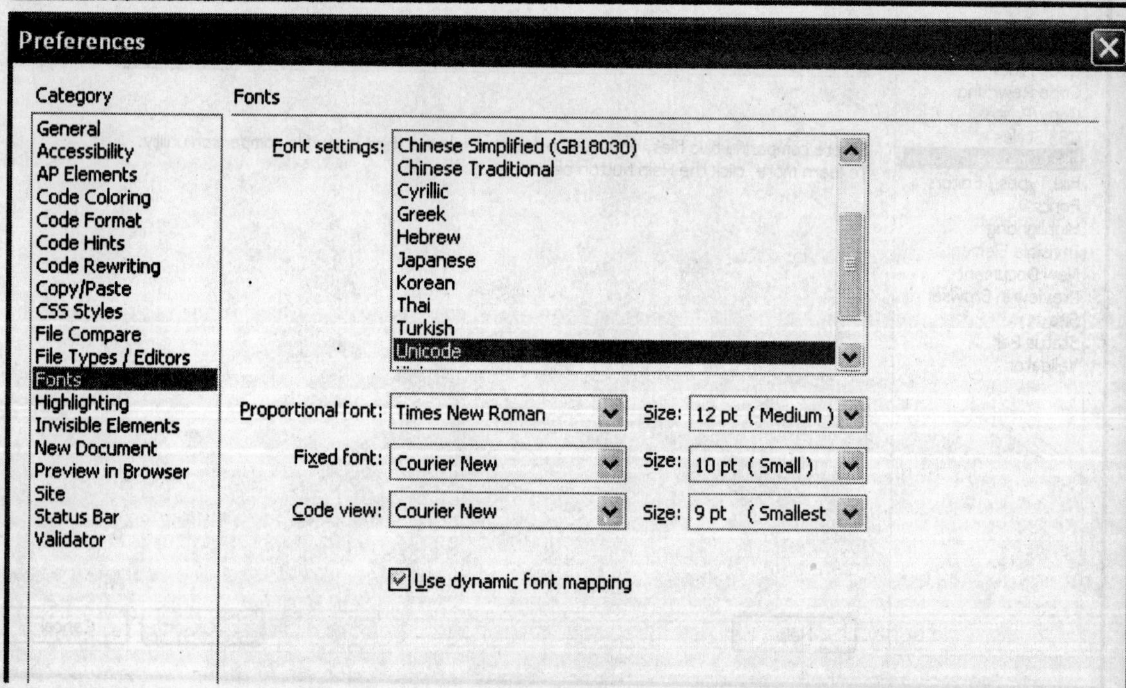
Preferences
Category
General
Accessibility
AP Elements
Code Coloring
Code Format
Code Hints
Code Rewriting
Copy/Paste
CSS Styles
File Compare
File Types / Editors
Fonts
Highlighting
Invisible Elements
New Document
Preview in Browser
Site
Status Bar
Validator
Fonts
Font settings:
Chinese Simplified (GB18030)
Chinese Traditional
Cyrillic
Greek
Hebrew
Japanese
Korean
Thai
Turkish
Unicode
Proportional font: Times New Roman
Size: 12 pt (Medium)
Fixed font: Courier New
Size: 10 pt (Small)
Code view: Courier New
Size: 9 pt (Smallest
Use dynamic font mapping

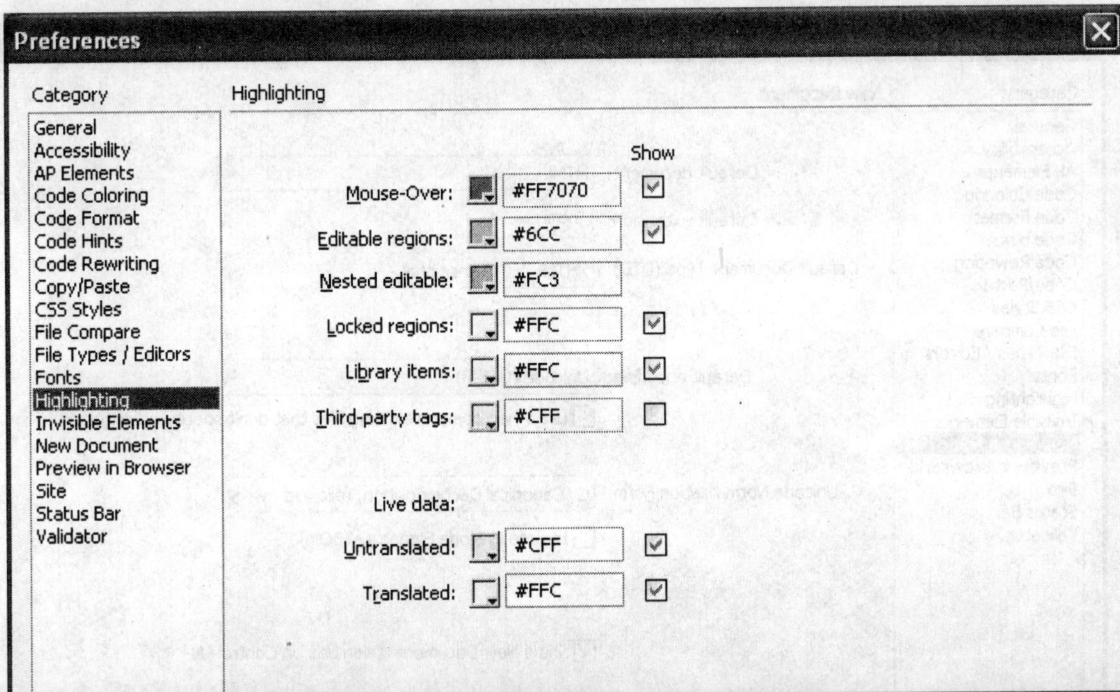
Preferences
Category
General
Accessibility
AP Elements
Code Coloring
Code Format
Code Hints
Code Rewriting
Copy/Paste
CSS Styles
File Compare
File Types / Editors
Fonts
Highlighting
Invisible Elements
New Document
Preview in Browser
Site
Status Bar
Validator
Highlighting
Show
Mouse-Over: #FF7070
Editable regions: #6CC
Nested editable: #FC3
Locked regions: #FFC
Library items: #FFC
Third-party tags: #CFF
Live data:
Untranslated: #CFF
Translated: #FFC

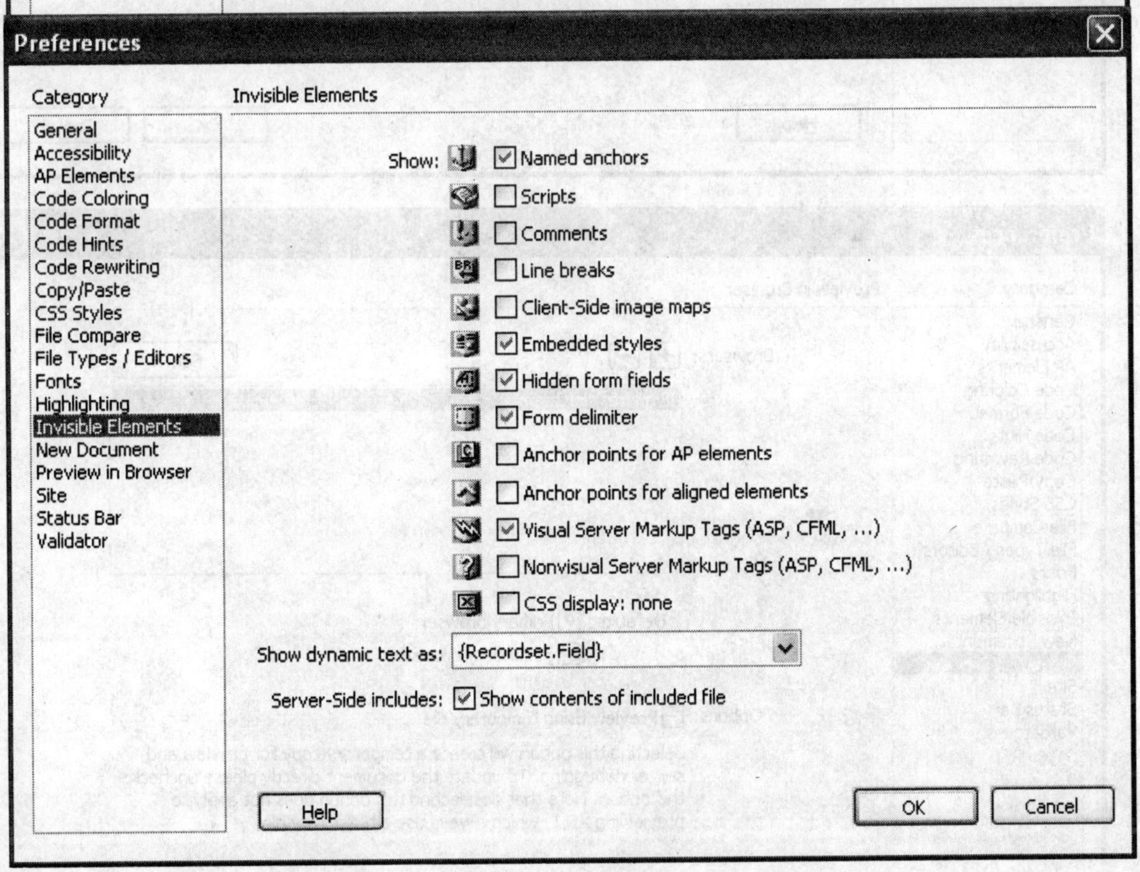
Preferences
Category
General
Accessibility
AP Elements
Code Coloring
Code Format
Code Hints
Code Rewriting
Copy/Paste
CSS Styles
File Compare
File Types / Editors
Fonts
Highlighting
Invisible Elements
New Document
Preview in Browser
Site
Status Bar
Validator
Invisible Elements
Show:
Named anchors
Scripts
Comments
Line breaks
Client-Side image maps
Embedded styles
Hidden form fields
Form delimiter
Anchor points for AP elements
Anchor points for aligned elements
Visual Server Markup Tags (ASP, CFML, ...)
Nonvisual Server Markup Tags (ASP, CFML, ...)
CSS display: none
Show dynamic text as: {Recordset.Field}
Server-Side includes: Show contents of included file
Help
OK
Cancel

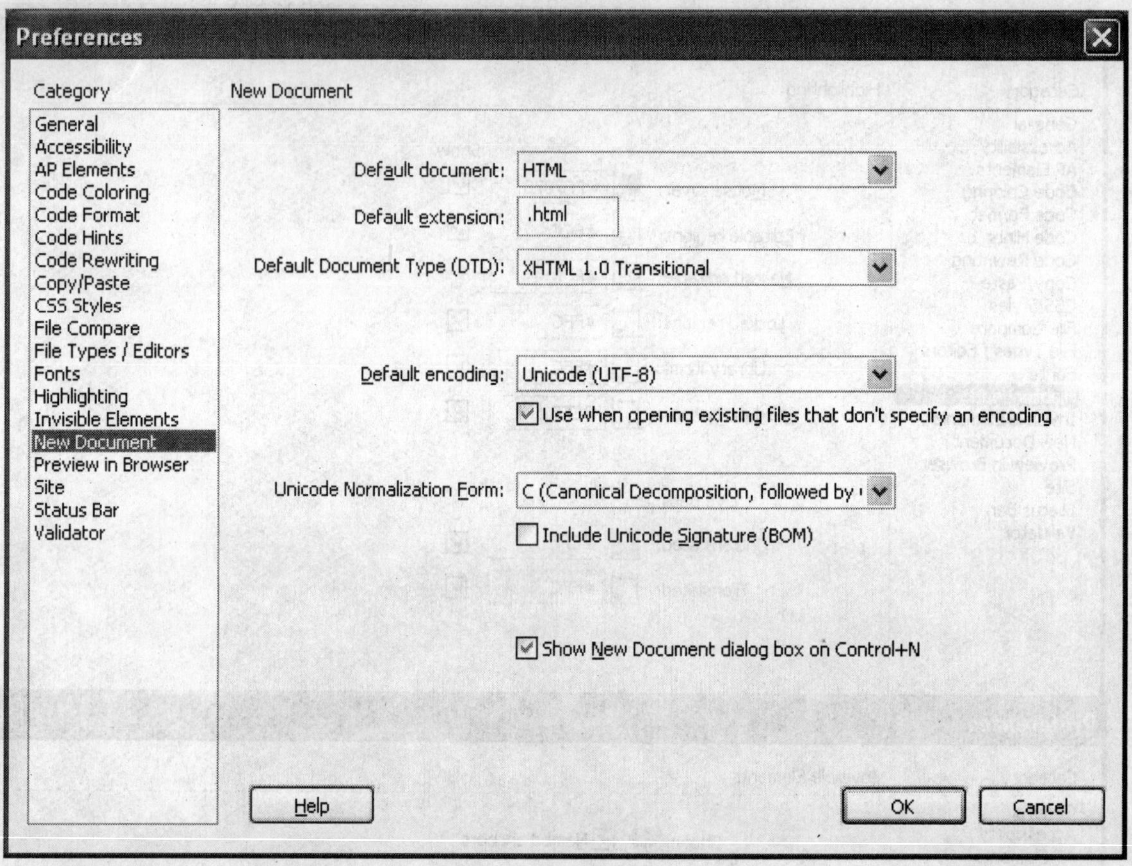
Preferences
Category
New Document
General
Accessibility
AP Elements
Code Coloring
Code Format
Code Hints
Code Rewriting
Copy/Paste
CSS Styles
File Compare
File Types / Editors
Fonts
Highlighting
Invisible Elements
New Document
Preview in Browser
Site
Status Bar
Validator
Default document: HTML
Default extension: .html
Default Document Type (DTD): XHTML 1.0 Transitional
Default encoding: Unicode (UTF-8)
Use when opening existing files that don't specify an encoding
Unicode Normalization Form: C (Canonical Decomposition, followed by
Include Unicode Signature (BOM)
Show New Document dialog box on Control+N
Help
OK
Cancel

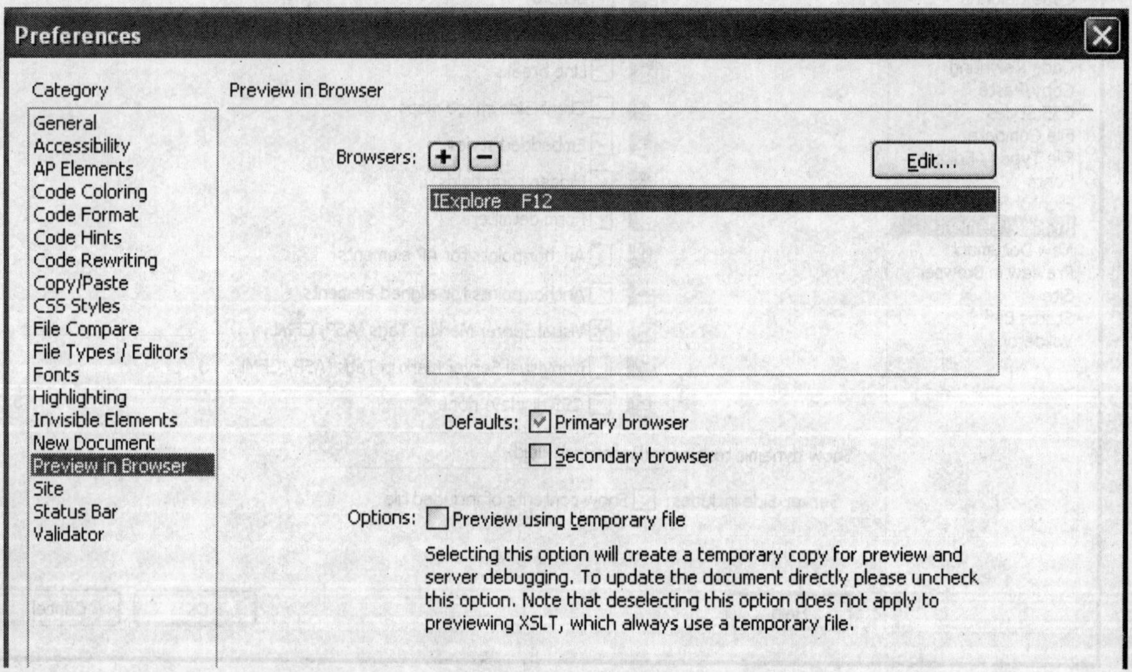
Preferences
Category
Preview in Browser
General
Accessibility
AP Elements
Code Coloring
Code Format
Code Hints
Code Rewriting
Copy/Paste
CSS Styles
File Compare
File Types / Editors
Fonts
Highlighting
Invisible Elements
New Document
Preview in Browser
Site
Status Bar
Validator
Browsers:
Edit...
IExplore F12
Defaults: Primary browser
Secondary browser
Options: Preview using temporary file
Selecting this option will create a temporary copy for preview and server debugging. To update the document directly please uncheck this option. Note that deselecting this option does not apply to previewing XSLT, which always use a temporary file.

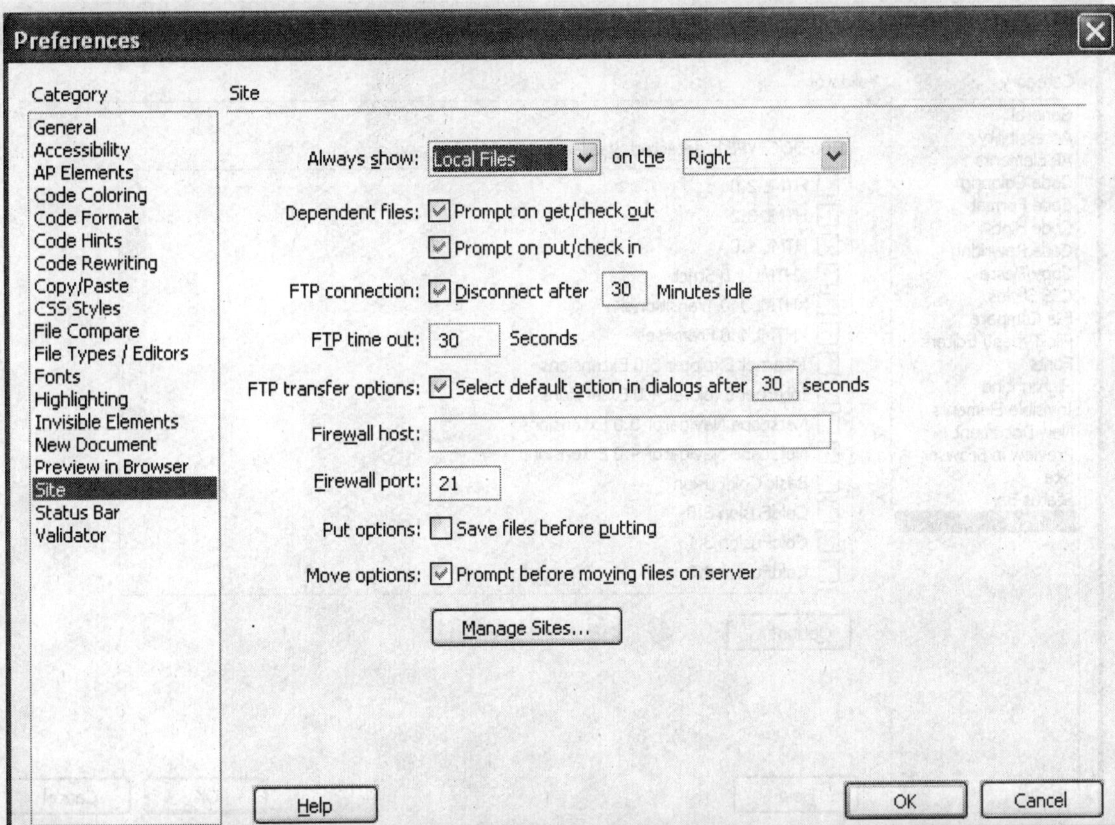
Preferences
Category
General
Accessibility
AP Elements
Code Coloring
Code Format
Code Hints
Code Rewriting
Copy/Paste
CSS Styles
File Compare
File Types / Editors
Fonts
Highlighting
Invisible Elements
New Document
Preview in Browser
Site
Status Bar
Validator
Site
Always show: Local Files on the Right
Dependent files: Prompt on get/check out
Prompt on put/check in
FTP connection: Disconnect after 30 Minutes idle
FTP time out: 30 Seconds
FTP transfer options: Select default action in dialogs after 30 seconds
Firewall host:
Firewall port: 21
Put options: Save files before putting
Move options: Prompt before moving files on server
Manage Sites...
Help
OK
Cancel

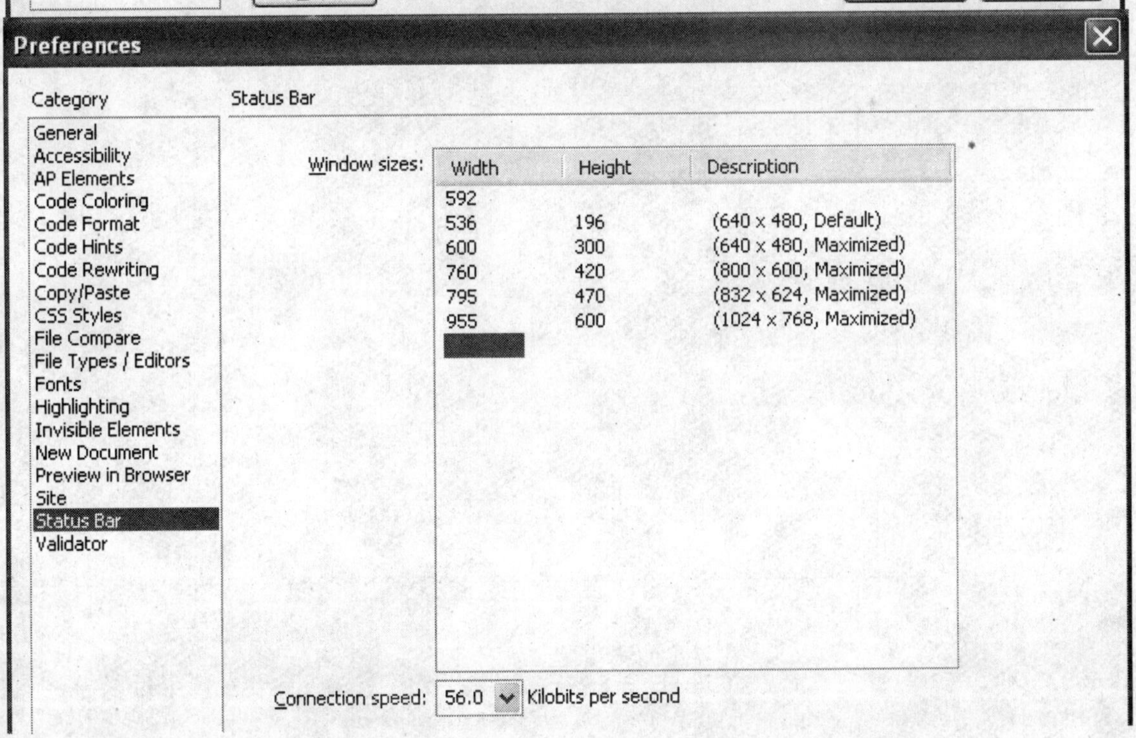
Preferences
Category
General
Accessibility
AP Elements
Code Coloring
Code Format
Code Hints
Code Rewriting
Copy/Paste
CSS Styles
File Compare
File Types / Editors
Fonts
Highlighting
Invisible Elements
New Document
Preview in Browser
Site
Status Bar
Validator
Status Bar
Window sizes:
Width Height Description
592
536 196 (640 x 480, Default)
600 300 (640 x 480, Maximized)
760 420 (800 x 600, Maximized)
795 470 (832 x 624, Maximized)
955 600 (1024 x 768, Maximized)
Connection speed: 56.0 Kilobits per second

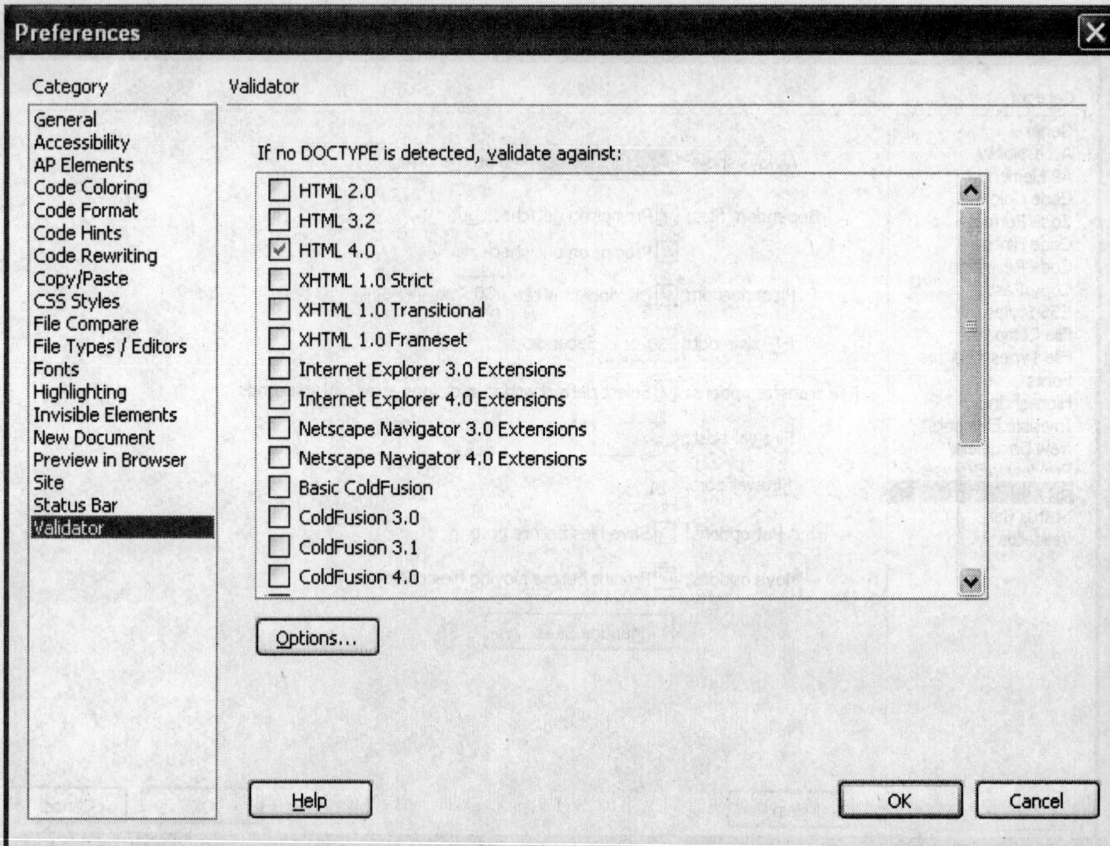
Preferences
Category
General
Accessibility
AP Elements
Code Coloring
Code Format
Code Hints
Code Rewriting
Copy/Paste
CSS Styles
File Compare
File Types / Editors
Fonts
Highlighting
Invisible Elements
New Document
Preview in Browser
Site
Status Bar
Validator
Validator
If no DOCTYPE is detected, validate against:
HTML 2.0
HTML 3.2
HTML 4.0
XHTML 1.0 Strict
XHTML 1.0 Transitional
XHTML 1.0 Frameset
Internet Explorer 3.0 Extensions
Internet Explorer 4.0 Extensions
Netscape Navigator 3.0 Extensions
Netscape Navigator 4.0 Extensions
Basic ColdFusion
ColdFusion 3.0
ColdFusion 3.1
ColdFusion 4.0
Options...
Help
OK
Cancel

2 Creating a New Page in Dreamweaver CS4

Introduction

As mentioned in the last chapter, Dreamweaver is used to create Web page. In this chapter, you will learn about creating a New Web page.

Creating a New page

For creating a new page, do the following:

1. Click at New from the file menu.
2. A dialog box appears, as shown here, asking you to select the Category and the Basic Page. I have selected here the HTML and Basic Page.

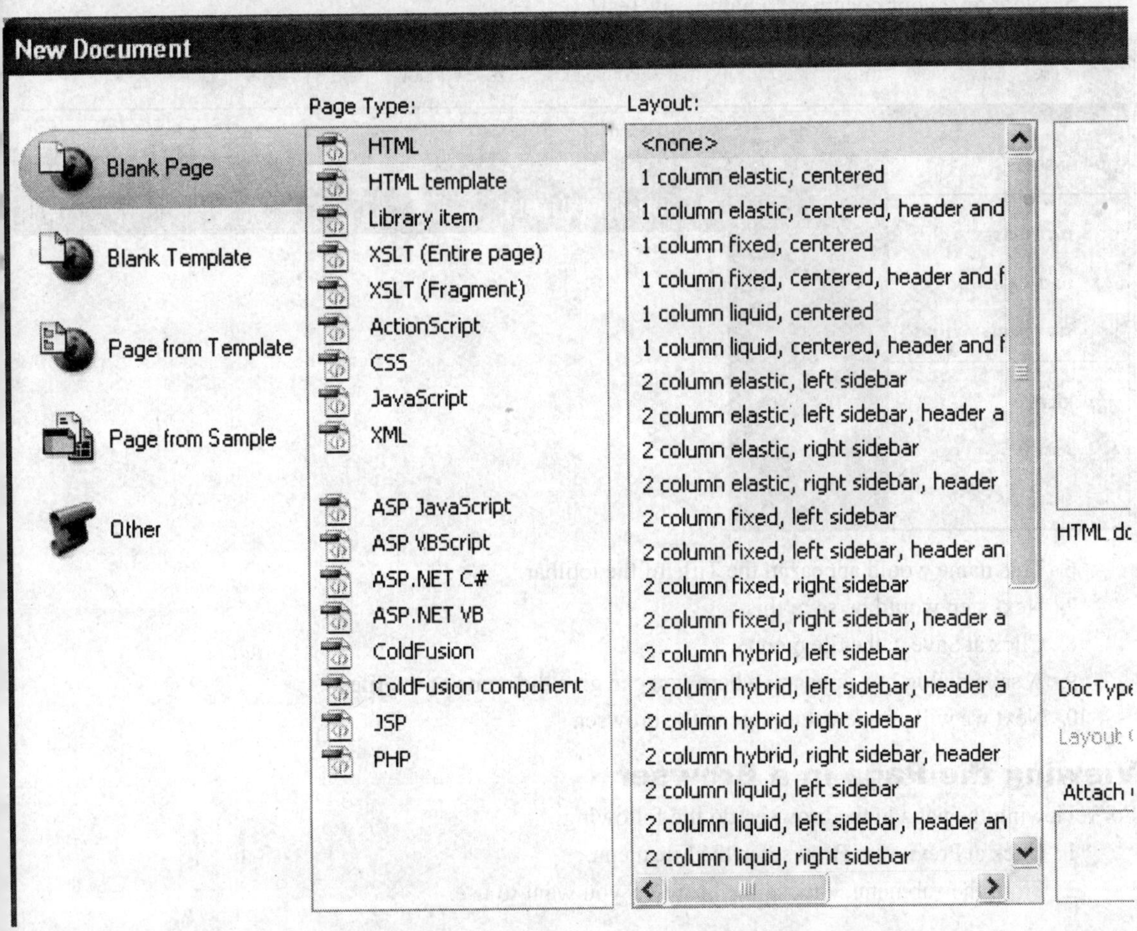

3. Click at Create to start.
4. In the windows taskbar too, you can see the name Untitled Document.

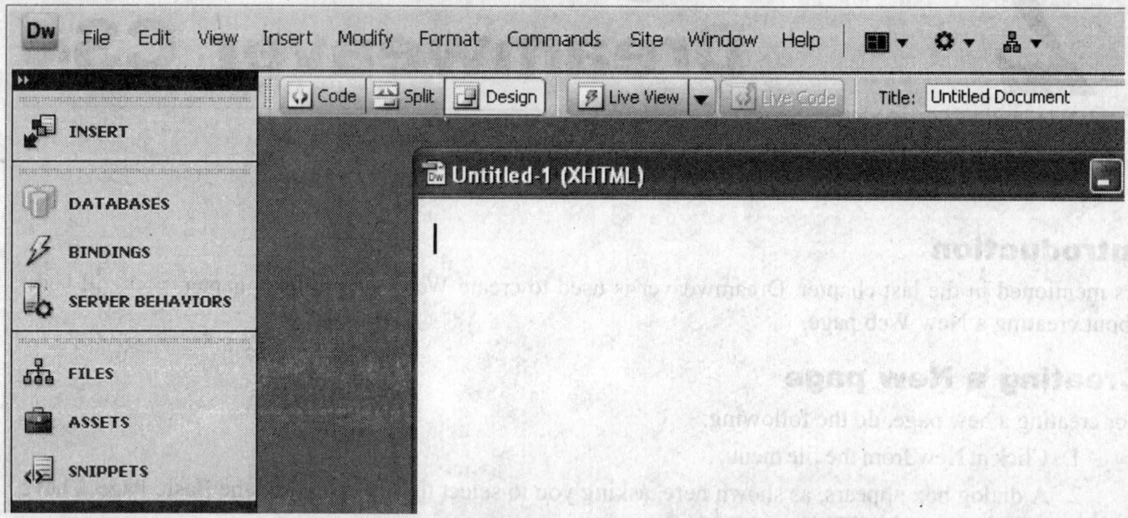

5. Now give your document a name, say Test1.

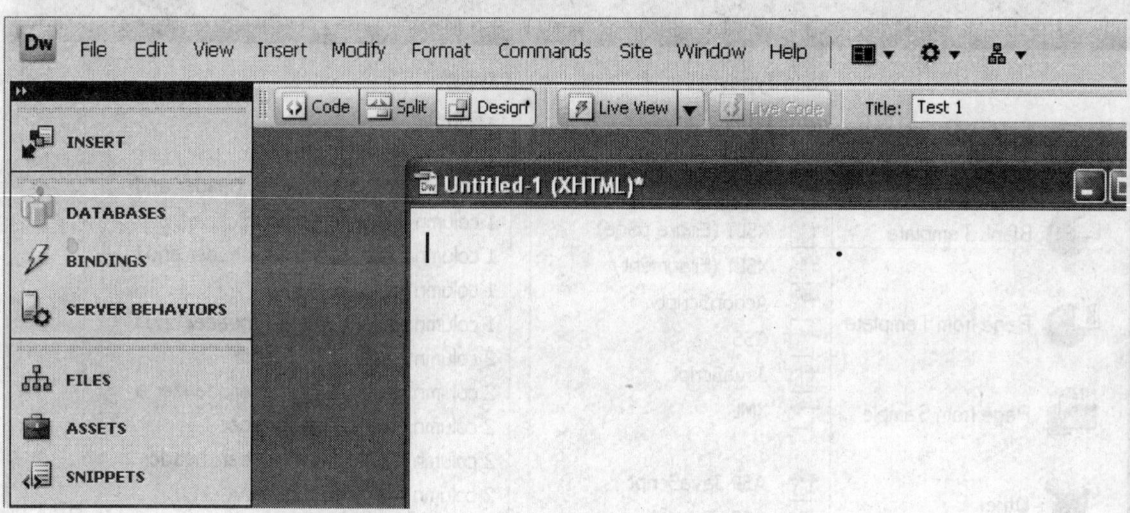

6. This name would appear in the Title of the toolbar.
7. Next step would be save this.
8. Click at Save in the file menu.
9. A save dialog box appears, where you can give the name of the file.
10. Next we will preview this page in the browser.

Viewing the Page in a Browser

For reviewing the page in the browser, do the following:

1. Click at Preview in Browser in the File menu.
2. From the submenu, choose the browser, you want to use.

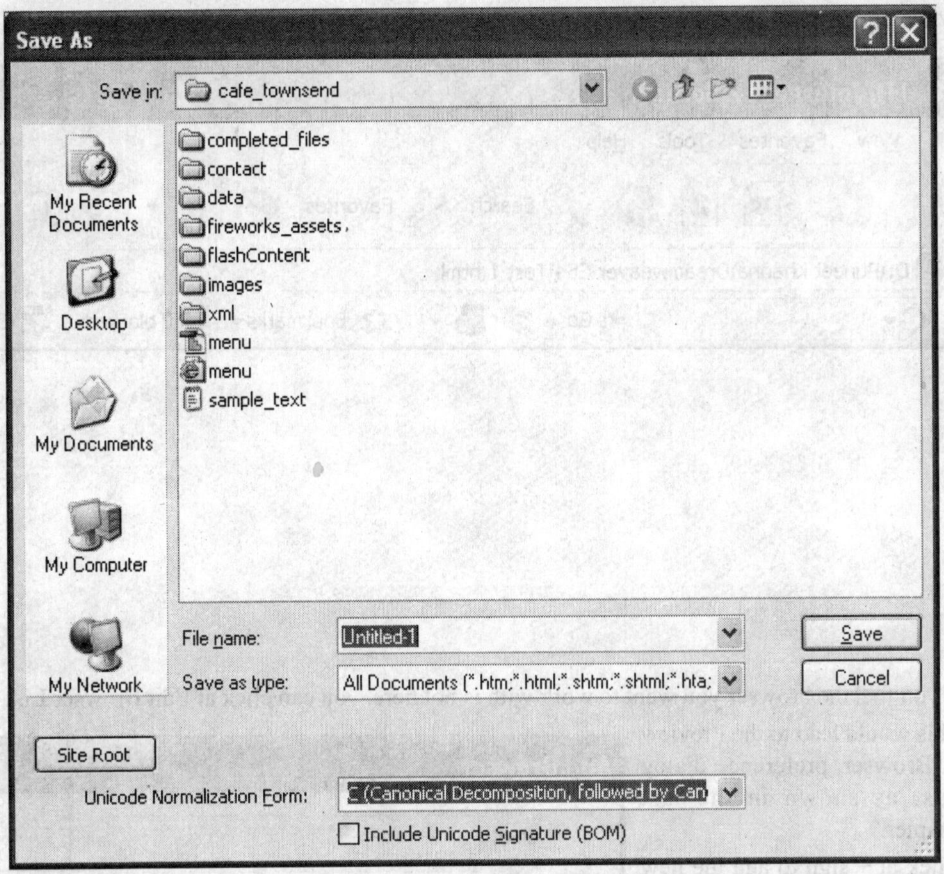
Save As
Save in: cafe_townsend
completed_files
contact
data
fireworks_assets
flashContent
images
xml
menu
menu
sample_text
My Recent Documents
Desktop
My Documents
My Computer
My Network
File name: Untitled-1
Save as type: All Documents (*.htm;*.html;*.shtm;*.shtml;*.hta;
Save
Cancel
Site Root
Unicode Normalization Form: C (Canonical Decomposition, followed by Can
Include Unicode Signature (BOM)

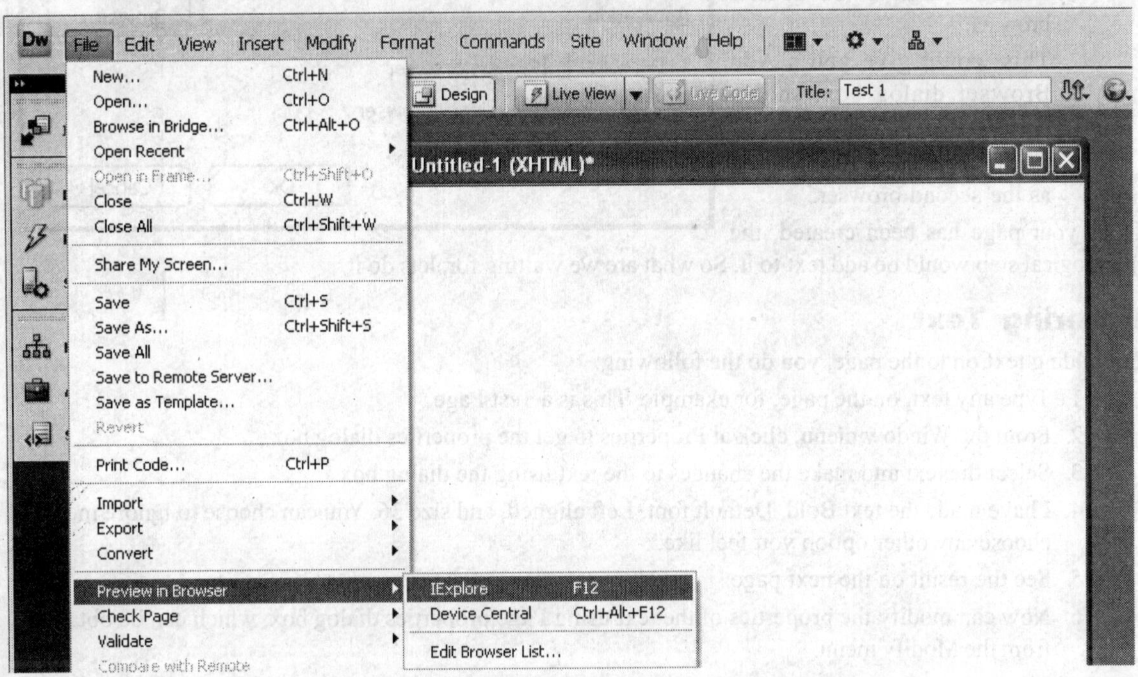
File Edit View Insert Modify Format Commands Site Window Help
New... Ctrl+N
Open... Ctrl+O
Browse in Bridge... Ctrl+Alt+O
Open Recent
Open in Frame... Ctrl+Shift+O
Close Ctrl+W
Close All Ctrl+Shift+W
Share My Screen...
Save Ctrl+S
Save As... Ctrl+Shift+S
Save All
Save to Remote Server...
Save as Template...
Revert
Print Code... Ctrl+P
Import
Export
Convert
Preview in Browser
Check Page
Validate
Compare with Remote
IExplore F12
Device Central Ctrl+Alt+F12
Edit Browser List...
Design
Live View
Live Code
Title: Test 1
Untitled-1 (XHTML)*

3. When chosen, Microsoft Internet Explorer, here you get the result, as shown here.

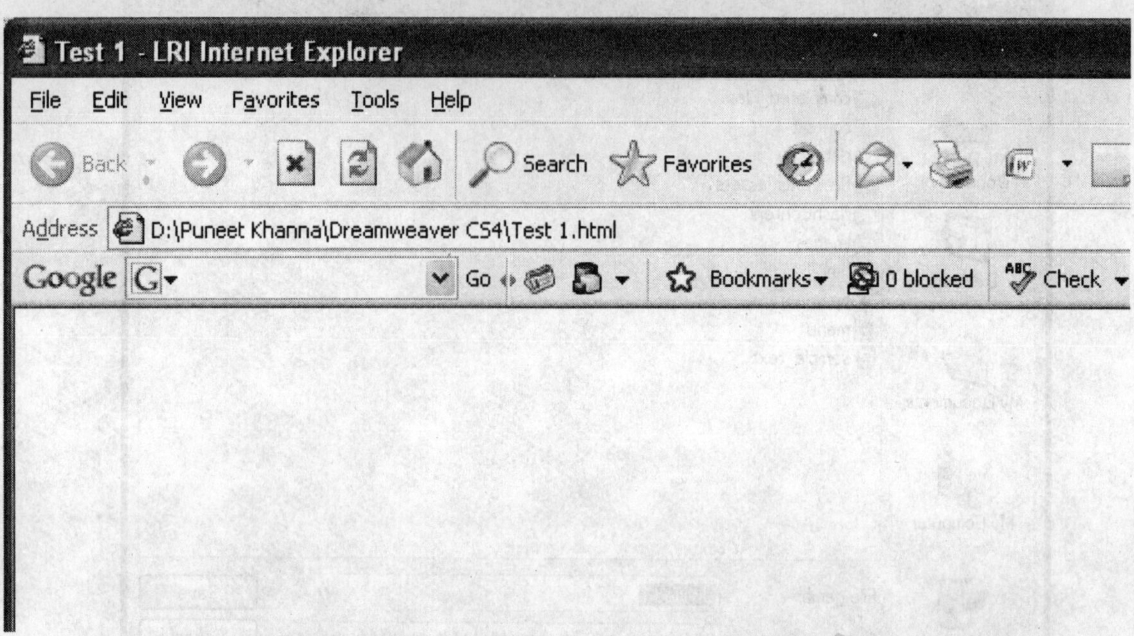

4. If you feel the browser you want to work with is not here. you can click at Edit Browser List.
5. This would lead to the Preview in Browser, preference dialog box, as shown in the last chapter.
6. Click at + sign to add the new browser.
7. This would give you a Add Browser dialog box, shown here.
8. Click OK to have this browser, as the second browser.

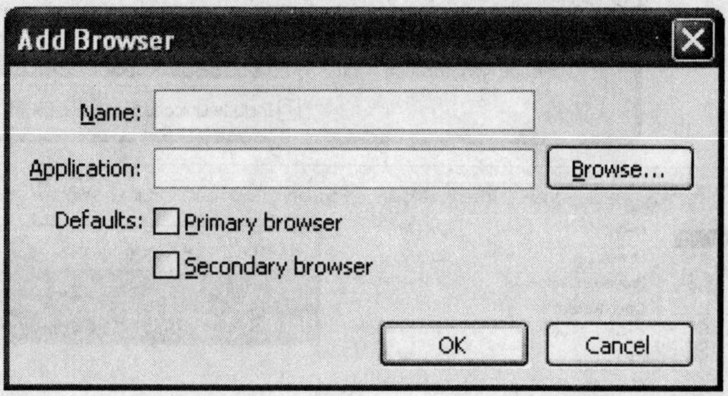

Once your page has been created, the next logical step would be add text to it. So what are we waiting for, lets do it.

Entering Text

For adding text on to the page, you do the following:

1. Type any text, on the page, for example, This is a Test Page.
2. From the Window menu, click at Properties to get the properties dialog box.
3. Select the text and make the changes to the text using the dialog box.
4. I have made the text Bold, Default font, Left aligned, and size 36. You can choose to ignore me and choose any other option you feel like.
5. See the result on the next page.
6. Now can modify the properties of the text using Page properties dialog box, which can be obtained from the Modify menu.

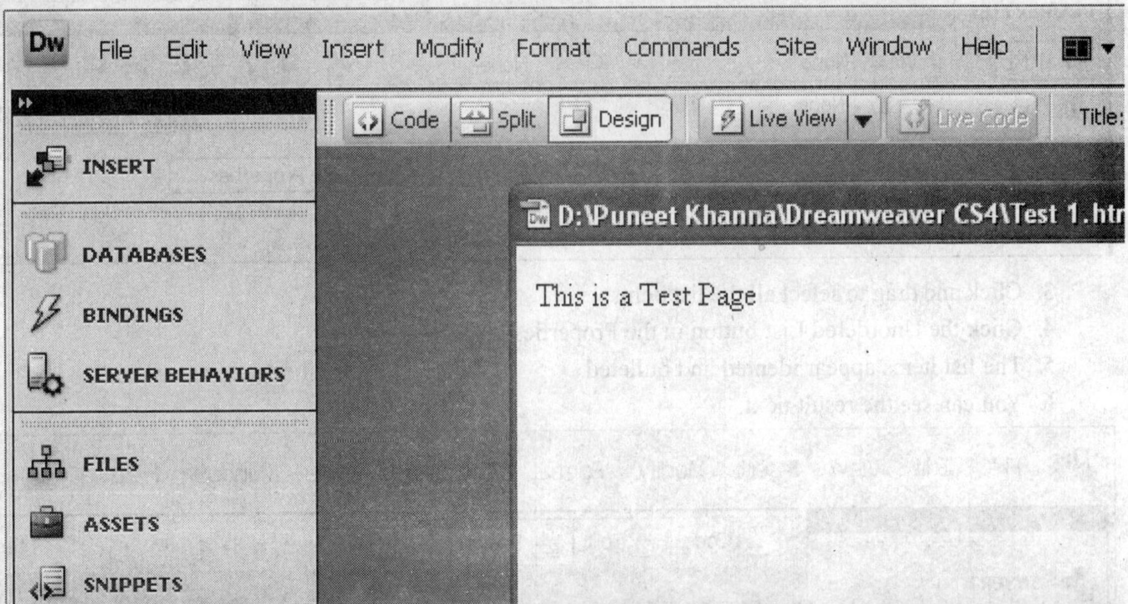

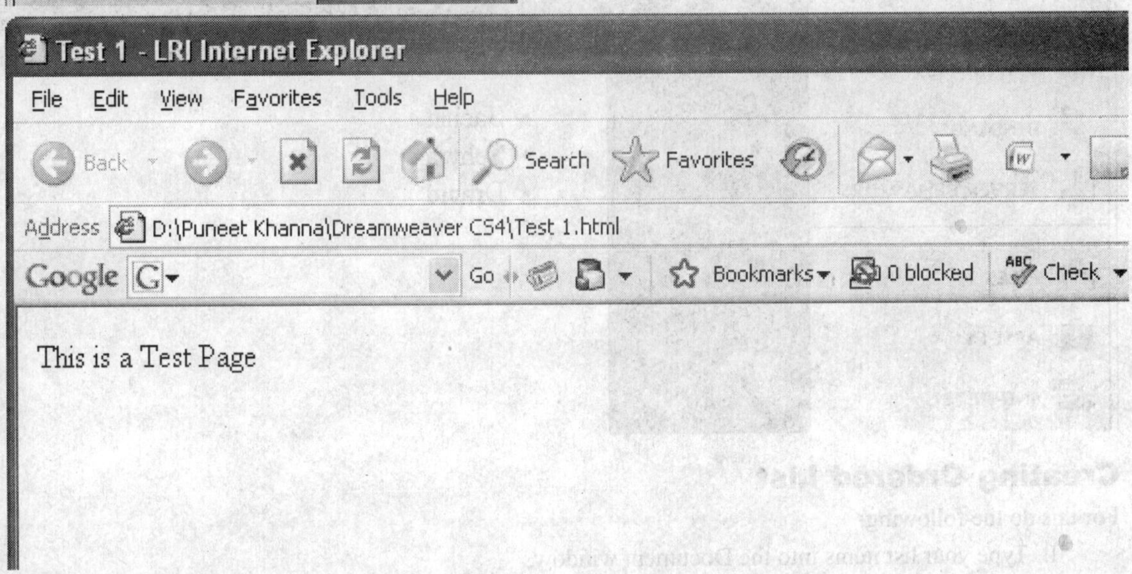

Adding a line

Add a horizontal rule to your Web page by selecting the horizontal rule object from the HTML command in the Insert menu. The Property inspector presents the properties of the horizontal rule. You can give the rule a name, and you can set width and height values in either or percent of the screen. You can set the alignment and turn shading on and off.

Creating Unordered List

For this do the following:

1. Type your list items into the Document window.
2. Click between the items and press Enter to place each item in a separate paragraph.

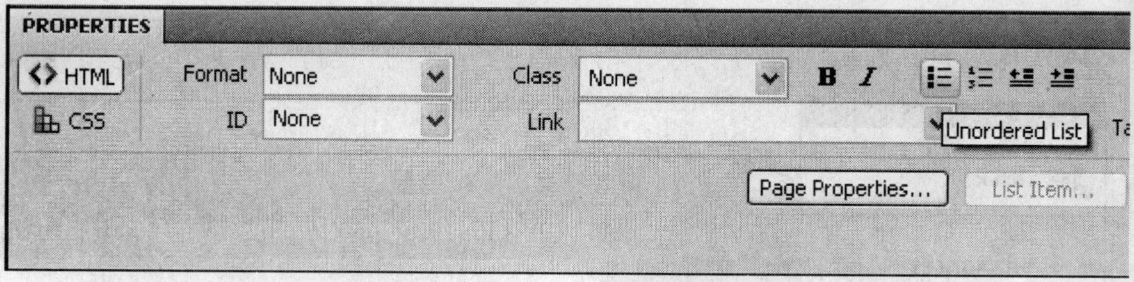

3. Click and drag to select all the list items.
4. Click the Unordered List button in the Properties inspector.
5. The list items appear idented and bulleted.
6. You can see the result next.

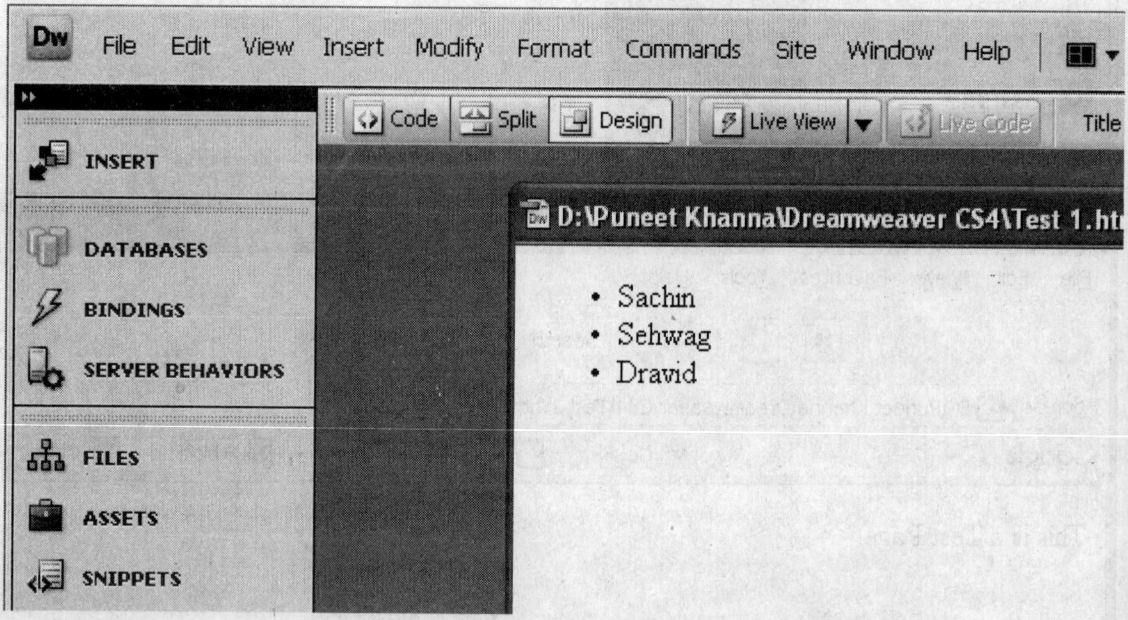

Creating Ordered List

For this do the following:

1. Type your list items into the Document window.
2. Click between the items and press Enter to place each item in a separate paragraph.
3. Click and drag to select all the list items.
4. Click the Ordered List button in the Properties inspector.
5. The list items appear idented and bulleted.
6. You can see the result of this below.

Changing Font

For this do the following:

1. Select the text whose font you want to change.
2. Click Text menu.

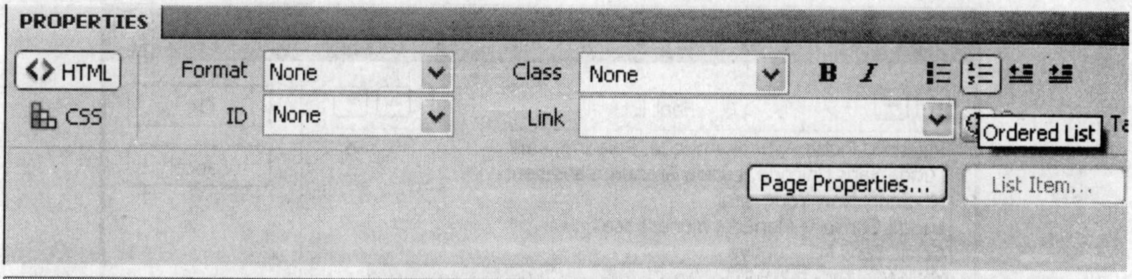

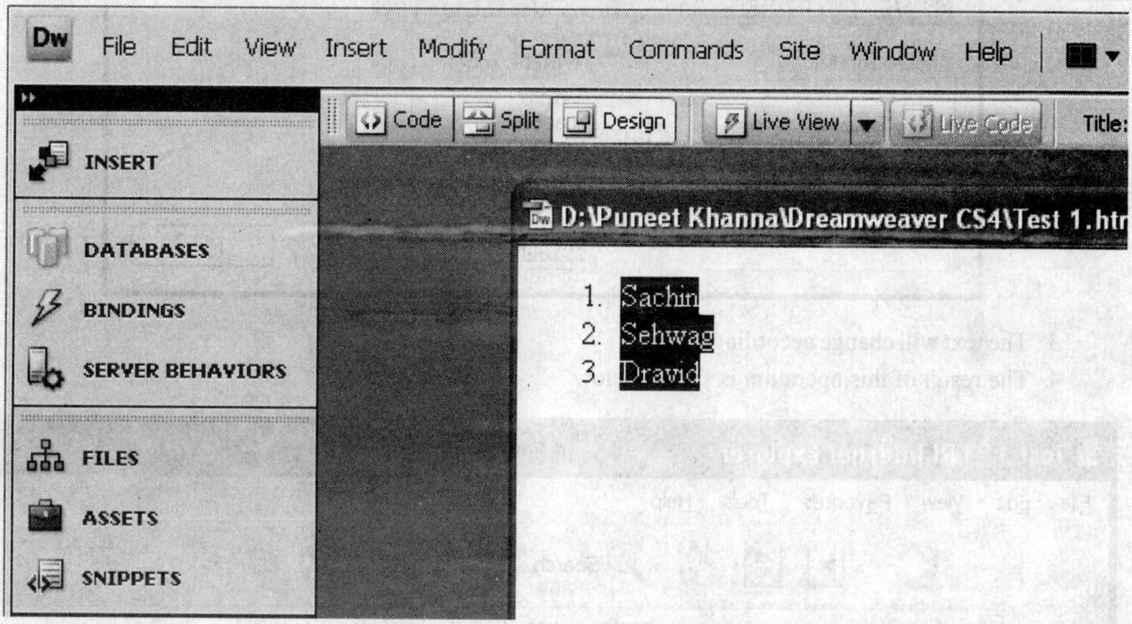

3. Click Font sub-menu.
4. A list of available fonts appears.
5. Select the font which you want to use.
6. The text changes to the new font.

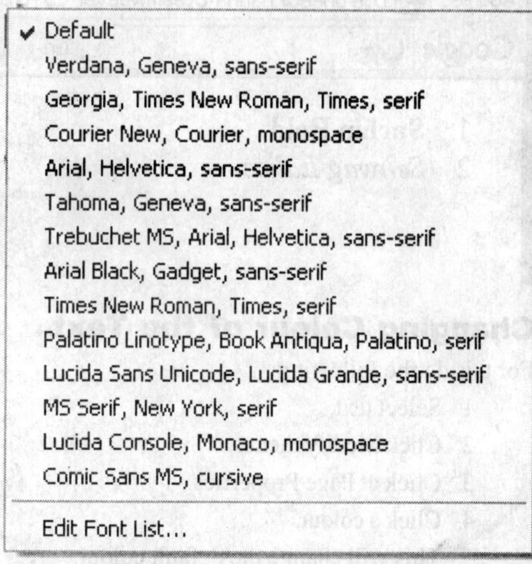

Adding New Font

For this do the following:

1. Select text, Font, and then Edit Font List.
2. A dialog box appears with the fonts available to you in your computer.
3. Select the font which you want to add.
4. Repeat this for other fonts too.
5. Click to have the font.

Making Text Bold/Italics

For this do the following:

1. Select text.
2. Click at B for Bold or I for Italics in the properties dialog box.

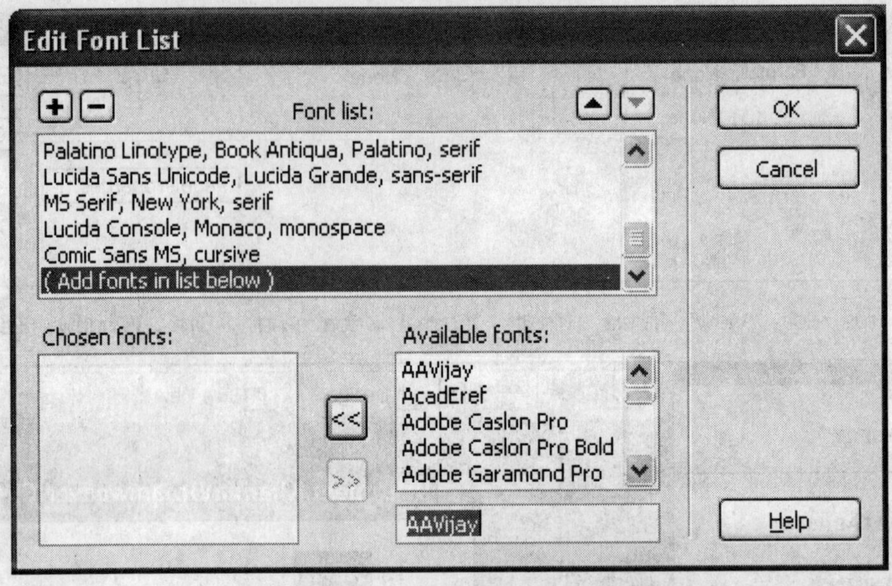

3. The text will change accordingly.
4. The result of this operation is shown below.

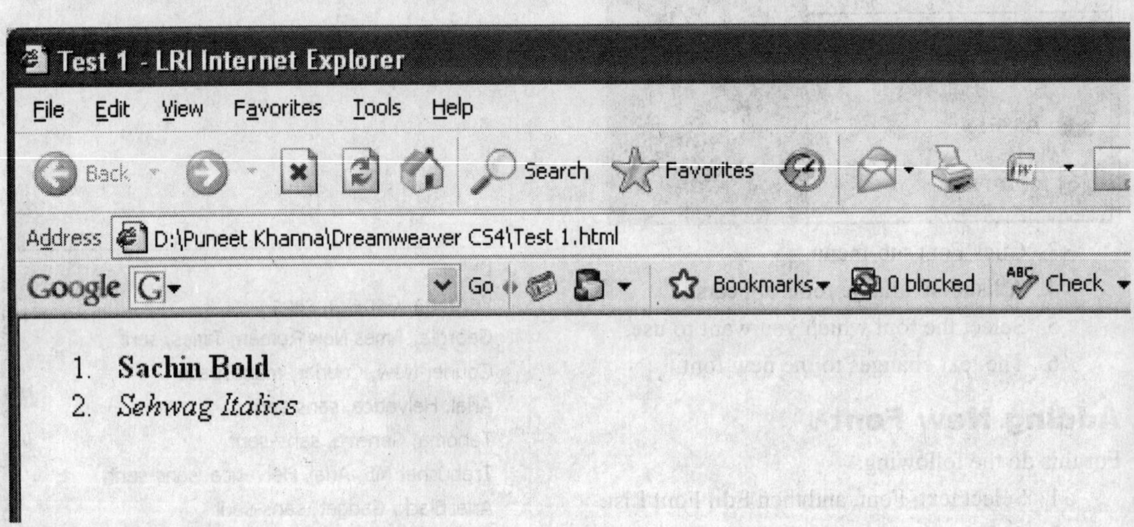

Changing Colour of the Text

For this do the following:

1. Select text.
2. Click Modify menu.
3. Click at Page Properties.
4. Click a colour.
5. This will change the default colour.
6. For changing the colour of the text, select text and apply colour from the properties dialog box.
7. The result of this operation is shown below.

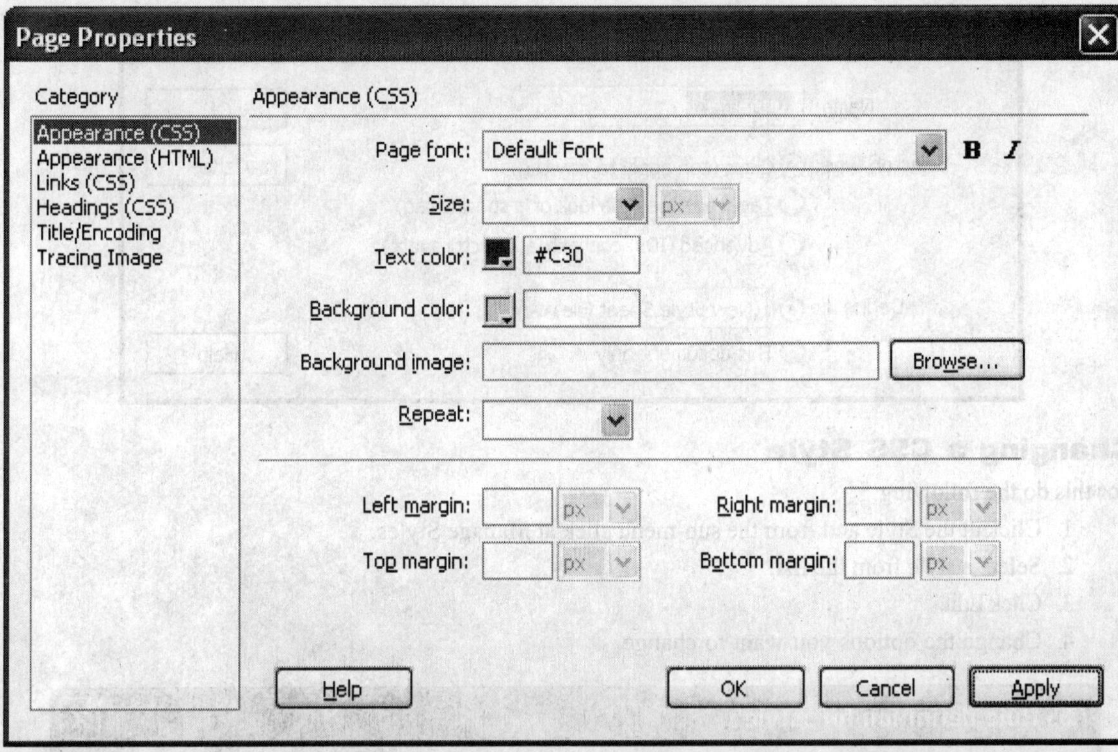

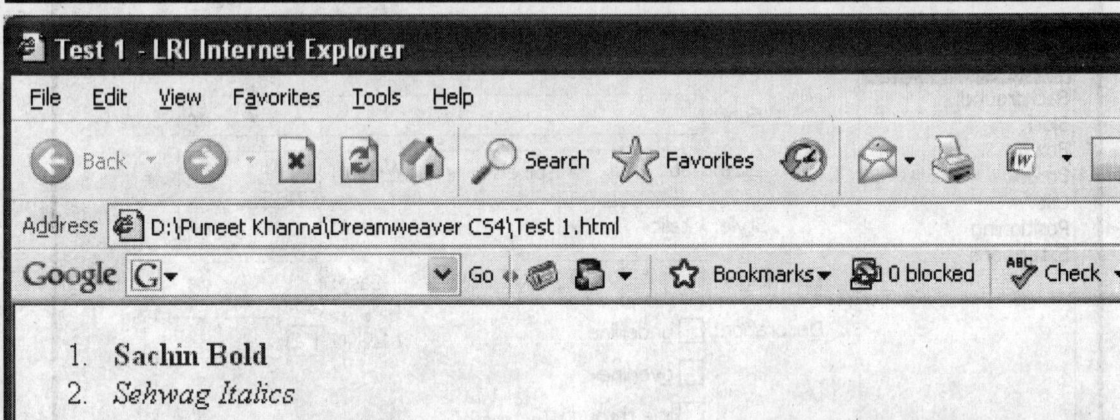

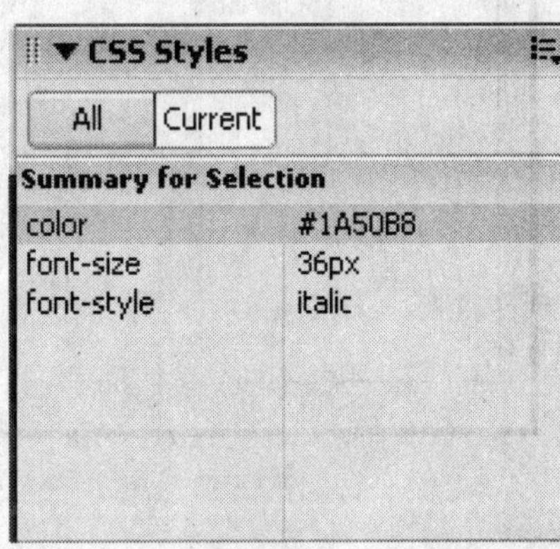

Creating a New CSS Style

For this do the following:

1. Click at CSS Styles button on the Properties.
2. The CSS Styles panel appears.
3. Click at the New.
4. The New CSS Style dialog box appears.
5. Give it a name and select the other options too.
6. Click Ok.
7. The new style appears in the CSS styles panel.

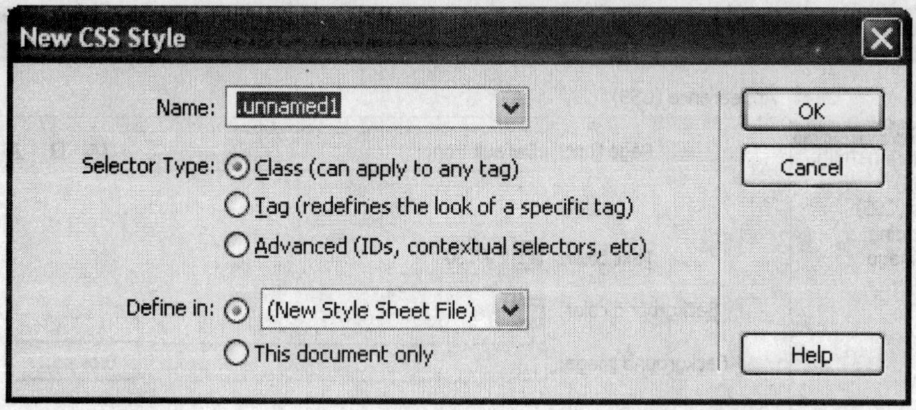

Changing a CSS Style

For this do the following:

1. Click at the Style and from the sub-menu click at Manage Styles.
2. Select a style from the list.
3. Click Edit.
4. Change the options you want to change.

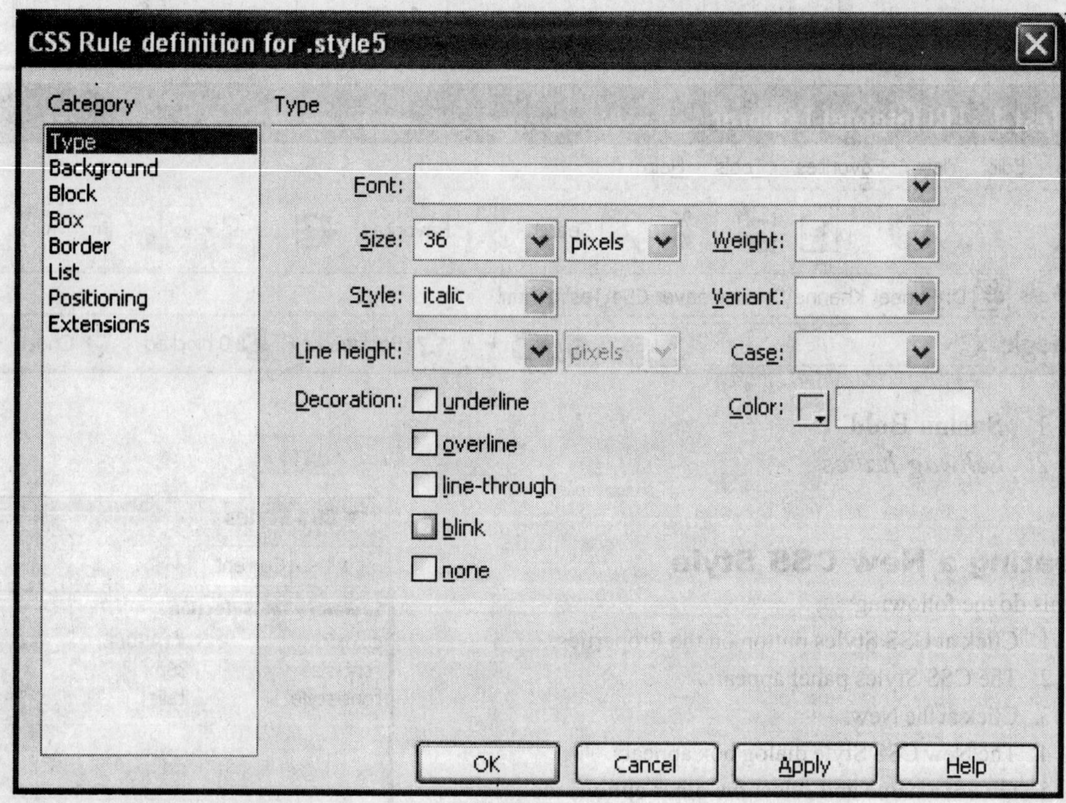

3 Adding Graphics and Multimedia

Introduction

Now we will add various type of graphics and multimedia files in our page. First among them is a simple image which we will insert.

Adding an Image

For adding an image to your page, do the following:

1. Place the cursor where you want to insert the image.
2. Click at Insert menu.
3. Click at Image.
4. Alternatively you can click at Insert Image icon on the Objects panel.
5. The select image source dialog box appears.

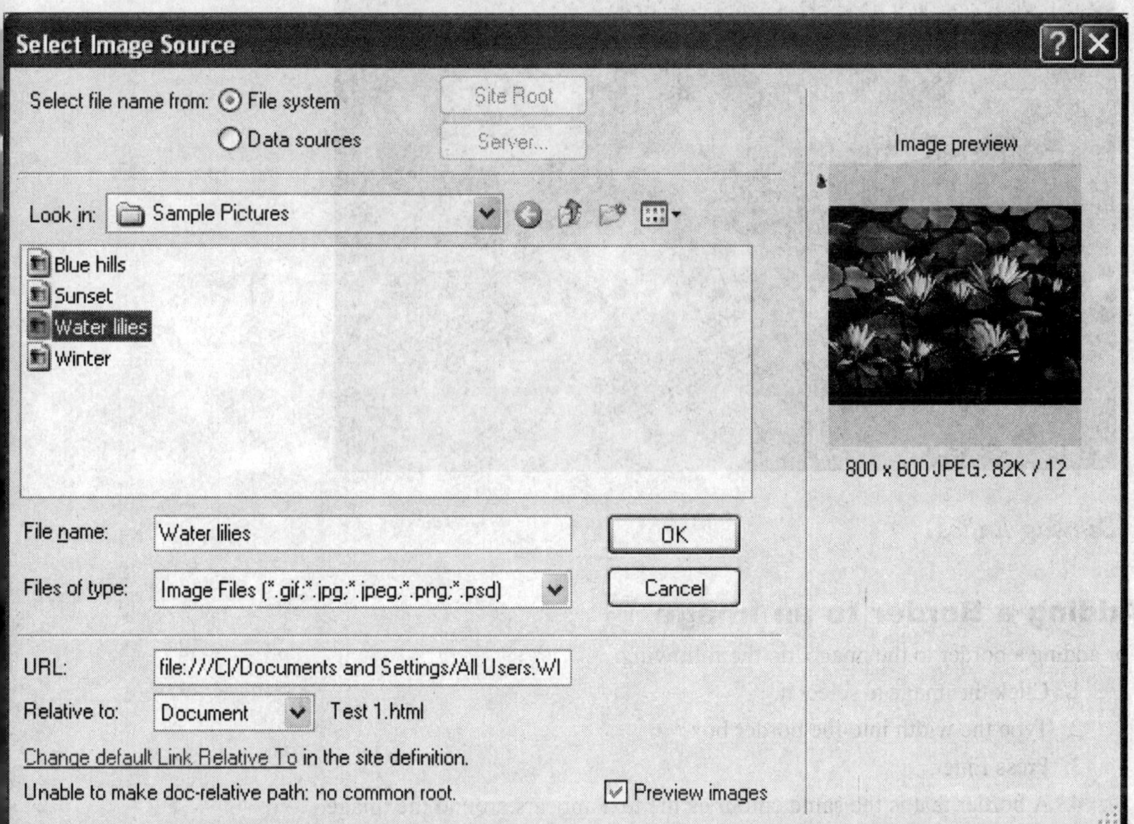

6. Click at the folder button to reach the folder where your file is.
7. Click at the image file.
8. A preview of the image appears.
9. Click select.
10. The image appears where you positioned your cursor in the Web page.

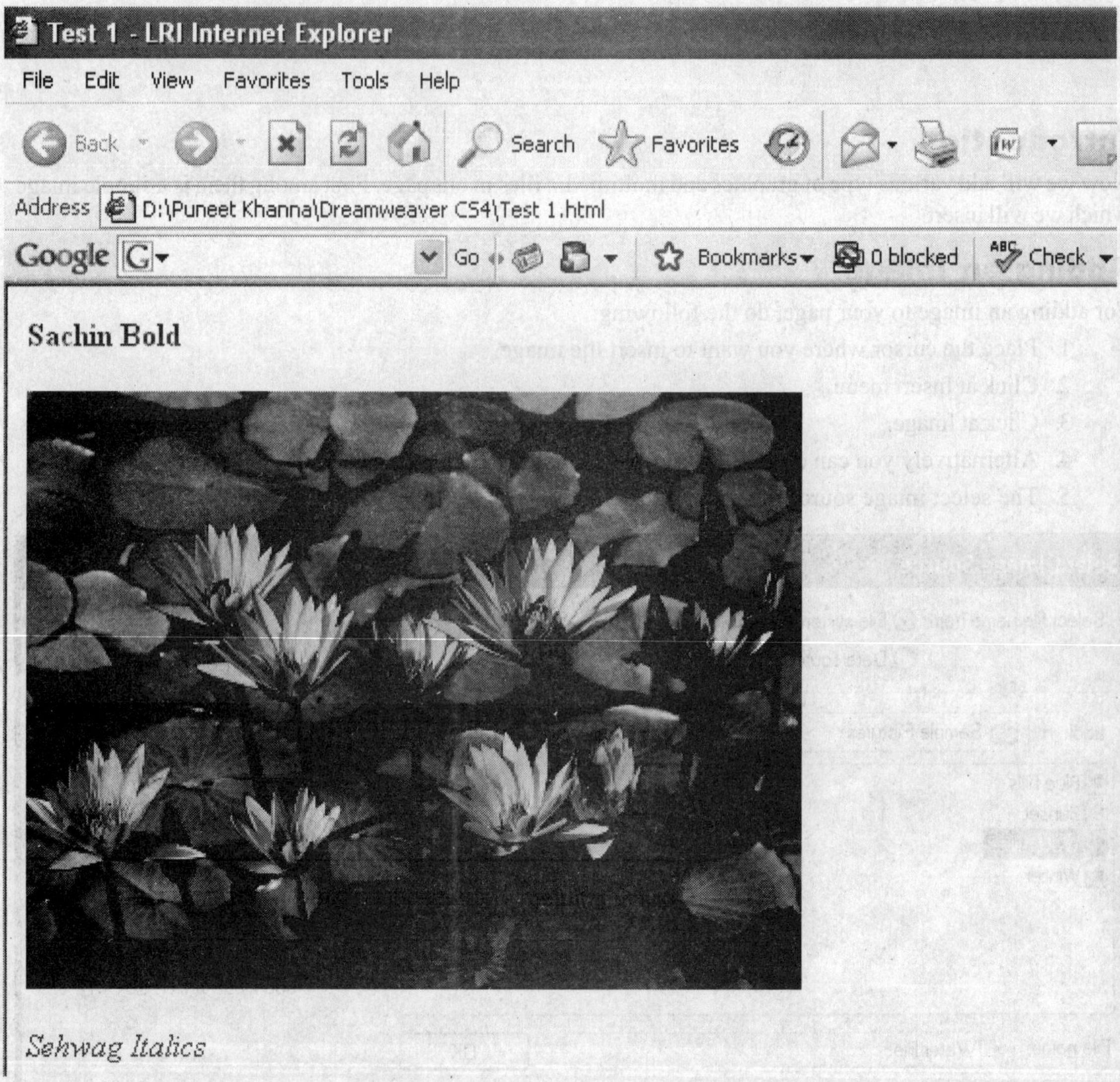

Adding a Border to an Image

For adding a border to the image, do the following:

1. Click the image to select it.
2. Type the width into the border box.
3. Press Enter.
4. A border that is the same colour as the text appears around the image.

5. See how the image looks now.

Resizing the Image

You can resize the image by changing its size in terms of height and width. For this, do the following:

1. Change the pixel dimensions as in terms of height and width.
2. The image appears in new shape.
3. Please make sure that the new dimensions are proportionate to the ones given before, else your image would look distorted.
4. Still however the best is to do it proportionatly, as describe in the next para.
5. In the figure on the last page, the dimensions have been changed.

Changing Dimensions by Dragging

For dragging the image to reshape, do the following:

1. Click the image to select it.

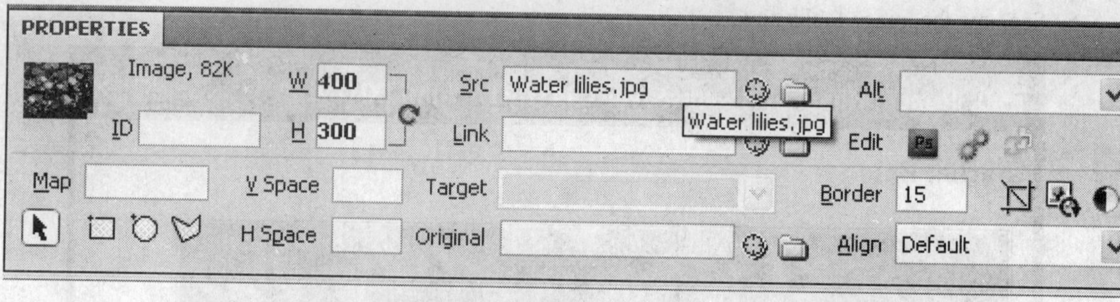

2. Click and drag the handle at the edge of the image.
3. You can even enter the % of the images in the height and width columns.
4. To proportionately reduce/increase the size of the image, you must have Shift key pressed.
5. This way the image would be reduced/increased in proportions.
6. You will see the result below.

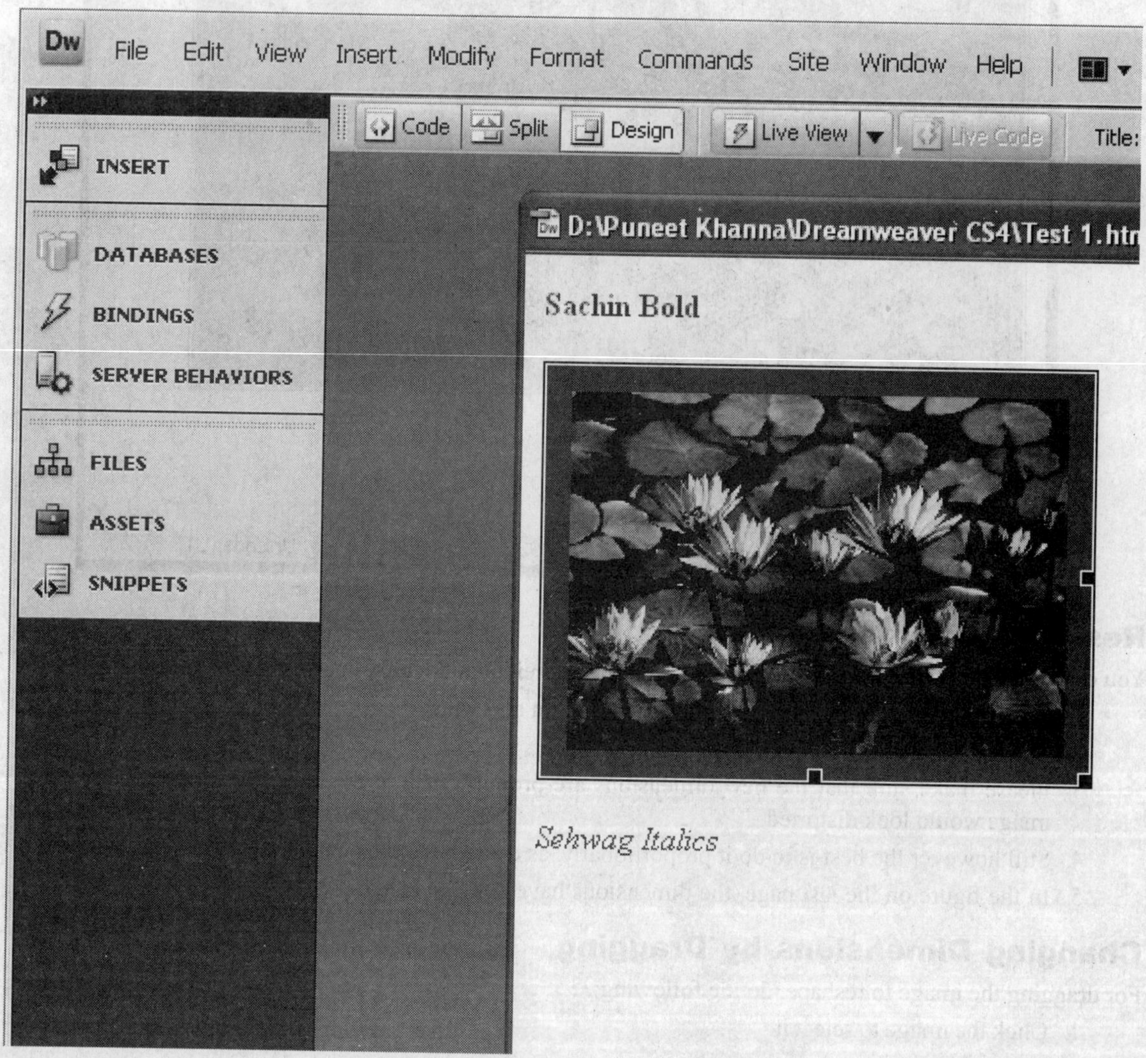

Wrapping Text around Image

There are 2 ways this can be done, i.e., leaving the space around the image on left and right or top and bottom. This is how it is done:

1. Click the image to select it.
2. Type the desire amount of space in vertical space.
3. Press Enter to see the space above and below the image.
4. Similarly you can add space on left and right by adding space to the horizontal space.
5. Both options are covered in the figure shown below.

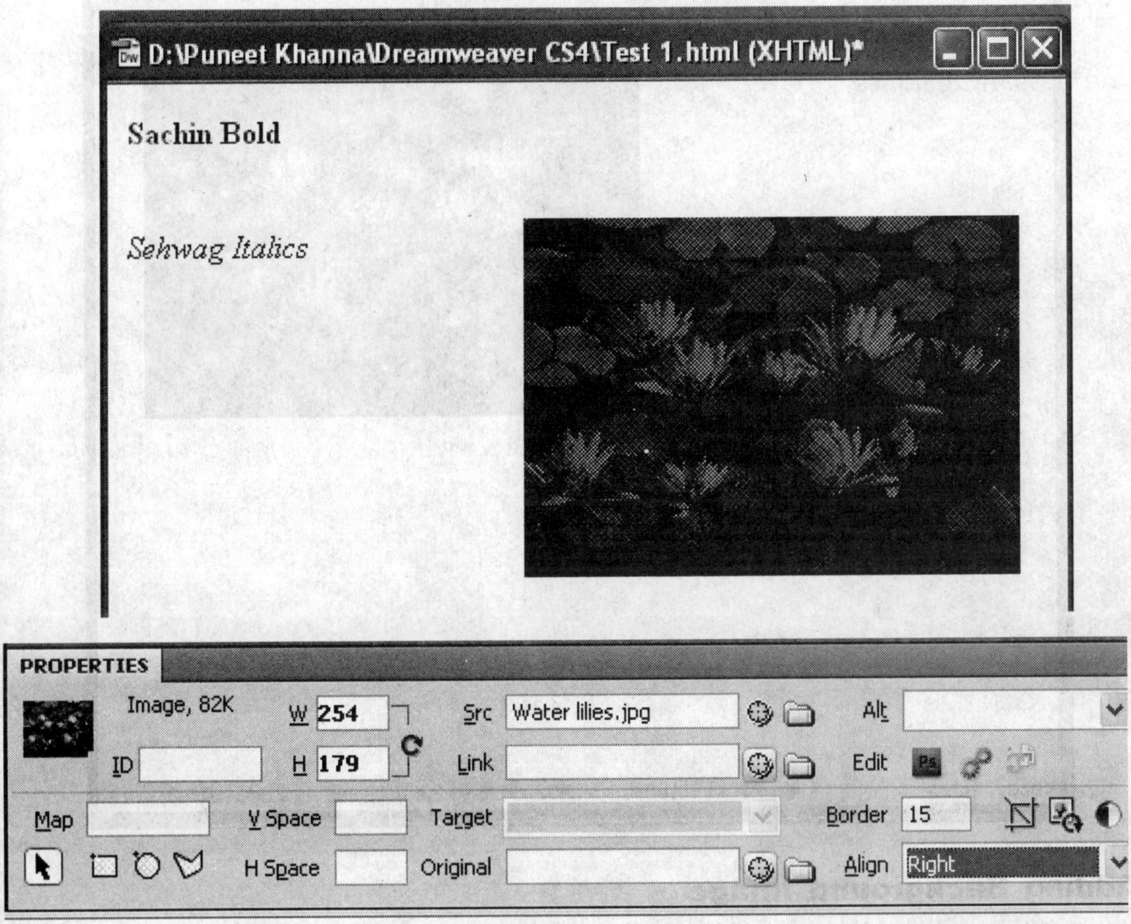

Adding Horizontal Rule

A horizontal rule can be added into your page and then it can be customized using the options from the properties dialog box. This is how it is done:

1. Place your cursor where you want to place your line.
2. From the Insert menu, click at HTML and then Horizontal rule.
3. A line will appear in your page.

4. Type the horzontal rule dimensions in the width and height boxes.
5. Click shading to shade the rule.
6. Select the alignment too, if needed.

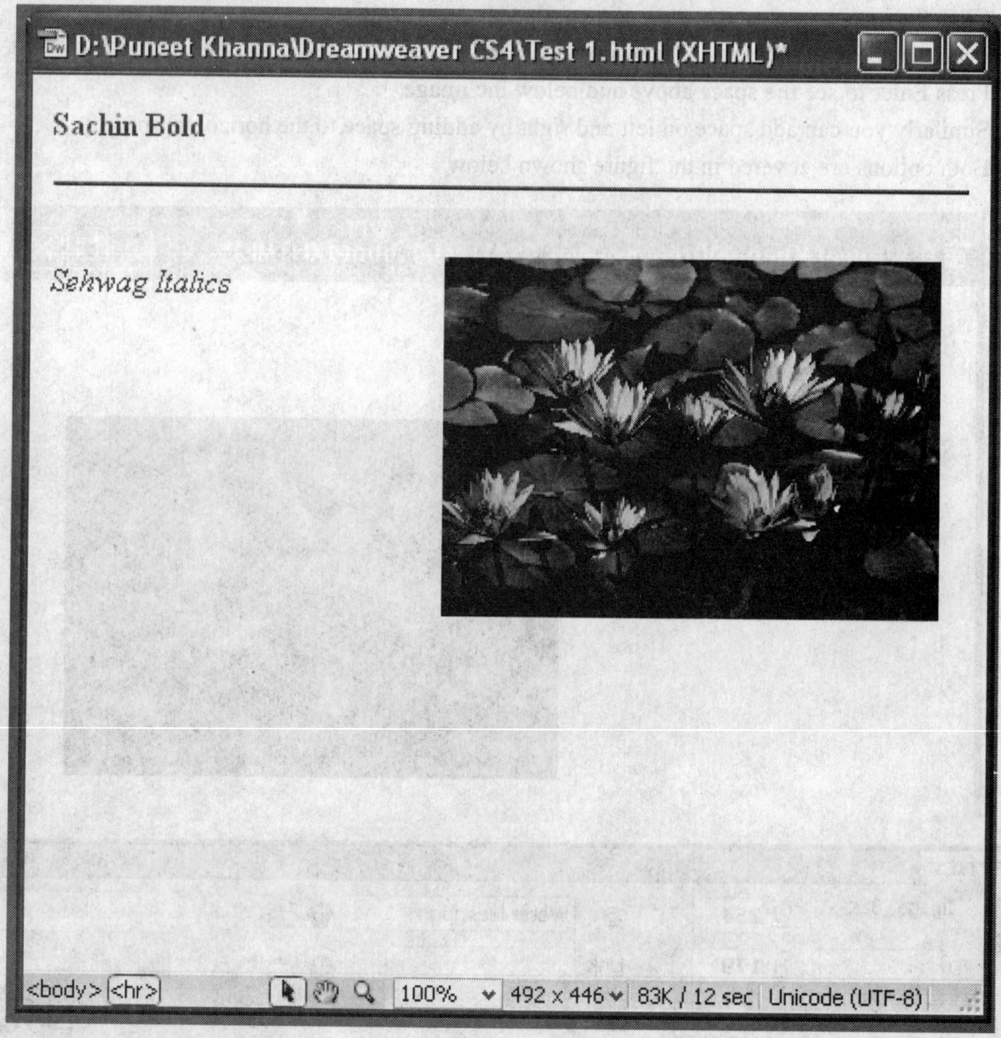

Adding Background Image

You can choose to have a background in your page. This is how it is done:

1. Click at the Modify menu.
2. Click at Page Properties.
3. Click at Background Image.
4. Click at Browse.
5. Select the figure you want to be included as the background image.
6. A preview image appears.
7. Click at Select. The image filename and path appears in the background image box.

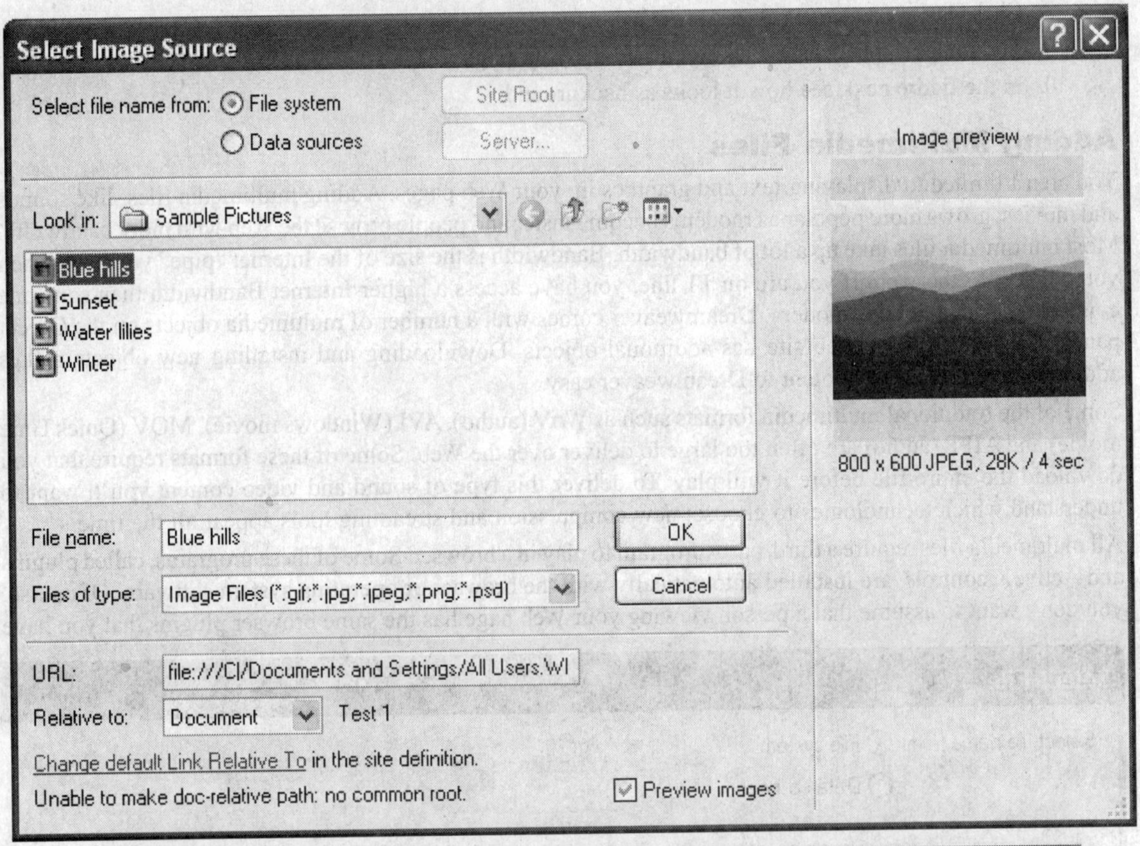
Select Image Source
Select file name from:
File system
Data sources
Site Root
Server...
Image preview
Look in:
Sample Pictures
Blue hills
Sunset
Water lilies
Winter
800 x 600 JPEG, 28K / 4 sec
File name:
Blue hills
OK
Files of type:
Image Files (*.gif;*.jpg;*.jpeg;*.png;*.psd)
Cancel
URL:
file:///C|/Documents and Settings/All Users.WI
Relative to:
Document
Test 1
Change default Link Relative To in the site definition.
Unable to make doc-relative path: no common root.
Preview images

D:\Puneet Khanna\Dreamweaver CS4\Test 1.html (XHTML)*
Sachin Bold
Sehwag Italics

8. Click Ok.
9. The image appears as a background on the your page.
10. In the figure next, see how it looks as background.

Adding Multimedia Files

You aren't limited to displaying text and graphics in your Web pages. Adding multimedia files, like sounds and movies, grows more popular as modems become faster and people browse the Web with more bandwidth. Most multimedia files take up a lot of bandwidth. Bandwidth is the size of the Internet "pipe" you have when you connect to the Web. If you are on T1 line, you have access a higher Internet Bandwidth than someone connecting with a 56kbps modem. Dreamweaver comes with a number of multimedia objects on the Object panel. The Macromedia Web site has additional objects. Downloading and installing new objects makes adding different types of content to Dreamweaver easy.

Some of the traditional multimedia formats such as WAV (audio), AVI (Windows movie), MOV (QuickTime movie) and AIFF (audio) are often too large to deliver over the Web. Some of these formats require that you download the entire file before it will play. To deliver this type of sound and video content you'll want to understand which technologies to choose; new compression and streaming tools appear all the time.

All multimedia files require a third-party program to play in a browser. Some of these programs, called plugins and ActiveX controls, are installed automatically with the browser or operating system software. Of course, you don't want to assume that a person viewing your Web page has the same browser plugins that you have

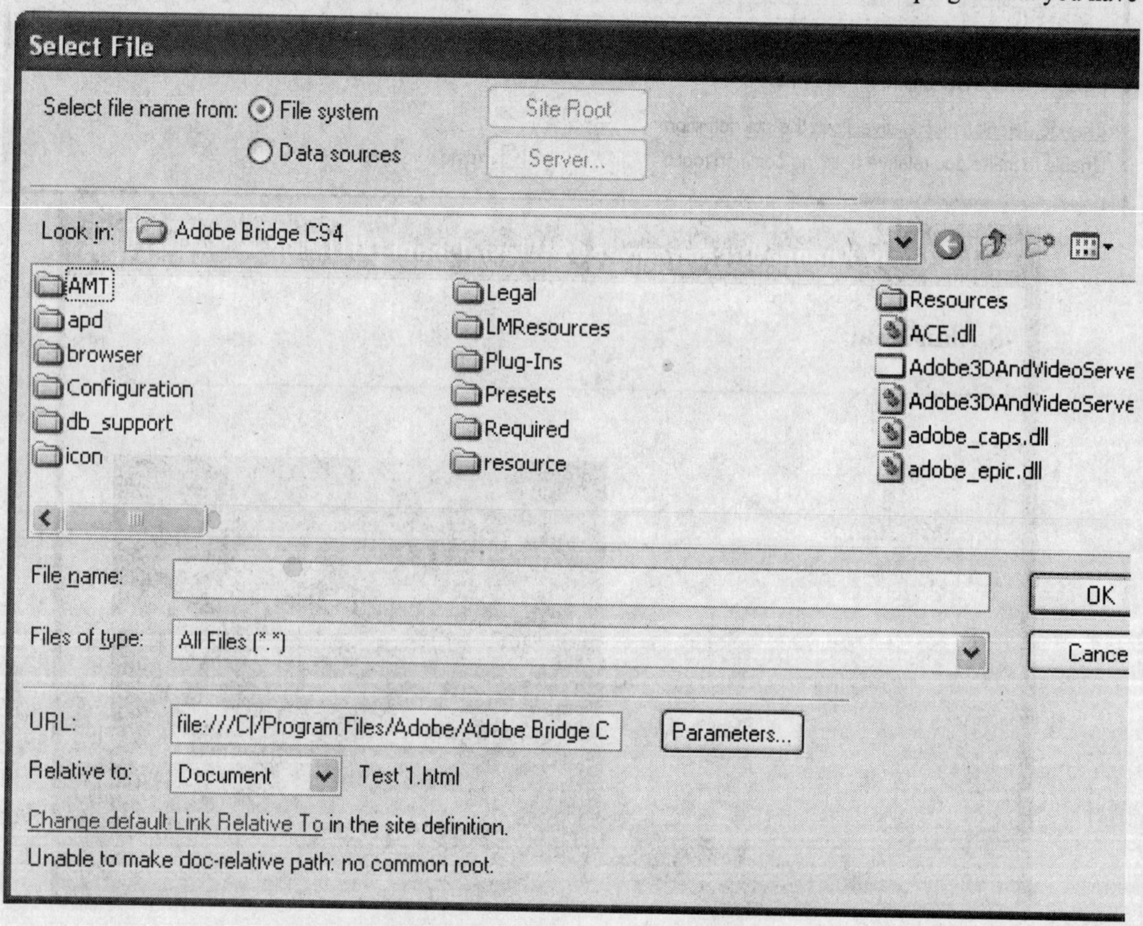

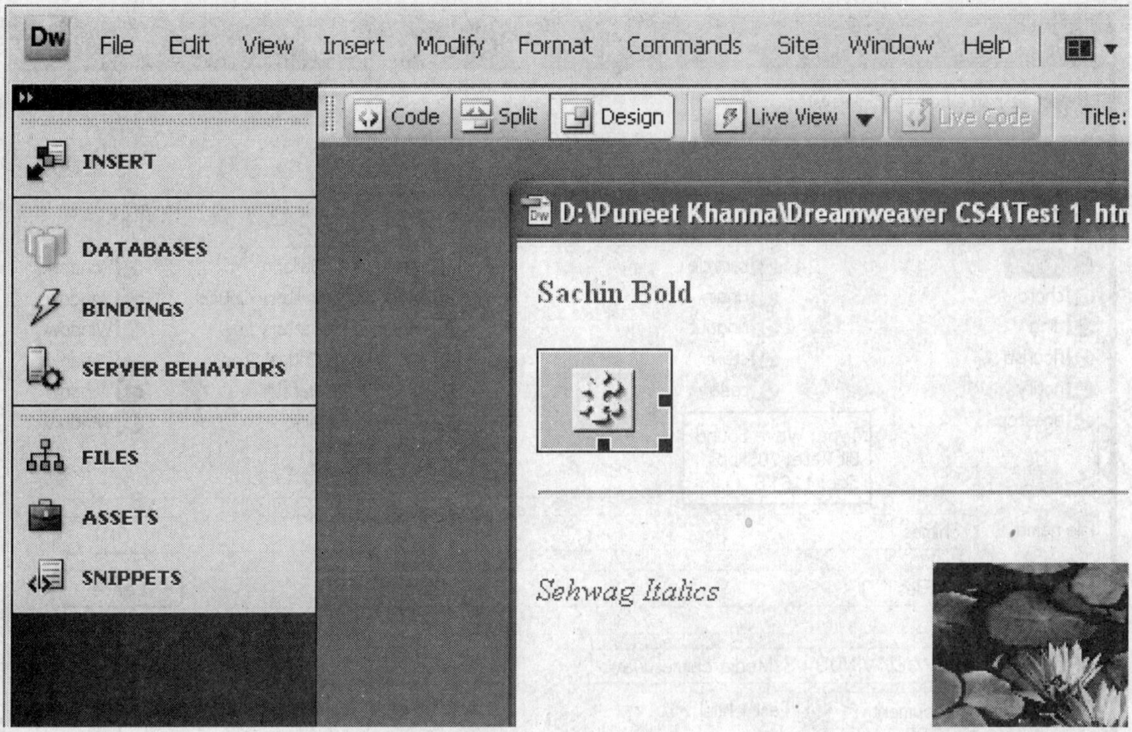

installed. You always want to give the viewer information on how to obtain a necessary third-party program. Dreamweaver has several features that improve your ability to successfully and multimedia files to a Web page. Dreamweaver gives you access to the properties that allow you to provide information on where to download a plugin. Dreamweaver enables you to add both Internet Explorer and Netscape specific plugin HTML code. There is a Dreamweaver behaviour that will detect whether the viewer has a specific plugin.

Add a Sound File

Adding a sound file to a Web page can sometimes add to the experience. And, it's a good way for you to get familiar with adding multimedia files. You use the Plugin object form the Special panel of the Object panel (or the Plugin command form the Media submenu of the Insert menu) to insert a sound into a Web page.

To insert a Plugin object

1. Place cursor where you want to insert your plugin.
2. Click at Insert menu and select Plugin from the Media submenu.
3. A select file dialog box appears.
4. Select the file which you want to place.
5. Click select.
6. A plugin icon appears in the Document window.
7. Type the URL of the side where the user can download the plug-in.
8. You can test some of the multimedia files.
9. In the figure shown here, I have used CHIMES.WAV file which gives the sound of a dog bark.

Notice the Property inspector for the Plugin object has some properties that are similar to ones you have seen while working with images. Selecting a file fills in the Src box.

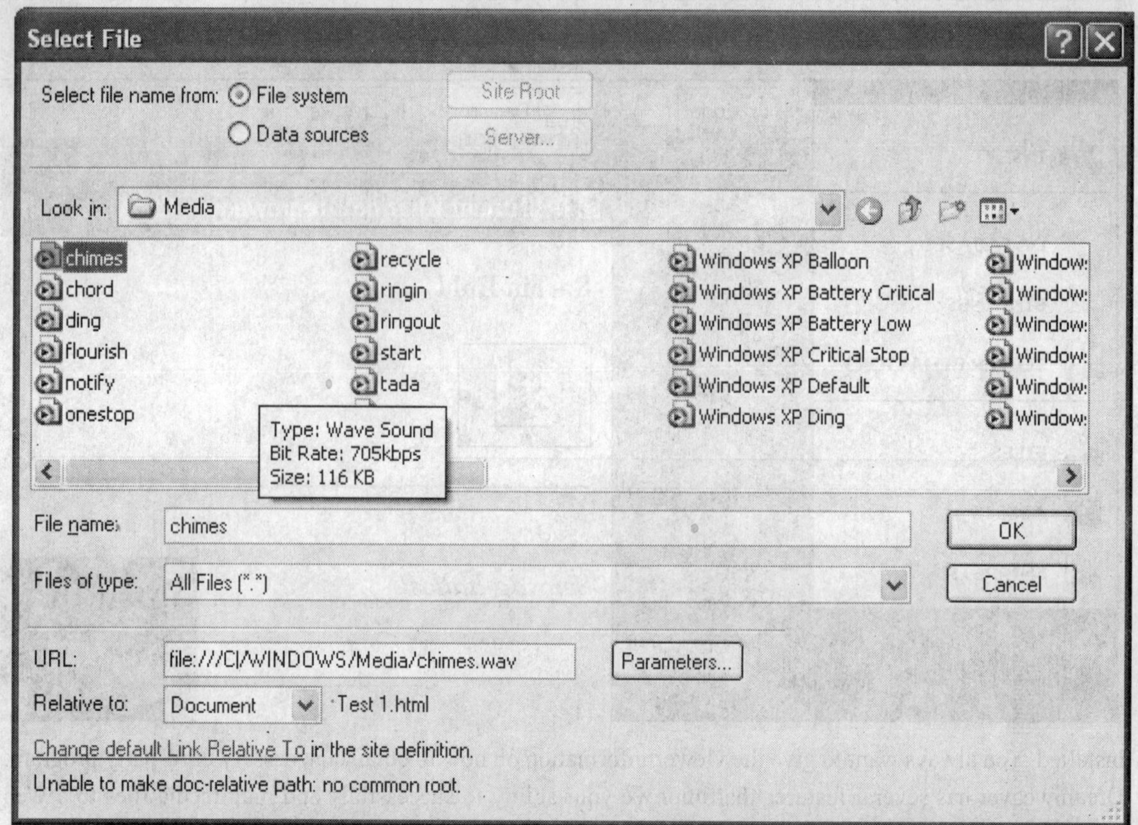
Select File
Select file name from: File system
Data sources
Site Root
Server...
Look in: Media
chimes
chord
ding
flourish
notify
onestop
recycle
ringin
ringout
start
tada
Windows XP Balloon
Windows XP Battery Critical
Windows XP Battery Low
Windows XP Critical Stop
Windows XP Default
Windows XP Ding
Type: Wave Sound
Bit Rate: 705kbps
Size: 116 KB
File name: chimes
OK
Files of type: All Files (*.*)
Cancel
URL: file:///C|/WINDOWS/Media/chimes.wav
Parameters...
Relative to: Document
Test 1.html
Change default Link Relative To in the site definition.
Unable to make doc-relative path: no common root.

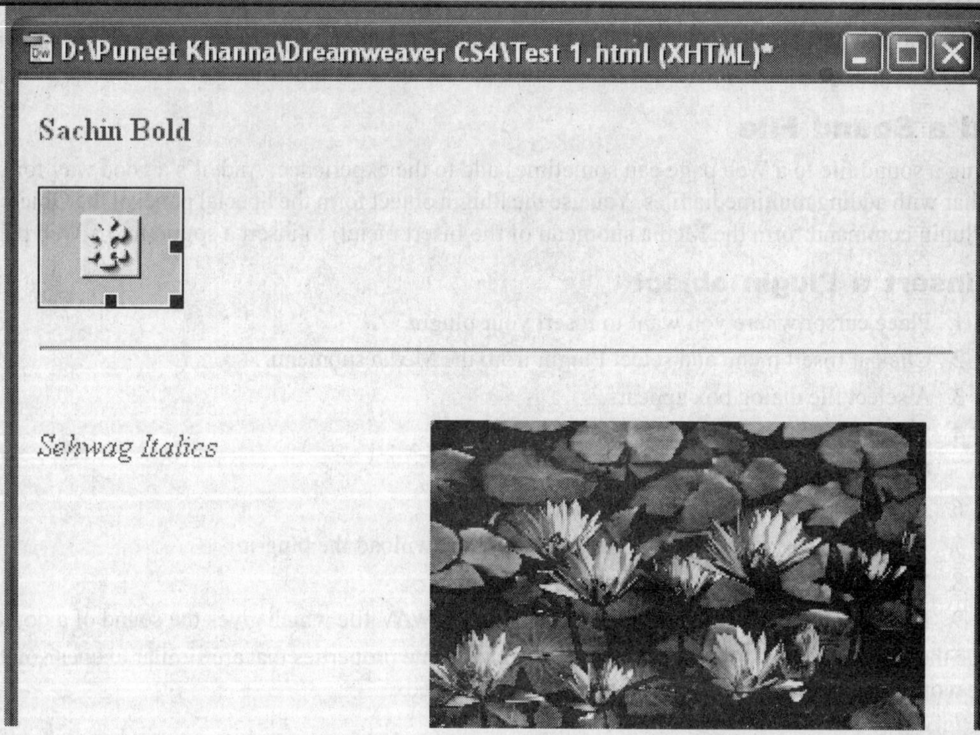
D:\Puneet Khanna\Dreamweaver CS4\Test 1.html (XHTML)*
Sachin Bold
Sehwag Italics

There is an Align drop-down menu, similar to the one for images, which affects how other objects align with the Plugin object. Other familiar properties are W (width), H (height), V align (vertical) and H align (horizontal). You can also add a border to the Plugin object.

When delivering multimedia, much depends on which browser and plugins the user has. Some plugins and some sound file formats are more popular than others are.

The popularity of file format is constantly evolving. These days, the RealMedial and MP3 sounds formats are popular and quite common on the Web. MIDI files are common, too.

Some of the most popular sound file formats, are given below.

Common Web Sound Formats

Format	Streaming?	Description
AIFF	No	A popular Macintosh sound format. Not idea for longer sounds because of its large file size.
WAV	No	A popular Windows sound format. Not ideal for longer sounds because of its large file size.
u-Law (.au)	No	Originally, a popular Web sound format from Sun, but not as common now.
QuickTime	Yes	Apple's movie format can also play sounds. File sizes can be large.
MIDI	No	Open standard sound format that uses defined MIDI sounds on the user's computer. Files are very compact.
RealMedia	Yes	Real-time streaming audio and video format.
Shockwave Audio	Yes	Real-time streaming audio format.
MP3 (MPEG 3)	Yes	Compact file size with excellent sound quality. This open standard sound format has become very popular.
Liquid Audio	Yes	Small file sizes with excellent sound quality.
Beatnik	No	Sound format combining MIDI and digital audio.

Add Looping to the Sound

Dreamweaver offers the flexibility to deal with advanced attributes of objects and even attributes that haven't been created yet, through the Parameters dialog box. Selecting the Parameters buttons opens the Parameters consist of two parts: a parameter name and a value.

Many plugins have optional or required parameters that you can set in the Parameters dialog box. The parameters available for sounds, such as loop and autostart, may or may not be available for other formats. Different plugins have different parameters available. Various options of common sound parameters are given below.

Common Sound Parameters

Parameters	*Values*
loop	TRUE, FALSE, N (number of times playing)
autostart	TRUE, FALSE
hidden	TRUE, FALSE
volume	0-100
playcount	N (number of times playing-IE only)

After selecting the Parameters button, click the + button to add a parameter.

- To make the sound loop, type loop as the parameter name. Tab or click in the value column and type TRUE. The default is false so if you only want the sound to play once you do not need to enter the loop parameter. Netscape will recognise a number as the value of the loop parameter and will play the sound that many times.
- To create the same effect with Internet Explorer, add the playcount parameter in addition to loo.

You can enter multiple parameters in the Parameters dialog box. After you have finished adding parameters, click the OK button. To edit a parameter, select the Parameter button align and click in the parameter you want to change. To delete a parameter, click the – button. Use the arrow keys to rearrange the order of the parameters.

Creating Flash Text

Now you can add by creating Flash objects directly in Dreamweaver. You do not need to have Flash installed on your computer to have this functionality. You can now create Flash Text and Flash buttons right in Dreamweaver.

The Flash Text object enables you to create and insert a Flash movie consisting of text into your Web page. Insertn Flash text has advantages over using simple HTML text:

- Flash text can be anti-aliased. Anti-aliasing blends text with the background so that the edges of the letters look smoother.
- You can use any font available on your computer. The viewer does not need to have the font installed on their computer.
- The text can be larger than HTML text.

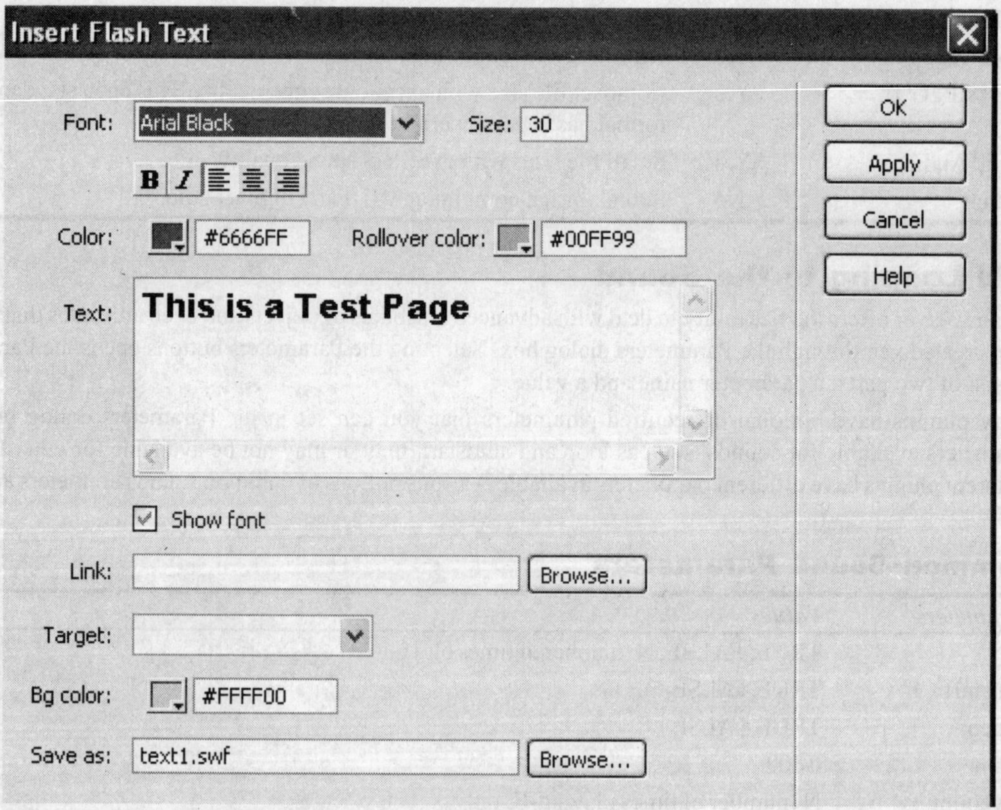

To insert a Flash Text object into your Web page

1. Select the Flash Text object from the Object panel or the Interactive Images submenu of the Insert menu.
2. The Insert Flash Text dialog box appears (shown in figure. Select the Font, Size, Style (Bold or Italic) and alignment. Select the Color, which is the initial color of the text and Rollover color, which is the color the user will se when they place their cursor over the text.
3. Type the text you want to appear in the Text box. Make sure the Show Font check box is selected beneath the box so you can see what the font you have selected looks like.
4. Enter a URL in the Link text box, or use the Browse button to browse to a Web page. It's a good idea to only link to local Web pages in the same directory where you save your Flash text movie. Document relative links do not work in some browsers if the files are no in the same directory.
5. Using the Target text box, you can target a window for the link.
6. Select a background color from the Bg Color drop-down list.
7. Dreamweaver creates a separate flash movie for your Flash text. Enter a name for the Flash movie in the Save As box.
8. Click OK. You'll see the text appear in the Dreamweaver document window.

You can edit your Flash text movie after you have inserted it into a Web page by selecting the Edit button in the Properties inspector when the movie is selected in the document window. You can view the changes you make in the Insert Flash Text dialog box without closing the dialog box by selecting the Apply button.

In the document window, the Flash Text can be resized by either dragging the resize handles or entering new

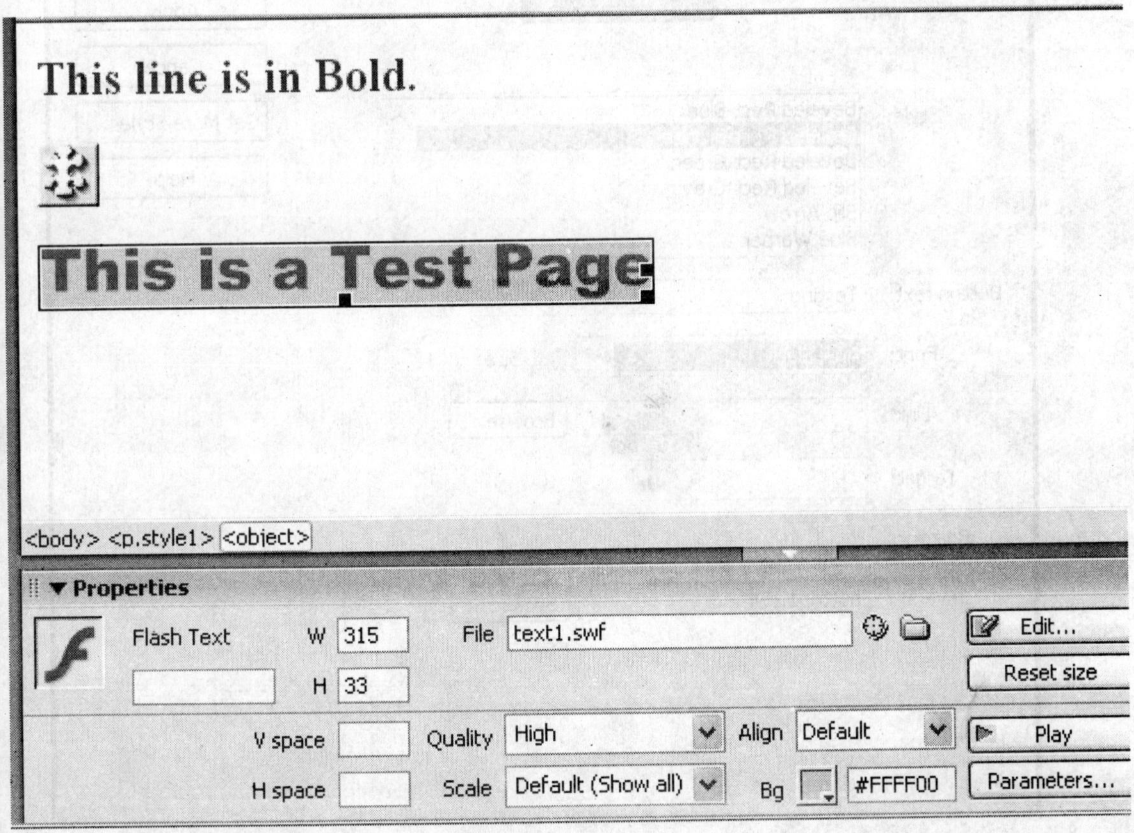

W (width) and H (height) attributes into the Property inspector. Select the Reset Size button to return to the original dimensions of the movie.

Create a Flash Button

Dreamweaver comes with a number of templates for creating Flash buttons right in Dreamweaver. Like the Flash Text object you just created, Dreamweaver creates Flash button movies automatically. To insert a Flash button into your Web page.

1. Select the Insert Flash Button object from the Object panel or the Interactive Images submenu of the Insert menu.
2. The Insert Flash Button dialog box appears.
3. Select a button style from the Style list. A preview of the button appears in the Sample window at the top of the dialog box. You can click on the preview to see what the down state of the button looks like and any animation effects that the button might have.
4. Add text to a button in the Button Text field. Only buttons that already have the default "Button Text" text in the Sample window will display this text. You cannot and text to buttons that do not already display text.

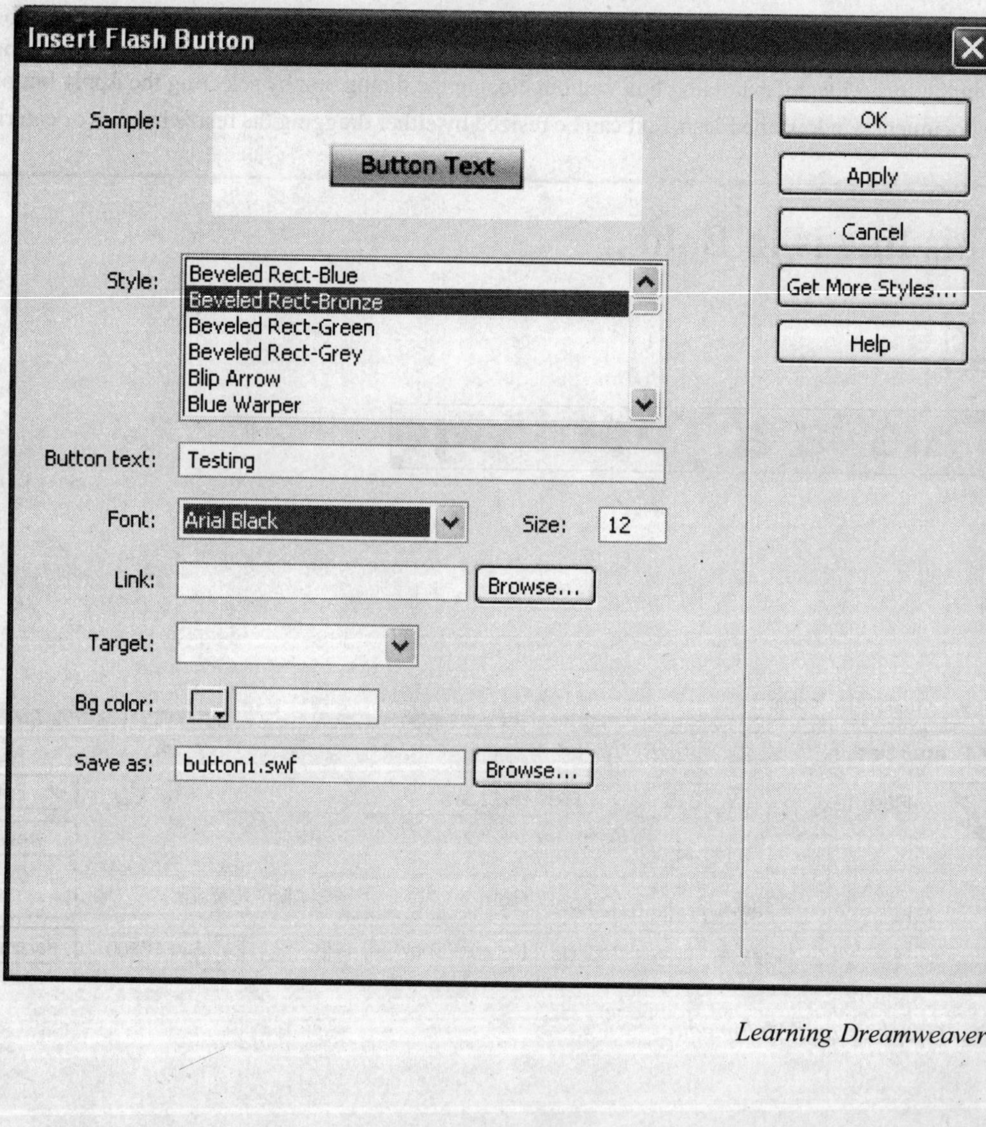

5. Set up font and font size for the button text in the Font and Font Size text boxes. You can choose from different fonts in the Font drop-down list.
6. Enter a URL for a hyperlink and a target, if necessary, in the Link and Target text boxes, respectively. As when you created Flash text, you need to be careful about document-relative addressing. It's best to save the Flash movie in the same directory as the linked Web page.
7. Add a background color from the Bg drop-down list. This color appears around the button, not within the button art.
8. Click OK. You'll see the button appear in the Dreamweaver document window.

You can edit the Flash button as you did the Flash text above. Both the button and then text movies are saved as Flash .swf files and can be edited in Flash. Some buttons can be used as groups. For instance, a number of e-commerce buttons are available to create a purchasing and checkout application.

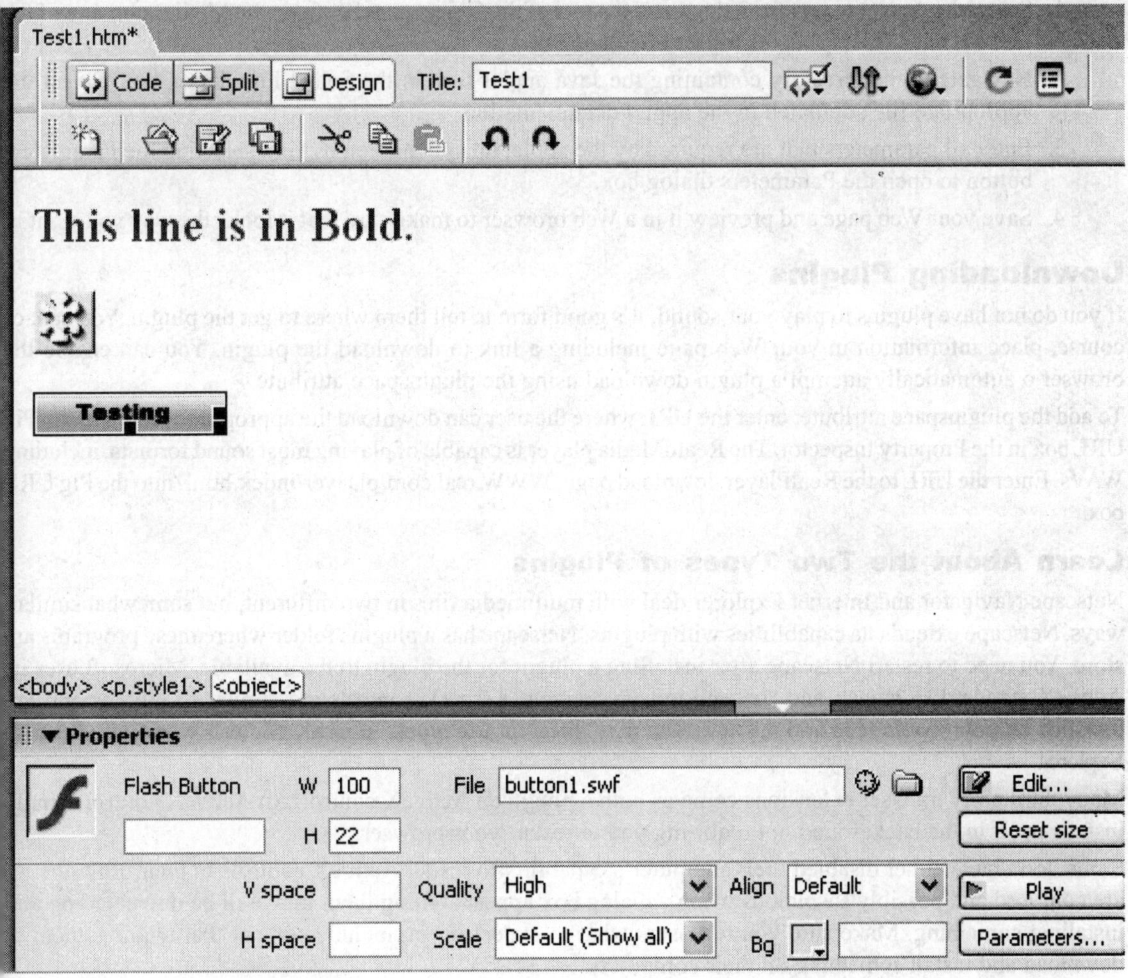

Insert a Java Applet

Java is a programming language used to create self-contained programs called applets. Java applets run within the browser window just like the other multimedia objects you've been working with in this color. You can put a Java applet into your page, add parameters, and add some interesting multimedia to your Web page.

Java and JavaSript are not the same thing. Nor are they really related. JavaScript is a scripting language that is used in Web page development to set the properties of a Web page. Java is a compiled programming language that is used to develop applications.

To insert a Java applet into your Web page, you must have all of the appropriate files for the applet. The number and type of files may vary. You will need to read the documentation for the applet that you are using. Some users have Java turned off in their browser, so you should be careful about including information vital to the Web page in a Java applet.

Any Java applet that you intend on using in your Web page should come with instructions on how to set it up. Be sure to read the instructions carefully and enter all the parameters correctly or the applet might not work. If you do not set up the applet correctly, users sill simply see an empty grey box on the page.

To insert applet into a Web page

1. Select the Applet object from the Special panel of the Object panel or from the Media submenu of the Insert menu. This opens the Select File dialog box.
2. Navigate to the directory containing the Java applet files in the Select File dialog box. Select the appropriate file stipulated in the applet documentation.
3. Enter all parameters that are required by the applet documentation by first selecting the Parameters button to open the Parameters dialog box.
4. Save your Web page and preview it in a Web browser to make sure that it looks the way you want it.

Downloading Plugins

If you do not have plugins to play your sound, it's good form to tell them where to get the plugin. You can, of course, place information in your Web page including a link to download the plugin. You can enable the browser o automatically attempt a plugin download using the pluginspace attribute.

To add the pluginspace attribute, enter the URL where the user can download the appropriate plugin in the Plg URL box in the Property Inspector. The RealdMedia player is capable of playing most sound formats, including WAVs. Enter the URL to the RealPlayer download page, WWW.real.com/plaayer/index.html, into the Plg URL box.

Learn About the Two Types of Plugins

Netscape Navigator and Internet Explorer deal with multimedia files in two different, but somewhat similar, ways. Netscape extends its capabilities with plugins. Netscape has a plugins folder where these programs are stord. You need to restart Netscape after installing a plugin for the plugin to the available. Microsoft uses its ActiveX standard to launch and run multimedia content. ActiveX controls are similar to plugins and are installed on your machine to add the ability to play different file types. ActiveX controls work with Internet Explorer.

Many third party browser extensions come as both a plugin an ActiveX control. An ActiveX control usually installs itself in the background not requiring you to restart your browser.

Some users have either disabled their computer's capability to install ActiveX controls in their browsers, or are confused and possibly suspicious when a dialog box appears telling them they will be downloading and installing something. Make sure you tell users what to expect if you include content that requires them to download and install something on their computers.

Installing plugins and ActiveX controls registers the appropriate MIME type in the browser. MIME (Multipurpose Internet Mail Extensions) types enables your browser to recognise a extension. Your browser can the launch the correct plugin to play the file.

4 Working with Tables in Dreamweaver CS3

Introduction

So far you have seen how the text and graphics are used by Dreamweaver. In this chapter we will see how the software handles tables and the data in them. But, first of all let us create a table.

Inseting a Table

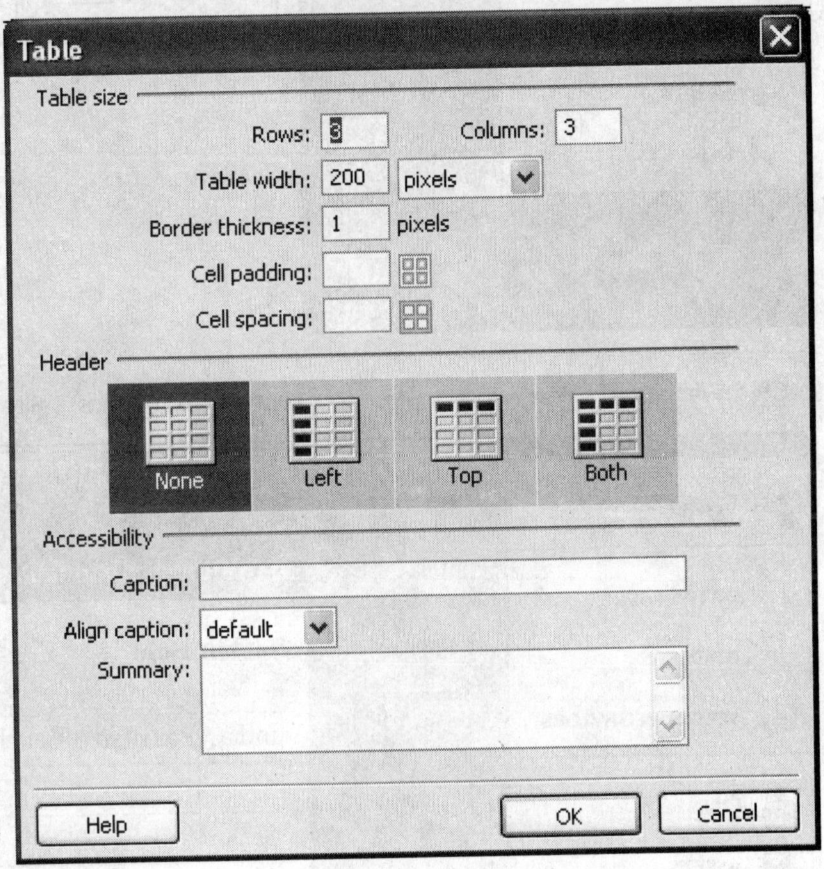

For this do the following:

1. Place the cursor where you want to insert the table.
2. Click at Insert menu and choose Table.
3. A Table dialog box appears.
4. Type the number of rows and columns you want in your table.
5. You can set the width in pixels or as a percentage by clicking and selecting your choice of measurements.
6. Type a border size in pixels.
7. You can set other options too and then click Ok.

Inseting Text into Tables

For this do the following:

1. Click inside a table cell.
2. Type your text in the cell.

Inseting a Table within a Table

For this do the following:

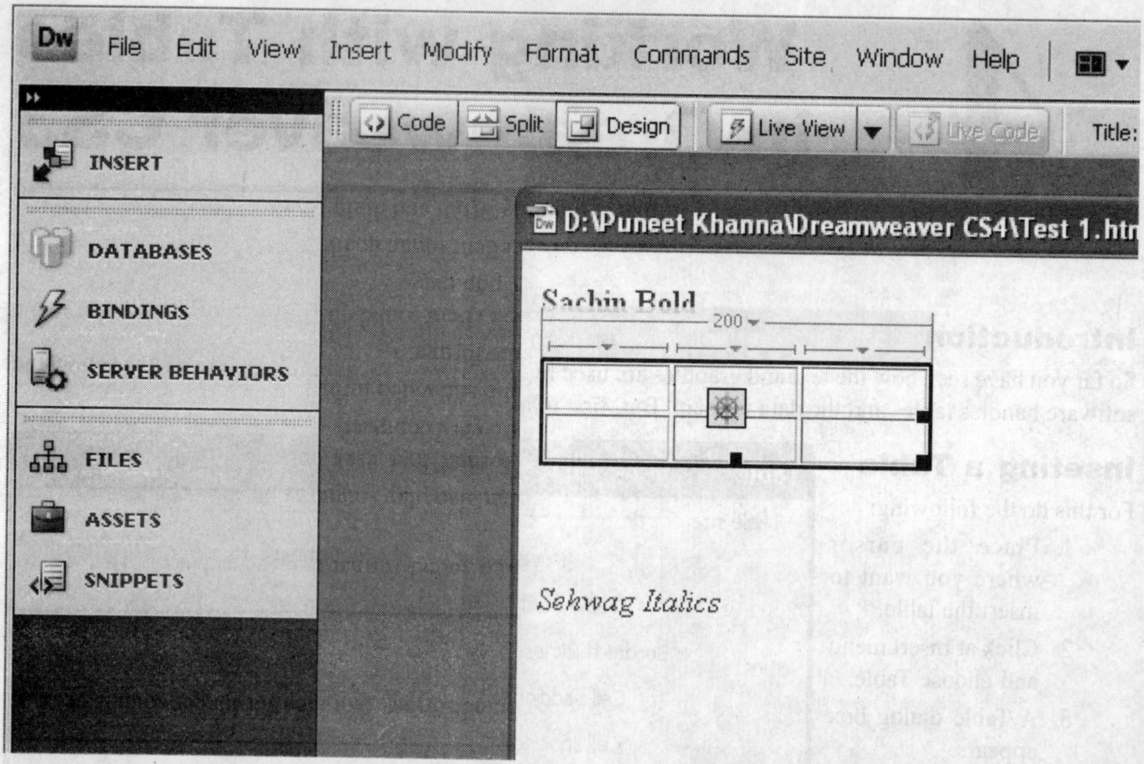
Dw
File
Edit
View
Insert
Modify
Format
Commands
Site
Window
Help
Code
Split
Design
Live View
Live Code
Title:
INSERT
DATABASES
BINDINGS
SERVER BEHAVIORS
FILES
ASSETS
SNIPPETS
D:\Puneet Khanna\Dreamweaver CS4\Test 1.htm
Sachin Bold
200
Sehwag Italics

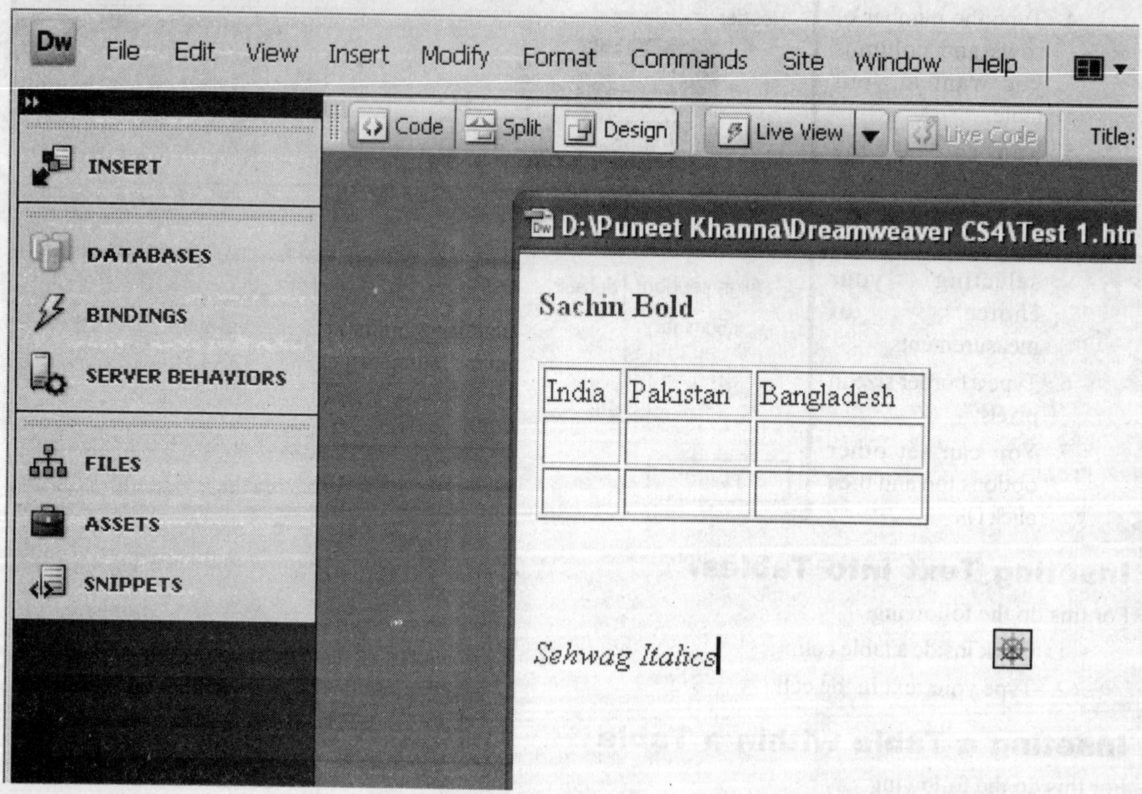
Dw
File
Edit
View
Insert
Modify
Format
Commands
Site
Window
Help
Code
Split
Design
Live View
Live Code
Title:
INSERT
DATABASES
BINDINGS
SERVER BEHAVIORS
FILES
ASSETS
SNIPPETS
D:\Puneet Khanna\Dreamweaver CS4\Test 1.htm
Sachin Bold
India
Pakistan
Bangladesh
Sehwag Italics

1. Click inside a table cell.
2. Click at table icon.
3. Type your measurement to define the characteristics of the table.
4. Click Ok.
5. A new table appears within the table cell.

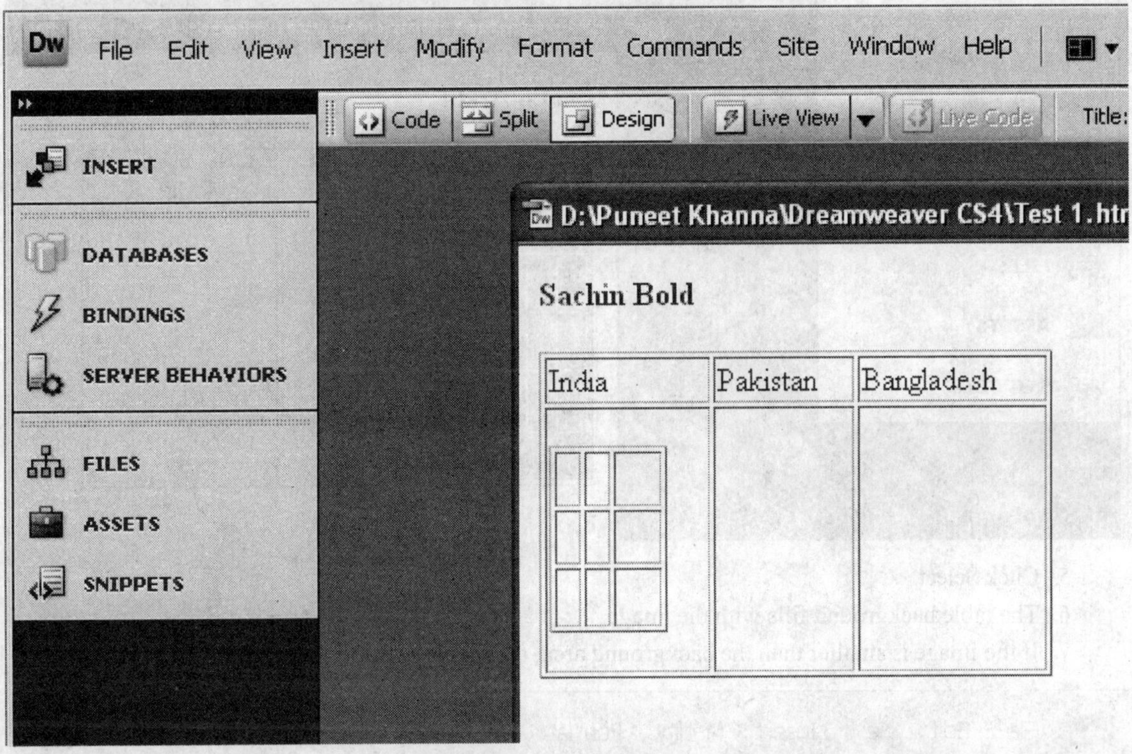

Changing Background Colour of a Table

For this do the following:

1. Click the upper left corner to select the table.
2. Click the Bg Colour.
3. Click a colour.
4. You can click the System Color Picker button to select a custom color.
5. You can click the Default Color button to specify no colour.
6. The background colour fills the cells of the table.
7. You can also type a colour name or a hexadecimal colour code directly.

Inserting Image in a Table

For this do the following:

1. Click the upper left corner to select the table.
2. Click the Insert Image icon.
3. The Select Image Source dialog box appears.
4. Click an image file.

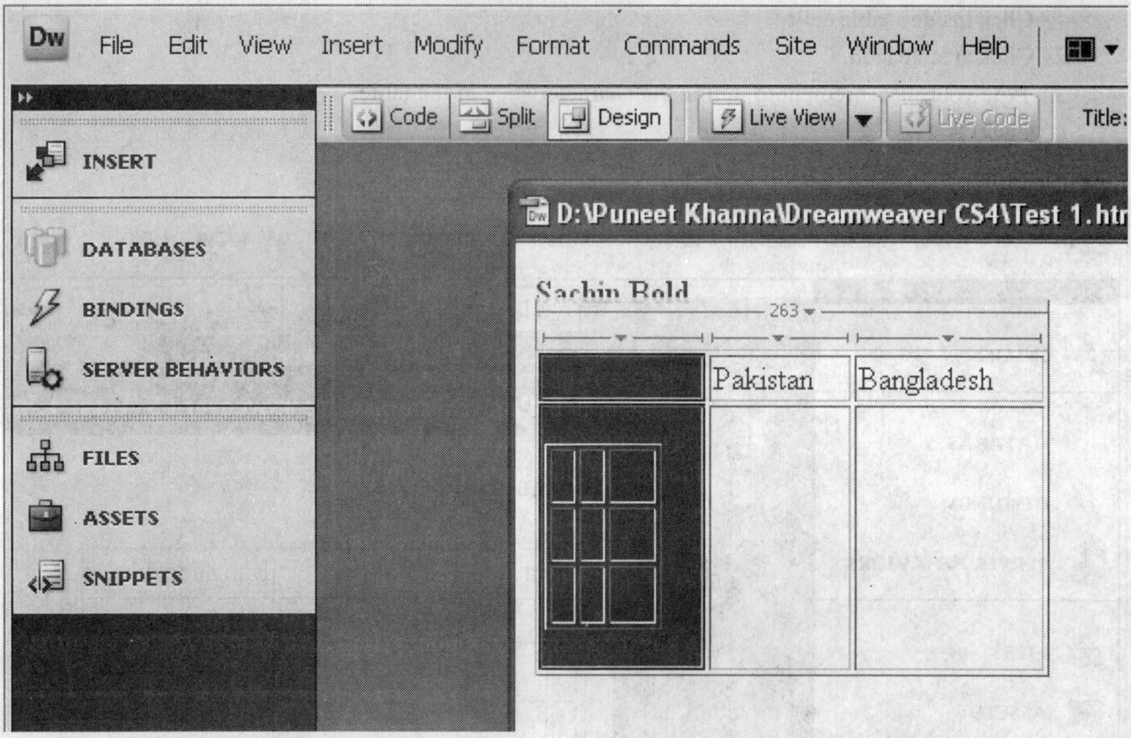

5. Click Select.
6. The table background fills with the image.
7. If the image is smaller than the background area, the image tiles to fill the entire table.

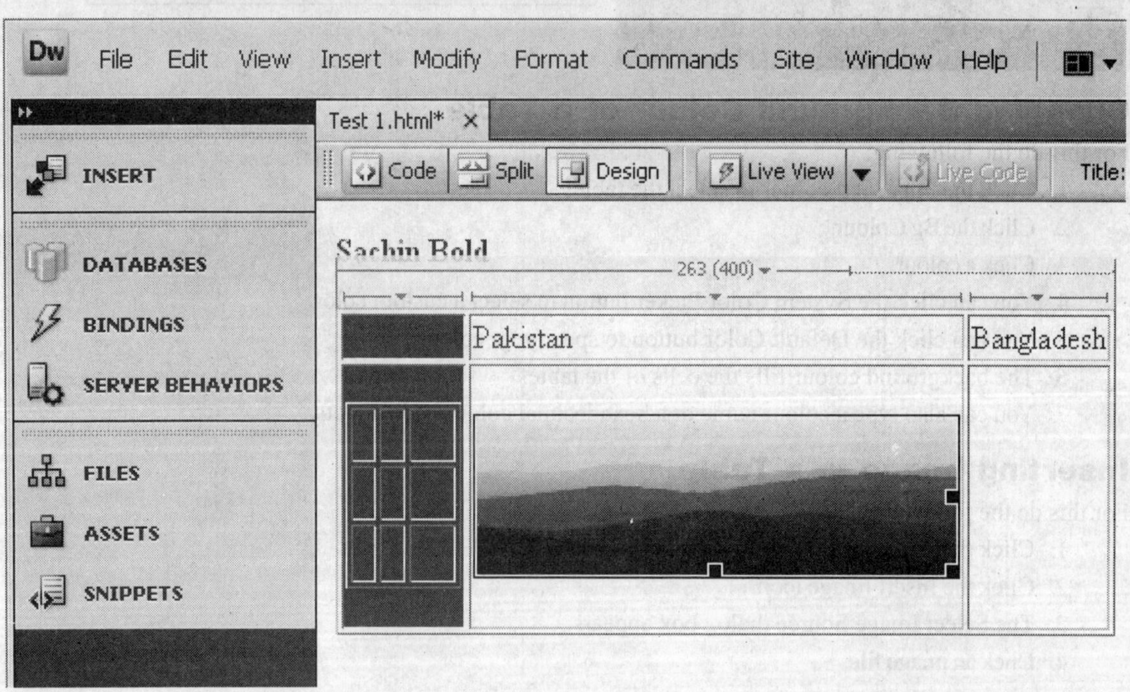

Inserting Rows or Columns in a Table

For this do the following:

1. Click the cell directly below where you want to insert a row or directly to the right of where you want to insert a column.
2. Click the Modify menu.
3. Click Table.
4. Click Insert Row or Insert Column.
5. An empty row or column appears in the table.
6. To insert multiple rows or columns you can repeat the above steps.

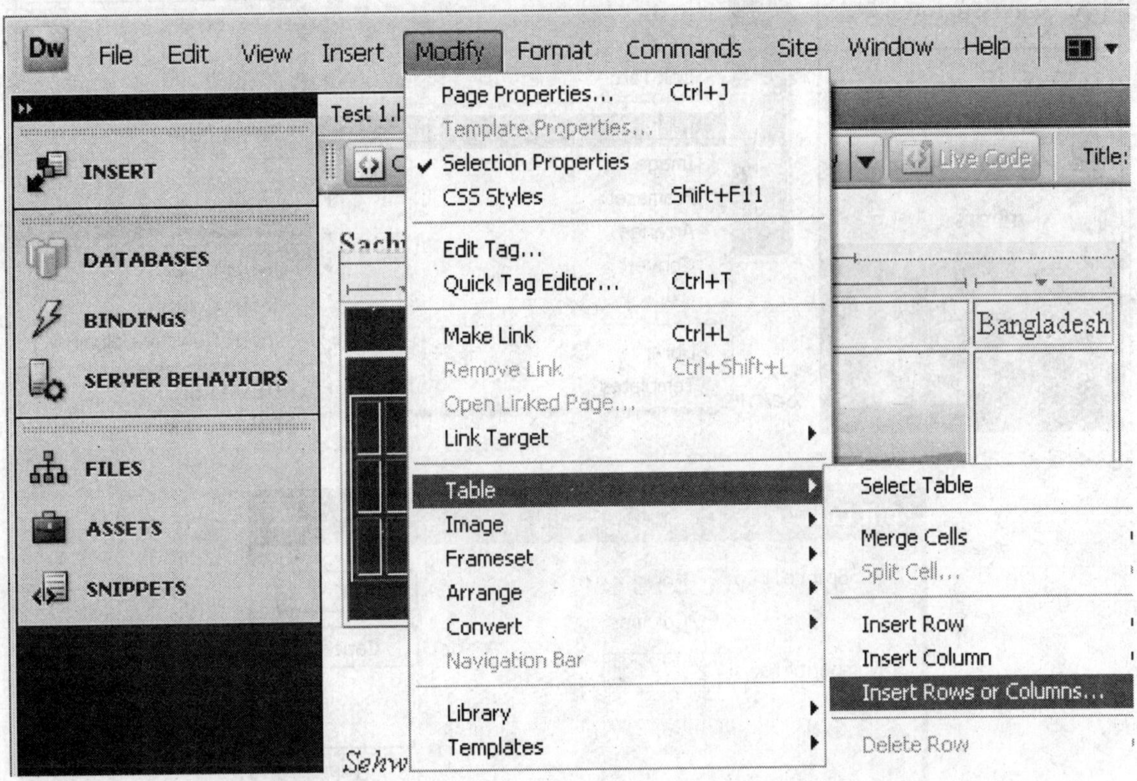

Splitting a Table Cell

For this do the following:

1. Click inside the cell that you want to split.
2. Click the Modify menu.
3. Click Table.
4. Click Split Cell.
5. You can also split a cell by clicking the Split cell button.
6. The Split Cell dialog box appers.
7. Click Rows or Columns to specify how to split the cell.
8. Type the number of rows or columns.

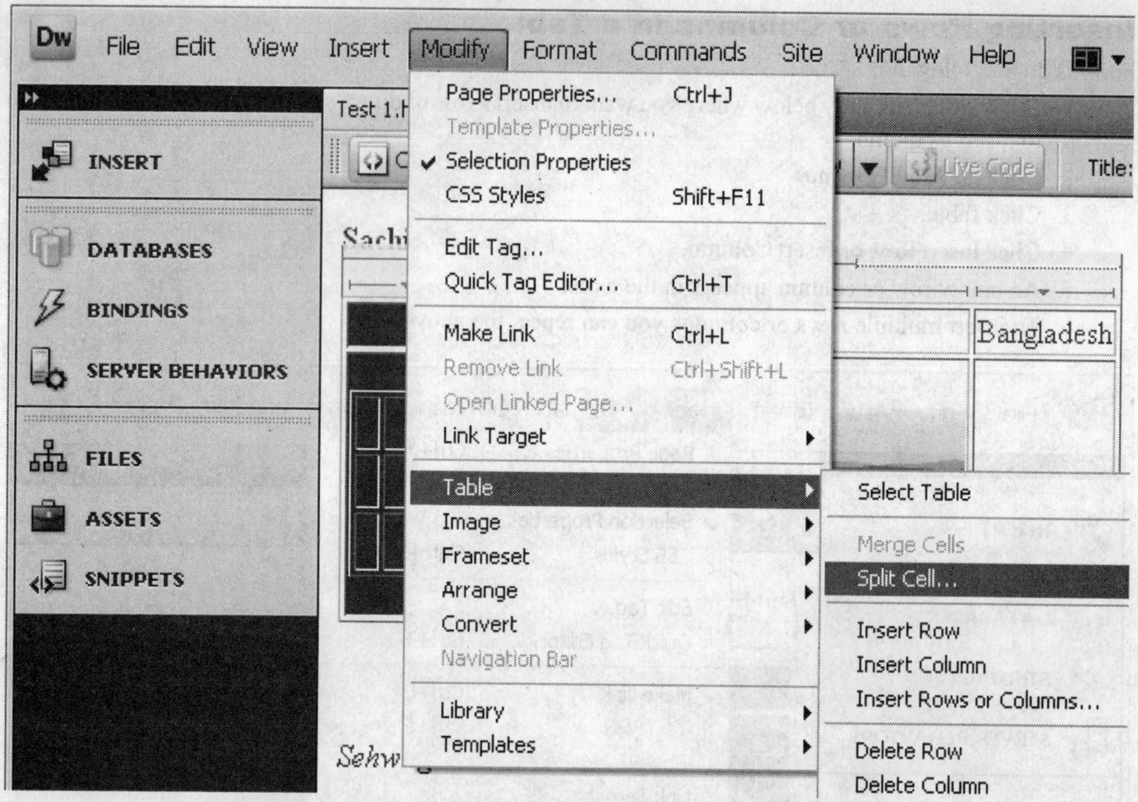

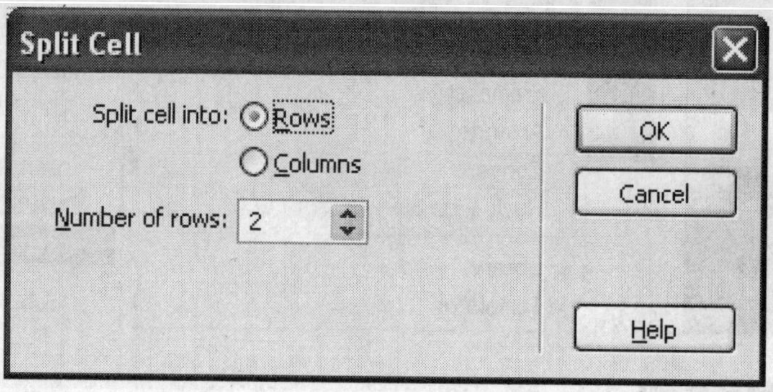

9. Click Ok.
10. The table cell splits.

Merging Cells of a Table

Instead of splitting, you may have to merge two cells. For this do the following:

1. Press Shift while selecting the two cells which you want to merge.
2. Click the Modify menu.
3. Click Table.
4. Click Merge Cells.

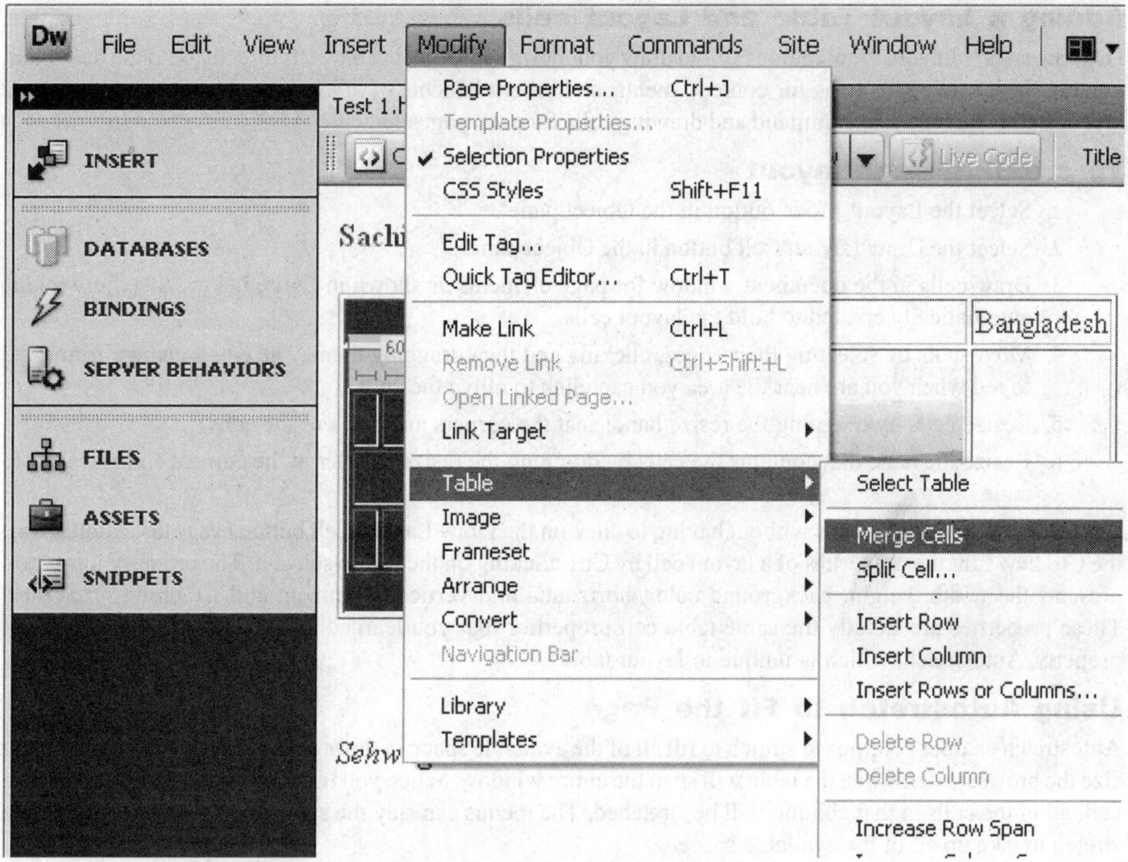

5. You can also split a cell by clicking the Merge cell button.
6. The table cells merge.

Designing Your Page Layout Using Tables

In the last paragraph, we explored some of the properties of tables and table cell. You used tables in Web pages in he same way you might use tables in a spreadsheet or a word processing application – to present data in an organised way. Now, you will apply more properties and new commands, using tables to aid with Web page layout.

Page layout refers to designing the way the page look when viewed in the browser. You position text, menus and other page elements in an efficient and attractive way.

Tables give Web developers the ability to make page elements appear in a specific place on the screen. Dreamweaver enables you to work in Layout views so that you can draw table elements directly onto the document window. This makes it easy to create tables for page layout.

Using Layout View

Dreamweaver CS4 includes a Layout view, enabling you to easily draw, move and edit table cells. To run on Layout view, select the Layout View button the Object panel. When you turn on Layout view, the two layout buttons on the Object panel become active. One of these buttons draws a layout table while the other button draws an individual layout cell. These have been described in the last chapter.

Adding a Layout Table and Layout cells

Dreamweaver's Layout view enables you to draw your design in table in table cells directly onto the document window. You can create areas for content, menus and other elements of a Web page by selecting the Draw layout Cell command and command and drawing cells for each page element.

To create a page layout

1. Select the Layout Mode button in the Object panel.
2. Select the Draw Layout Cell button in the Object panel.
3. Draw cells in the document window for page elements as shown in figure below. A layout table is automatically created to hold the layout cells.
4. Move cells by selecting their edges, clicking and then dragging them. The edges change from blue to red when you are near the area you can click to move the cells.
5. Resize cells by dragging the resize handles at the corners and sides of the cells.
6. Resize the table that contains the cells by dragging the resize handles at the corners and sides of the table.

To create multiple layout cells without having to click on the Draw Layout Cell button every time, hold down the Ctrl key. Edit the properties of a layout cell by Ctrl-clicking on the cell to select it. The property inspector, presents the width, height, background color, horizontal and vertical alignment and wrapping properties. These properties are exactly the same table cell properties that you learned earlier. There's one additional property, Autostretch, which is unique to layout tables.

Using Autostretch to Fit the Page

Autostretch enables columns to stretch to fill all of the available space in the browser window. No matter what size the browser window is, the table will span the entire window. When you turn on Autostretch for a specific cell, all of the cells in that column will be stretched. The menus can stay the same width, but the content can stretch to take up all of the available space.

Dreamweaver will automatically add spacer images to your table cells to make sure that they remain the size that you intend in all browsers. The spacer image trick is an old trick used by Web developers to ensure that table ells don't collapse. A transparent one pixel GIF is stretched to a specific width. This image is not visible in the browser.

To turn on Autostretch

1. Select a cell by Ctrl-clicking it.
2. Select the Autostretch radio button in the property inspector.
3. The Choose Spacer Image dialog box appears, as shown on next page. You have three choices:

   Create a spacer image file: Dreamweaver creates an invisible one pixel GIF image, adds it to the top cell of each column and stretch it to the column width. When you select this option, Dreamweaver asks you where you'd like to store the spacer.gif image that Dreamweaver creates.

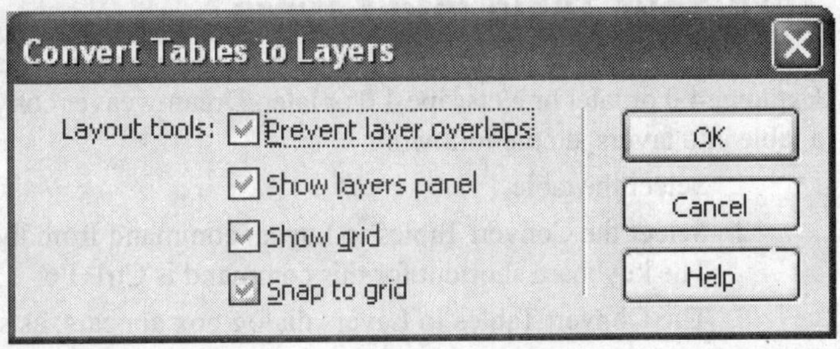

   Use an existing spacer image file: If you've already created a spacer image, select this option. Dreamweaver asks you to navigate to where the image is stored.

   Don't use spacer images for Autostretch tables: If you select this option, Dreamweaver warns you tat your cells may collapse and not maintain the widths that you have set.

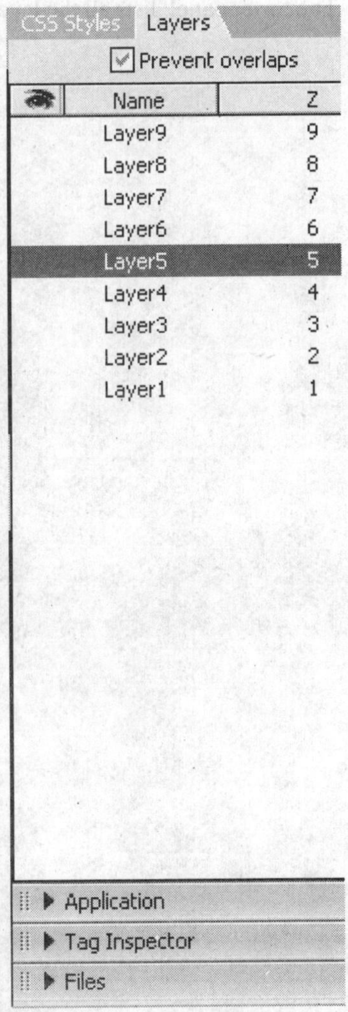

You can also apply the Autostretch command for an entire column by selecting the dropdown menu in the column heading, shown in figure. Each column heading displays the width of the column in pixels. You can also simply add a spacer image to the column by selecting the Add Spacer Image command. When a column has a spacer image added, the line at the top of the column appears thicker.

Create or select a spacer image for an entire site by opening the Layout View category of Dreamweaver preferences. Note that you can also change the colors of how layout objects appear in Dreamweaver and whether or not spacer images are automatically inserted in this preferences category.

Align Table Cell Content

The vertical alignment drop-down menu sets the alignment for the content of an individual cell or a group of cells. Align the content of a cell or a group of cells vertically – from top to bottom. When setting the vertical alignment, you have the following options:

- Default is usually the same as middle alignment of the cell contents.
- Top aligns the cell contents at the top of the cell.
- Middle aligns the cell contents in the middle of the cell.
- Bottom aligns the cell contents at the bottom of the cell.
- Baseline is applied to multiple cells in a row, aligning the bottom of the objects across all cells. For instance, if you have very large text in the first cell and small text in the second cell, the bottom of both liens of text will be aligned with baseline vertical alignment.

Align the contents of a cell or a group of cells horizontally – from left to right – with the Horizontal Alignment drop-down menu. When setting the horizontal alignment, you have the following options:

- Default usually is the same as the left for cell content and center for header cell content.
- Left aligns the cell contents on the left of the cell.
- Center aligns the cells contents in the center of the cell.
- Right aligns the cell contents on the right of the cell.

Turn Your Table into Layers

Layers allow absolute placement of objects on the page but require a recent browser version, such as Internet Explorer 4.0 or later or Netscape 4.0 or later. Dreamweaver converts a table into a group of layers. To convert a table into layers, do the following:

1. Select the table.
2. Select the Convert Tables to Layers command from the Convert submenu under the Modify menu. The keyboard shortcut for this command is Ctrl+F6.
3. The Convert Tables to Layers dialog box appears, as shown.
4. You'll explore the properties controlled by the check boxes in the Convert Tables to Layers dialog box in the next hour. For now, accept the default and click OK.

The Layer panel, lists all the layers that Dreamweaver created from the table.

5 Working with Forms in Dreamweaver CS3

Introduction

Now we will create a form to collect input. Dreamweaver gives you easy access to a number of different form elements, including text boxes, radio buttons, check boxes, lists, drop-down menus and buttons to capture user choices.

With forms, you can collect information, such as comments or orders and interact with your users. In your form you can ask for your user's name and e-mail address or you can have them sign a guest book or provide feedback on your Web site. You can send this information back to the Web server if you'd like. Dreamweaver enables you to validate information so that you know it's in the correct format.

Creating a Form

When you add a form to a Web page, Dreamweaver represents it as a red, dashed-line box, if you have Form Delimiter checked in the Invisible Elements category in Preferences dialog box. Make sure you have this option selected so you can see the outline of the form.

While creating a form, it might be helpful to have the Forms panel active in the Object panel. The first step in creating a form is to insert a form into your Web page to hold all the form objects that will collect user input.

Adding a Form

1. Place cursor where you want to insert the form.
2. Select the Form command from the Insert menu or select the form object in ht Forms panel of the object panel.
3. A message box, shown in figure may appear telling you that you will not be able to see the form unless you view the invisible elements. Select the Invisible Elements command from Visual Aids submenu of the View menu, if necessary.
4. You see a red, dashed-line box that represents the form as shown in figure below.

You can format the area within a form with tables, horizontal rules, text and order items that would normally be in a Web page. The only items that will be collected, however, are the names of the form elements and the data the user enters in the form. The text and formatting object you place within the form will not be submitted.

To select a form, click on the edge of the form outline. The Property inspector shows the three properties you can enter for a form:

- Form Name is necessary if you plan to apply any behaviour (or your own custom scripts) to form. It's a good idea to always name forms. Dreamweaver puts a default form process the form data.
- Action is a URL that points to an application, usually a script, on the server that will process the form data.
- Method tells the application on the server how the data should be processed.

Give your form a name. To format a form; click within the form so the insertion point appears with the form outline. Now you can type or insert objects and they will be inside of the form.

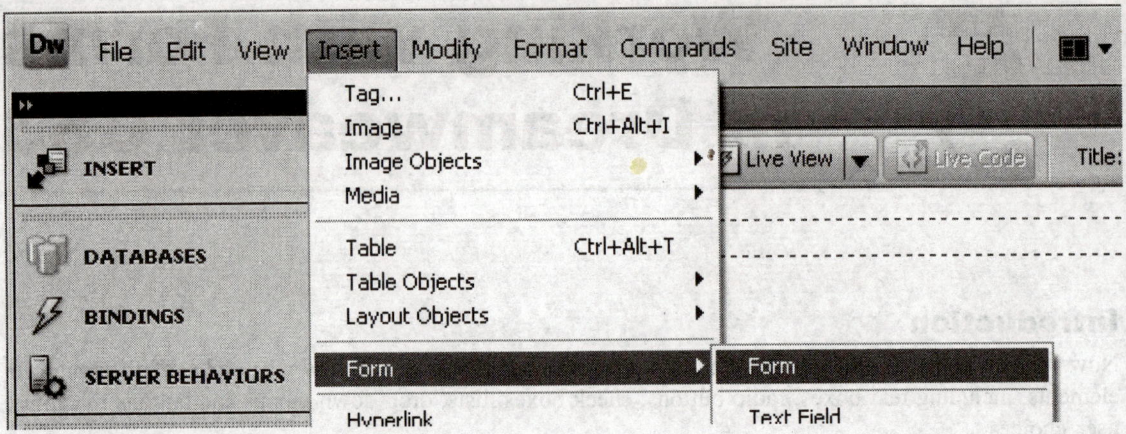

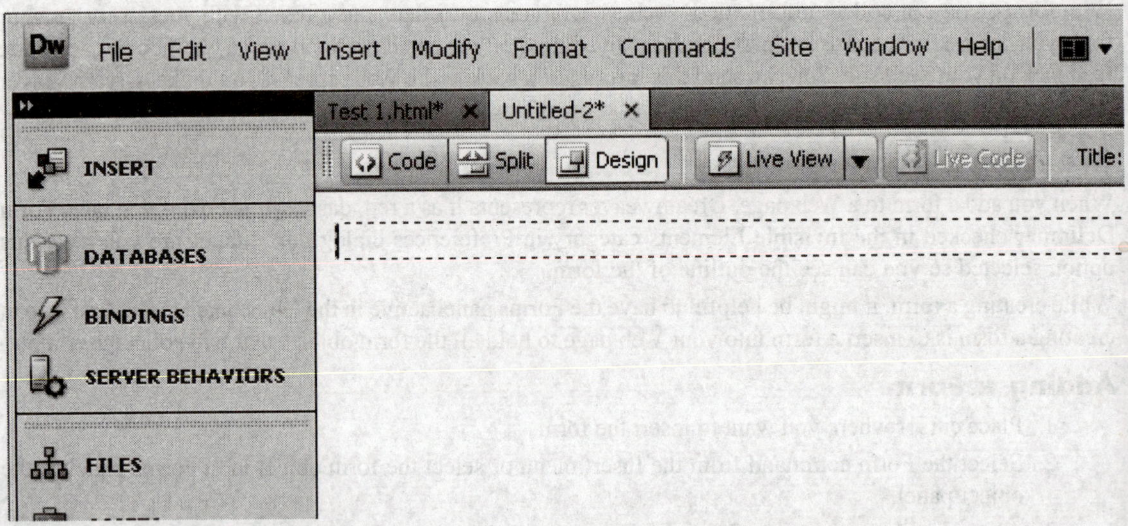

Adding Text Fields

Text fields are commonly used in forms. Single-line text fields enable you to type in a name, address, phone number or another short piece of text information. Text fields can also have multiple lines suitable for comments or lengthy pieces of information.

Create a group of text fields designed to collect the user's first and last name, email, address and comments. Begin by inserting a single-line text field into your Web page to collect the user's first name:

1. Make sure the insertion point is within a form.
2. Select the Text Field object from the Object panel or select theText Field command from the Form Object submenu in the Insert menu.
3. A text field appears in the form a shown in figure.

To add another text field directly to the right of the first one, place the insertion point after the text field and insert another text field for the user's last name. Add another single-line text field for the user's email address; place the insertion point after the second text field you created and press the Enter key to add a new paragraph within the form before you insert the text field. In another new paragraph, place a fourth text field to collect user comments. The form should look like figure.

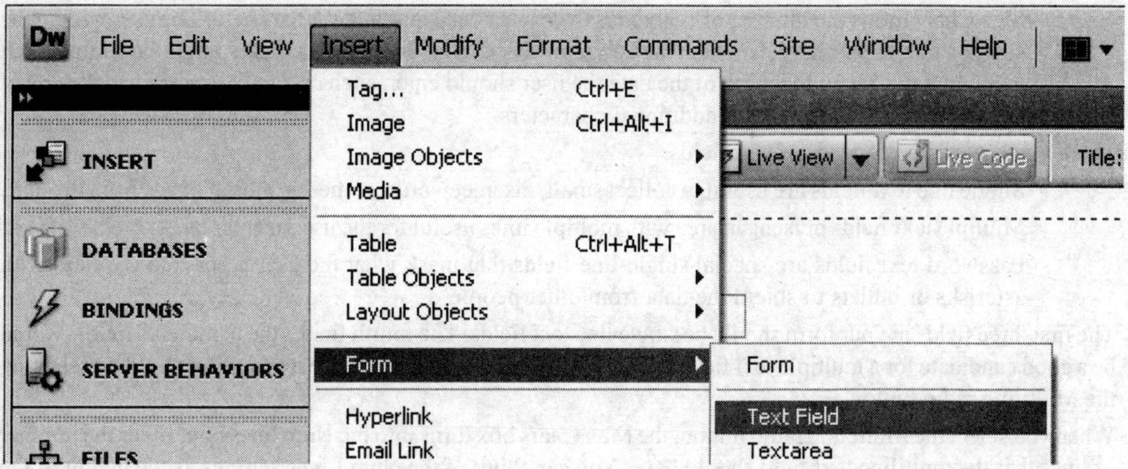

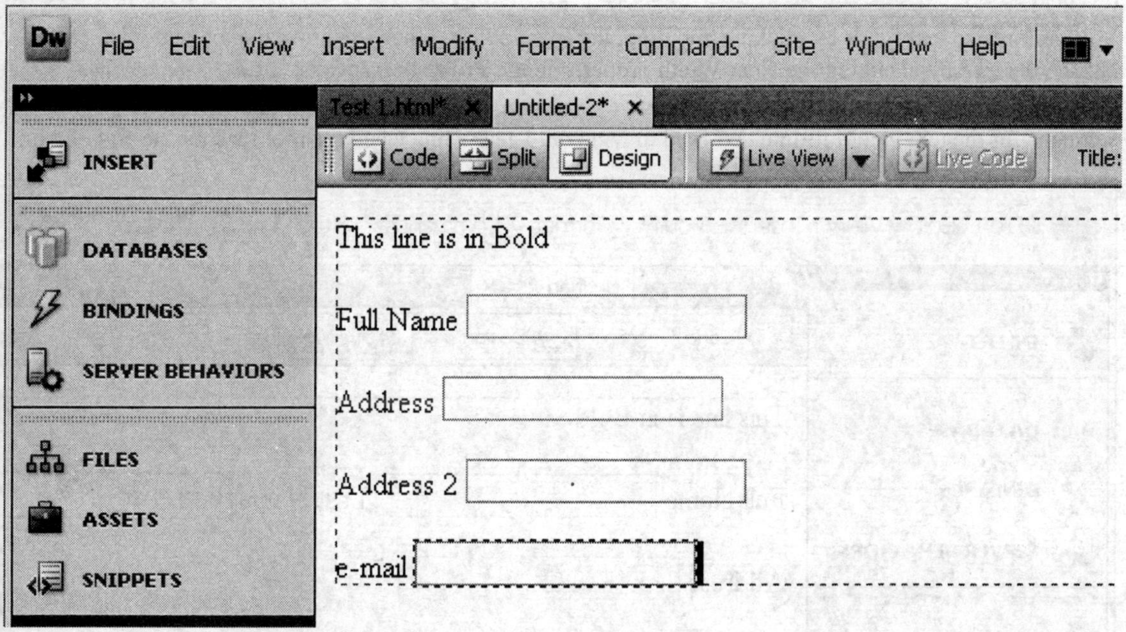

Apply Text Field Attributes

When you have a text field selected, the Property inspector presents the text field attributes. Dreamweaver fills in a unique default name. Rename all four text fields in your form with meaningful and unique names; possible names would be firstname, lastname, email and comments. As with other Dreamweaver objects, it is a good idea not to use spaces and punctuation your names. Some scripts and applications are not designed to deal with form element names that contain spaces and punctuation.

You can set both the size of the text field and the number of character a user can ether into it. There are two different width settings for a text field:

- Char Width sets the size of the text field and the number of characters that are visible in the field. If there are more characters in the text field than this width setting, they will be submitted but simply won't be visible.

- Max Chars limits the number of characters that a user can enter into the text field. The user will not be able to enter more characters than the value of Max Chars. Setting Max Chars might be useful when you know the absolute length of the data the user should enter, such as a social security number and do not want the user to enter additional characters.

There are three different types of text fields:

- Single line text fields are useful to collect small, discreet words, names or short phrases from the user.
- Multiple text fields present an area with multiple lines useful for the user to enter larger blocks of text.
- Password text fields are special single-line fields that mask what the user types into the field with asterisks or bullets to shield the data from other people.

The first three fields in your form should be single line text fields. The fourth field – the comments field – would be a good candidate for a multiple text field. Select the comments field and make it a multiline field by selecting the Multiline radio button.

When you select the Multi line radio button, the Max Chars box turns into the Num lines box. Enter the number of lines that the multiline text field should have. You can think of the Num Lines settings as the height of the text field.

You can't resize text fields by clicking and dragging like you can other Dreamweaver objects. You can only change the size by changing the Char Width property in the Property inspector.

The Wrap drop-down menu also becomes active once you have created a multiline text field. The default setting is for the text in a Multiline text field to wrap onto a new line when the user reaches the end of a line.

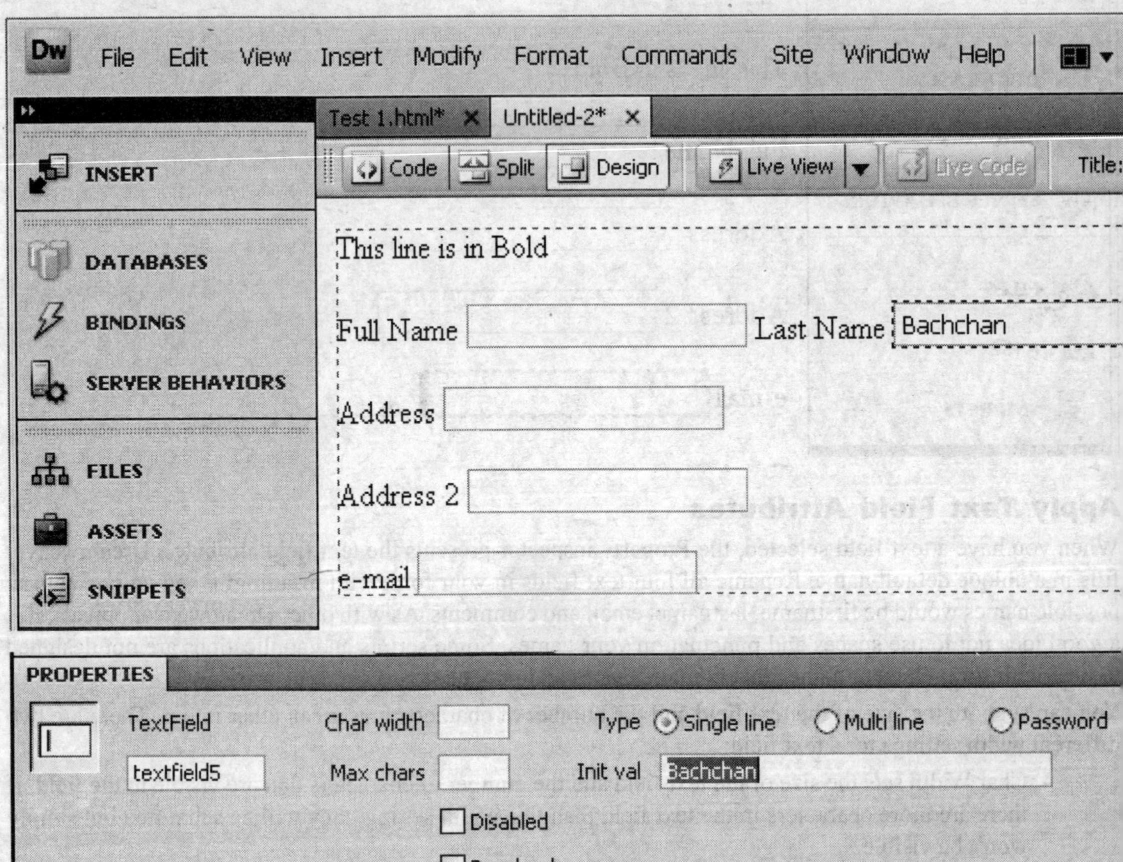

You can turn wrapping off by choosing the Off command from the Wrap drop-down menu. There are two additional wrap settings: physical and virtual. Physical enable sthe lines of text to wrap at the end of the box by placing a hard return (CRLF character) there. Virtual enables the lines of text to wrap at the end of the box but no character is inserted.

You can add default text that initially appears in the text field. Enter text into the Init Val box in the Property inspector so that text will be present when the user initially loads the form. This text could be instructions or a default value that the user could change if they wanted to.

Adding Labels

You've created the text fields into which the user will enter data, but you also need to add instructions, labels another element to the form to make it usable. Add a label in front of each of the text fields describing what text the user should enter into the field. You might want to place the labels and the text fields into a table to have better control over how the objects line up.

Adding Radio Buttons

These are another type of form element that you can use to collect user input. Radio buttons can be grouped so that the user can select only one button of the group; when the user selects a different member of the group, the previously selected button is de-selected. To group radio buttons, they all must have the same name. To create a group or radio buttons

1. Place cursor within a form where the radio buttons will be located.
2. Selected the Radio Button object from the Object panel or select the Radio Button command from the Form Object sub menu of the Insert menu.
3. Enter the name of the radio button group into the name box in the far left of the Property inspector, as shown in the figure on the next page. Remember that all of the radio buttons in the group need to have the same name.
4. Enter a checked value for the radio button in the Checked Value. This value is sent to your script or server application that processes the form.
5. Choose whether the button will be checked or unchecked when the user first loads the form by selecting either the Checked or Unchecked options beside the Initial State setting.

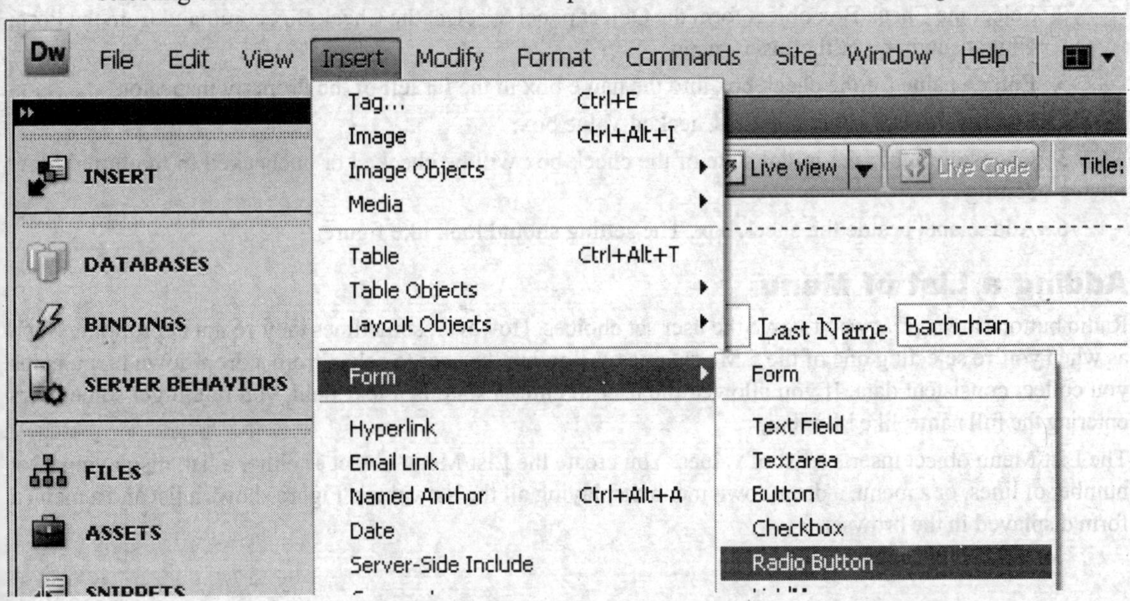

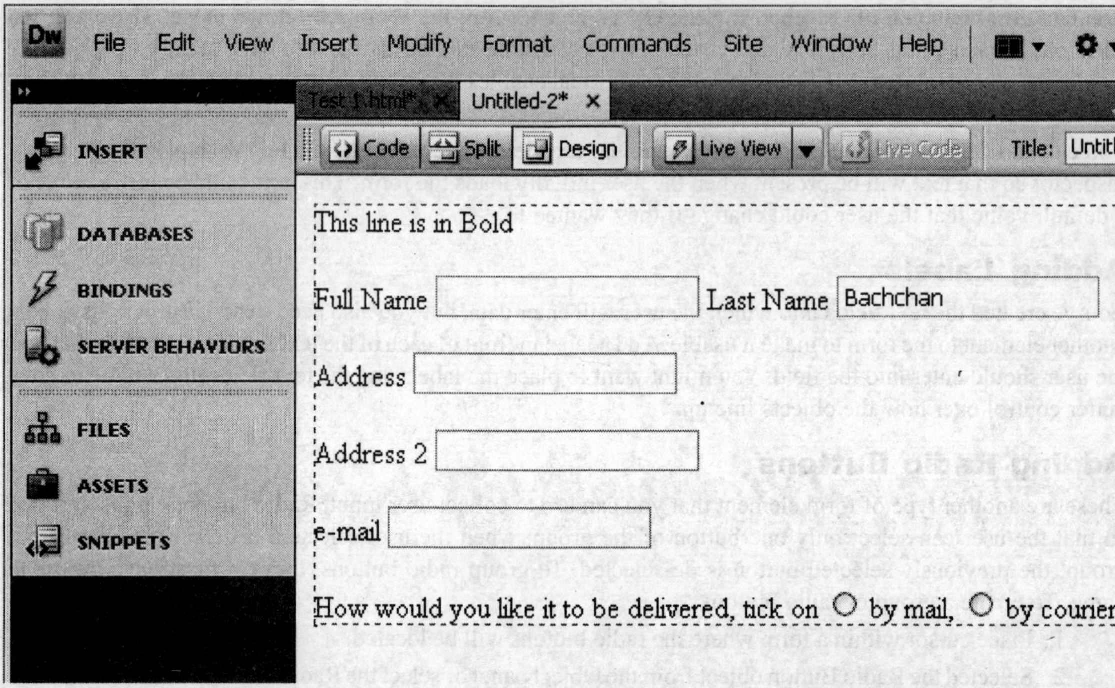

6. Place a label beside the button so that it is easy for the user to tell which answer they are choosing.
7. Repeat steps one through six for all of the members of the radio button group.

Adding Check Boxes

Check boxes collect user input when the user either checks or unchecks the box. They differ from radio buttons because they are not grouped; instead they act independently. To add a check box to your form

1. Place cursor within a form whether the check box will be located.
2. Select the Check Box object form the Object panel or select the Check Box command from the Form Object submenu of the Insert menu.
3. Enter a name for the check box into the name box in the far left of the Property inspector.
4. Enter a checked value into the Checked Value box.
5. Choose whether the initial state of the check box will be checked or unchecked in the Initial State setting.
6. Add a label beside the check box. The setting should look like figure.

Adding a List of Menu

Radio buttons are a great way to give the user set choices. However, sometimes they're not appropriate, such as when you're selecting one of the 5 Metro cities. Allowing the user to select from a drop-down menu helps you collect consistent data. If you allowed the user to enter a state in a text field, you might get some users entering the full name, like Mumbai,.

The List/Menu object inserts a list of values. You create the List/Menu object as either a list, displaying a set number of lines, or a menu, a drop-down menu displaying all the list values. Figure shows a list and a menu a form displayed in the browser.

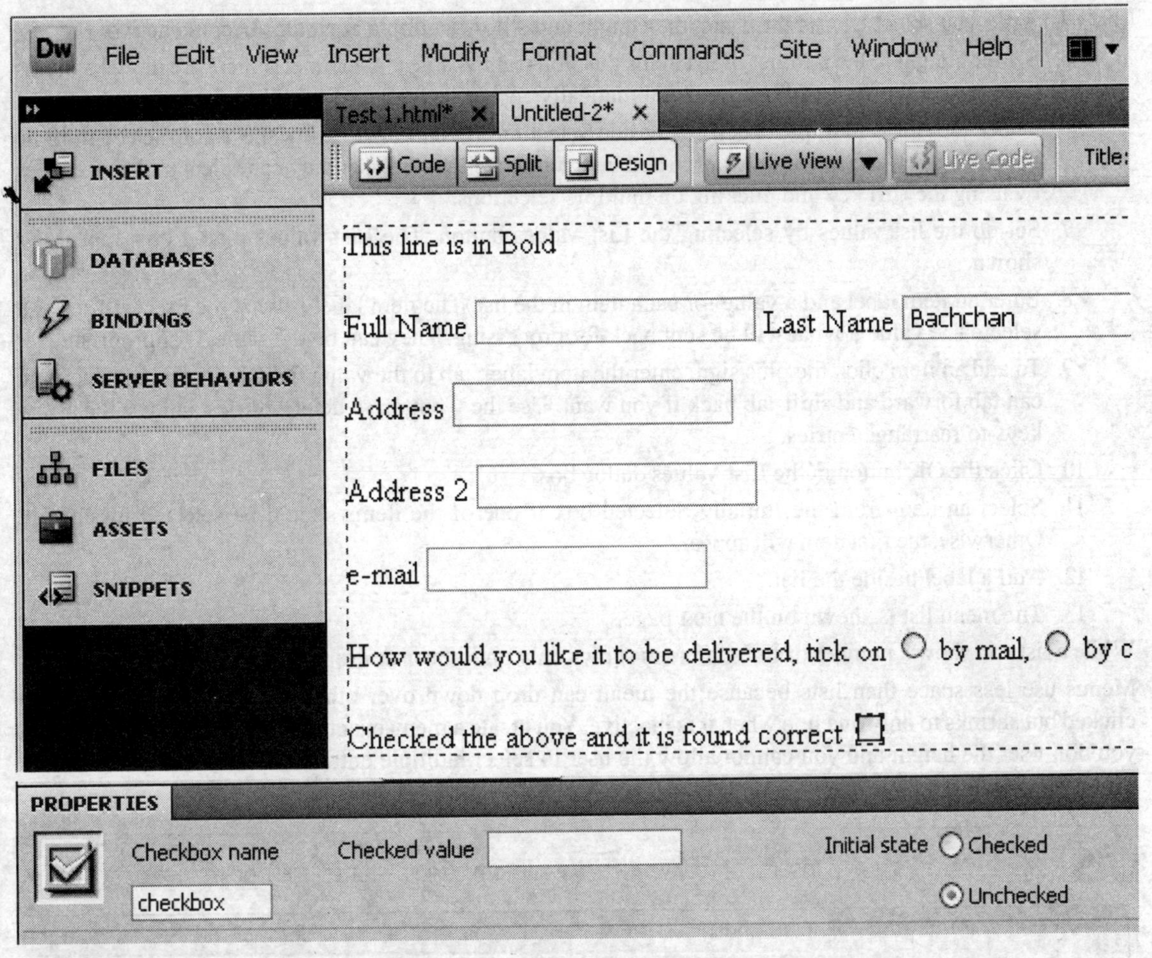

Creating a list

1. Place cursor within the form where the list will be located.
2. Select the List/Menu object from the Object panel or select the List/Menu command from the Form Object submenu of the Insert menu.
3. Enter the name of the list into the name box in the far left of the Property inspector.

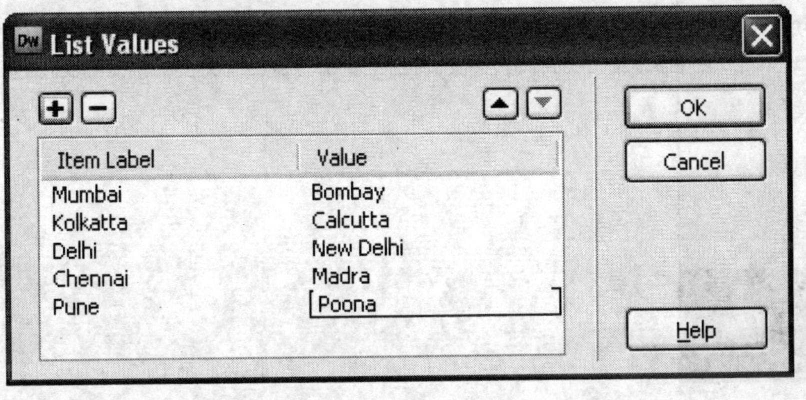

4. After you select List as the Type, the Height and Allow Multiple attributes become active.
5. Set the Height to the number of list items that you want visible at one time. If there are more list items than can be shown, scrollbars will automatically appear.
6. Check the Allow multiple check box beside Selections if you want to allow the user to select multiple values in the list. You might want to add instructions telling the user they can select multiple entries by using the Ctrl key and clicking on multiple selections.
7. Set up the list values by selecting the List Values button. The List Values dialog box appears as shown.
8. Enter an item label and a value for each item in the list. The item label is what the user will see and select. The value it what will be sent back for processing. They can be the same, if appropriate.
9. To add an item click the plus sign, enter the item label, tab to the value field, and enter a value. You can tab forward and shift-tab back if you want. Use the – button to delete entries and use the arrow keys to rearrange entries.
10. Click the OK button in the List Values dialog box.
11. Select an item from the Initially Selected box if one of the items should be selected by default. Otherwise, the first item will appear.
12. Add a label beside the list.
13. The menu list is shown on the next page.

While a list can show a number of lines, a menu shows only until the user drops the menu down by clicking. Menus use less space than lists because the menu can drop down over other objects on the page when clicked but shrinks to only one line when it is inactive. You create a menu exactly like you do a list except that you don't set the height and you cannot allow the user to select multiple entries.

Turn your list into a drop-down menu by selecting the Menu option as the type.

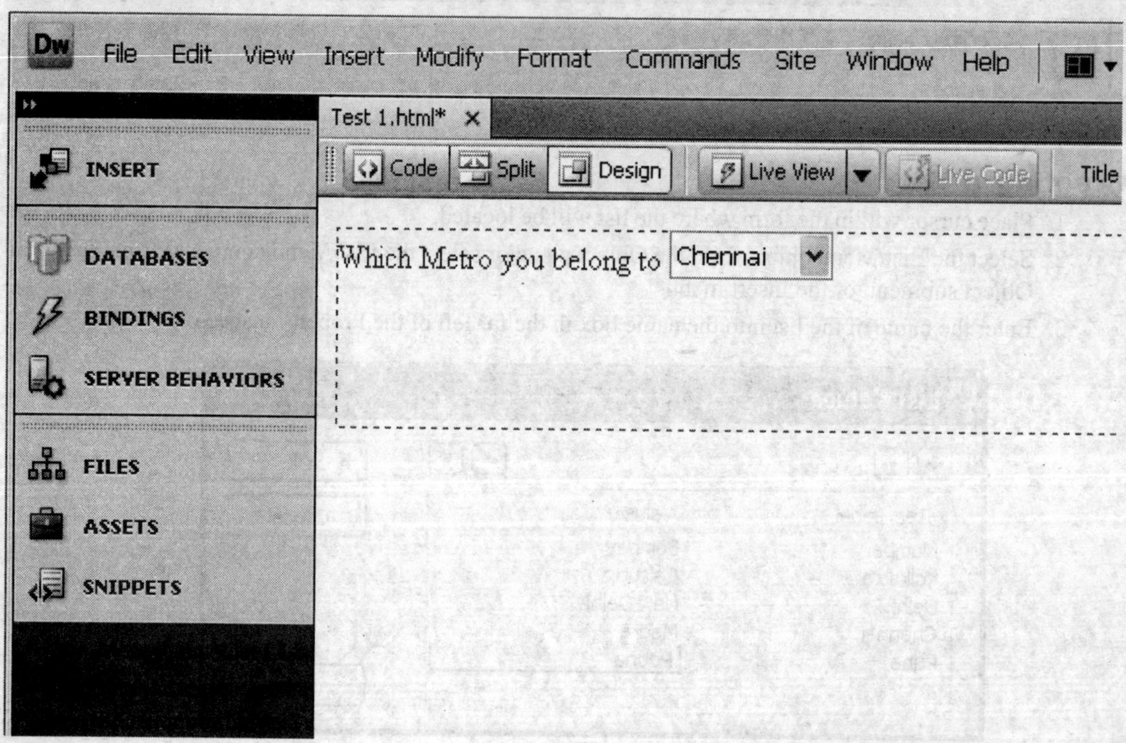

Adding Push Buttons and Picture Buttons

There are four different types of buttons that you can add to your forms:

- The **Submit button** triggers sending the data the user has entered into a form to a script or an application on the server. The Submit button triggers the action that you've set in the form's Action box in the Property inspector.
- The **Reset button** erases all of the data the user has entered in the form. It also reloads any initial values.
- An **Image button** acts like a Submit button. All of the data in the form is submitted and the coordinates of where the user clicked are sent too.
- A **generic button** has no automatic function. You can add functionality to a generic button by applying a behaviour to it.

Adding Submit and Reset Buttons

First, add a Submit and Reset button to your form. Usually the Submit button is one the left and the Reset button is beside it on the right. Add a button to the form by positioning the insertion point and then selecting the Button object from the Object panel (or the Button command from the Form Object submenu in the Insert menu). Select submit form as the action for the left button and select Reset form as the action for the right button. The button should look like those in the figure shown below.

You can accept the default names that Dreamweaver gives the Submit and Reset buttons, or you can give them new names. You can change the label of either button; a button does not need to say "Submit" to function as a Submit button. Each from must have a Submit button to send the form data. The Reset button is optional. You only want to have one Submit button per form.

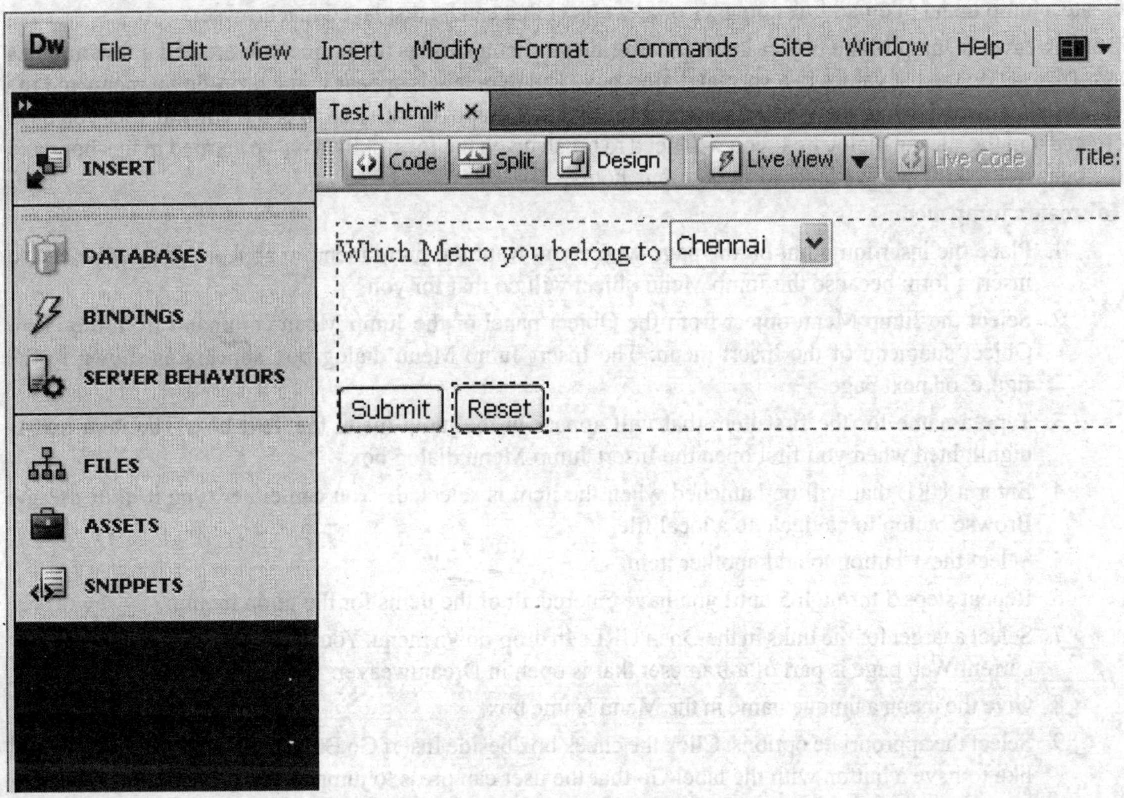

Adding an Image Field to Submit a Form

You can replace a Submit button with an image field. When the user clicks on the image, the form contents are submitted and the coordinates of the location where the user clicked on the image are sent too. You could capture and process the coordinate information if you wanted to.

First, make sure the insertion point is inside of a form. Add an image field by selecting the Image Field object form the Object panel or the Image Field command from the Form Object submenu of the Insert menu. The Select Image Source dialog box enables you to navigate and select a standard Web image file. The Property inspector displays the name, width, height, source, alt text and alignment attributes. You set these attributes as you would for any image.

Adding a generic Button

You can add a generic button anywhere on your Web page. It does not have to be within a form because it cannot submit form contents. Add a generic button by selecting the Button object from the Object panel or the Button command form the inert menu. Name the button, give it a label and select None as the action. Now you can apply a behaviour to this button that can be triggered by a button click.

Sometimes it is difficult to delete a form from the page. The easiest way to delete a form is to right-click on the form to view the context menu. Choose the Remove Tag <form> command. If the Remove Tag command does not say <form>, you have the wrong object selected. You could, of course, always select the <form> tag in the tag selected to deleted the form.

Creating a Jump Menu

A jump menu is a list of links that allows the viewer to jump to other Web sites or different Web pages within the current site. Dreamweaver's Jump Menu object makes it easy to set up this type of jump menu. You can create a jump menu of email links, images or any object that can be displayed in a browser.

Dreamweaver's Jump Menu object inserts a drop-down menu similar to the one you created a few minutes ago. You set up the list values in a special dialog box. The item labels appear in the drop-down menu and the values contain the URL to the Web pages where the user will jump. If you need to edit the menu after you have created it in the special dialog box, you will need to brush up on the form skills you've learned in this hour and the behaviour skills you've learned in previous hours.

To create a jump menu

1. Place the insertion point on the page where you want the jump menu to appear. You don't need to insert a form because the Jump Menu object will do that for you.
2. Select the Jump Menu object from the Object panel or the Jump Menu command from the Form Object submenu of the Insert menu. The Insert Jump Menu dialog box appears as shown in the figure, on next page.
3. Type a name for the first item that will appear in the jump menu the Text box. The item text is highlighted when you first open the Insert Jump Menu dialog box.
4. Enter a URL that will be launched when the item is selected. You can either type it in or use the Browse button to navigate to a local file.
5. Select the + button to add another item.
6. Repeat steps 3 through 5 until you have entered all of the items for the jump menu.
7. Select a target for the links in the Open URLs In drop-down menu. You will only target options if your current Web page is part of a frameset that is open in Dreamweaver.
8. Give the menu a unique name in the Menu Name box.
9. Select the appropriate options. Click the check box beside Insert Go Button After Menu of you would like to have a button with the label Go that the user can press to jump. Even if the button is present

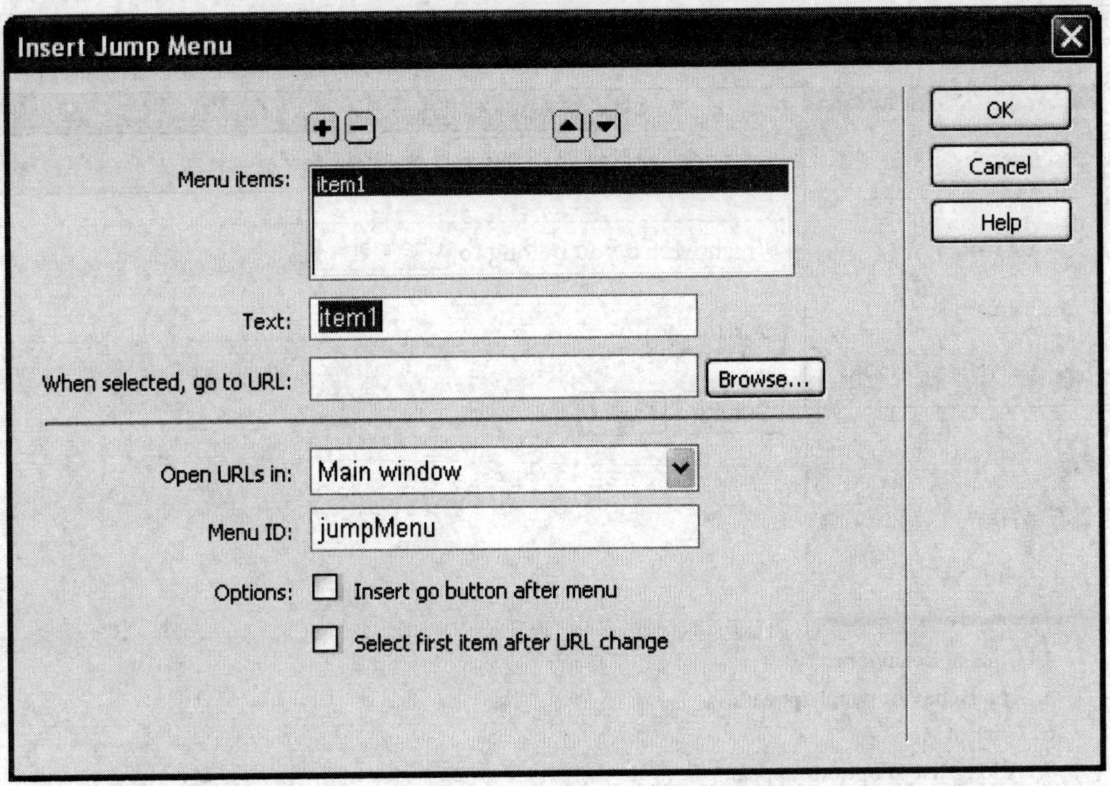

the user will still automatically go to the link once they have chosen it. The Go button enables the user to launch the first link without having to first launch another link.

10. Select the check box beside Select First Item After URL Change if you want the first item to be reselected after each jump selection.
11. Click OK. The jump menu within a form is inserted into your Web page.

A common way to create a jump menu is to have the first item be the text "Choose One..." and leave it without a link. Because you never want to select this item, the inability to select the first item in the drop-down menu won't be a problem. Select the check box that makes the first item always selected after you have jumped somewhere and the "Choose One..." selection reappears.

You can edit the jump menu by editing the Jump Menu behaviour. Select the List/Menu object that the Jump Menu command creates and double-click the Jump Menu behaviour in the Behaviours panel. Rearrange the list with the up and down arrow buttons. You can turn on or off the Select First Item After URL Change setting. You cannot add a Go button by editing the Jump Menu behaviour. You can add it manually, through. Create a generic button by inserting a button into the form, giving it the label "Go" and setting its action to None. Apply the Jump Menu Go behaviour to the button triggered by the onClick event.

Validating the Form

You can double check the information a user enters in a form to make sure that it is a valid information. For this do the following.

1. Click inside the red dashed box that forms part of the form.
2. Click at <form> at the bottom of the page to select the form.
3. Click at Windows menu.

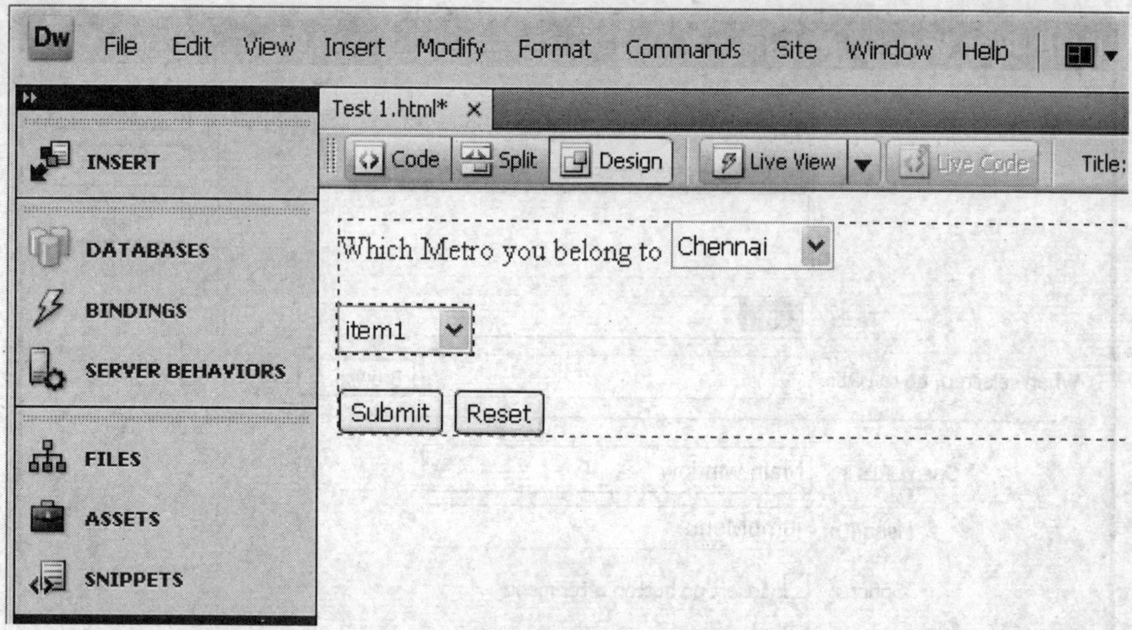

4. Click at Behaviors.
5. The Behavior panel appears.
6. Click at +.
7. A long list of options appear.
8. Click at Validate form.
9. A dialog box appears with all the field names in it.
10. Click a form field.
11. You can click Required to require a value in the selected form field.
12. Specify the type of data to accept in the form field.
13. You can repeat this step for other fields too.
14. Click Ok.
15. Behavior panel has OnSubmit button now.

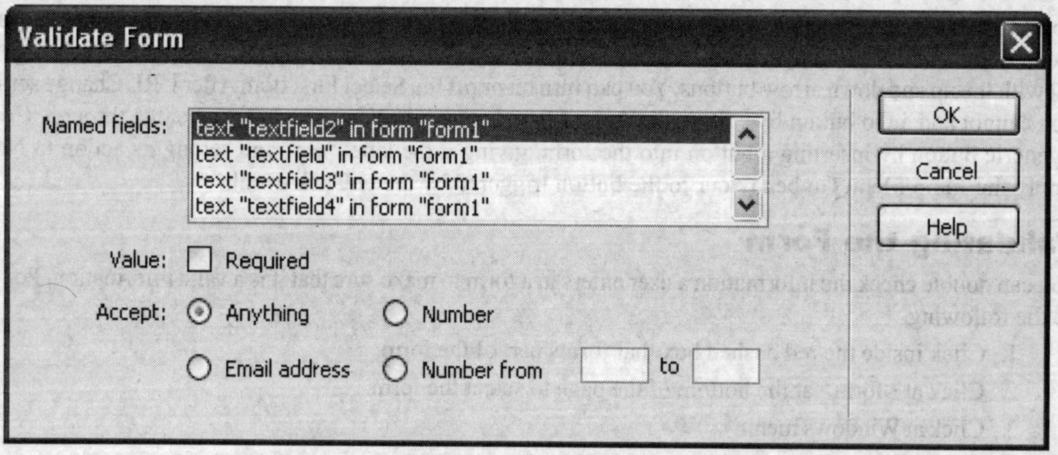

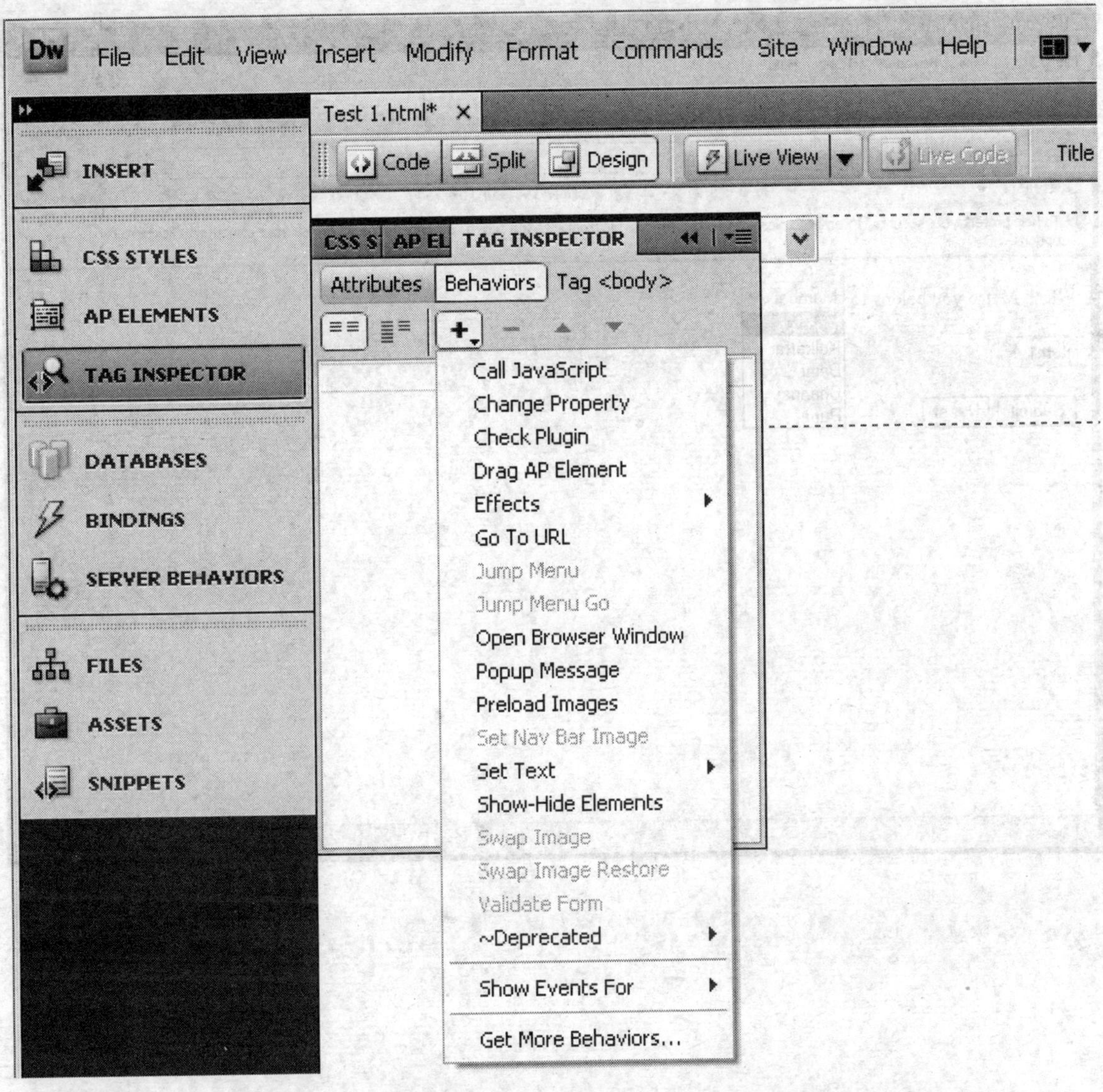

16. The OnSubmit.even applies validation to the form when the user clicks the submit button.
17. You can click down arrow button and select a different event.
18. Select Preview in Web browser from File menu.
19. Preview the Web page in a browser of your choice.
20. If you submit the form with invalid content the browser generates a pop-up alert.

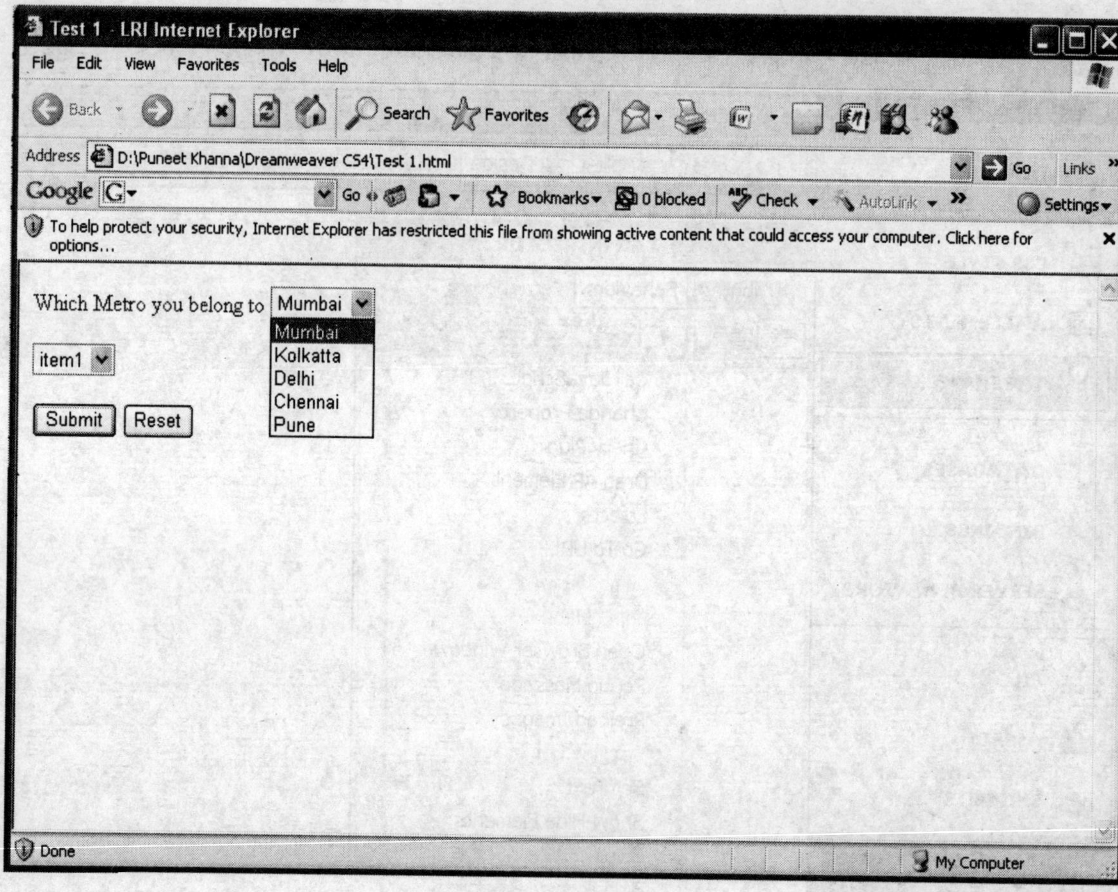
Test 1 - LRI Internet Explorer
File Edit View Favorites Tools Help
Address D:\Puneet Khanna\Dreamweaver CS4\Test 1.html
To help protect your security, Internet Explorer has restricted this file from showing active content that could access your computer. Click here for options...
Which Metro you belong to
Mumbai
Kolkatta
Delhi
Chennai
Pune
item1
Submit
Reset
Done
My Computer

6 Working with Frames in Dreamweaver CS4

Introduction

Your Web page can be divided into parts both horizontally and vertically. Each of this part is called a frame and is a new page in itself, where you can have text and image too.

Dividing a Page into Frames

For this do the following:

1. Click at Modify menu.
2. Click at Frameset submenu.
3. Click at one of the Split command, depending upon the one which you want to use.
   Split frame Left
   Split frame Right
   Split Frame Up
   Split Frame Down
4. The window splits into frames.
5. If your earlier page had some text, it would be shifted to one side.
6. Scroll bars appear if the content extends outside the frame borders.
7. In the figure on the next page, I have chosen the Split frame Left option.

Adding Contents to Frames

For this do the following:

1. Press and hold Alt key and then click inside a frame to select it.
2. You can also select a frame by clicking it in the Frames panel.
3. If the frame panel is not displayed, do that by selecting Windows menu and Frames.
4. Click at Browse for Files icon in the properties box.
5. The select HTML file dialog box appears.
6. Click at down arrow and select the folder that contains the HTML file.
7. Click the file.
8. Click Select.
9. The document appears in the frame, as shown on the next page.

Adding New Content to a Frame

For this do the following:

1. Click at Inside the frame.
2. Type the text that you want to display.

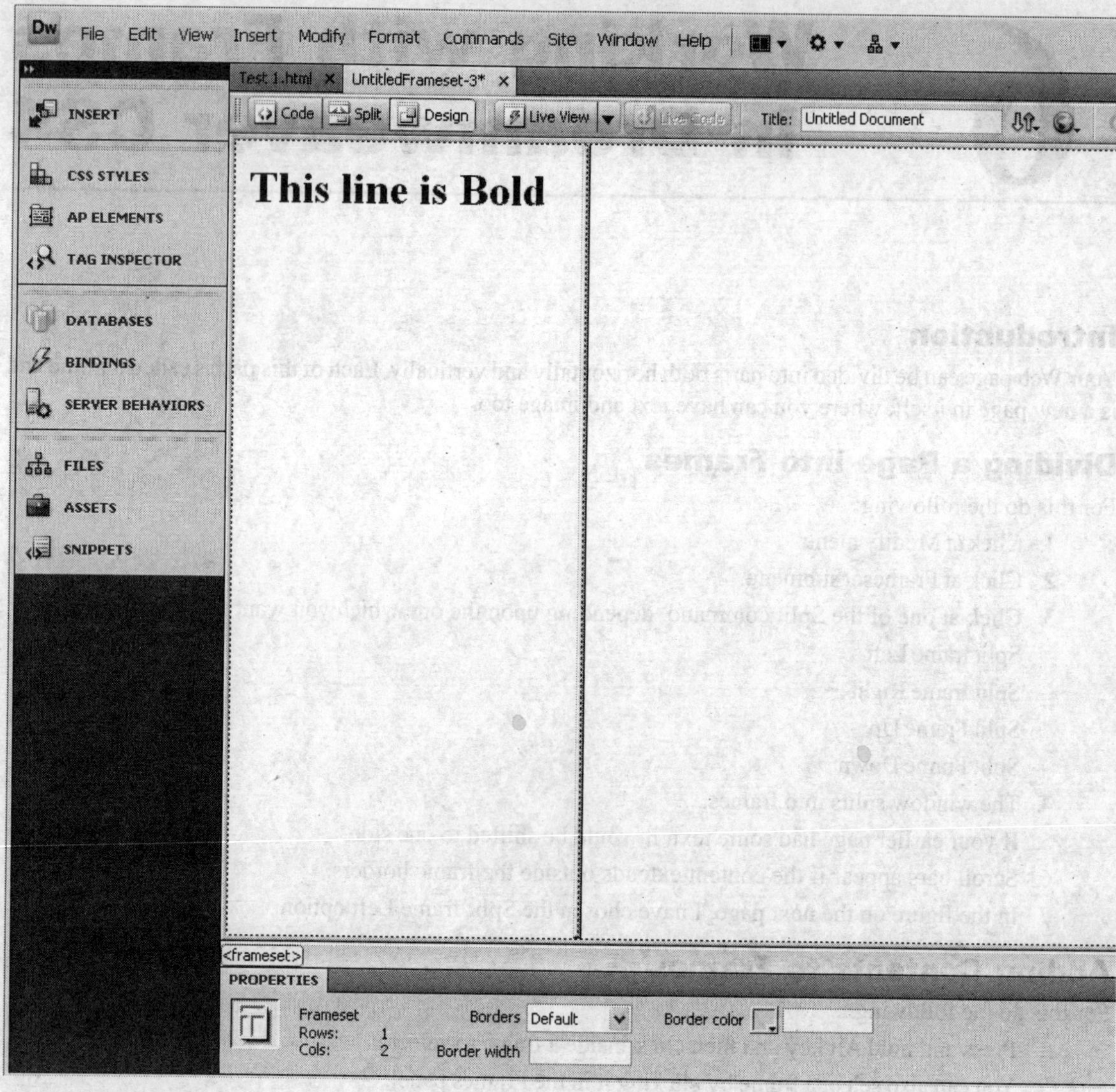

3. You can click button in the Objects panel to add images, tables, and other elements.

Saving Frames Pages

For this do the following:

1. Click inside the frame that you want to save.
2. Click File menu.
3. Click at Save Frames.
4. The Save As dialog box appears.
5. Click at down arrow and select the folder where you want to save the framed page.
6. Type a name for the page with an .htm or .html file extension.
7. Click Save.
8. Repeat above steps for the other framed pages in your document.

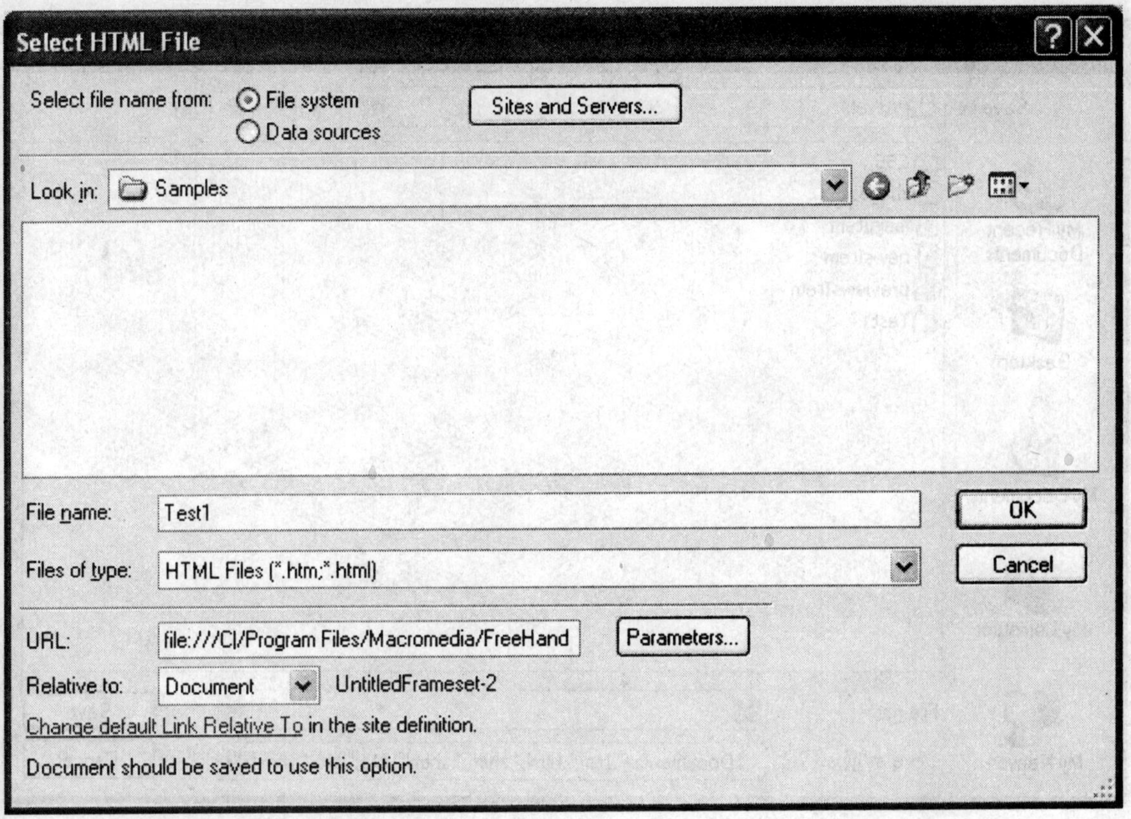

9. Save each page as a different filename.

Saving the Frameset

For this do the following:

1. Click anywhere on the frame border to select the frameset.
2. Click at File menu.
3. Click at Save Frameset As.
4. The Save As dialog box appears.
5. Click at down arrow and select the folder where you want to save the frameset.
6. Type a name for the frameset with an .htm and or .html file extension.
7. Click Save.

Naming Frames

For this do the following:

1. Press and hold Alt key and then click inside a frame to select it.
2. You can also select a frame by clicking it in the Frames panel.
3. If the frames panel is not ther on the screen, it can be called from Windows menu and Frames submenu.
4. Type a name for the frame.
5. Press Enter.

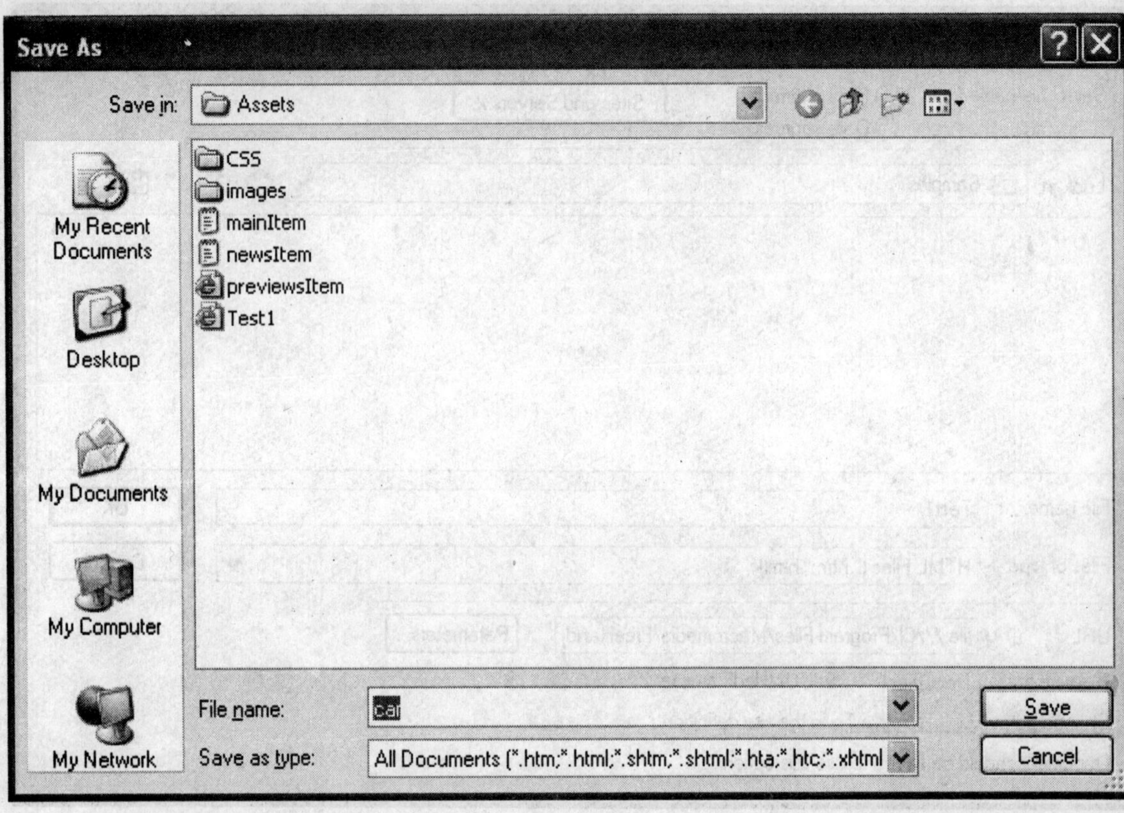

6. The name of the frame appears in the Frames panel.
7. Here I have given the name as Test Frame.

Deleting Frames

For this do the following:

1. Place the cursor over the border of the frame that you want to delete.
2. Click and drag the border to the edge of the windows.
3. The frame is deleted.

Hyperlinking to a Frame

For this do the following:

1. Name the frames of your frameset.
2. Click and drag to select the text or image that you want to turn into a hyperlink.
3. Click at Browse for File.
4. The Select File dialog box appears.
5. Click down arrow and select the folder containing the destination file.
6. Click the destination file.
7. Click Select.
8. Click the Target down arrow.
9. Click to select a frame where the target file will open.

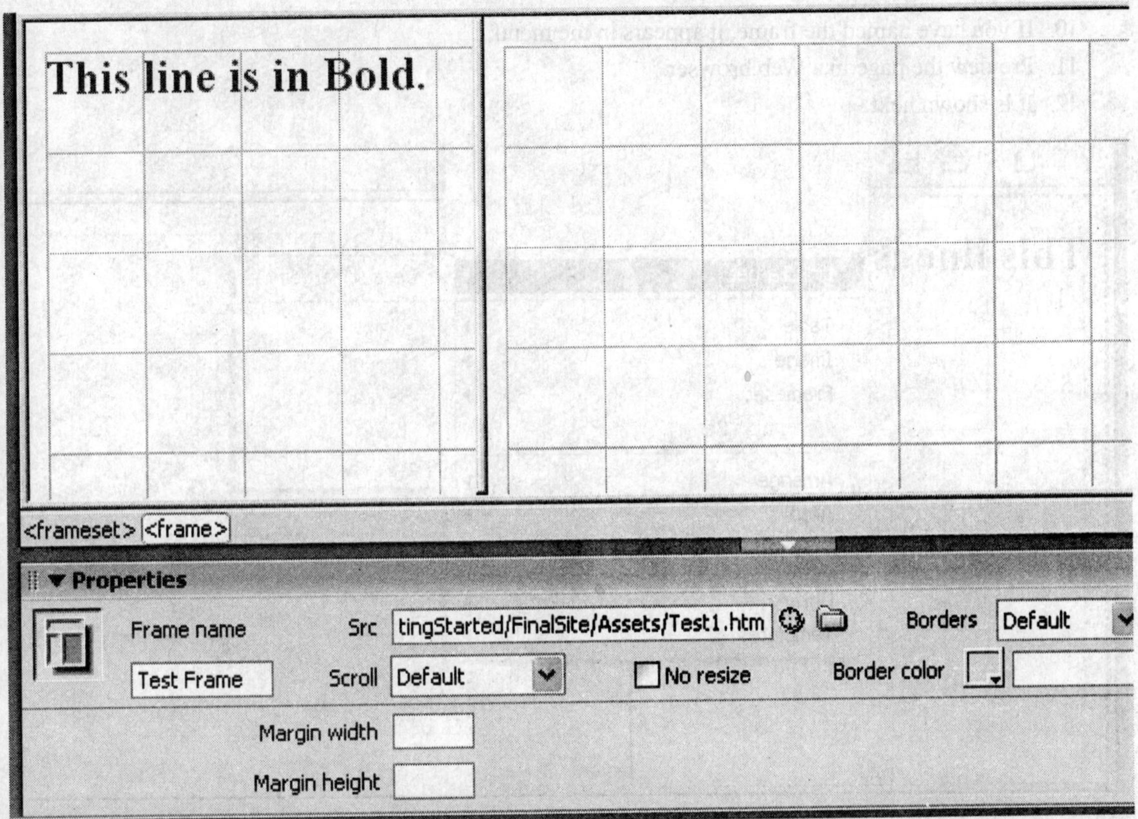
This line is in Bold.
<frameset> <frame>
Properties
Frame name
Test Frame
Src
tingStarted/FinalSite/Assets/Test1.htm
Borders
Default
Scroll
Default
No resize
Border color
Margin width
Margin height

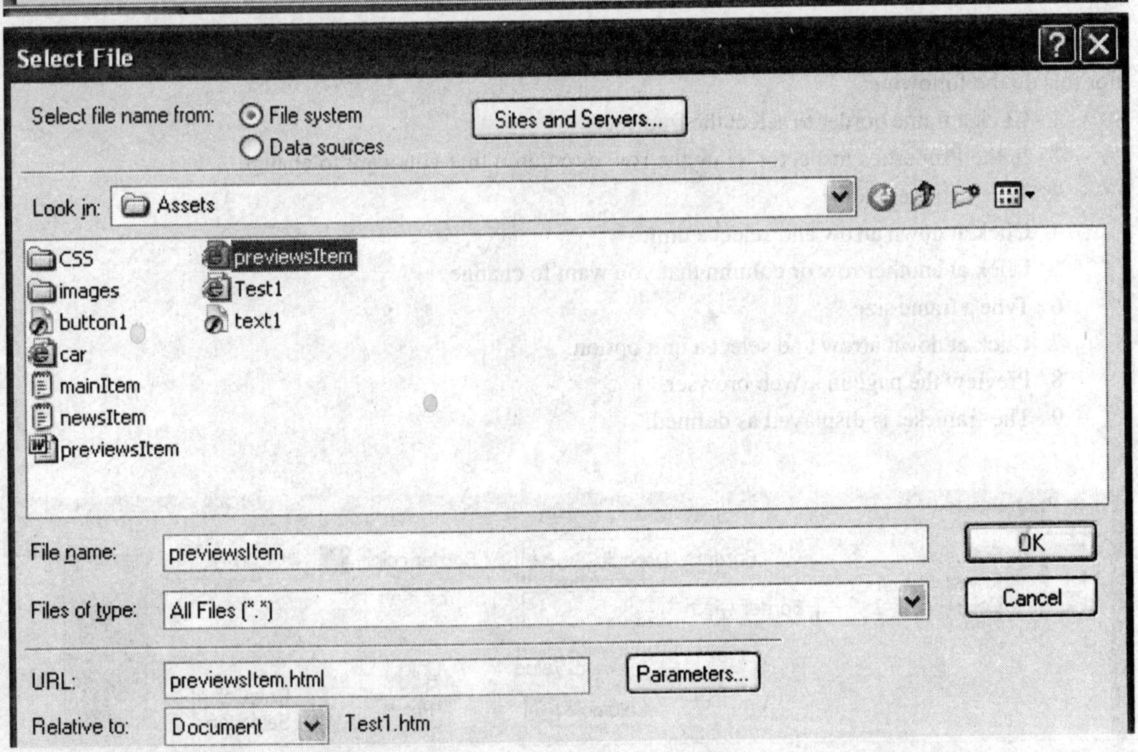
Select File
Select file name from:
File system
Data sources
Sites and Servers...
Look in:
Assets
CSS
images
button1
car
mainItem
newsItem
previewsItem
previewsItem
Test1
text1
File name:
previewsItem
OK
Files of type:
All Files (*.*)
Cancel
URL:
previewsItem.html
Parameters...
Relative to:
Document
Test1.htm

10. If you have named the frame, it appears in the menu.
11. Preview the page in a Web browser.
12. It is shown next.

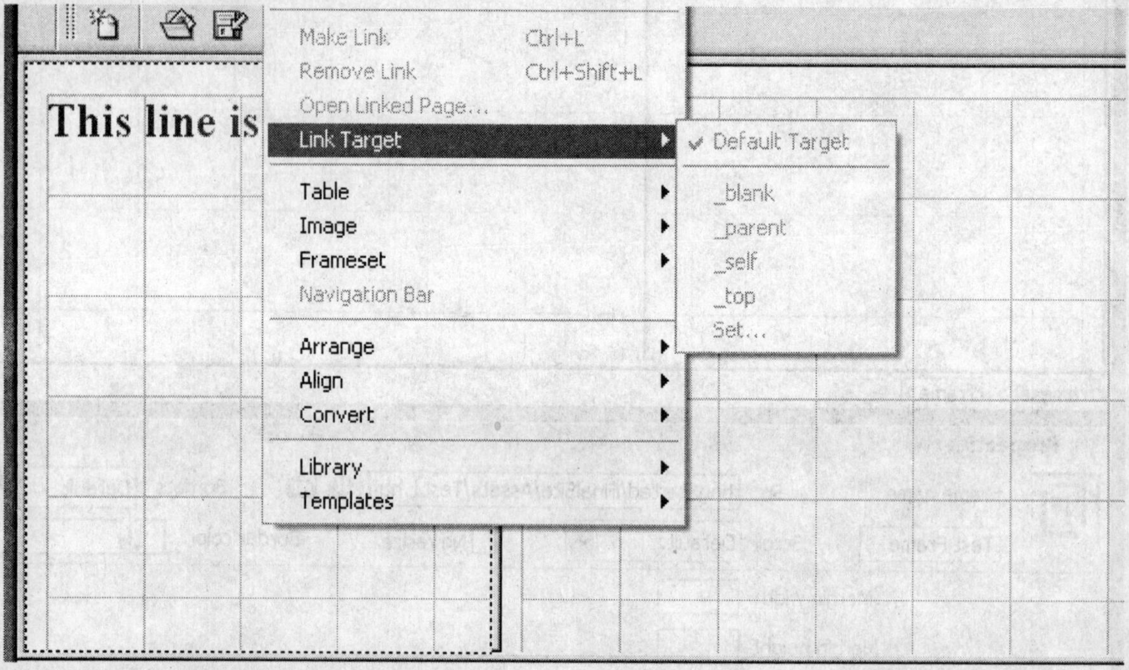

Changing Frame Dimensions

For this do the following:

1. Click a frame border to select the frameset.
2. In the Properties inspector, click the row or column that you want to change.
3. Type a frame size.
4. Click at down arrow and select a unit.
5. Click at another row or column that you want to change.
6. Type a frame size.
7. Click at down arrow and select a unit option.
8. Preview the page in a Web browser.
9. The frameset is displayed as defined.

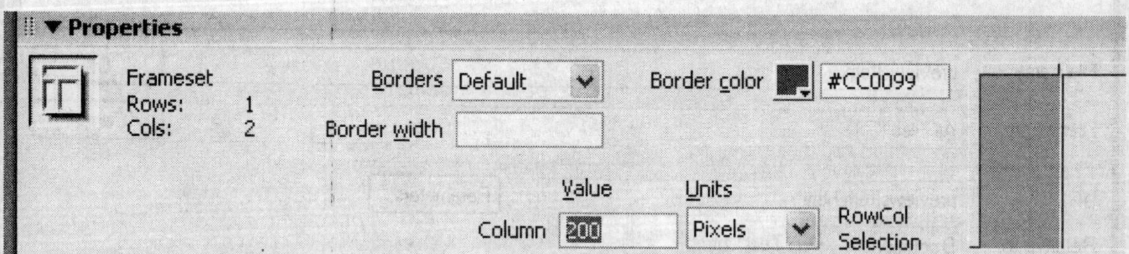

Setting Frame Borders

For this do the following:

1. Click the frame border to select the frameset.
2. Click at down arrow and select Yes or Default to keep the borders.
3. Type a border width.
4. Click a colour.
5. The frame border appears at the specified settings.
6. See the result next.

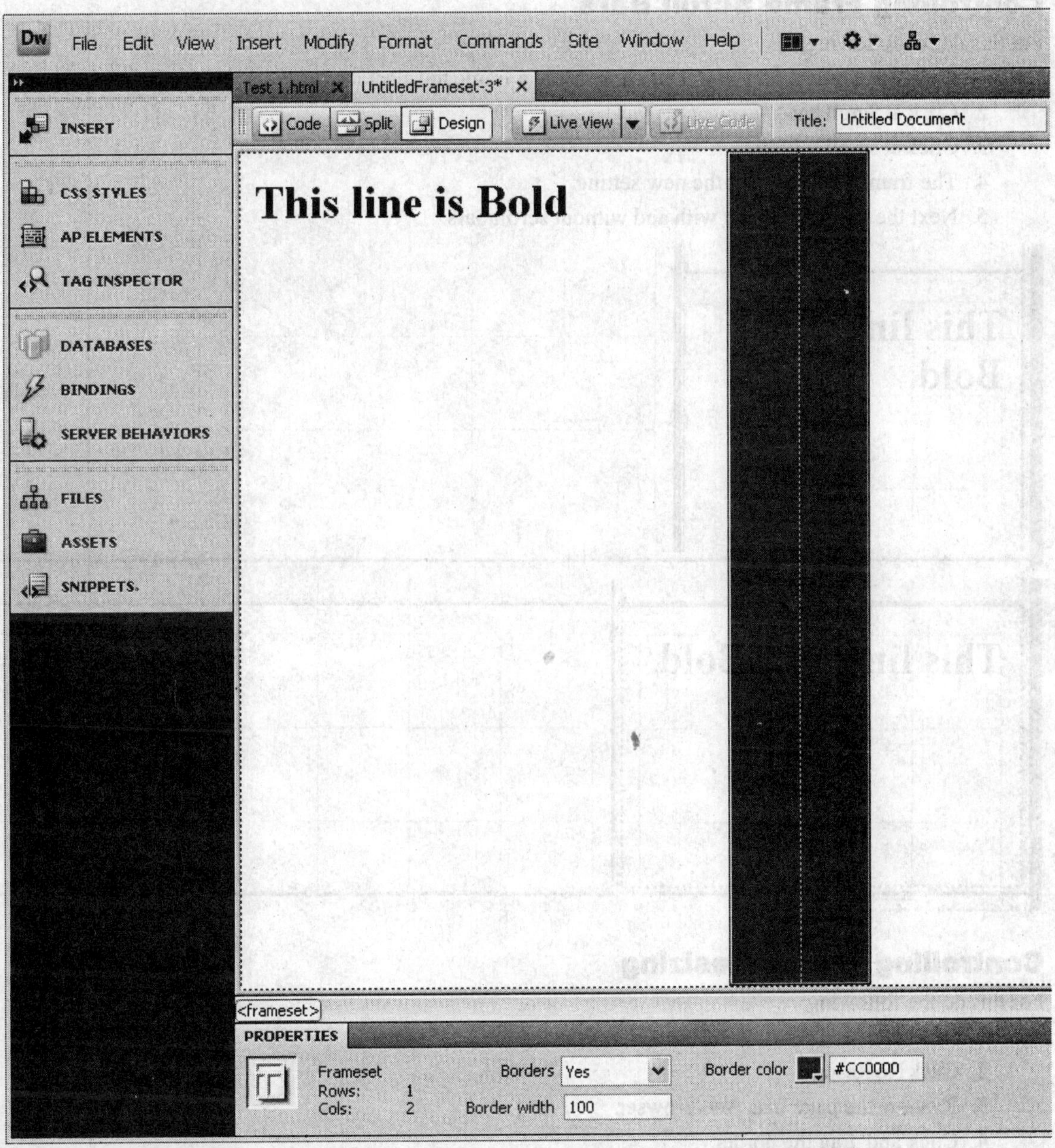

Turning off the Borders

For this do the following:

1. Click the frame border to select the frameset.
2. Click the Borders button.
3. Click No.
4. Preview the page in a Web browser.
5. The frame border does not appear now.

Controlling Frame Scroll Bars

For this do the following:

1. Press and hold Alt key and then click inside a frame to select it.
2. Click at Scroll bar.
3. Click at scroll setting.
4. The frame appears with the new setting.
5. Next the frame is shown with and without scroll bars.

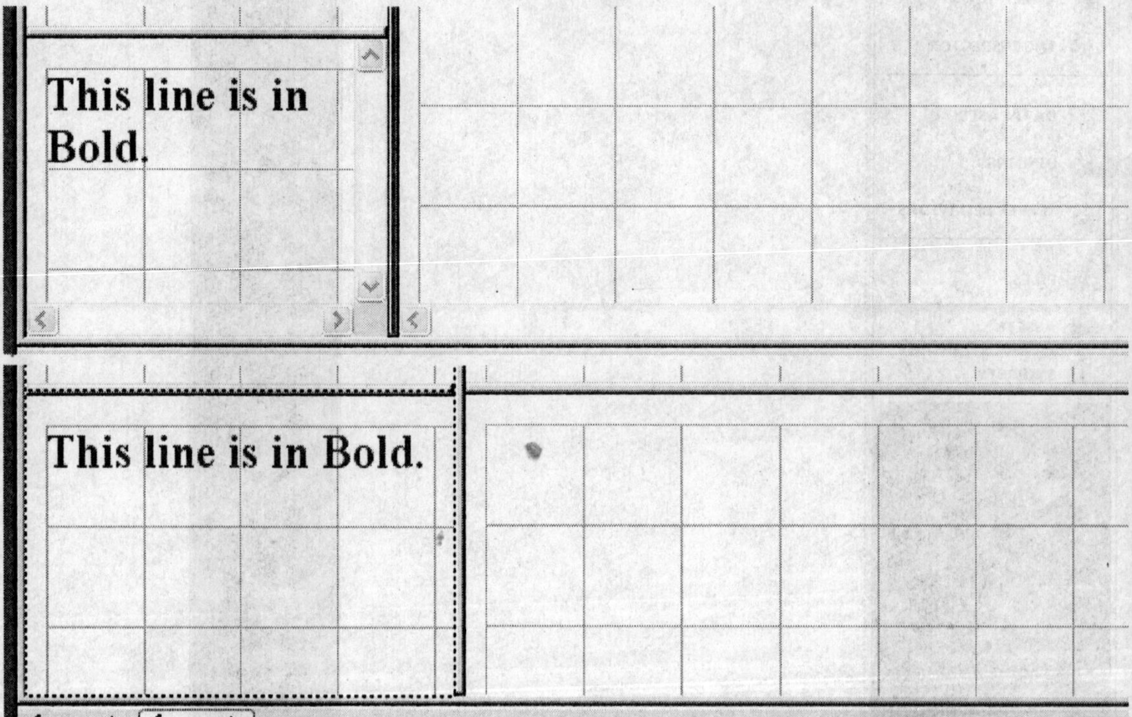

Controlling Frame Resizing

For this do the following:

1. Press and hold Alt key and then click inside a frame to select it.
2. Click No Resize.
3. Preview the page in a Web browser.
4. Click and drag the border.

5. The browser prevents you from resizing the frame.

Adding Noframes Content

For this do the following:

1. Click the frame border to select the frameset.
2. Click Modify menu.
3. Click at Frameset.
4. Click Edit NoFrames Content.
5. A blank NoFrames content window is displayed.
6. Click inside the window.
7. Add the content that you want to display.
8. A browser cannot display frames will display the NoFrames content when your framed site is opened.
9. Open your page in a text based browser or any other browser that cannot display frames.
10. The NoFrames content appears.

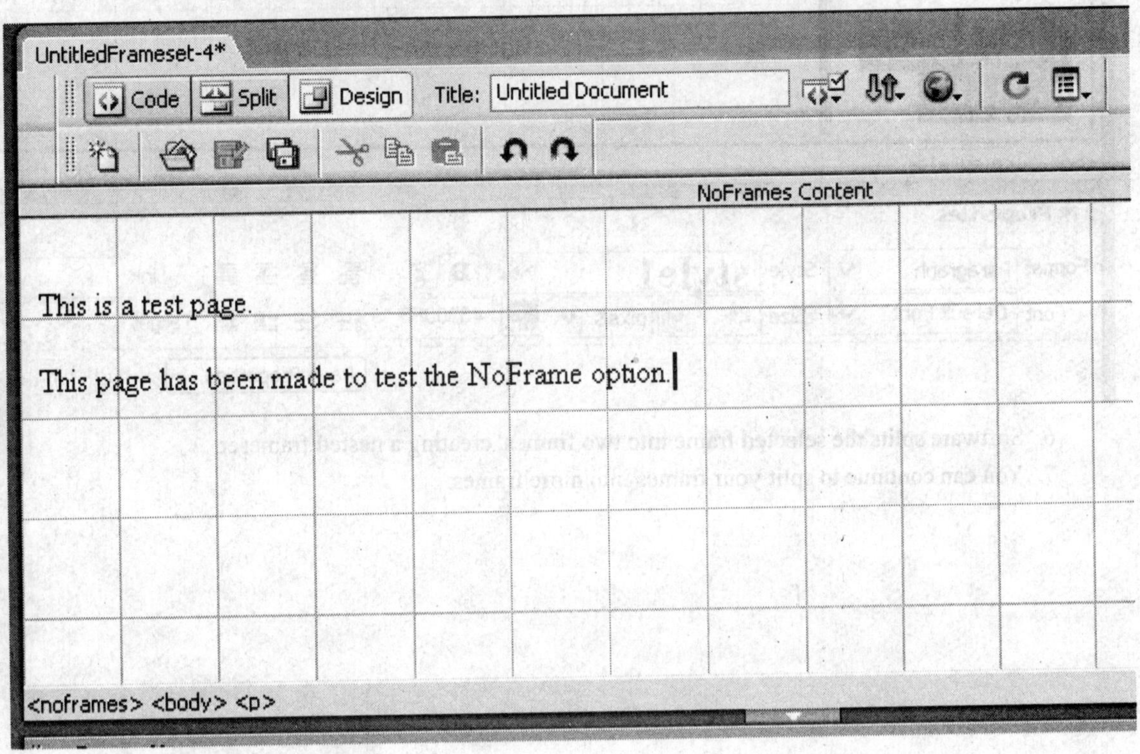

Nesting Page Frames

For this do the following:

1. Click inside the frame that you want to subdivide.
2. Click at Modify menu.
3. Click Frameset submenu.
4. Click at Split command.
5. You can optionally click a predefined frame design in the Objects panel.

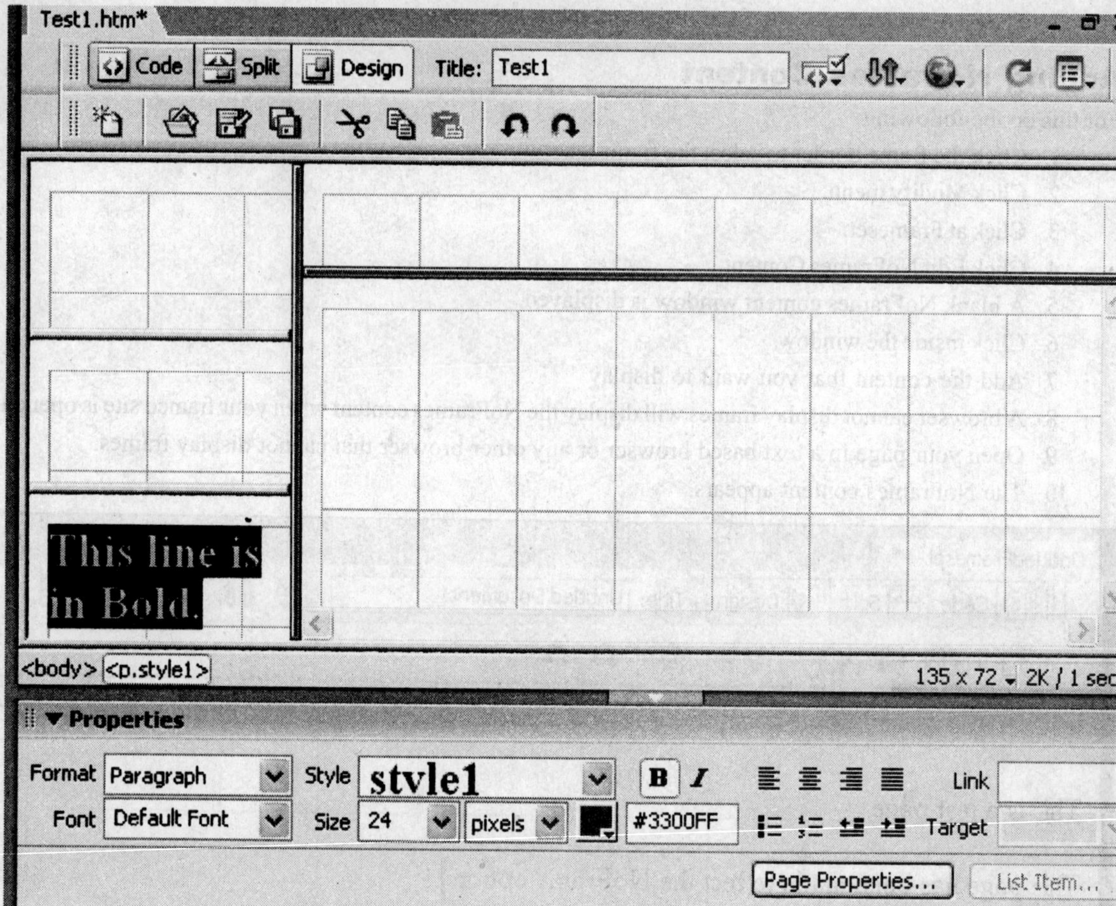

6. Software splits the selected frame into two frames, creating a nested frameset.
7. You can continue to split your frames into more frames.

7 Working with Stylesheets in Dreamweaver CS4

Introduction

The styles allow you to set various parameters in a particular style and then use it wheneve needed. Those of you who have worked with various word processing software must have used styles very often.

Creating a HTML Tag

For this do the following:

1. Click at Text menu.
2. Click at CSS Styles submenu.
3. Click at New Style.
4. The New Style dialog box appears.
5. Click at Tag.
6. Click This Document Only to create an embedded style sheet.
7. Click OK.
8. You are asked to save the style with a name.
9. Once saved you are given the Style definition for font, dialog box.
10. Select the Type category, you can customize font characteristics.
11. You can select other categories to define more style information.
12. Click OK.
13. Dreamweaver adds the new style to any content formatted with the redefined tag.
14. You can also apply the style by formatting new content with the tag.

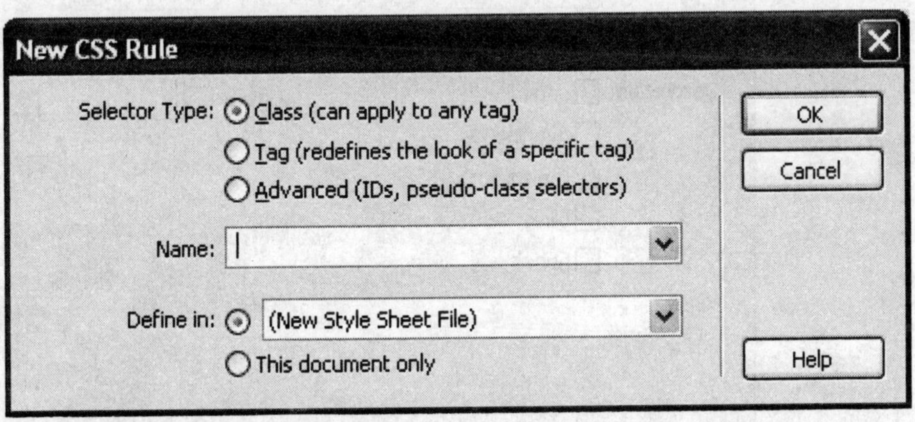

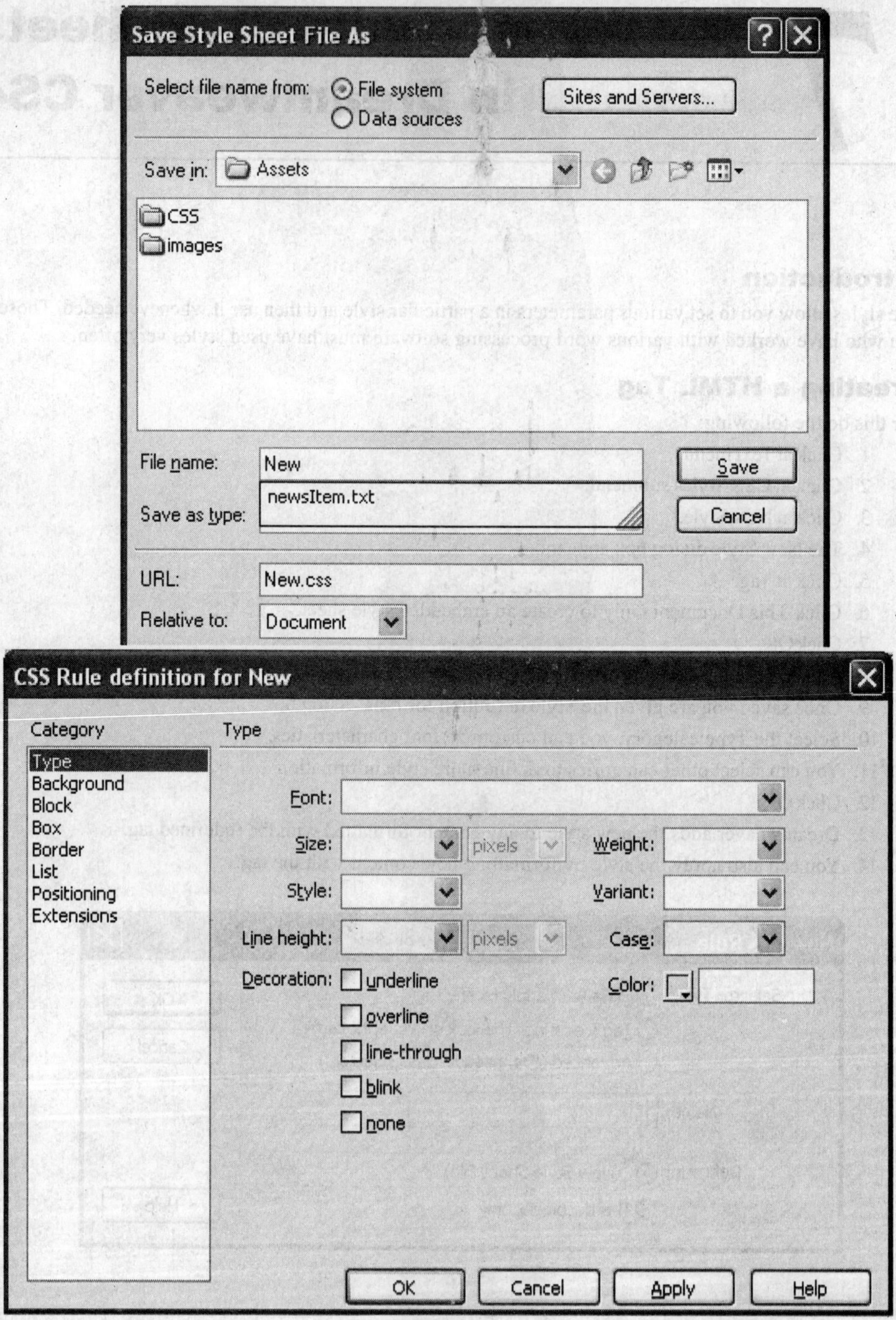
Save Style Sheet File As
Select file name from:
File system
Data sources
Sites and Servers...
Save in:
Assets
CSS
images
File name:
New
newsItem.txt
Save as type:
Save
Cancel
URL:
New.css
Relative to:
Document
CSS Rule definition for New
Category
Type
Background
Block
Box
Border
List
Positioning
Extensions
Type
Font:
Size:
pixels
Weight:
Style:
Variant:
Line height:
pixels
Case:
Decoration:
underline
overline
line-through
blink
none
Color:
OK
Cancel
Apply
Help

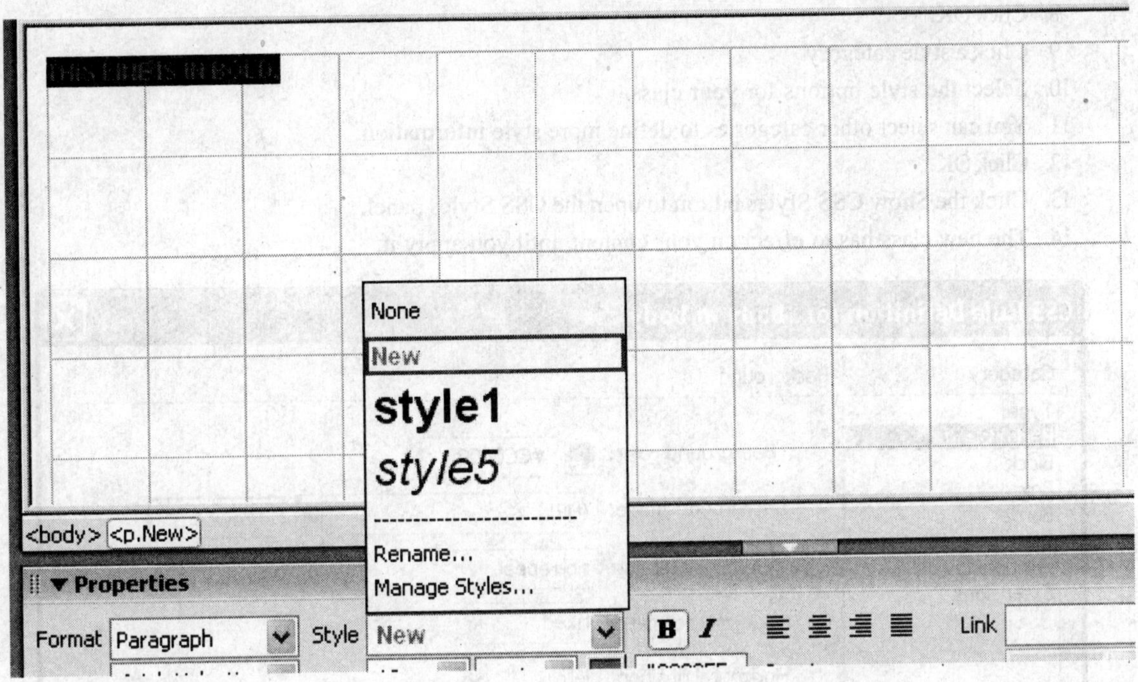

Creating a Class

You can define specific style attributes as a style sheet class. You can then apply that class to elements on your Web page.

For this do the following:

1. Click at Text menu.
2. Click CSS Styles.
3. Click New Style submenu.
4. The New Style dialog box appears.

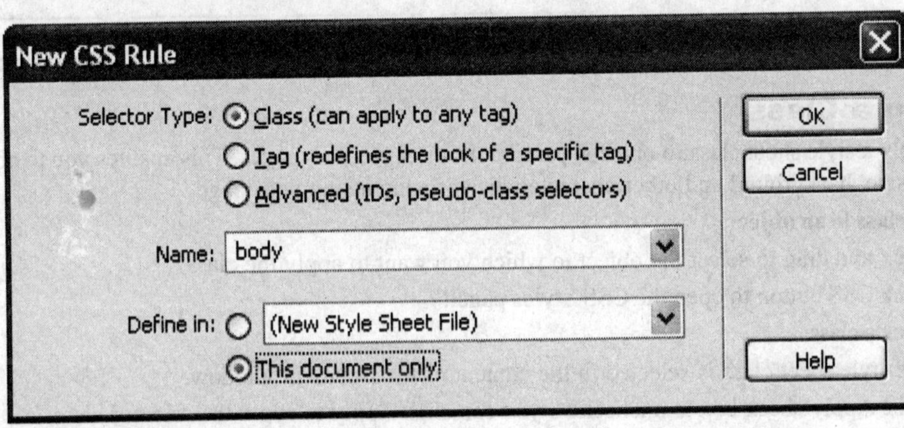

5. Click Make Custom Style.
6. Type the name of the class.
7. Click This Document Only to create an embedded style sheet.

8. Click OK.
9. Click a style category.
10. Select the style options for your class.
11. You can select other categories to define more style information.
12. Click OK.
13. Click the Show CSS Styles button to open the CSS Styles panel.
14. The new class has to effect on your content until you apply it.

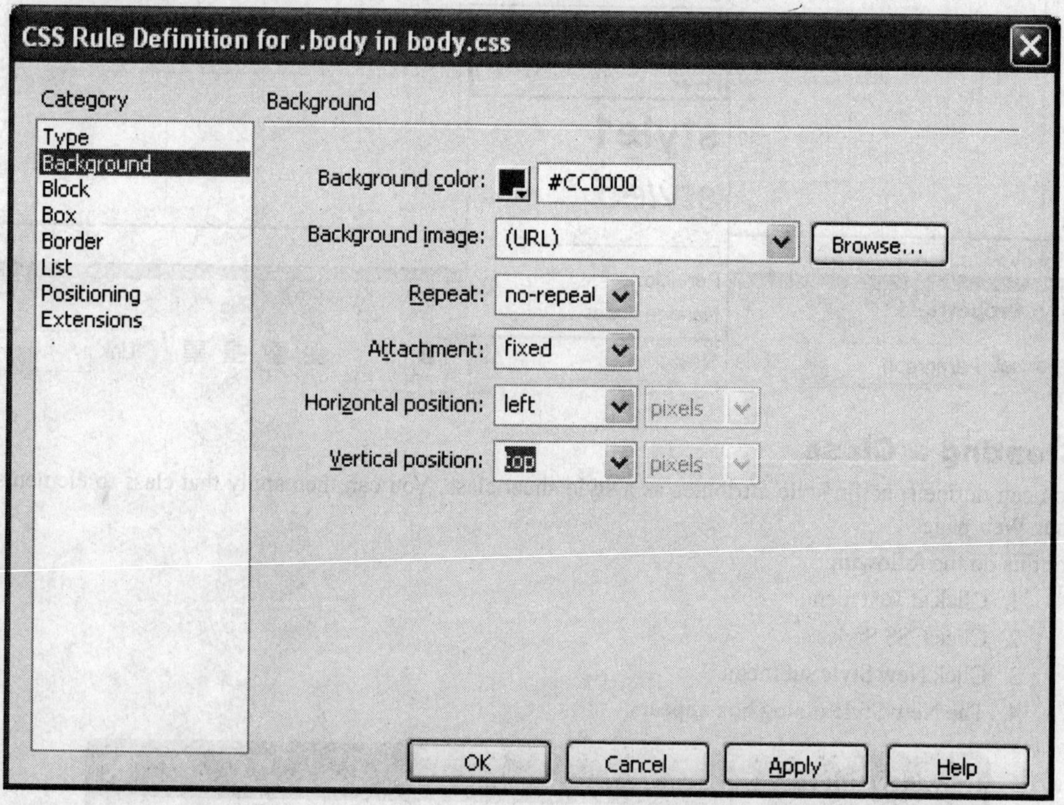

Applying a Class

You can apply a style sheet class to objects, paragraphs or entire Web pages. This enables you to change the color, font, size, background and other characteristics of contents on your page.

Applying a class to an object:

1. Click and drag to select the object to which you want to apply the class.
2. Click CSS button to open the CSS Styles panel.
3. Click a class.
4. The style sheet class is selected in the content of the Docment window.
5. If the Apply check box is unchecked, you can click Apply to apply the selected class.

Apply a class to Paragraph:

1. Click inside the paragraph.
2. Click <p> in the tag selector.

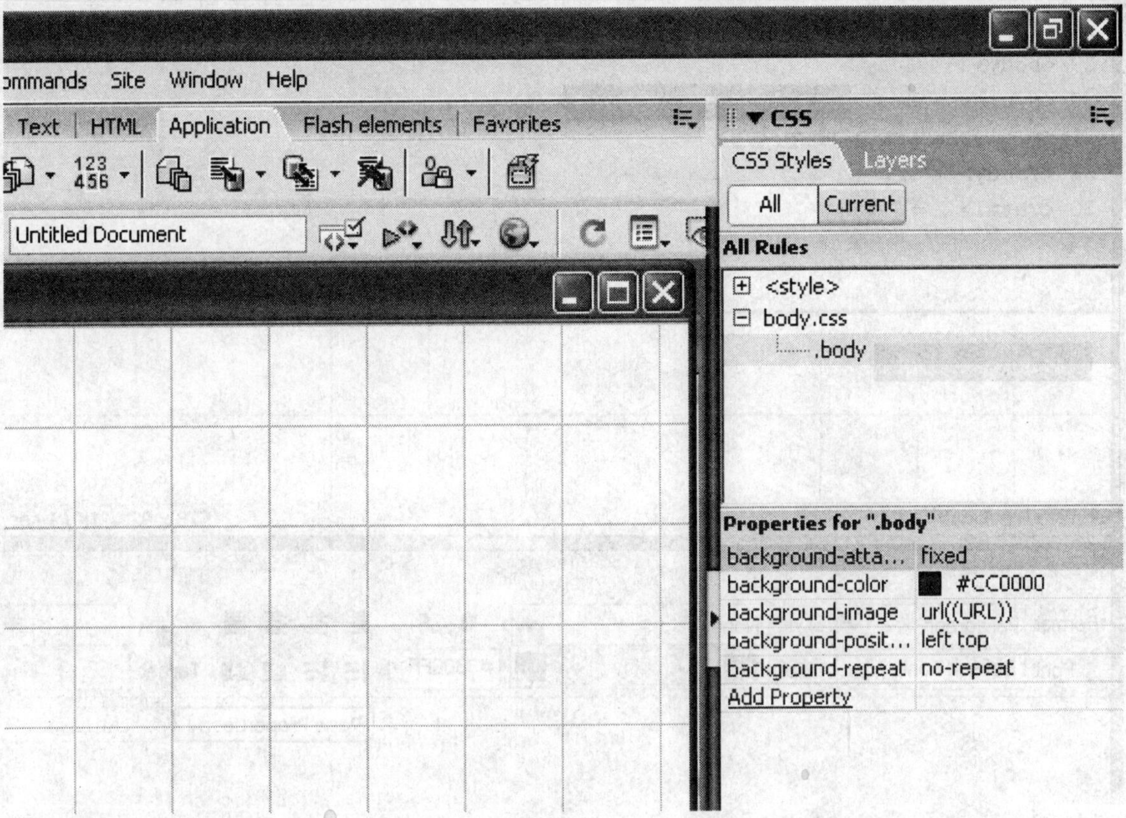

3. Click the class.
4. Dreamweaver applies the style sheet class to the selected paragraph in the Document window.

Apply a class to the Entire body of a page:

1. Click inside the Document window.
2. Click <body> in the tag selector.
3. Click the class.
4. Dreamweaver applies the style sheet class to the entire body of the page in the Document window.

Editing a Style Sheet Class

You can edit the style rules of a class. This will change all instances where you have applied the class on your pages.

For this do the following:

1. Click open CSS Styles button to open the CSS Styles panel.
2. The CSS Styles panel displays the classes available to that page.
3. Double-click the class that you want to edit.
4. Click a style category.
5. Edit the style definitions.
6. Change the background color to a different shade.
7. You can also click another category to modify more style definitions.

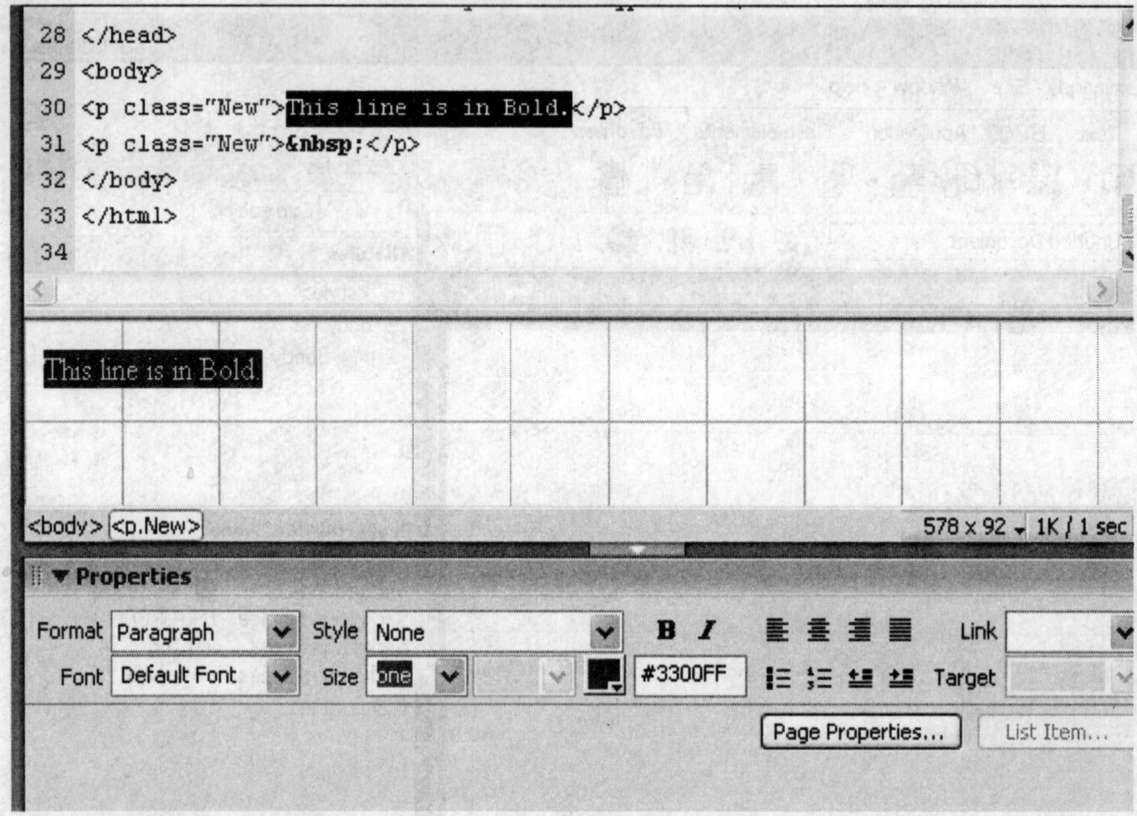

8. Click OK.
9. Preview the page in a Web browser.

Using CSS selectors to Modify Links

You can use style sheet selectors to customize the links on your page. Selectors let you customize your links in ways that you cannot the HTML.

For this do the following:

1. Click Text menu.
2. Click CSS Styles submenu.
3. Click New Style.
4. The New Style dialog box appears.
5. Click Use Advanced button which includes CSS Selector.
6. Click This Document Only to create an embedded style sheet.
7. Click OK.
8. Click a style category.
9. Select the style options for your link.
10. In the Type category, you can change the characteristics of your text links.
11. You can click other categories to define more style information.
12. Click OK.
13. Preview the page in a Web browser.

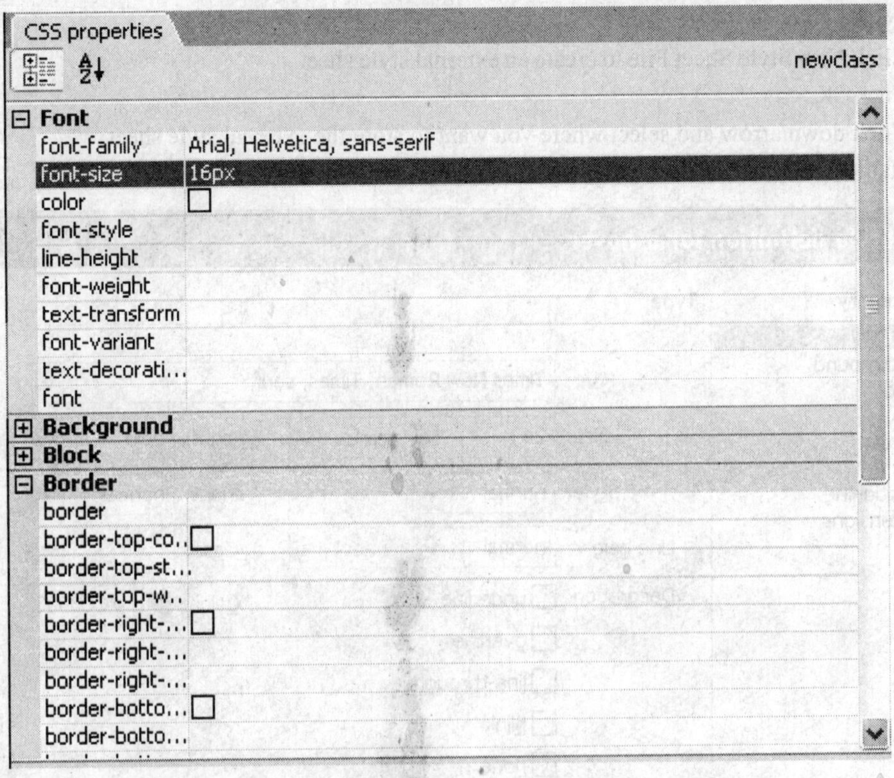

Creating an External Style Sheet

External style sheets enable you to define a set of style sheet rules and apply them to many different pages – even pages on different Web sites. This capability lets you keep a consistent look and feel across many pages and streamline style updates.

1. Click Text menu.
2. Click CSS Styles submenu.
3. Click New CSS Style.
4. The New CSS Style dialog box appears.
5. Click Make Custom Style.

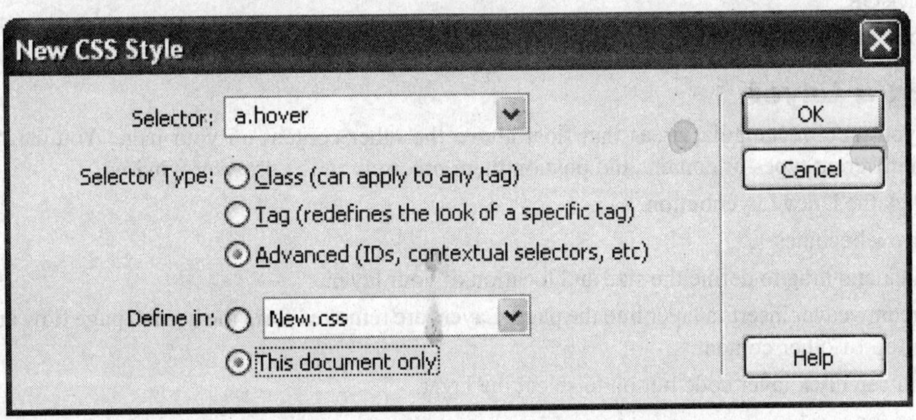

6. Type a class name.
7. Click New Style Sheet File to create an external style sheet.
8. Click OK.
9. Click down arrow and select where you want to store the external style sheet.
10. Name the style sheet file with a .css extension.

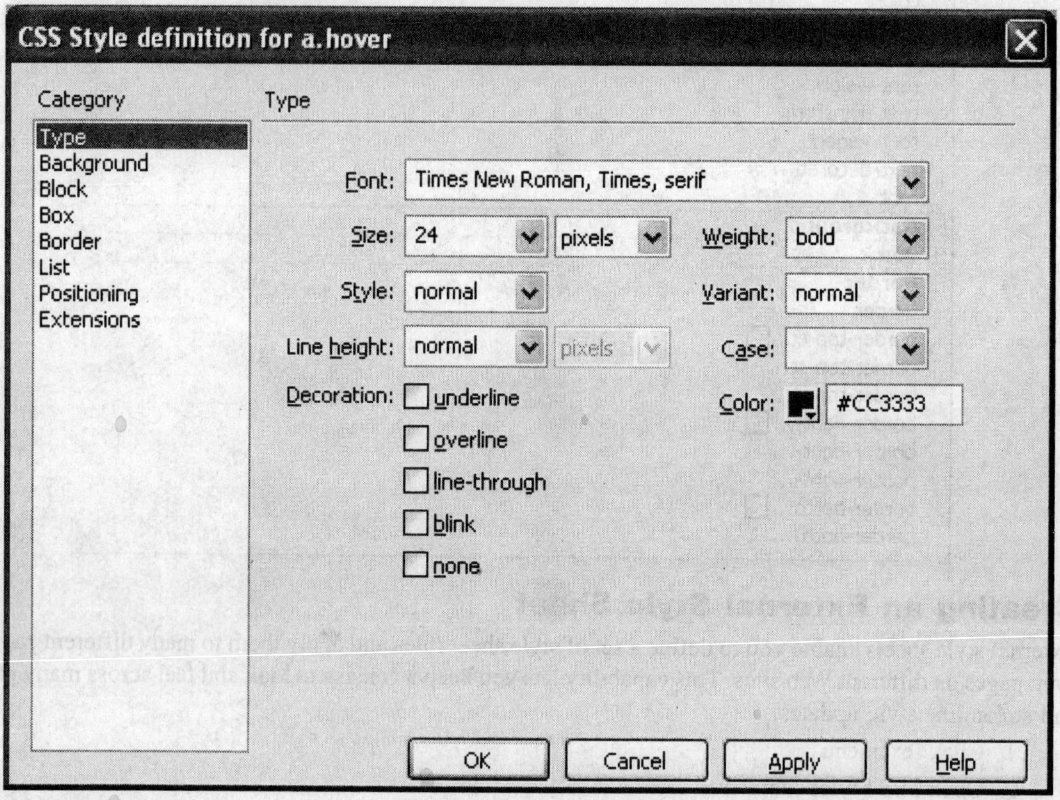

11. Click Save.
12. Click a style category.
13. Select the style options for your style sheet.
14. Click OK.
15. You can repeat above steps to add more style rules to the external style sheet.

Creating a Layer

Layers let you crete rectangular areas that float above the other content on your page. You can fill these blocks with different types of content and postion them precisely in the browser window.

1. Click the Draw Layer button.
2. Arrow becomes +.
3. Click and drag to define the size and location of your layer.
4. Dreamweaver inserts a layer into the page. Layers are removed form the normal page flow and can sit on top of other content.
5. You can click layer code button to select the layer.

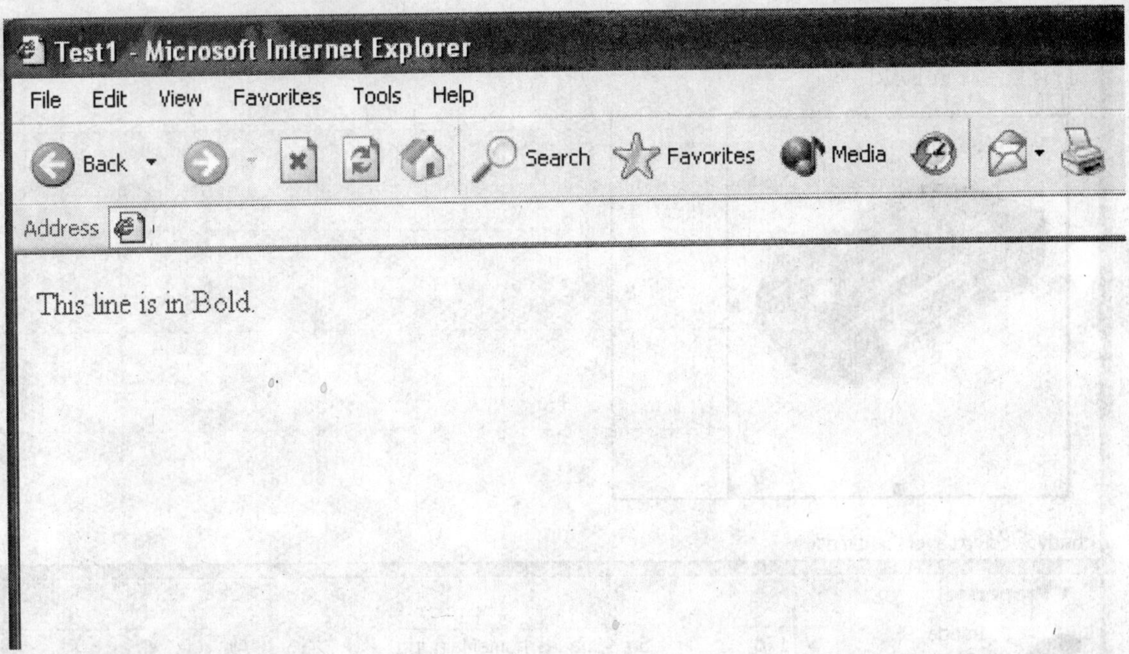

Adding Content to a layer:

1. Click inside the layer.
2. Click Insert menu and Image to insert an object.
3. Fill out any necessary dialog boxes to define and insert the object.
4. An image object appears inside the layer.
5. To add text, you can click inside the layer and type. You can also style the text in a layer.

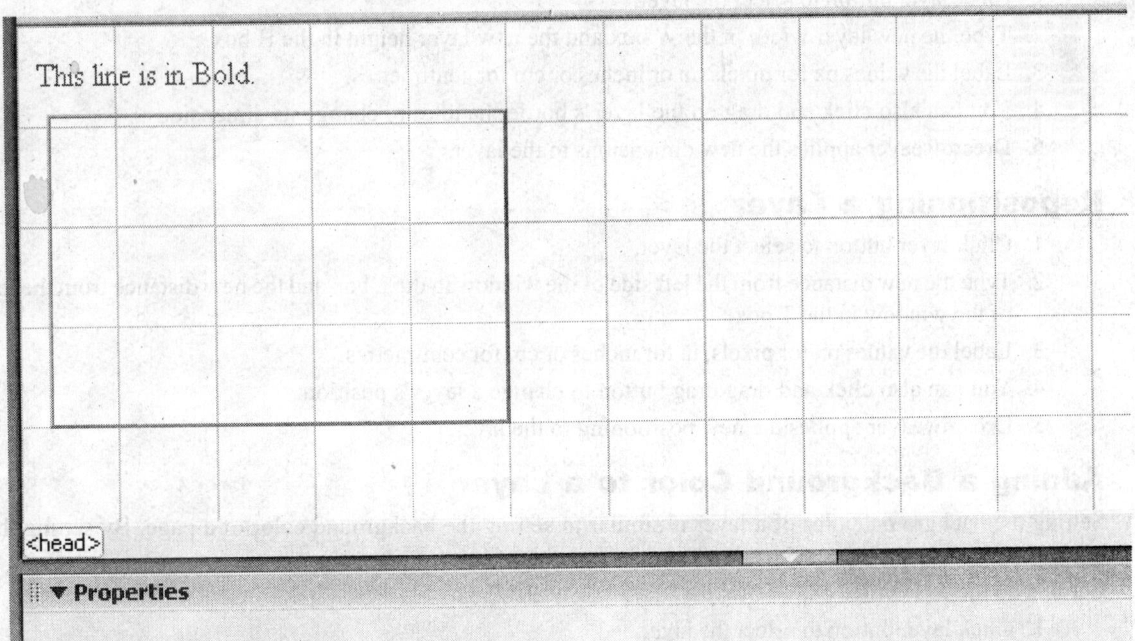

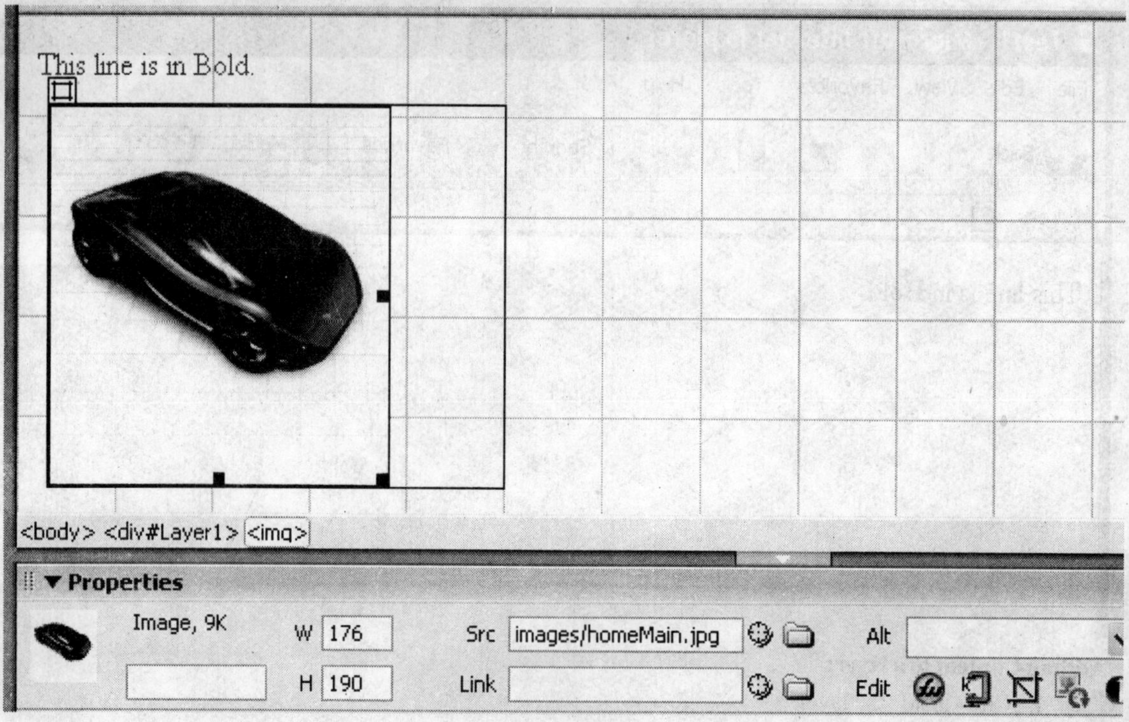

Resizing a Layer

Every layer has specific position and dimension settings that define its place in the page. You can adjust the position and dimensions of a layer to make it fit attractively with the rest of the content on your page.

1. Click layer button to select the layer.
2. Type the new layer width in the W box and the new layer height in the H box.
3. Label the values px for pixels, in or inches or cm for centimetres.
4. You can also click and drag on the layer's border handles to change its dimensions.
5. Dreamweaver applies the new dimensions to the layer.

Repositioning a Layer

1. Click layer button to select the layer.
2. Type the new distance from the left side of the window in the L box and the new distance from the top of the window in the T box.
3. Label the values px for pixels, in for inches or cm for centimetres.
4. You can also click and drag drag button to change a layer's position.
5. Dreamweaver applies the new positioning to the layer.

Adding a Background Color to a Layer

Setting the background color of a layer is similar to setting the background color of a page. By setting the background color, you can make a layer stand out or blend in on a page.

For this do the following:

1. Click layer button to select the layer.

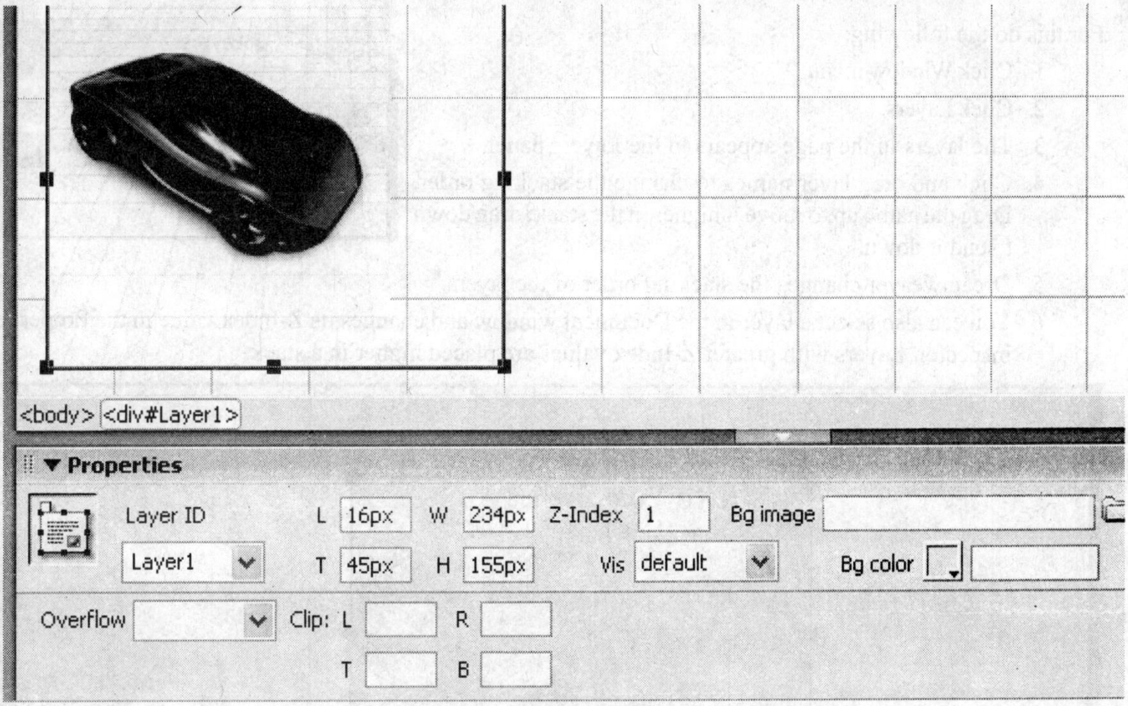

2. Click the Bg Color button.
3. Click a background color.
4. The layer background changes to the new color.
5. You can click the Bg Image button to select a background image for the layer.

Changing the Stacking Order of Layers

You can change the stacking order of layers on a page to change how they overlap one another. You can then hide parts of some layers under other layers.

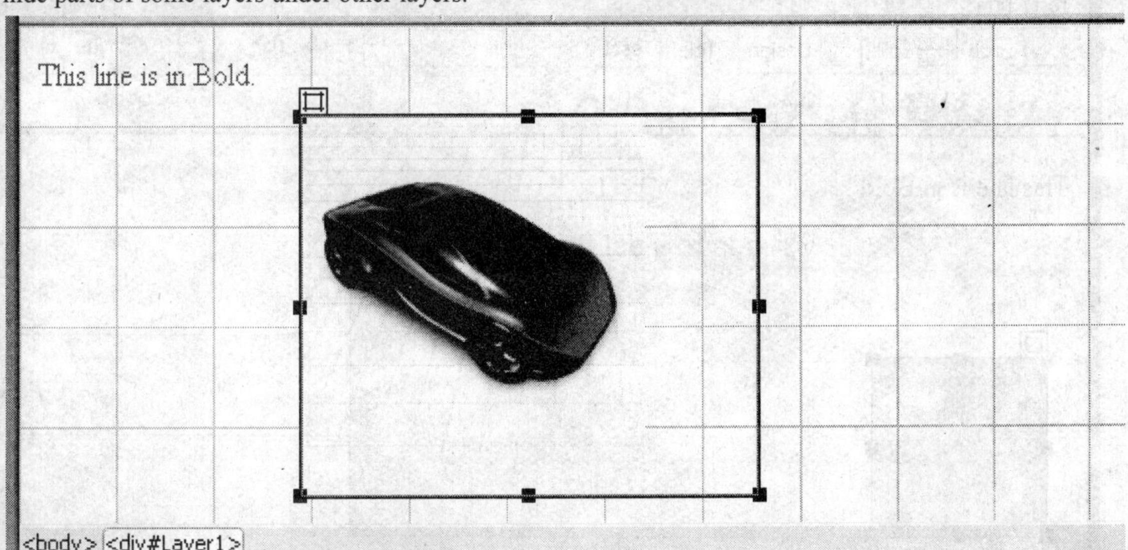

For this do the following:

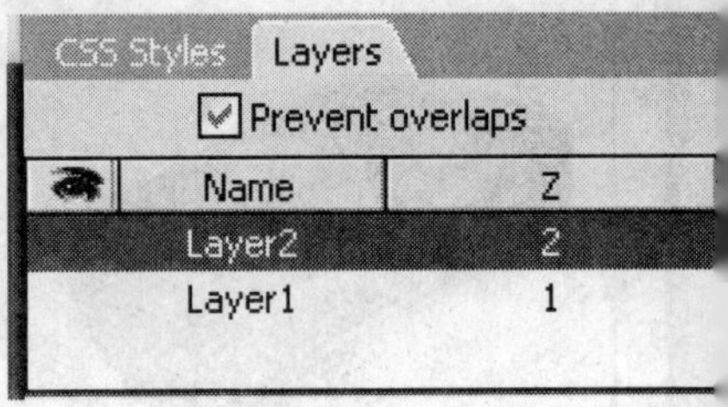

1. Click Window menu.
2. Click Layers.
3. The layers in the page appears in the Layers panel.
4. Click and drag layer names to change the stacking order. Drag the name up to move it higher in the stack; drag down t send it down.
5. Dreamweaver changes the stacking order of the layers.
6. You can also select a layer in the Document window and changes its Z-Index value in the Properties inspector. Layers with greater Z-Index values are placed higher in a stack.

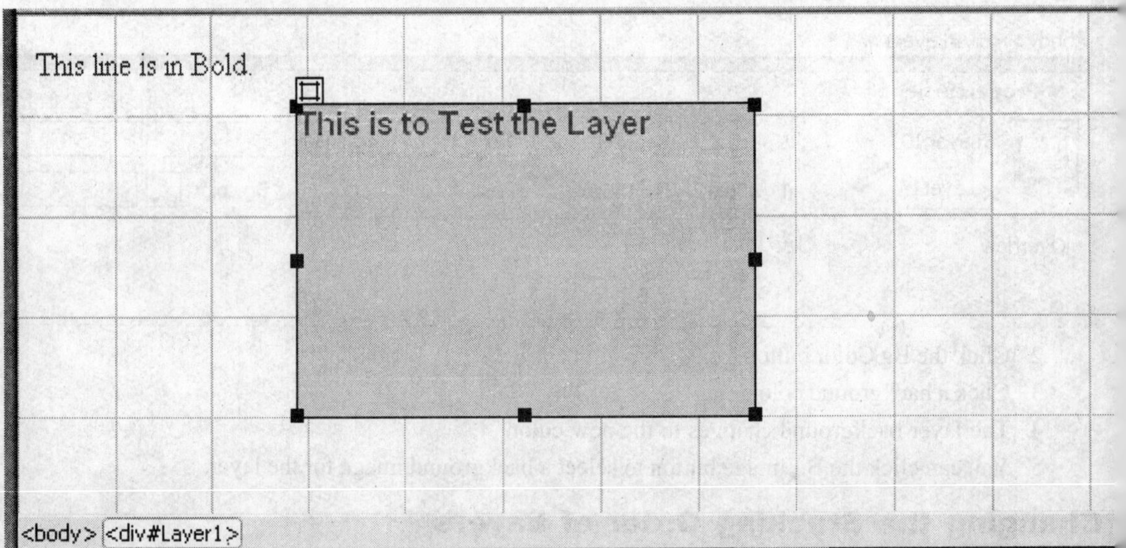

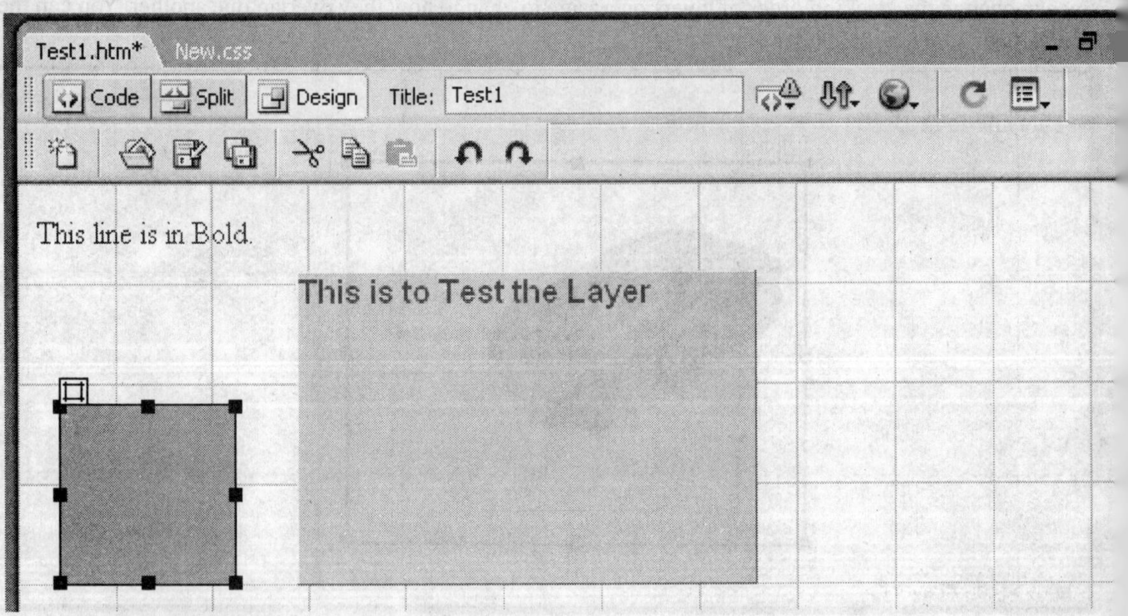

8 Creating and Applying Templates

Introduction

Templates are there to help you start working on a Web page with ready made background. These are there to help you create Web pages with ready made informations. You can even create your own templates.

Creating a Template

First create a template, save it to the Template category of the Asset panel and then use it to create a new Web page within your Web site. Others that are working on the same Web site can use the template, too and you can use templates created by others.

You need to define a Web site before Dreamweaver can insert a template. Dreamweaver creates a directory called Templates in the root of your Web site where it stores the original template files. Dreamweaver keeps the code of a template in a file in the Template directory and inserts a copy of the code when you insert a template in a Web page. A template differs form a library item because the template is an entire Web page, not just a portion of one.

Use the Template Category of the Asset Panel

When you are creating and applying templates, open the Template category of the Asset panel. The template category shows all of the templates that exist in the current Web site. Each Web site that you create can have a different set of templates.

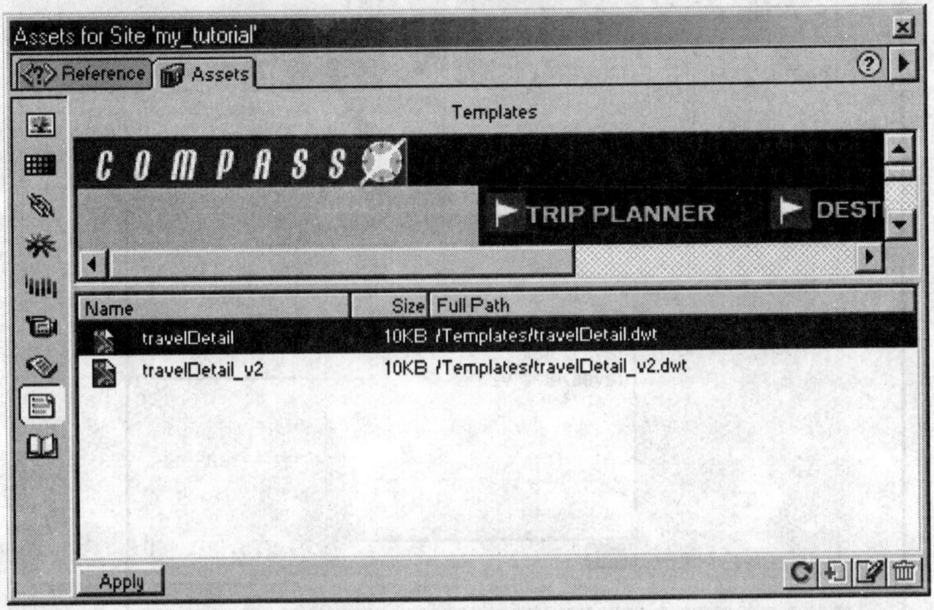

The Template category of the Asset panel is divided into two halves. The top half displays the contents of the template. The bottom half lists the names of the templates in the Web site. The buttons at the bottom include the following:

- The Apply button applies the currently selected template to the Web page.
- The new Template button creates a new, blank template.
- The Open Template button opens the template in its own Dreamweaver document window for editing.
- The Delete Template button removes the template from the Templates director. This doesn't affect any instances of the templates except that the template can no longer be updated site wide.

Creating a template from an Existing Web page

There are two ways to create templates:

- From an existing Web page – after you decide to create a template out of a Web page, you save the page as a template.
- From scratch, as a new empty template – you can create a new template, open it up and add objects to the template just like it was a regular Web page.

Once you apply a template to your Web page a copy all of the content that the template contains gets inserted into the page. You no longer need to have the original template present for the Web page to display. When you upload your Web page onto a remote Web site you do not need to upload the Templates directory. You

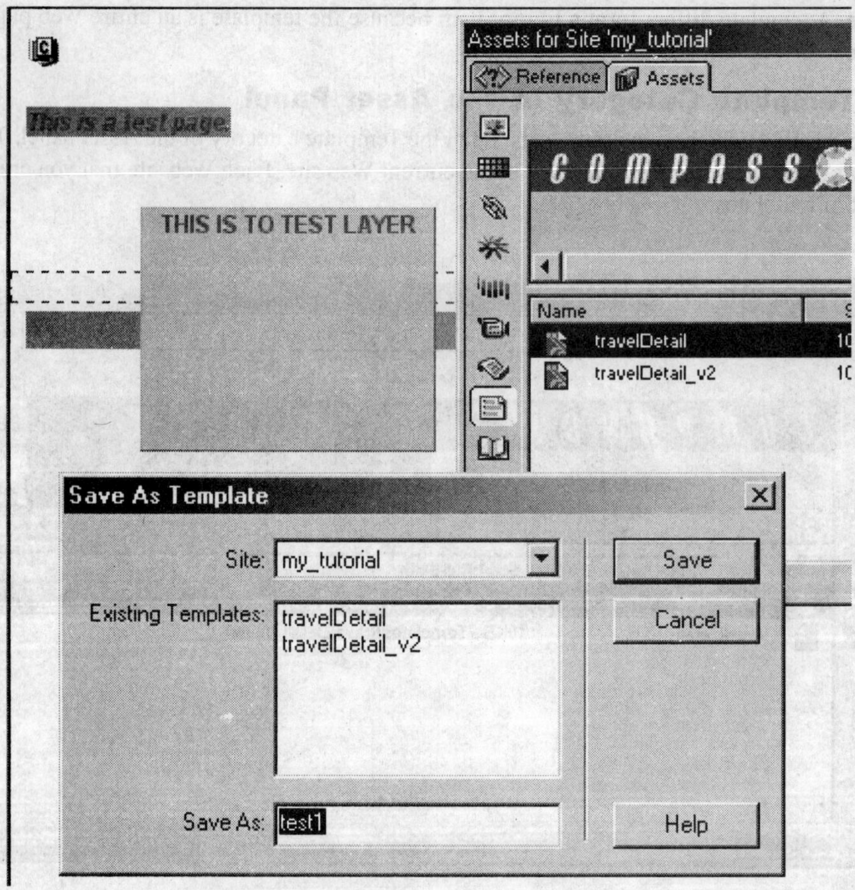

might want to upload the template onto your server so that others can use the templates too. You'll want to keep the directory in case you want to make changes to templates throughout your Web site.

Crete a template from an existing Web page:

1. Select the Save As Template command under the File menu.
2. The save As Template dialog box appears as shown in figure. Enter a meaningful name for the template.

Dreamweaver creates an individual file for each template. The file extension for templates is .dwt. If you look in the Templates directory of your web site you will see one .dwt file for each template you have in your Web site.

Create a Template from Scratch

To create a new empty template and then add objects to it.

1. Click the New Template button at the bottom of the Template category of the Asset panel.
2. Dreamweaver creates a new blank template as shown in figure. A message appears in the top half of the Template category of the Asset panel telling you how to get started adding content to the blank template.
3. Give the template a name.
4. Double-click the template in the Template category of the Asset panel.
5. Dreamweaver opens the template in a separate document window. You can tell that you have a template open because Dreamweaver displays <<Template>> along with the name of the template in the title bar as shown.
6. Insert objects into the template's document window just like you would any Web page.
7. Close the document window and save the template. Your changes will be reflected in the Template category of the Asset panel. Don't worry right now about the message you receive about your template not having any editable regions. You'll add some editable regions in a few minutes.

The Template category of the asset panel has a pop-up menu that contains useful commands, shown in figure. Different commands are available depending on what is currently selected.

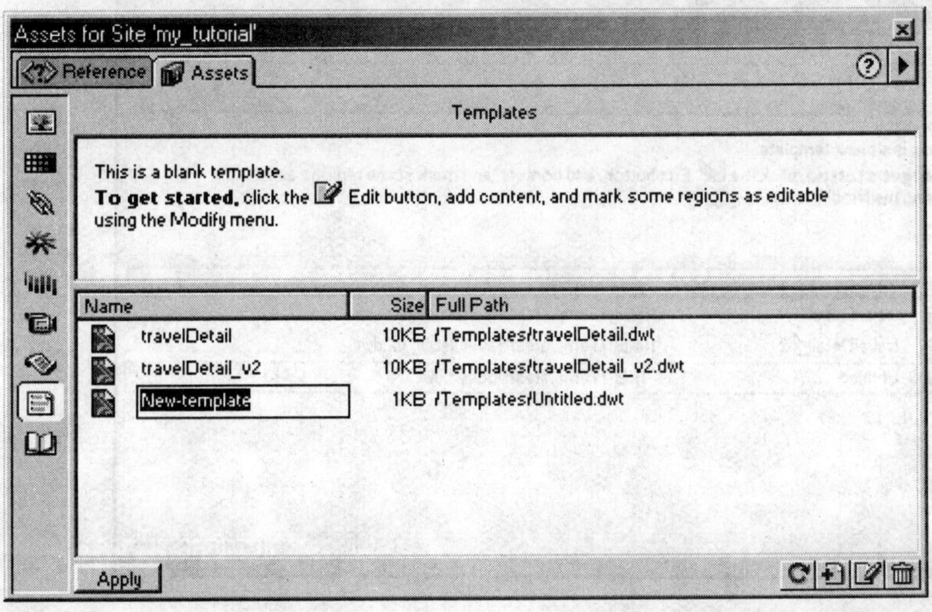

Make an Existing Region Editable

Before you apply a template to a Web page, you need to mark regions of the template as editable. By default, all regions in the template are locked. Mark regions as editable if you will need to change, add or update the content in the region.

Leave all regions locked that do not need to be changed. If you need to make changes to a locked region, you can change the original template file and update all of the Web pages that are linked to that template. The Template commands to manipulate Editable Regions are located in the Templates submenu in the Modify menu, shown in figure on the next page.

To make an existing region editable

1. Open a template and select the region that needs to be editable.
2. Select the Mark Selection as Editable command from the Templates submenu in the Modify menu.
3. The New Editable Region dialog box appears as shown in figure. Give the region a meaningful name.

After you create an editable region, the name of the region is listed at the bottom of the Templates submenu in the Modify menu while you are working on the template. Select one of the region name sin the menu to highlight that region in the document window.

Dreamweaver gives you the ability to create editable regions on various objects in a template. For instance, you can make a layer editable. You will be able to move the layer or change nay of its properties after you apply the template to a Web page. Or, you can leave the layer locked and create an editable region within the layer. Then you can't move the layer or change the layer properties when you've applied the template but you can put content within the layer.

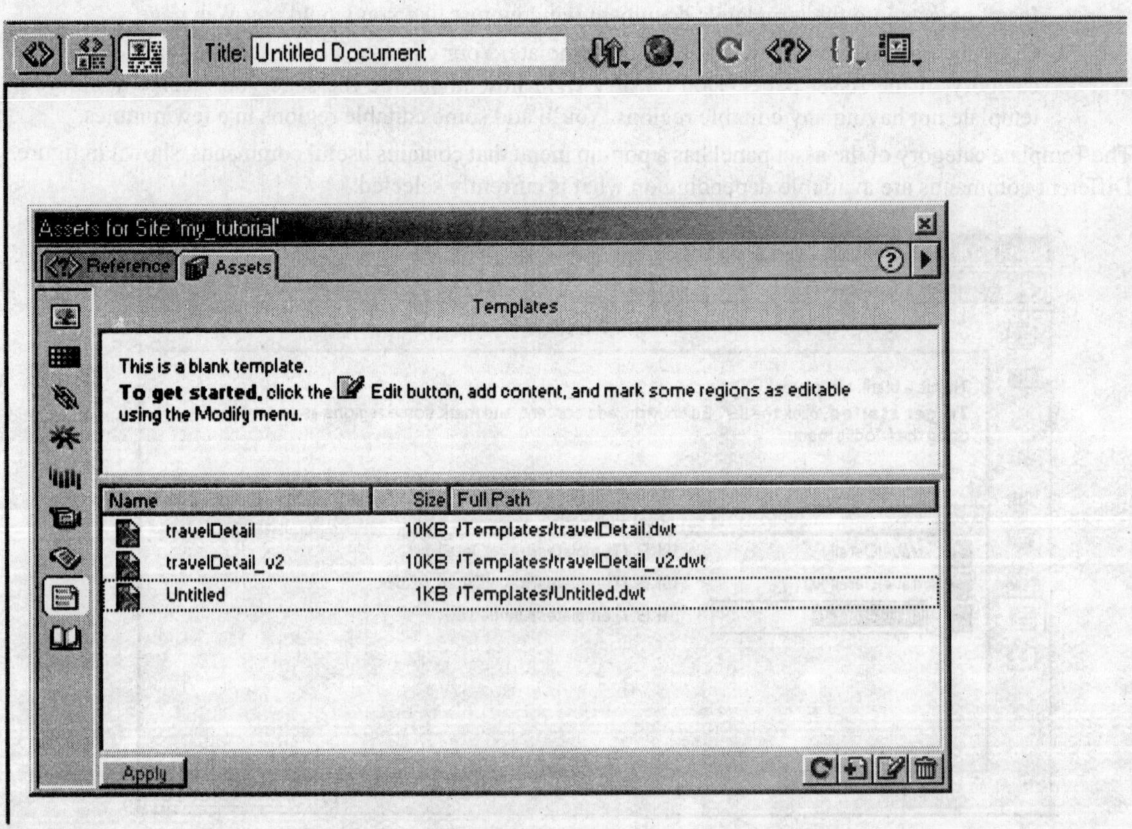

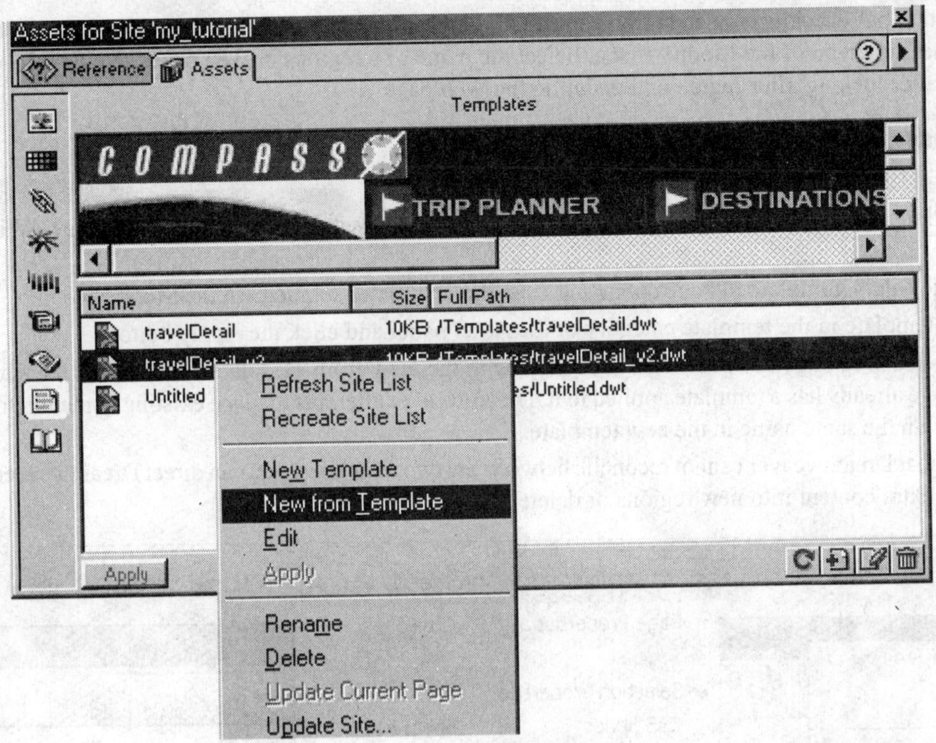

You can import or export the editable regions of a Dreamweaver template as XML. Use the commands under the Import and Export submenus of the File menu.

Dreamweaver highlights editable regions so that they are easy to pick up out in the document window. The highlights only appear in Dreamweaver and not in the browser. The highlights only appear if Invisible Elements is checked in the View menu. Set the highlight color in the Highlighting category in Dreamweaver preferences. The editable regions are highlighted only while editing the original template file. Just the opposite is true in a Web page with a template applied: The locked regions are highlighted.

Make a New Editable Region

You can create a new, blank region in a template. Seelct the New Editable Region command from the Templates submenu in the Modify menu. Name the new region in the New Editable Region dialog box. The editable region appears in a highlighted rectangular outline as shown in figure.

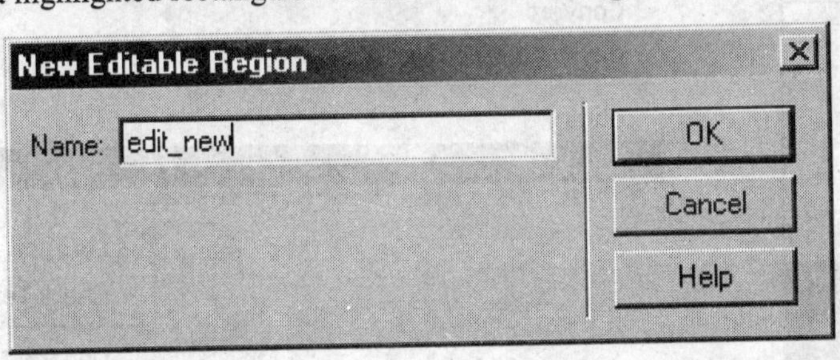

If Dreamweaver displays the message that the selection is already a part of an editable region, then you need to move the selection. Examine the tag selector for the tag <mm:editable>. If you see this tag, you need to modify your selection until that tag is no longer part of the selection.

To lock a region that has previously been marked as editable, select the Unmark Editable Region command from the Templates submenu of the Modify menu. Select the name of a regions in Web pages, you will lose that information after locking after region and updating the Web pages.

Apply a Template to a Web Page

You can apply templates in three different ways:

- Simply drag the template form the Template category of the Asset panel and apply it to a new Web page.
- Select the Apply Template to Page command from the Templates submenu in the Modify menu.
- Select a template in the template category of the Asset panel and click the Apply button.

Apply a template to a Web page or open a new Web page with the New from Template command in the file menu. If a Web page already has a template applied to it, Dreamweaver attempts to place existing content into editable regions with the same name in the new template.

If there is content that Dreamweaver cannot reconcile between the two templates, you can direct Dreamweaver to either save the extra content into new regions or delete it.

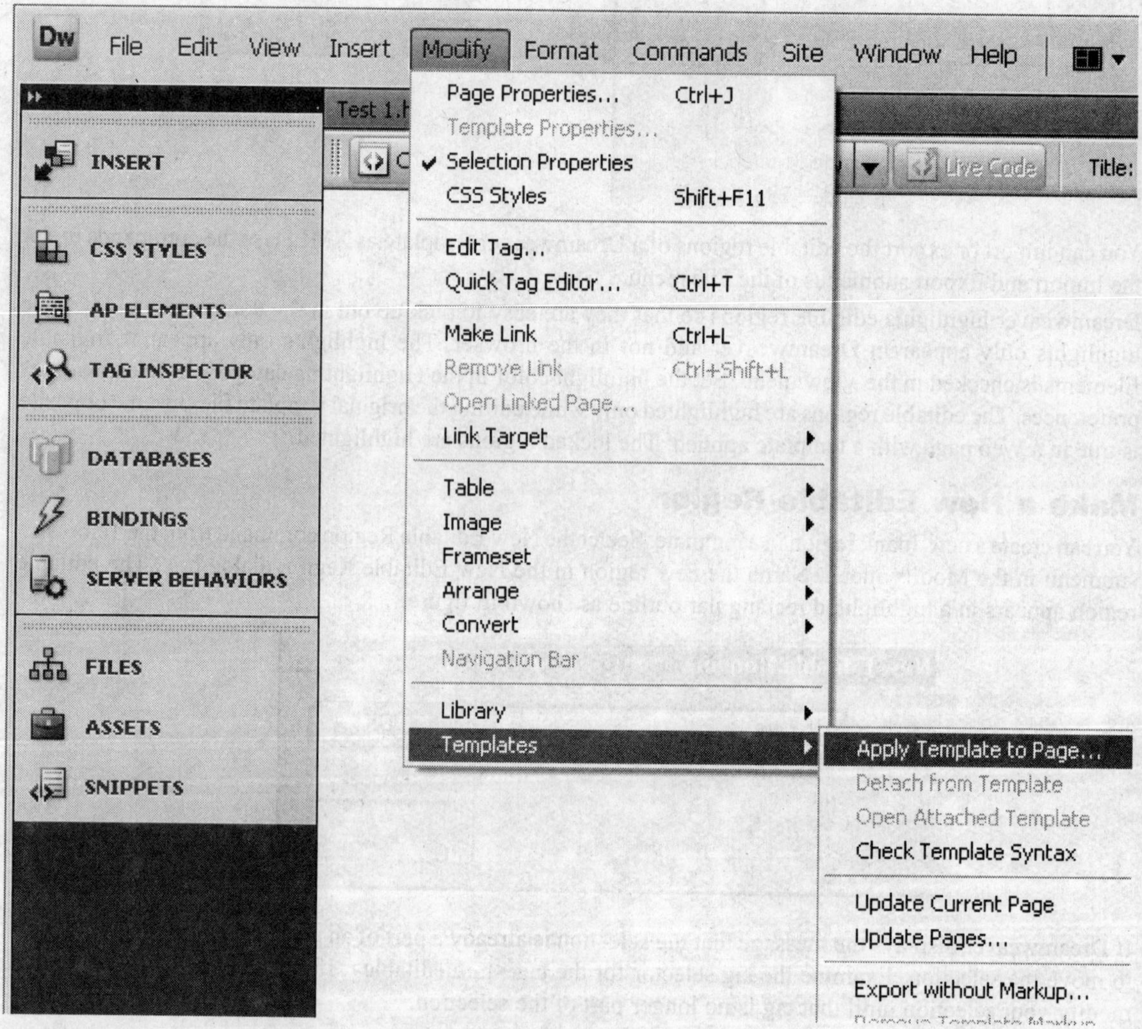

Make Changes to a Template

Edit templates by opening the template to add or change its contents. You can open the template from the Template category of the Asset panel or you an open the template from the Site Manager. Edits to locked objects are applied to all of the Web pages that use the template. Edits to editable objects have no effect on Web pages that use the template.

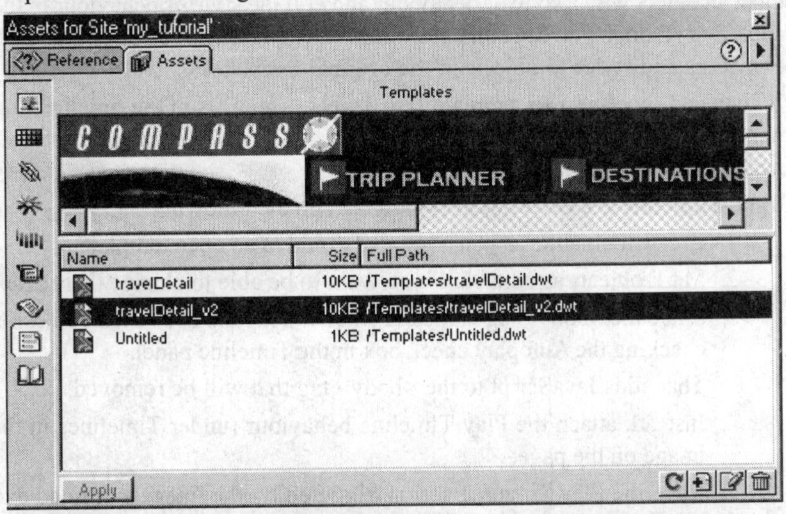

Update Pages That Contain the Template

After you edit and save a template, Dreamweaver will ask you whether you want to update files. Select files and then the Update button to automatically update the linked templates.

The Update Pages dialog box displays statistics on how many files were examines, updated and could not be updated. The Show Log check box needs to be checked to display these statistics. Select the Close button to close the Update Pages dialog box.

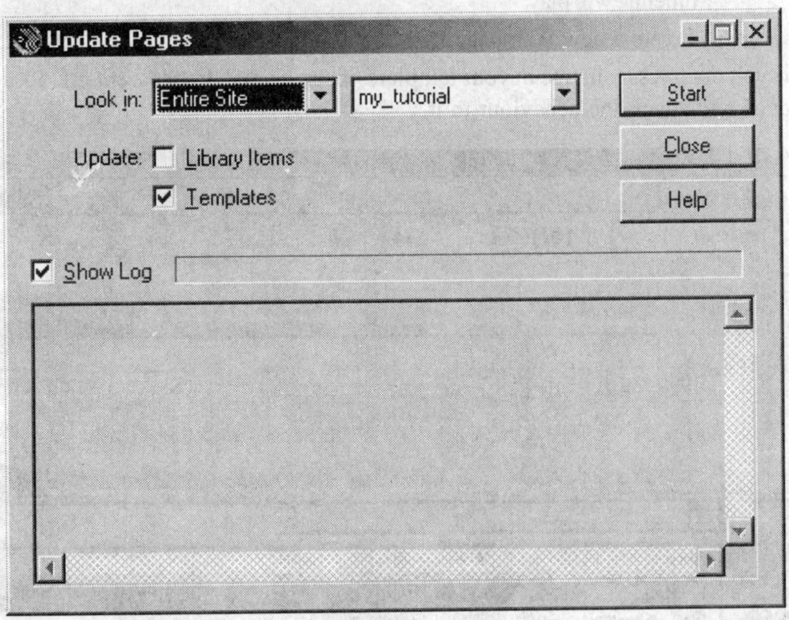

Certain files in the Web site may not be updated because you do not have these files checked out.

When you have checked in/ check out turned on in you Web site, files that are not checked out to you are marked as read-only. Dreamweaver will not be able to update any files marked read-only.

You can also manually update files linked to templates. Right-click on the template in the Template category f the Asset panel and select either the Update Page command, to update the current Web page or the Update Pages command, to update the entire Web site.

The Update Page command acts immediately and no dialog box appear. When you issue the Update Pages dialog box appears as shown in figure.

Click the Start button to update all of the linked templates in the Web site.

Use Behaviours, Styles and Timelines in Templates

You can use behaviours, styles and timeliness in templates. Styles and JavaScript will be applied to a Web page based on the template. To edit styles and behaviours in the Web page, objects they are applied to must be editable.

Select an object with a style or behaviour and edit the style or behaviour in the CSS Style panel or Behaviour panel. Even though you can edit behaviours and styles in a Web page linked to a template, you can only apply behaviours and styles to objects in the original template.

You can add timeliness to template. The layers or images in the timeline must be marked as editable if you intend on allowing them to be changed. If you don't need the timeline content the changed, leave the layer on image locked and it will still animate.

To add a timeline to a Dreamweaver template, do the following:

1. Create a timeline as you normally would in an open template.
2. Mark objects as editable if you want to be able to change them after the template is applied.
3. Since the <body> tag is locked when a template is applied you can't trigger the timeline to play by checking the Autoplay check box in the Timeline panel.

   That adds JavaScript to the <body> tag that will be removed.
4. Instead, attach the Play Timeline behaviour (under Timelines in the Behaviours inspector) to any image on the page.

   Have the Play Timeline action triggered by the image's onLoad event. When the image loads, the timeline will play.
5. Create a new Web page with the template. Change any objects that need to be edited.

If you not have an image in your template, insert a small transparent gif (1 x 1 pixels) somewhere in your Web page and attach the behaviour to it.

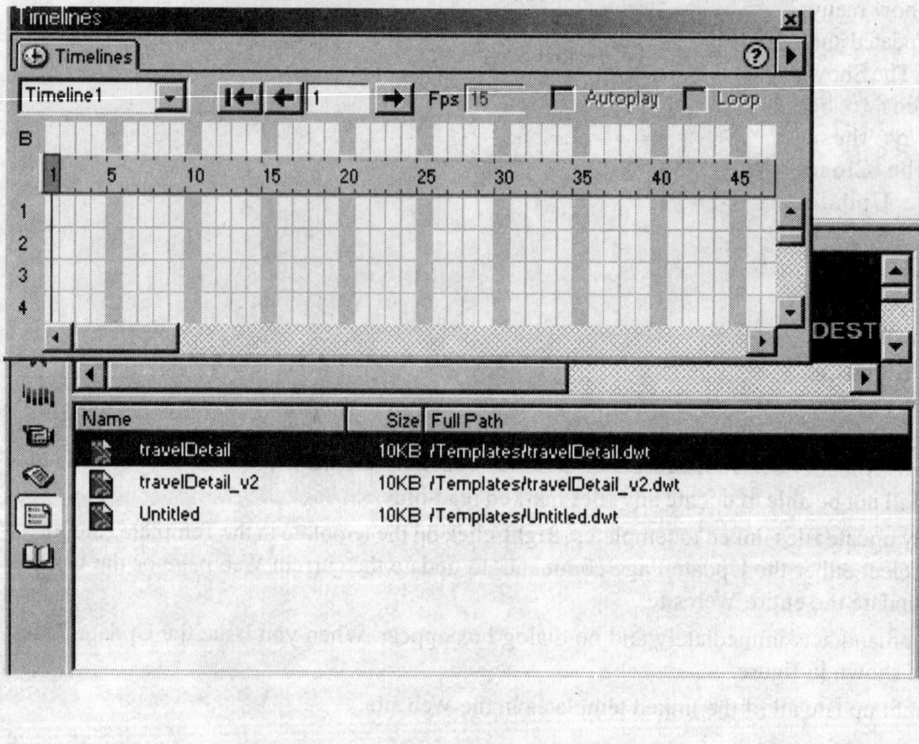

9 More Commands of Dreamweaver CS4

Creating a Custom Snippet

Snippets are bits of code that are available from Dreamweaver's Snippets panel. You can use any of the multiple snippets available when you install Dreamweaver. You can also create custom snippets out of code that you use respectively. This can speed up development of Web pages as well as maintain consistency in your code.

First, let's explore the existing snippets that are available in Dreamweaver. Some of these snippets may not interest you, but some may speed up your daily work in Dreamweaver. The lower half of the Snippets panel displays categories of snippets, along with descriptions of what are snippets to (you might have to enlarge the Snippets panel to see the descriptions). The upper portion of the Snippets panel gives you a preview of the selected snippet. The default Snippets panel, has the following categories:

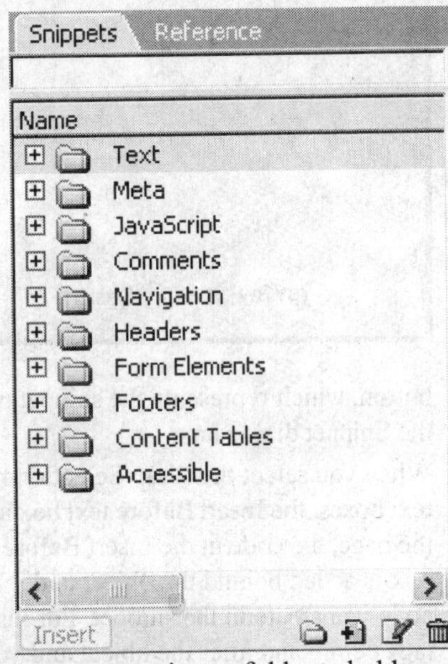

- Text
- Navigation
- Meta
- JavaScript
- Headers
- Form Elements
- Footers
- Content Tables
- Comments
- Accessible

You can create a new snippet out of an object or some code that you use often. You can create a new snippet within an existing category or you can create a new folder for your own personal snippets. To create a new snippets folder to hold your custom snippets, click the New Snippet Folder button. Give your new folder a name. Now you can store new snippets in this folder or move existing snippets into the folder for easy access.

Click the New Snippet button to begin creating a snippet of code to store in the Snippets panel. In the Snippet dialog box that appears, you enter a name and a description for the snippet. You can select either the Wrap Selection radio button or the Insert Block radio button. The Wrap Selection setting divides the dialog box into two halves; the top half is inserted before the current selection and the bottom half is inserted after. The Insert Block setting inserts the snippet as a block of code instead of wrapping it around other objects.

The snippet content goes into the Insert Code text box. The easiest way to insert code into a snippet is to first create the code in Dreamweaver, either in Design or Code view. When you select the New Snippet command with the code selected. Dreamweaver automatically places the code into the Insert Code text box. You can select how you'd like the snippet preview to appear in the Snippet panel by Design view or the Code radio

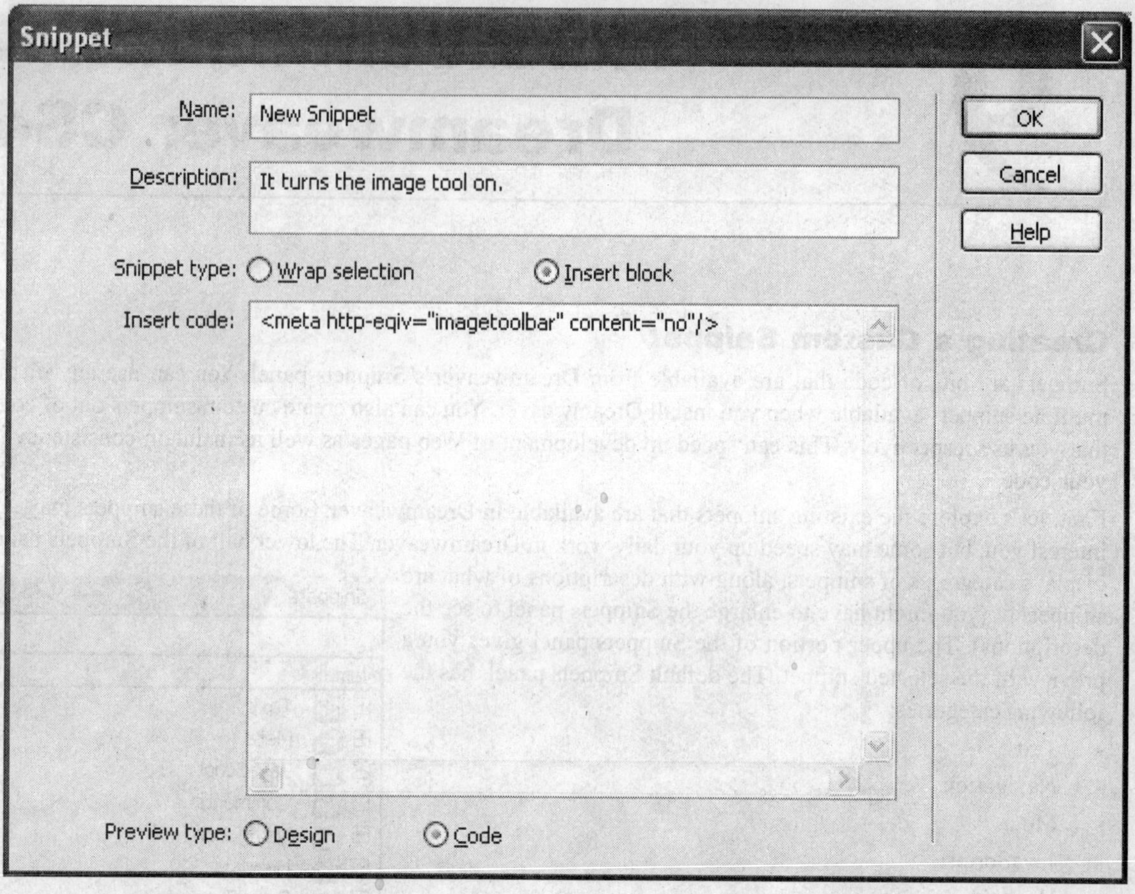

button, which represents the snippet preview in Code view. These radio buttons are located at the bottom of the Snippet dialog box.

When you select the Wrap Selection radio button when creating a snippet, you enter code into two different text boxes: the Insert Before text box and the Insert After text box. When you apply the snippet to an object on the page, the code in the Insert Before text box is added before the object and the code in the Insert After text box is added behind the object code. You need to create this type of snippet to package an object within the code you create in the snippet. For instance, if you want an object to be within a hyperlink, you need to add tags before and after the object and you need to create with Wrap Selection selected to get the Insert Before and Insert After text boxes.

Editing the Keyboard Shortcuts

You can edit all the keyboard shortcuts in Dreamweaver by using the Keyboard Shortcuts dialog box, which you can open by selecting Edit, Keyboard Shortcuts. Instead of modifying the existing set of keyboard shortcuts, you should create your own set. Drop down the Current Set drop-down menu to see the existing keyboard shortcuts sets: Adobe Standard, BBEdit.

Dreamweaver and Homesite. If you are used to the keyboard shortcut or any of these other Web editors, you can use those shortcuts sets by selecting them in this menu.

You do not want to modify the Adobe Standard keyboard shortcut set because you might need to revert to it later. Instead, you want to create your own version of that keyboard shortcut set by duplicating; you do this by clicking the Duplicate Set button. Then you give your new set a name and make sure it is selected in the Current Set drop-down menu. Then you are ready to customize any of the keyboard shortcuts you want.

You select commands from several categories in the Commands drop-down menu: Menu Commands, Site Panel, Code Editing, Document Editing, Site Window and Snippet. Select one of the categories and then select a command from the list. If the command already has a keyboard shortcut, it will show up in the Shortcuts list at the bottom of the dialog box. You can either modify the existing keyboard shortcut for that command or add an additional shortcut by clicking the + button.

To add or edit a keyboard shortcut, place the cursor in the Press Key text box at the bottom of the dialog box and press the key combination that you'd like to use for the keyboard shortcut. The keys are recorded in the Press Key text box. If that shortcut already exists for another command, you will see an error message. You should press different keys until you come up with a unique keyboard shortcut for the command. Click the Change button to apply the shortcut to the command.

Click OK to save your custom keyboard shortcuts. Make sure you test the shortcuts to ensure that they work the way you want them to. You can always open the Keyboard Shortcuts dialog box and edit your shortcuts later if you need to.

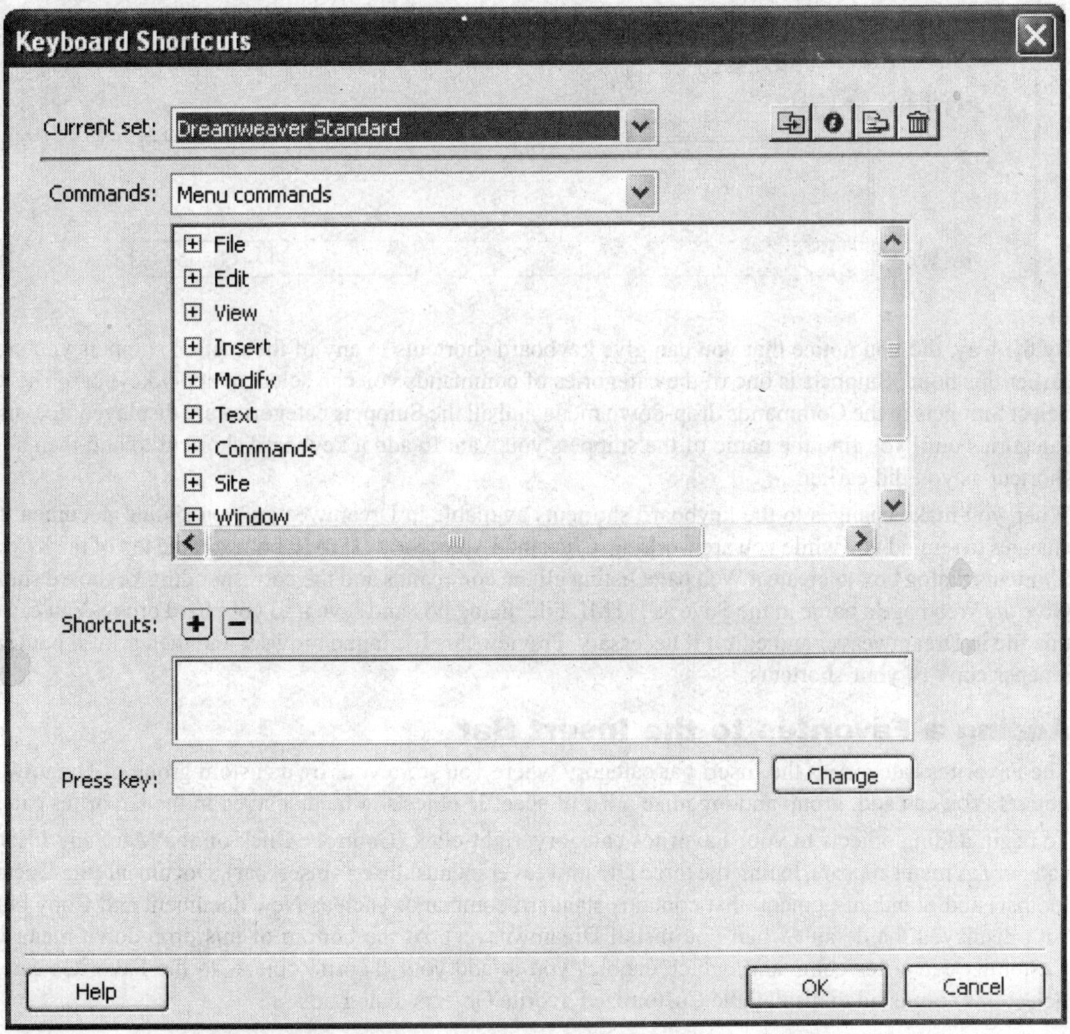

By the way, did you notice that you can give keyboard shortcuts to any of the custom snippets you created earlier this hour? Snippets is one of the categories of commands you can select to apply keyboard shortcuts. Select Snippets in the Commands drop-down menu and all the Snippets categories are displayed. Expand the categories until you find the name of the snippets you want to add a keyboard shortcut to and then add the shortcut as you did earlier.

When you make changes to the keyboard shortcuts available in Dreamweaver, you should document those changes to remind you while you are working. Click the Export Set as HTML button at the top of the Keyboard Shortcuts dialog box to create a Web page listing all the commands and the corresponding keyboard shortcut. Give the Web page a name in the Save as HTML File dialog box and save it to your hard drove. You can open this file in Dreamweaver and edit it if necessary. Preview this file in the browser and then print it out to have a paper copy of your shortcuts.

Adding a Favorites to the Insert Bar

The Favorites category is the Insert bar category where you store your own custom group of Dreamweaver objects. You can add, group and organize a list of specific objects to be displayed in the Favorites category.

To begin adding objects to your Favorites category, right-click (Control+ Click on the Mac) any Insert bar category. A menu appears, listing the three Dreamweaver menus: Insert (Insert bar), Document (the Document toolbar) and Standard (a menu that contains standard commands such as New document and Copy but that isn't displayed the default when you install Dreamweaver). At the bottom of this drop-down menu is the Customize Favorites command, which enables you to add your favorite objects to the Favorites category Select this command to display the Customize Favorite Objects dialog box.

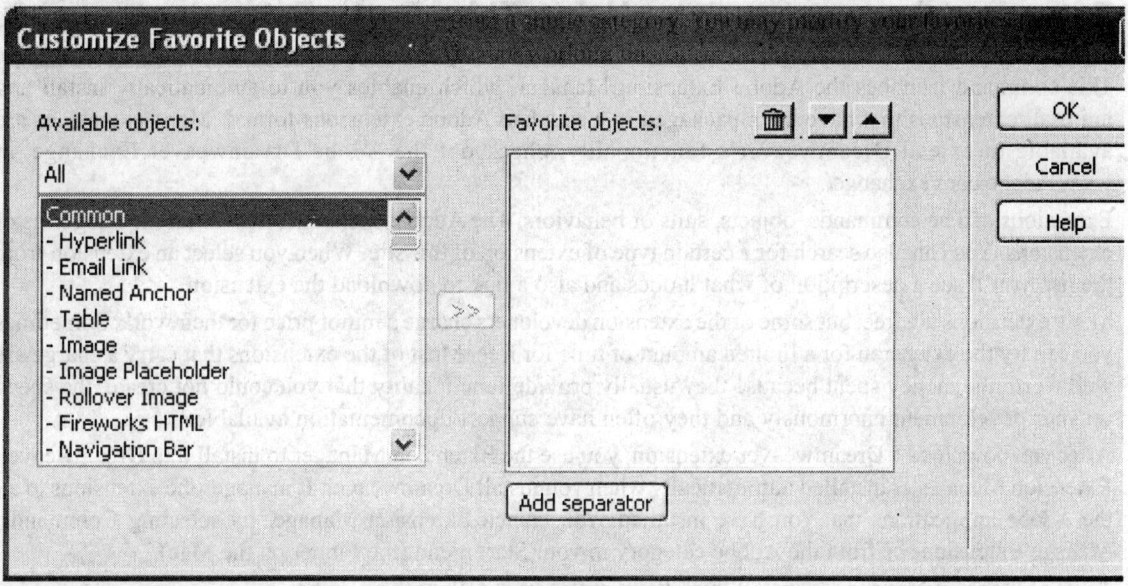

Select objects from the available Objects list on the left side of the dialog box, which shows all the objects listed in the Insert bar. Select an object in the Available Objects list and click the arrow button in the middle of the dialog box to move that object to the Favorites Object list on the right side of the dialog box. Use the up and down-arrow buttons to reorder the Favorites Objects list. Add a separator to the list, by clicking the Add Separator button; the separator is added below whatever you have selected in the Favorite Objects lists.

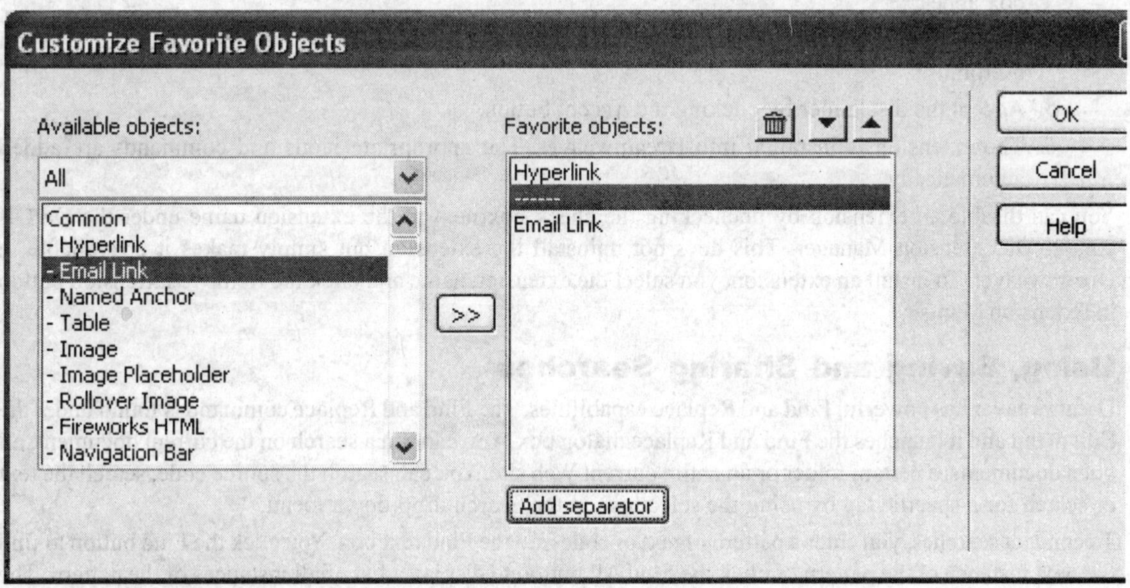

After you click OK to save your list of favorites, those objects will appear in the Favorites category of the Inert bar. The objects are not deleted from their original categories but are simply duplicated in the Favorites category so that you can access them easily from a single category. You may modify your favorites from time to time, depending on the type of projects you are working on.

Extending Dreamweaver by Using Third-Party Extensions

You can easily install third-party extensions to Dreamweaver by selecting Commands, Manage Extensions. This command launches the Adobe Extension Manager, which enables you to automatically install and uninstall extensions that have been packaged in a standard Adobe extensions format. Many extensions are available to extend Dreamweaver's functionality; check out the Adobe Dreamweaver Exchange, at www.Adobe.com/exchange/.

Extensions can be commands, objects, suits or behaviors. The Adobe Exchange, lists different categories of extensions. You can also search for a certain type of extension of this site. When you select an extension from the list, you'll see a description of what it does and also a link to download the extension.

Many extensions are free, but some of the extension developers charge a minor price for their work. Sometimes you can try the extension for a limited amount of time for free. Most of the extensions that carry a charge are well worth the money spent because they usually provide functionality that you could not create, the speed up your development enormously and they often have support documentation available.

After you download a Dreamweaver extension, you use the Extension Manager to install it to Dreamweaver. Extension Manager is installed automatically when you install Dreamweaver. It manages the extensions to all the Adobe applications that you have installed. You launch Extension Manager by selecting Commands, Manage Extensions or from the Adobe category in your Start menu (the Finder on the Mac).

To use Extension Manager to install third-party extensions, follow these steps;

1. Download an extension file from the Dreamweaver Exchange Web site. An extension file has the .mxp file extension.
2. Launch Extension Manager.
3. Click the Install New Extension button in Extension Manager. The Select Extension to Install dialog box appears.
4. Browser to the directory where you saved the file you download. Select the file and click the Install button.
5. Accept the disclaimer by clicking the Accept button.
6. The extension is installed into Dreamweaver. The appropriate icons and commands are added automatically.

You can disable an extension by unchecking the check box next to the extension name under the On/Off column of Extension Manager. This does not uninstall the extension but simply makes it unavailable in Dreamweaver. To install an extension, you select the extension name and click the Remove Extension button in Extension Manger.

Using, Saving and Sharing Searches

Dreamweaver has powerful Find and Replace capabilities. The Find and Replace command is found under the Edit menu and it launches the Find and Replace dialog box. You can run a search on the current document, all open documents, a certain folder or an entire current Web site. You can search the source code, search the text or search for a specific tag by using the selections in the Search drop-down menu.

To conduct searches, you enter a pattern of text or code into the Find text box. You click the Find button to find the next instance of the pattern or click the Find All button to display a list of all instances of the pattern. The list is displayed in the Results panel group, beneath the Property inspector.

The Text and Source Code search categories are self-explanatory: You search for text within the Web page by using a Text search and you search for code within Dreamweaver's Code view using the Source Code search.

The Specific Tag search is a little more complicated, however. You use the Specific Tag search to find HTML tags in your code and modify the tag, modify an attribute of a tag or strip the tag out of the code completely.

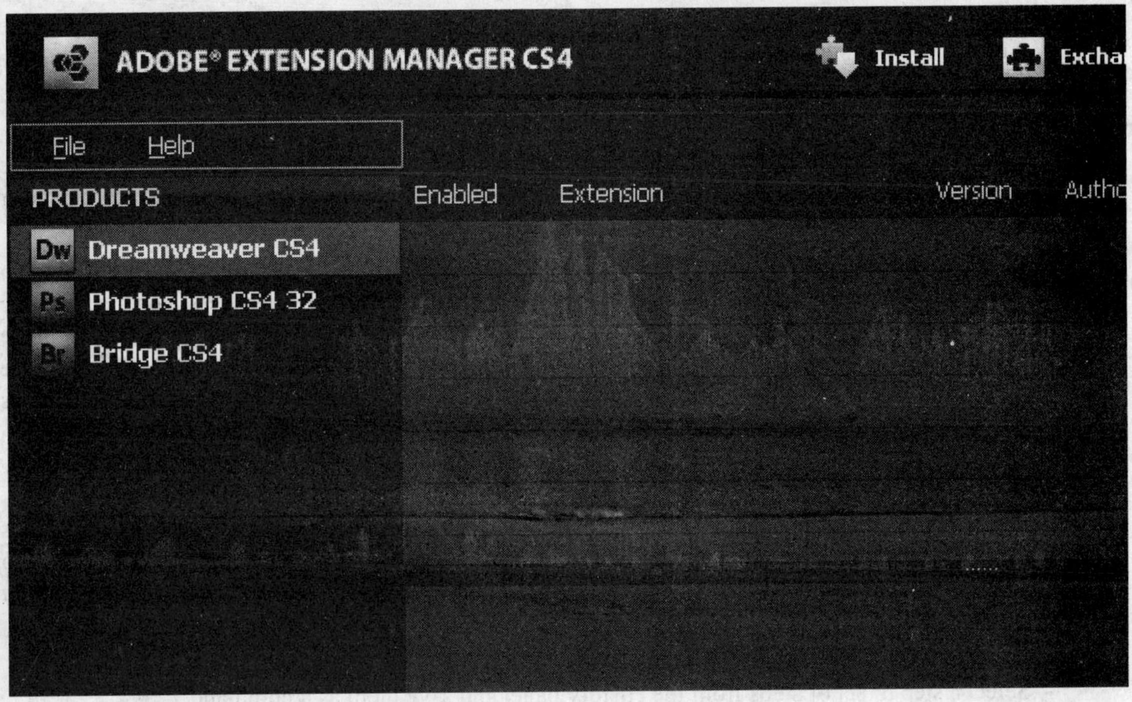

For instance, you might want to search your Web site for font tags because these tags have been replaced by Cascading Style Sheets (CSS) styles, the more modern way of formatting page display. You can use a specific tag search to accomplish this:

1. In the Find and Replace dialog box, set the scope of your search in the Find In drop-down menu.
2. Select Specific Tag from the Search drop-down menu.
3. Select Font from the list of tags directly to the right of the Search drop-down menu.
4. If you are looking for font tags with a specific attribute - say the face attribute or the size attribute – enter the search characteristics in the Attributes section. Add or subtract attributes by using the + and – buttons. If your tag search has no attribute, click the – button to delete the initial attribute that is listed.

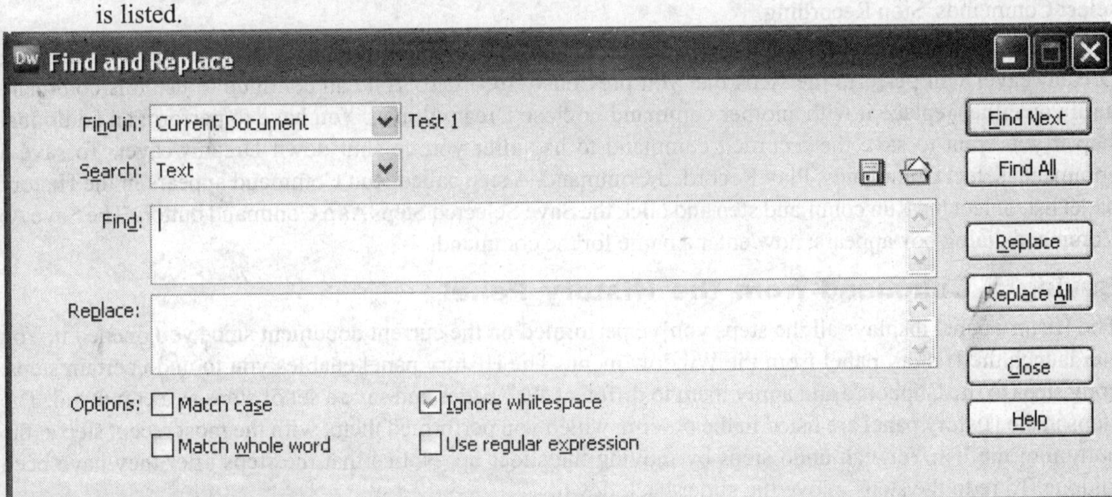

5. Set what will happen to the font tags by using the Action drop-down menu. To simply strip all the tags out of your site, use the Strip Tag action. To replace the font tags with a CSS style, use the Change tag action and select Span from the drop-down menu to the right.
6. Click the Find All button to display all the search findings.
7. Find-tune your search by selecting the Find and Replace command again. Your search parameters are retained by Dreamweaver. If your search returns the correct findings, select the Replace command or the Replace All command.
8. In the Search panel, double-click each of the entries to apply a CSS style to the selection.

If you're created a complicated search that you'd like to reuse later or share with others, you can save the search as a Dreamweaver query file. To do this, click the Save Query button to save the current query in the Find and Replace dialog box. Dreamweaver prompts you to browser to a location and then save a file with the .dwr file extension. To load this query, click the Load Query button. You can share these .dwr files with others so that they can run the query, too.

Making a Menu Command

Dreamweaver enables you to record and save a step or set of steps as a command. These recorded commands are like macros created in other applications, such as Word and Excel. Commands enables you to save a complicated set of steps to apply wherever you need to accomplish a repetitive task. There are two different ways to accomplish this:

- Record a set of steps as you perform them and then play them back.
- Select a step or set of steps from the History panel and save them as a command.

Recording a Command

Dreamweaver enables you to record a set of steps and then play them back. Dreamweaver can record only a single set of steps in this way. When you record a new set of steps, the previous set will be replaced. You can use a recorded set of steps again and again until you either record a new set of steps or close Dreamweaver.

To record a set of steps, first select the type of object that you will apply your steps to. If you've created a command that modifies text, you need to apply the command to text; it will not work if you apply it to a dissimilar object. You will not be able to select objects while recording because Dreamweaver cannot record the selection step. After you've selected an appropriate object in the Document window, select Commands, Start Recording. The cursor will change into a different cassette icon. Perform the steps to record and then select Commands, Stop Recording.

Apply the recorded command by selecting an object and then selecting Commands, Play Recorded Command. Dreamweaver will perform the steps that you previously recorded. You can continue to use this command until you either replace it with another command or close Dreamweaver. You have to perform an additional step if you want to save the recorded command to use after you've shut down Dreamweaver. To save a command, select Commands, Play Recorded Command. A step called Run Command appears in the History panel list. Select the Run command step and click the Save Selected Steps As a Command button. The Save As Command dialog box appears; now enter a name for the command.

Saving a Command from the History Panel

The History panel displays all the steps you've performed on the current document since you opened it. You can launch the History panel from the Window menu. The History panel enables you to undo certain steps, copy steps to the Clipboard and apply them to different Web pages and save a set of steps as a command. The steps in the History panel are listed in the order in which you performed them, with the most recent step at the bottom of the list. You can undo steps by moving the slider up. Notice that the steps after they have been undone. To redo the steps, move the slider back down.

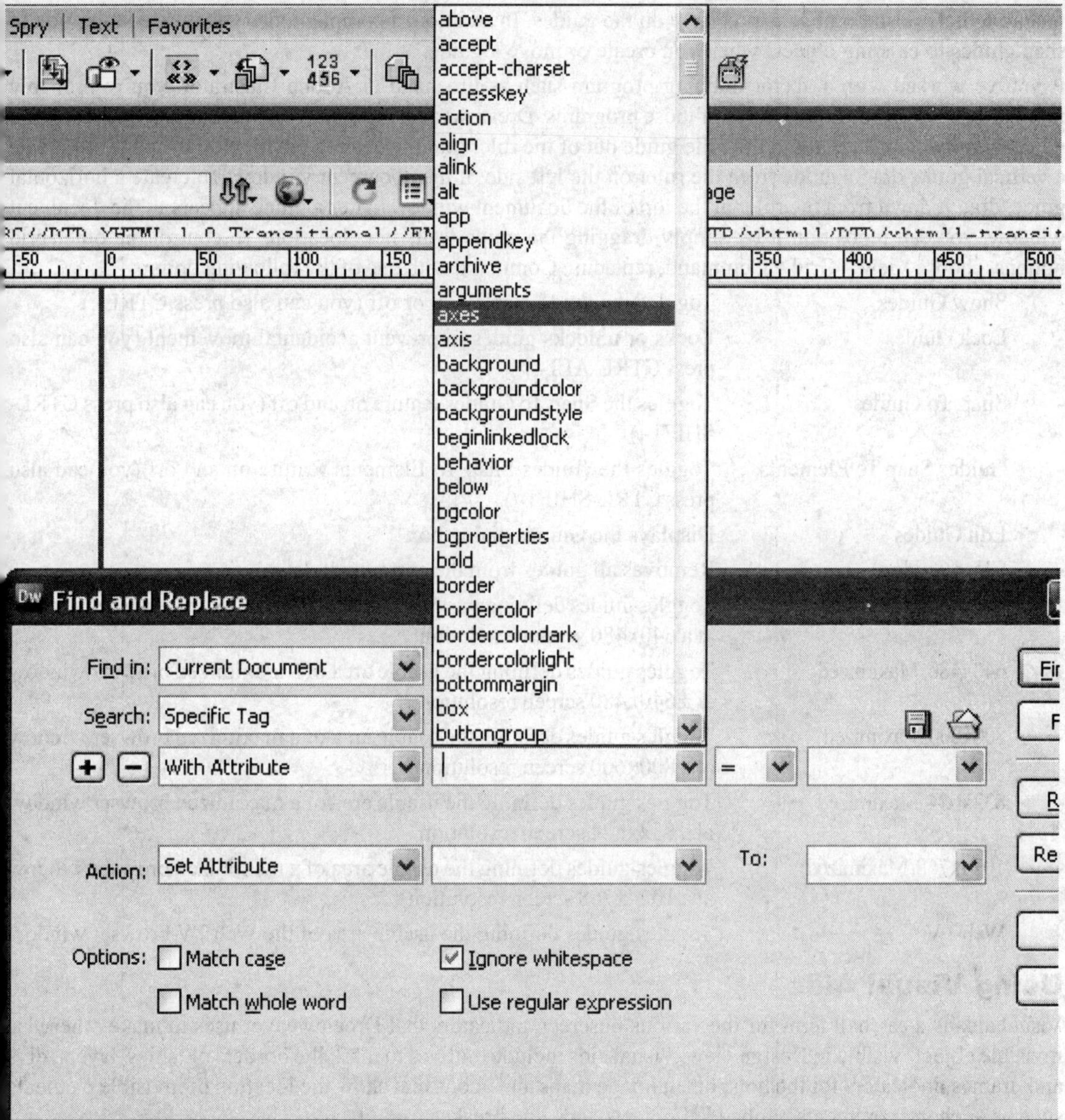

You can save a set of steps from the History panel as a command. Select the steps in the panel by dragging the ursor over them. Click the Save Selected Steps as Command button. When the Save As Command dialog box ppears, name the command. This new command now appears at the bottom of the Commands menu. To run our custom commands, select them from the Commands menu. Select Commands, Edit Command List to ename or delete a command.

sing Guides

Guides are yet another onscreen marker to help you position and align objects on the page. Guides are similar o the grid feature except that you can freely position guide lines, whereas grid lines are evenly spaced across he entire document. Like grid lines, you can show or hide guide lines and you can activate the Snap to Guide feature to help position objects precisely on the guides. In addition, a complementary feature enables you to snap guides to existing objects when you create or move a guide.

If you've worked with a vector drawing program such as Freehand or Adobe Illustrator, you're probably familiar with the guide line features of those programs. Dreamweaver's guides work the same way. To create a guide, simply click a ruler and drag the guide out of the ruler into the desired position on the page. To create a vertical guide, drag a guide from the ruler on the left side of the document window. To create a horizontal guide, drag it down from the ruler at the top of the document window. After a guide appears in the document window, you can reposition it by simply dragging the guide to its new location. To control the other grid options, choose View > Grid > Command, replacing Command with one of the following options:

- Show Guides — Toggles the guide display on or off (you can also press CTRL-;)
- Lock Guides — Locks or unlocks guides to prevent accidental movement (you can also press CTRL-ALT-;)
- Snap To Guides — Toggles the Snap To Guides feature on and off (you can also press CTRL-SHIFT-;)
- Guides Snap To Elements — Toggles the Guides Snap To Elements feature on and off (you can also press CTRL-SHIFT-/)
- Edit Guides — Displays the Guides dialog box
- Clear Guides — Removes all guides from the current window
- 640x480, Default — Toggles guides defining the usable area of a default-sized browser window at a 640x480 screen resolution
- 640x480, Maximized — Toggles guides defining the usable area of a maximized browser window at a 640x480 screen resolution
- 800x600,Maximized — Toggles guides defining the usable area of a maximized browser window at a 800x600 screen resolution
- 832x624, Maximized — Toggles guides defining the usable area of a maximized browser window at a 832x624 screen resolution
- 1024x768, Maximized — Toggles guides defining the usable area of a maximized browser window at a 1024x768 screen resolution
- Web TV — Toggles guides defining the usable area of the Web TV browser window

Using Visual Aids

Visual aids is a catchall term for the various onscreen indicators that Dreamweaver uses to make otherwise invisible objects visible in Design view. Visual aids include outlines to mark the borders of tables, layers, divs and frames, indicators for the hotspots in image maps and icons that show the location of invisible elements such as anchors, comments, embedded objects and line breaks.

Dreamweaver CS3 adds some new visual aids to highlight certain CSS block elements. This is a big help when you're working with CSS layouts. Specifically, the new CSS-related visual aids work with divs and other block elements that use absolute or relative positioning. Inline elements and block elements with static positioning aren't highlighted.

You have complete control over which visual aids are visible as you work with your page in Design view. You can activate some or all, of the visual aids to make it easier to see and manipulate invisible page elements. Or you can hide the visual aids to reduce the clutter in the Design View window. Choose View > Visual Aids > Command, replacing Command with one of the following options to turn elements on and off:

Hide All — Suppresses the display of all the visual aids (you can also press CTRL-SHIFT-I) Repeat the command to restore the previously selected assortment of visual aids

CSS Layout Backgrounds	Shows (or hides) the background color of CSS block elements and suppresses other background colors
CSS Layout Box Model	Shows (or hides) shading to indicate margins and padding on the selected CSS block elements
CSS Layout Outlines	Shows (or hides) the outline of CSS block elements
Layer Outlines	Shows or hides the outlines displaying the size and location of layers
Table Widths	Shows or hides table width dimensions
Table Borders	Toggles the table border display on or off
Frame Borders	Toggles the frame border display on or off
Image Maps	Shows or hides the hotspots in image maps
Invisible Elements	Toggles the invisible elements icon display on or off. Invisible elements include named anchors, scripts, comments, hidden form fields and more. You can adjust settings in the Preferences dialog box to select which icons Dreamweaver displays when you enable viewing Invisible Elements.

Using the Zoom and Magnification Tools

One of the small but very useful new features of Dreamweaver is the ability to change the magnification of the document window. You can use it to zoom in for a closer look at a detail on your page or to zoom out for an overview of the entire page layout. This is a common feature in image editors (such as Fireworks and Photoshop) and vector drawing programs (such as Freehand and Illustrator), but it's new to the world of web design.

Dreamweaver includes several tools to enable you to interact with the magnification feature. They are listed next.

- To zoom in (make the document appear larger), choose View | Zoom In, press CTRL – = or click the Zoom tool on the status bar and then click the document.
- To zoom out (make the document appear smaller), choose View | Zoom Out, press CTRL – hyphen (-) or click the Zoom tool on the status bar and then ALT-click the document.
- To zoom to a specific magnification, choose View | Magnification | percent or select the magnification percent from the Set Magnification list on the status bar. In addition to standard magnification percents, your can also choose the Fit Selection, Fit All and Fit Width options.
- To reposition the zoomed document within the document window, use the scroll bars or click the Hand tool on the status bar and then drag the document.
- To return the pointer to its normal operation after using the Zoom or Hand tools, click the Select tool on the status bar.

Knowing The Panels

In addition to the Insert bar, the Property Inspector panel and the Files panel, Dreamweaver includes an assortment of other panels that provide tools for performing a variety of tasks. Here's a list of the Dreamweaver panels and a brief summary of their purposes, arranged according to their default grouping in the panel dock. Coverage of a couple of specific panels follows the list.

The CSS Panel Group The CSS Panel group contains panels you're likely to use as you create web pages in Design view:

- **The CSS Styles panel** Provides a place to manage Cascading Style Sheet styles and apply them to your web page. The CSS Styles panel is greatly expanded in Dreamweaver CS3 so that it now consolidates all CSS information in one location. It includes all the features of Dreamweaver CS3's CSS Styles panel and the Relevant CSS portion of the Tag Inspector, plus more.

- **The Layers panel** This is where you keep track of layers on your web page. You can use the panel to select a layer for editing and to make layers visible or hidden.

The Application Panel Group You'll use panels from the Application Panel group if you develop dynamic database-driven web pages.

- **The Databases panel** Shows the databases that are available for the current site and allows you to define new database connections.
- **The Bindings panel** Shows the recordsets (query results) that are available for the current page and allows you to define new recordsets.
- **The Server Behaviors panel** Enables you to insert server behaviors into your web page to create and manipulate dynamic data.
- **The Components panel** Makes ColdFusion components available for editing and use in your ColdFusion-based web pages.

The Tag Inspector Group Older versions of Dreamweaver included a separate Tag Inspector panel, then Dreamweaver CS3 dramatically expanded its capabilities by adding the Relevant CSS view and making it a panel group. Now, in Dreamweaver CS3, the CSS part has moved to the CSS Styles panel, which returns the Tag Inspector to its role of listing the formatting attributes and behaviors attached to any HTML tag.

- **Attributes** Enables you to view and adjust various attributes of the selected tag.
- **The Behaviors panel** Enables you to attach behaviors to HTML tags on your web page and to edit existing behaviors.

The Files Panel Group Entries in the Files Panel group help you manage your site files.

- **The Files panel** This is the home of the collapsed version of the Files panel. It's an abbreviated version that shows only one file list (usually the Local view) instead of the two side-by-side panels.
- **The Assets panel** Creates a master list of resources such as image files, templates and Flash files located both in your current site and in a Favorites list. The Assets panel helps you quickly find and reuse images and other resources you've used on other pages in the site.
- **The Snippets panel** A collection of code blocks that you can paste into your web documents.

The History Panel Group The History Panel group is an optional panel group. It appears only if you open the History panel by choosing Window > History. The History panel is where Dreamweaver keeps track of your recent actions as you create and edit your pages. You can select actions from the History panel and replay them to perform repetitive tasks.

The Code Inspector Panel The Code Inspector panel doesn't appear docked in the panel dock – at least, not by default. Instead, it appears as a separate, undocked panel with its own title bar and border. You can dock the Code Inspector panel into the panel dock if you want, but its size would probably make that awkward. The Code Inspector panel provides yet another place for you to view and edit the HTML code for your web page. It's exactly the same view you get in the Document window in Code view, but the Code Inspector panel gives you the option to work in a separate window if you prefer to use it.

The Results Panel The Results panel shows the results of a search operation, report or log. Unlike other panels that you open in order to access resources that you want to add to your web page, this panel normally appears automatically to show the results of a task or command, such as running a site report or checking a page for compatibility with a target browser. The Results panel can show the results of several different operations and commands, each on separate tabs. Click a tab to view the related information. You can initiate most reports by clicking the green arrow at the upper-left corner of the tab.

- **The Search tab** Shows the results of a Find and Replace operation (choose Edit > Find and Replace or type CTRL > F) where you click the Find All button instead of stepping through each item one at a time in the Find and Replace dialog box.

- **The Reference tab** Your access point for an online library of reference material about HTML, CSS styles, accessibility standards and more.
- **The Validation tab** Shows a list of errors found when validating code in one or more documents.
- **The Target Browser Check tab** Shows a list of browser incompatibilities found during a target browser check on one or more documents.
- **The Link checker tab** Shows the results of a san for broken links. The Show list box lets you choose to display a list of broken links, external links or orphaned files.
- **The Site Reports tab** Shows the results of any of the reports you run from the Reports dialog box. (choose Site | Reports). The site reports check your web pages for a variety of common errors.
- **The FTP Log tab** Shows a log of FTP activity resulting from transferring files between the local and remote sites in the Files panel.
- **The Server Debug tab** Shows the debugging information for ColdFusion applications.

Setting the Color Scheme and Other Page Properties

The page properties settings enable you to specify a color scheme for your page and adjust several defaults. For example, you can determine whether your page has dark blue type on a white background, white type on a black background or any other combination.

Previous versions of Dreamweaver set the page properties by adding attributes directly to the <body> tag that defines the beginning and end of the main web page in the HTML code. That was the normal practice among web authors for years. However, current web standards call for separating presentation formatting from structural markup and Dreamweaver CS3 now follows that standard by placing the page properties settings in the CSS style sheet section of your document instead of the inside <body> tag. One advantage of setting the properties with CSS styles is that you have more options, so the Page Properties dialog box has been expanded to give you access to more of those options.

Dreamweaver lets you control several page settings and defaults:

Under Appearance:

- **Page Font, Size and Color** Sets the default font, size and color for body text that doesn't have any other formatting applied. If you leave these settings blank, the generic browser defaults for body text will apply. Those defaults are: a serif font (usually Times Roman), a medium size (about 12-point) and black (#000000).
- **Background Color** Sets the page background. You'll probably want to select a background color (such as white, #FFFFFF) to keep your page from reverting to the old browser-default color scheme of a dull gray background.
- **Margins** The left, right, top and bottom page margins control how close the objects you place on your page can come to the top and left edge of the browser window. If you don't specify the page margins, each browser will use its own, slightly different, default margin settings.

Under Links:

- **Links** Sets the color and formatting of text hyperlinks. Dreamweaver leaves these settings blank when you create a new page, which means that the browser's default link text formatting (usually blue text with an underline) is used. You can use the page properties settings to control the font and size for all links and to specify a different color for each of the four states of the text links on your page.
- **Link Font and Size** Sets the font and size for link text. Leave this blank to use the normal text font and size.
- **Link Color** Determines the base color for hyperlinks.

- **Active Links** Sets the color of text hyperlinks as they are clicked. Normally, the active links color appears only momentarily.
- **Visited Links** Controls the color of text hyperlinks the visitor has already viewed.
- **Rollover Links** Determines the color of text hyperlinks as the mouse pointer passes over the link.
- **Underline Style** Controls whether and when underlines appear on links.
- **Headings** Sets the color and formatting for each of the six standard headings.

To change the color settings for your page, perform the following steps:

1. Choose Modify > Page Properties to open the Page Properties dialog box.
2. Select Appearance in the Category list on the left, then adjust the settings in the main part of the dialog box by making selections from drop-down boxes (Page Font), entering values (Size and Margins) or clicking buttons (Bold or Italic). For color selections, click the Color Picker button for each setting and select the desired color from the Color Picker box that appears. You can select text and background colors in this category.
3. Repeat the process for the Links and Headings categories.
4. Click Apply or OK to record your color scheme for the current page. Dreamweaver updates the Document window to reflect your color choices.

You don't have to set a value for every option in the Page Properties dialog box. If you leave a setting blank, the visitor's browser will simply use its own default setting. You can also adjust most of these settings from other dialog boxes or panels in Dreamweaver and you might prefer to use one of the other techniques to handle these formatting tasks.

The Page Properties dialog box also gives you the option of specifying a background image, document encoding and a tracing image. Unless you work with web pages in foreign languages, you'll rarely need to change the document encoding.

The Tag Inspector Panel and Tag Attributes

The Tag Inspector panel is another way you can view and edit the formatting attributes of the 8 HTML tags that make up your web page. Its role was greatly expanded in Dreamweaver CS3 when Adobe added a CSS style property display to the Tag Inspector. Now, in Dreamweaver CS3, the CSS Properties list is part of the CSS Styles panel and the Tag Inspector returns to its original role of displaying the embedded attributes of the selected tag.

Like the Property Inspector, the Tag Inspector panel displays formatting information for the selected object and enables you to edit those settings interactively. The difference between the two panels is that the Property Inspector displays only the most-used settings, while the Tag Inspector is much more complete, displaying every possible attribute for the selected tag. Also, you can use the Property Inspector to apply character formatting to selected text passages, whereas the Tag Inspector works with entire paragraphs and other tags.

To open the Tag Inspector, choose Window | Tag Inspector or press F9. The Tag Inspector automatically displays the attributes of the currently selected tag. The Attributes tab lists the attributes available for the selected tag – that is, the attributes that can be applied to the tag itself rather than through CSS styles.

The two buttons at the top of the Attributes tab enable you to switch between a categorized list and a straight alphabetical listing of attributes. In category mode, you can click the +1- button beside a category name to expand/collapse the category. In alphabetical mode, any attribute with defined properties floats to the top of the list, followed by undefined attributes. The left column lists the possible attributes for the selected tag. The right column lists the properties of those attributes. To change an attribute, click the right column beside the attribute you want to change and then type in the appropriate value or click the arrow button and select a property from the drop-down list box that appears. (For web pages that are linked to a database, you can click the Dynamic Data button to select a field to supply the property data.)

Edit Code in Code View

Basically, when you edit code in Dreamweaver, you use the program as a fancy text editor. You can type HTML codes in Code view, just as you would any other text and you can select, move, insert, delete and edit HTML codes, just as you would any other text.

However, if you're like most Dreamweaver users, you'll rarely, if ever, enter HTML code from scratch. Instead, you'll probably let Dreamweaver build the code for the pages you create in Design view and then use Code view to examine that code and make occasional minor edits.

In addition to its basic text-editing capabilities, Dreamweaver provides some special features just to make life easier when you work with HTML code. Check out these tips and techniques for manipulating code:

- To indent a line of code in Code view, select the line(s) of code and choose Edit > Indent – Code or click the Indent Code button on the Coding toolbar or press CTRL-SHIFT->. Choosing Edit > Outdent Code or clicking the Outdent Code button on the Coding toolbar or pressing CTRL-SHIFT-< moves the selected line(s) to the left.
- To check for balanced tags, click the content inside the tag you want to check, then choose Edit | Select Parent Tag, click the Select Parent Tag button on the Coding toolbar or press CTRL-[. Dreamweaver highlights the tags enclosing the selected content. Choose Edit | Select Parent Tag again to highlight the next level of nested tags.
- To insert a comment in your code, place the insertion point at the location where you want to add the comment and click the Comment button in the Common category of the Insert bar or choose Insert | Comment. Alternatively, you can click the Apply Comment button on the Coding toolbar and choose Apply HTML Comment from the menu that appears. Dreamweaver inserts a comment tag (< ! >) into your source code and positions the insertion point in the middle awaiting your typed comment. (If you're in Design view, Dreamweaver opens the Comment dialog box, where you can type the comment text to be inserted into the web document.)

Use the Coding Toolbar

One of the new features of Dreamweaver CS3 is a toolbar full of buttons that make working with code a little faster and easier. The Coding toolbar appears along the left side of the document window in Code view and in the Code pane of Code and Design view, as well as the Code Inspector panel. You can toggle the Coding toolbar on or off by choosing View > Toolbars > Coding.

The Coding toolbar includes many useful features for working with code. Some of the buttons are simply convenient shortcuts for commands that are available on other Dreamweaver menus, but others offer access to entirely new code manipulation tools. Here's a list of the Coding toolbar buttons (from top to bottom) and what they do:

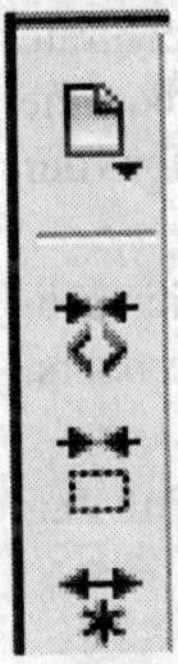

Open Documents Displays a list of currently open documents. Choose a file name to display that document in the Code view window for editing.

Collapse Full Tag Collapses (hides the contents of) the current tag.

Collapse Selection Collapses (hides the - contents of) the current selection.

Expand All Expands all collapsed code.

Select Parent Tag Selects the starting and ending tags surrounding the current cursor position or selection and all of the code enclosed by that tag.

Balance Braces Selects all the code enclosed by parentheses, braces or square brackets.

Line Numbers Toggles the display of the line numbers along the left side of the Code view window on or off.

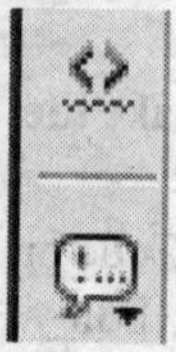

Highlight Invalid Code Toggles the highlighting the invalid code on or of.

Apply Comment Adds comment tags around the current selection or cursor position. When you click this button, a menu appears allowing you to choose the kind of comment you want to insert. You can choose from several types, including HTML comments (<!——>), /**/. //. ‘ and server comments.

Remove Comment Removes the comment tags surrounding the current cursor position.

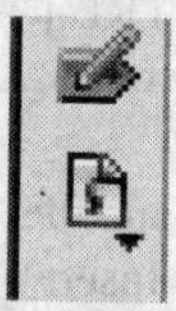

Wrap Tag Opens the Quick Tag Editor in Wrap Tag mode.

Recent Snippets Displays a list of recently used code snippets. Select a snippet from the list to insert it at the current cursor position.

Indent Code Selects the code block in which the cursor is located and indents it one level. Click the button again to increase the indent.

Outdent code Selects the code block in which the cursor is located and moves it to the left one indent level. Click the button again to reduce the indent another level.

Format Source code Opens a menu of code formatting options, including Apply Source Formatting and Apply Source Formatting to Selection (which automatically indents tags) and commands that open the Code Formatting category of the Preferences dialog box and the Edit Tag Library dialog box.

Collapse and Expand Code

Code collapse is another welcome new feature of Dreamweaver CS3. It makes working in Code view much easier by enabling you to hide selected blocks of code temporarily/ With the collapsed code hidden from view, it's much easier to scroll through your document and the document is less cluttered so you can concentrate on the code you're working on with fewer distractions from the adjacent code. Code collapse only affects the way Dreamweaver displays the code in Code view - it doesn't delete or otherwise alter the actual code for your web page.

You work with code collapse using a combination of toolbar buttons in the Coding toolbar, as well as icons in the blue bar along the left side of the document window, adjacent to the Coding toolbar and / or line numbers. Yu can use the following techniques to hide or show blocks of code with code collapse:

- To collapse a single tag, position the cursor anywhere within that tag and click the Collapse Full Tag button on the coding toolbar.

- To collapse a selection spanning several lines or tags, select the code you want to collapse and then click the Collapse Selection button on the Coding toolbar or click the minus (-) icon that appears in the blue bar.
- To expand a single tag or selection, select the collapsed code and click the plus (+) icon that appears in the blue bar alongside the collapsed item.
- To expand all the collapsed items in the current items in the current document, click the Expand All button on the Coding toolbar.

Using the Tag Inspector Panel

The Tag Inspector panel has gone through some changes in the last couple of versions of Dreamweaver. In Dreamweaver CS3, it was home to a display of CSS style properties as well as an interactive view of HTML tag attributes and behaviors in your document. Now, in Dreamweaver CS3, the CSS stuff is located in the CSS Styles panel where it belongs and the Tag Inspector panel is focused on the things that are attached to your document's HTML tags.

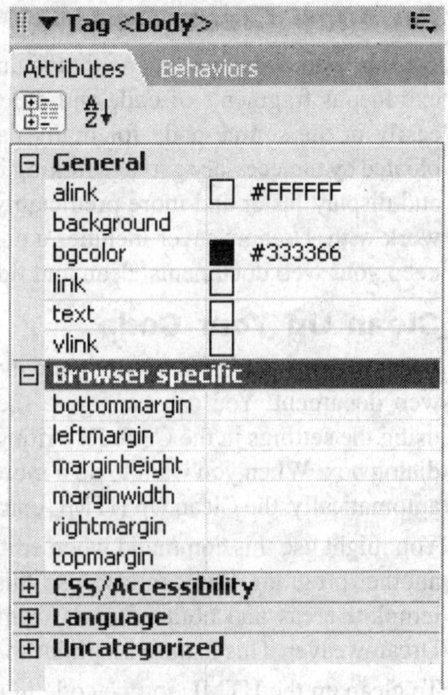

Choose Window > Tag Inspector or press F9 to open the Tag Inspector panel. When you click a tag (or anywhere within a tag) while you're in Code or Attributes. Desıgn view, the attributes for that tag appear in the Inspector. You can view and edit the tag's attributes in the Tag Inspector panel in much the same way you view and edit object properties in the Property Inspector. The difference is that the Tag Inspector offers a lot more detail.

The Tag Inspector contains two tabs. Click the Attributes tab to see a list of all the available attributes for the selected tag. The attributes appear in the left column and the associated values for each attribute appear in the right column. Click an attribute value field to select or enter a value. The two buttons at the top of the Attributes tab enable you to break the attributes into categories or display the entire list in alphabetical order.

Work with Code Snippets

Why build the code for a page footer or other common document feature manually on each page when you can cut and paste code from another page and edit it to fit your needs? Why indeed? Code Snippets enable you to organize and store blocks of code and insert them into your documents with a couple of mouse clicks. The Snippets panel comes stocked with a generous assortment of code snippets. You can add to or edit the snippets to build your own library of reusable code.

Choose Window > Snippets or press SHIFT – F9 to open the Snippets panel. By default, the panel appears in the File panel group. The Snippets panel is divided into two panes. The lower pane shows a tree-type list of folders and snippet icons. Use the usual plus and minus buttons to expand or collapse folders and the scroll bars to navigate the list. When you select a snippet icon in the list, a preview of that snippet appears in the upper pane of the Snippets panel.

The buttons along the bottom of the Snippets panel enable you to edit and use the snippets:

- Select a snippet and click the Insert button to insert the snippet code into your document at the current insertion point or around the current selection. You can insert snippets into your document in Design view or Code view.
- Click the New Snippet Folder button to add a new folder to the list in the Snippets panel. Type a name for the new folder and press ENTER.

- Select a portion of a web page in Design view or a block of code in Code view and then click the New Snippet button to open the Snippets dialog box with the selected code displayed. Edit the contents of the dialog box as needed and then click OK to add the snippet to the Snippets panel.
- Select a snippet in the Snippets panel and click the Edit Snippet button to open the Snippets dialog box with the code for the selected snippet displayed. Edit the contents 01 the dialog box as needed and then click OK to record your changes. Select a snippet in the Snippets panel and click the Remove button to delete the snippet from the list.
- Click and drag a folder or snippet icon to another location in the list to rearrange the snippet list.

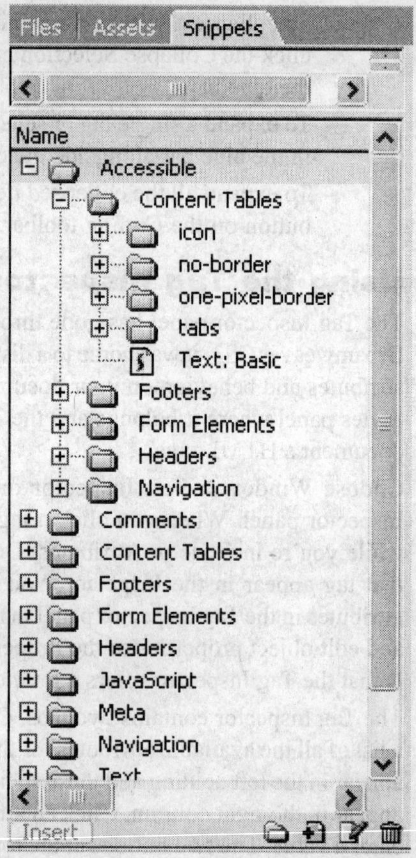

Produce Clean Code

A clean web document is one that is uncluttered by redundant tags, extraneous fragments of code and other debris that accumulates so easily in the source code for many pages. Documents that aren't bloated by unnecessary garbage lurking in the code not only download and display faster and more predictably, they're just plain easier to work with. Dreamweaver includes a number of features to help you keep your web documents clean and tidy.

Clean Up Your Code

Dreamweaver performs a basic code cleanup every time you open a web document. You can configure the automatic cleanup options using the settings in the Code Rewriting category of the Preferences dialog box. When you want to do a more thorough code cleanup on a web document than Dreamweaver does automatically, the Clean Up HTML command will get the job done.

You might use this command when editing an older web document or after opening a document produced in another program. You can also use this command to remove Dreamweaver – specific comments (such as template areas and library items) from a web document before sending it to someone who doesn't have Dreamweaver. This feature is similar to the Clean Up Word HTML command.

To clean up the HTML source code in a web document, follow these steps:

1. Open the document you want to clean up.
2. Choose Commands > Clean Up HTML. Dreamweaver opens the Clean Up HTML/ XHTML dialog box.
3. Select the cleanup options by clicking the check boxes in the dialog box. You can select any combination of the following:

- **Remove Empty Container Tags** Removes any pair of opening and closing tags that don't enclose any content. This cleans up any unneeded tags that were left behind after you deleted the content to which they applied.
- **Remove Redundant Nested Tags** Removes nested copies of the same tag, such as removing the bold <b> or <strong» tag around a word within a sentence that is also tagged as bold.
- **Remove Non-Dreamweaver HTML Comments** Removes any comments that were inserted into the code by other programs (or programmers).

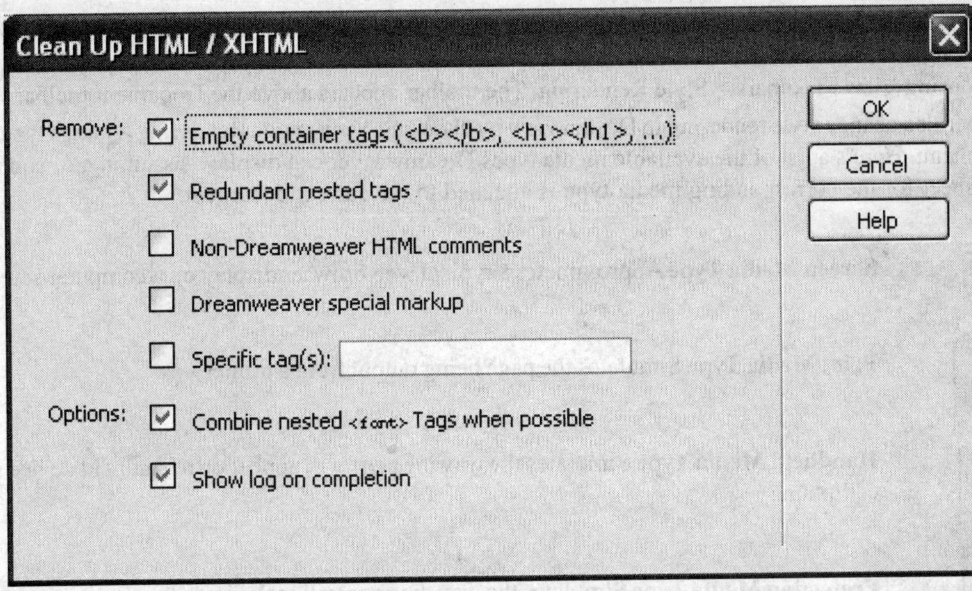

- **Remove Dreamweaver Special Markup** Removes any comments inserted into the source code by Dreamweaver. This includes comments that mark template areas and library items.
- **Remove Specific Tag(s)** Removes any tags identified in the text box to the right of the option. Use this option to remove valid but unwanted HTML tags, such as the obnoxious <blink> tag.
- **Combine Nested <font> Tags When Possible** Consolidates nested <font> tags that apply to the same text into a single pair of opening and closing tags with multiple attributes.
- **Show Log On Completion** Displays an optional alert box on completion of the cleanup process. It shows statistics on how many changes were made to the code.

4. Click OK to close the Clean Up HTML dialog box and begin the cleanup. Dreamweaver rewrites the HTML code, correcting the errors as specified. The process takes a few moments to complete – how long it takes depends on the size of the web document and the speed of your computer.

View Your Page With Different Style Sheets

One of the advantages of separating/presentational formatting from structure and content is that you can easily adapt the same content to a variety of different media by simply changing the rules in the CSS style sheet that provides the formatting instructions for a page. In fact, you can attach multiple CSS style sheets to your document and designate which style sheet should be used for each medium. For example, the beige text on a blue background that looks so good on a computer monitor may not print well, so you can create a separate CSS style sheet for the print media and define the text as an easy-to-read black on a white background. Dreamweaver gives you several tools for previewing the effects of different style sheets.

Select Media Style Sheets

If you have defined multiple CSS style sheets for your document, Dreamweaver normally uses the style sheet designated for screen media to render your page in Design view in order to produce a close approximation to the way your page will appear in a web browser viewed on a computer screen. However, one of the new features of Dreamweaver CS3 is the ability to select another media style sheet and preview its effects in Design view. This enables you to develop all your media style sheets interactively in Dreamweaver, not just the screen style sheet.

The easiest way to switch back and forth between style sheets is to use the buttons on the new Style Rendering toolbar shown in the following illustration. The toolbar is hidden by default, but you can turn it on by choosing View | Toolbars > Style Rendering. The toolbar appears above the Document toolbar.

You can also change style rendering in Design view by choosing View | Style Rendering > media type from the main menu. Here's a list of the available media types Dreamweaver can display –assuming, of course, that a style sheet for the corresponding media type is attached to the current document.

Screen Media Type Approximates a typical web browser display on a computer screen

Print Media Type Simulates the page being output from a printer

Handheld Media Type Simulates the way the page will appear on a handheld device such as a cell phone

Projection Media Type Simulates the way the page will look viewed via a projection device

TTY Media Type Simulates the page output from a teletype device

TV Media Type Simulates the way the page will look on a television screen

View or Hide CSS Styles

Along with the ability to switch back and forth between CSS style sheets for different media, Dreamweaver CS3 now gives you the option to disable CSS styles completely and display your page as plain unstyled content. This gives you a preview of the way your page will appear to someone viewing it in a browser that doesn't support CSS styles or one that has CSS style rendering turned off. It's also a good simulation of how your page content is presented to search engines and screen readers.

By default, Dreamweaver displays your page in Design view with CSS styles applied. To toggle CSS style display on or off, choose View | Style Rendering > Display Styles or click the Display CSS Styles button on the Style Rendering toolbar. The Display CSS Styles feature operates independently from the style sheet media type selection and it affects only the display in Design view. It doesn't change the way your page appears in a web browser.

Attach a Design-Time Style Sheet

In addition to the media type selection and the ability to hide CSS styles, Dreamweaver offers another way to control what style sheets Dreamweaver uses. The Design – Time style sheets feature lets you specify one or more style sheets that Dreamweaver will use or ignore as it displays your page in Design view. They're called Design – Time style sheets because they only affect Dreamweaver's Design view, not the way the page appears in a web browser.

Design – Time style sheets are a little more cumbersome to use, but they have the potential to be even more versatile than media type selections. You can use ht feature to preview any style sheet's effect on your page and you can selectively hide any style sheet so that it doesn't affect your page. You're not limited to the

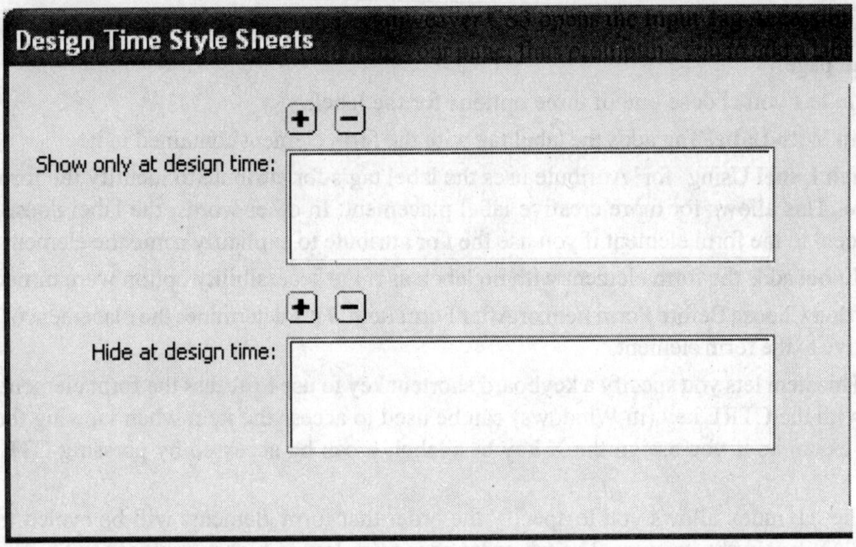

common media types and the Design – Time style sheets don't have to be attached to your document. As a result, you can use the feature to preview specialty style sheets for specific browsers or troubleshoot style sheet problems by disabling the suspected source of a problem.

To attach a Design – Time style sheet to your document (or hide style sheet from Design view), follow these steps:

1. Choose Text > CSS Styles > Design Time or right click in the CSS Styles panel and choose Design – Time from the context menu. Dreamweaver opens the Design Time Style Sheets dialog box.
2. Add or remove style sheets in the Show Only At Design Time box and Hide At Design Time box.
   - To add a style sheet to Dreamweaver's Design view display, click the plus (+) button above the Show Only At Design Time box to open the Select File dialog box. Locate and select the CSS style sheet and then click OK.
   - To hide a style sheet from Dreamweaver's Design view, click the plus (+) button above the Hide At Design Time box to open the Select File dialog box. Locate and select the CSS style sheet and then click OK.
   - To remove a style sheet from either list, select the style sheet and click the minus (-) button above the box.
3. Click OK. Dreamweaver closes the Design – Time Style Sheets dialog box and adjusts the Design view display to reflect the new style sheets. Style sheets that you add or hide in the Design – Time Style Sheets dialog box appear in the CSS Styles panel tagged with "design" or "hidden"

Label Form Objects with the <label> Tag

The traditional technique for labeling form elements was to enter text on the web page adjacent to the form element you wanted labeled. However, the current HTML specification provides the <label> tag specifically for this purpose.

This tag also adds functionality to the form element by associating the descriptive text for the form element directly with that element. This can be useful for speech – based browsers, so that the form elements can have spoken text associated with them. By default, Dreamweaver CS3 opens the Input Tag Accessibility Attribute dialog box every time you insert a form element into your page, thus prompting you to add a label to the form element.

Label Enter the text to be displayed for the label here. This is the descriptive text that identifies your form element on the page.

Style The style lets you choose one of three options for the label:

- **Wrap With Label Tag** adds the label tag with the form element contained in it.
- **Attach Label** Using 'for' Attribute uses the label tag's for attribute to identify the form element by name. This allows for more creative label placement. In other words, the label doesn't have to be adjacent to the form element if you use the f or attribute to explicitly name the element it's labeling.
- **No Label** adds the form element with no label, as if the accessibility option were turned off.
- **Position** Choose Before Form Item or After Form Item. This determines the placement of the label text relative to the form element.

Access Key This item lets you specify a keyboard shortcut key to use to access the form element. This key, in conjunction with the CTRL key (in Windows) can be used to access the item when viewing the form in the browser. For example, if you assign the X key to a label, it can be accessed by pressing CTRL – X in the browser.

Tab Index The tab index allows you to specify the order that form elements will be cycled through when pressing the TAB key in the browser. The tab order goes from low to higher numbers.

If for some reason you don't want to see the Input Tag Accessibility Attribute dialog box every time you insert a form element, you can disable it with the Accessibility options. To turn off accessibility options for form elements, do the following.

1. Choose Edit > Preferences and click the Accessibility category.
2. Uncheck the Form Objects option in the Show Attributes When Inserting list
3. Click OK to apply the changes

Dreamweaver also provides an icon in the Forms category of the Insert bar to add a label to a form element manually. To add the label, select the form element that you want the label to be associated with and then click the Label button or choose Insert > Forms > Label. The selected form element is wrapped with a <label> tag. Dreamweaver switches to Code and Design view and highlights the label tag for editing. After completing your edits, click the Refresh button in the Property Inspector panel to display the results in Design view.

Define Fieldsets

Another form element typically used to improve accessibility is the fieldset. This element is used to group related form fields together, which can make the user interface more intuitive, as well as provide information that speech-based browsers can use to audibly render the page.

A fieldset works very much like a label – it's an HTML tag that encloses a form element. The difference is that the <fieldset> tag can contain more than one form element. It is typically displayed with a border surrounding the form elements. If you supply a legend that text appears above the bounding box on the left.

To add a fieldset to your form, do the following:

1. Select the form elements you want to enclose with the fieldset.
2. Click the Fieldset button in the Forms category of the Insert bar or choose Insert > Forms > Fieldset. Dreamweaver displays the Fieldset dialog box.
3. In the Label box, enter the text to use for the fieldset's <legend> tag. This is the text that will be displayed at the top left, above the fieldset's bounding box. Leave this blank to create the fieldset box without a text label.
4. Click OK to close the dialog box and insert the <fieldset> and <legend> tags into the HTML code for your page. Dreamweaver switches to Code and Design view for further editing if needed. Click the Refresh button in the Property Inspector panel to update the Design view display.

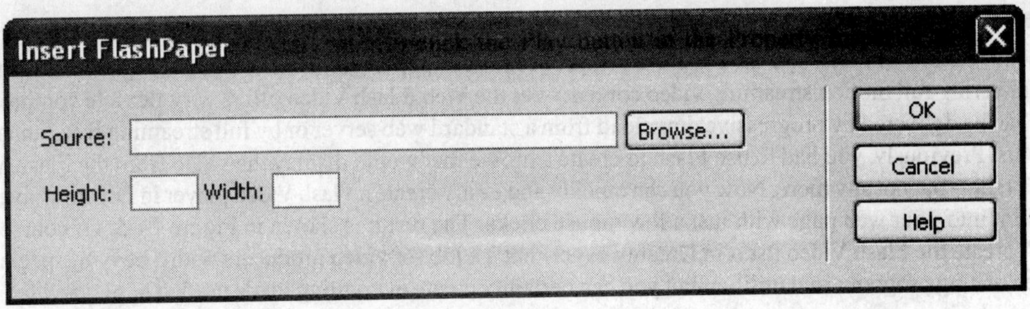

The HTML codeforafieldset looks like this:

```
<fieldset><legend>File Upload</legend>
<p><label>Filename :<br>
<input type="file" name="file1">
</label>
</p>
<p><label>Description:<br>
<textarea name= "textarea" ></textarea>
</label>
</p></fieldset>
```

Insert FlashPaper

FlashPaper is a utility that enables you to "print" word processing documents (and most anything else you can print) to a file that can be viewed with the Flash Player. It's a fast and easy way to create onscreen facsimiles of printed documents. In some ways, a FlashPaper document is like an Adobe PDF document. It retains all the fonts and formatting of a printed document in a transportable file format that can be viewed by someone who doesn't have the application that was used to create the original document. The difference is that FlashPaper is optimized for onscreen viewing using the Flash Player, which is available on nearly all computers and is far more widely available than the Adobe Reader software.

Naturally, since FlashPaper and Dreamweaver are both Adobe products, Dreamweaver makes it especially easy to add FlashPaper documents to your web page. Here's how:

1. In Design view, place your cursor at the location on the page where you want the FlashPaper document to appear.
2. Choose Insert > Media > FlashPaper or click the arrow beside the Media button in the Common category of the Insert bar and choose FlashPaper. Dreamweaver opens the Insert FlashPaper dialog box.
3. Enter the path and filename for the FlashPaper document file in the Source box or click the Browse button to open the Select File dialog box where you can locate and select the file. Enter the desired size of the FlashPaper document display in the Height and Width boxes and click OK. Dreamweaver opens the Object Tag Accessibility Attributes dialog box.
4. Enter the Title, Access Key and Tab Index in the respective boxes and click OK. Dreamweaver closes the dialog boxes and adds the FlashPaper object to your page.

Initially, the FlashPaper document appears as a gray box. You can edit the FlashPaper object properties in the Property Inspector as needed. You can also click the Play button in the Property Inspector to view the FlashPaper document in its viewer window, right there in the Dreamweaver Design view.

Insert FLV

Recent versions of Flash and the Flash Player have featured support for Flash Video – a highly efficient way of delivering full motion streaming video content over the Web. Flash Video offers very flexible compression and can be delivered by progressive download from a standard web server or by full streaming from enhanced servers. Previously, you had to use Flash to create a movie that would display the video from the Flash Video (FLV) file – but not any more. Now you can quickly and easily create a Flash Video player in Dreamweaver and insert it into your web page with just a few mouse clicks. The result is shown in Figure 14-5. Of course, you can't create the Flash Video itself in Dreamweaver-that's a job for video producers with a bevy of specialized video editing programs and utilities-but you can certainly create everything that's needed to playa video from your web site.

To add a Flash Video player to your web document, follow these steps:

1. In Design view, place your cursor at the location on the page where you want the Flash Video player to appear.
2. Choose Insert > Media > Flash Video or click the arrow beside the Media button in the Common category of the Insert bar and choose Flash Video. Dreamweaver opens the Insert Flash Video dialog box.
3. Select the video type-either Progressive Download Video or Streaming Video. (Streaming Video requires special software on the server. Progressive Download Video is another form of streaming

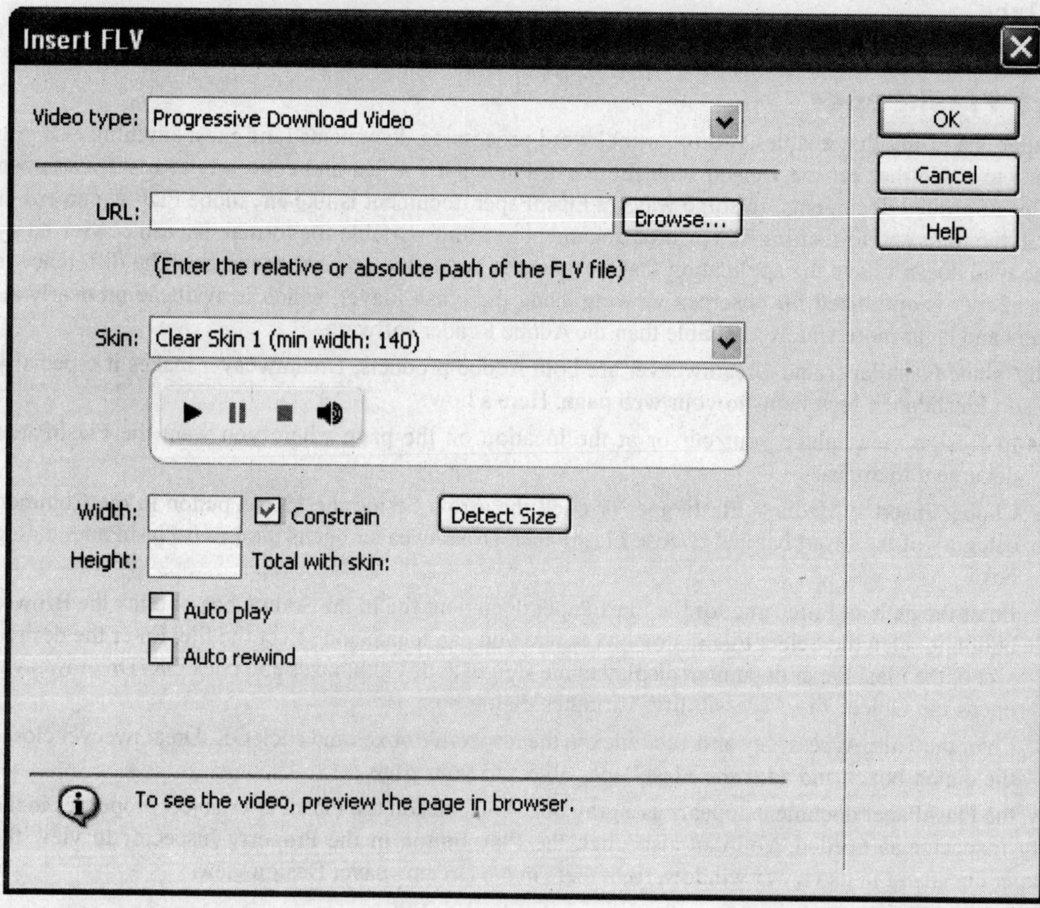

that works with any standard web server, so that's probably the one you'll want to use.) The other options in the Insert Flash Video dialog box change slightly depending on the video type you select.

4. Enter the path and filename of the FLV file in the URL box or click the Browse button to open the Select File dialog box where you can locate and select the file. (If you selected Streaming Video in step 3, enter the server address and the stream name.)
5. Select the Skin (the set of player control buttons), enter the width and height and choose the other options as appropriate. Then click OK to close the dialog box and add the Flash Video player to your web page.

Unlike most of the other media objects, Dreamweaver can't preview Flash Video in Design view. You'll need to preview your page in a browser in order to see the Flash Video. Even if you can't see the Flash Video in Design view, you can select its gray placeholder box and edit its properties in the Property Inspector.

Create a Pop – Up Menu

Pop – up menus are another popular navigation option. These dynamic menus can be linked to text links or images and are often used as submenus for nav bars. This enables visitors to link to a particular page of interest without having to wade through intermediate pages. To add a pop-up menu to a page

1. Position the insertion point cursor in your document at the location where you want to insert the pop-up menu.
2. Choose Show Pop-Up Menu from the Actions list in the Behaviors panel. The Show Pop – Up Menu dialog box appears.
3. Use the following options to complete your menu:

- **The Contents tab** establishes the menu item, enter the Text, Link and Target (optional) and then click the plus (+) sign to add a menu item to the list. Click the Indent button to add a submenu to your pop-up menu. Select an item in the list and use the up and down arrow arrow buttons to change the list order.
- **The Appearance tab** determines the font, color, size and alignment, as well as the colors for the up and over states for the menu items and whether the menu is horizontal or vertical.
- **The Advanced tab** controls the menu layout, including the cell dimensions, border width and color and the position of the text within the cells. This tab also enables you to set the delay between the mouseover and when the menu appears.
- **The Position tab** controls the positioning of the pop-up menu in relation to the image or text to which it is attached. The positioning can be set using one of four preset options or by manually typing coordinates that represent the distance in pixels from the top-left corner of the menu.

The trigger image or text becomes a link to the pop-up menu, so it will take on the formatting of other links in your document. If you wish to change the appearance of text, you can create and apply a CSS class to the trigger text.

The CSS Styles Panel

The newly expanded CSS Styles panel is your main access point for creating and editing style sheets in Dreamweaver CS3. To open the CSS Styles panel, choose Window > CSS Styles or click the CSS button in the Property Inspector.

The CSS Styles panel has two modes, which you can switch between using the two buttons located at the top of the panel.

Click the current button to display the formatting currently applied to the selected page element. In this mode, the upper portion of the CSS Styles panel displays a summary of the style properties affecting the current selection. The lower portion of the panel is an editable list of formatting properties.

Click the All button to see a list of styles currently associated with the document. That includes styles you create in the CSS Styles panel, styles that Dreamweaver creates automatically when you format text with the Property Inspector and styles from external style sheet that are attached to the document. The panel shows a style sheets and styles in a familiar tree – style list. Click the +/- box beside a style sheet name to expand or collapse the list of style rules within that style sheet. Again, the lower portion of the panel displays an editable list or properties of the style that is selected in the upper portion of the panel.

A set of buttons at the bottom of the CSS Panel enable you to modify the list display in the lower portion of the panel and manage styles and style sheets. The three buttons on the left let you select an alphabetical list of the available style properties (the default) or a categorized list or a view that shows only the properties set for the current rule or selection and hides all the rest of the properties. The four buttons on the right enable you to create new style sheets, attach external style sheets and edit or delete existing styles. These commands are also available in the pop-up menu that appears when you click the menu button in the upper - right corner of the panel or right - click within the panel.

Create a CSS Style Sheet in Dreamweaver

You can create two different kinds of CSS style sheets: internal style sheets and external style sheets. An internal style sheet is a collection of styles embedded in the code of the existing web document. External style sheets reside in an external file that can be referenced much as you reference another HTML page using hypertext link. If your site is small and there are style differences between pages, you'll probably want to use internal style sheets for each page. If, however, you're trying to create a consistent appearance for your entire site, you can create an external style sheet and apply it to multiple pages (or even multiple sites), thus simplifying the formatting of those pages considerably.

In each type of style sheet, you can create a collection of styles or rule declarations, each of which is simply a list of formatting specifications. You can create three different and distinct kinds of styles:

- **Custom styles (also called Classes)** Can be applied to any text selection or other object.
- **Tags** Redefine formatting for HTML tag styles.
- **Advanced selectors** Pseudo-classes, contextual selectors, IDs and so on.

Although you can create, apply and edit styles and style sheets from other places in Dreamweaver, the CSS Styles panel is your primary tool for managing CSS styles. For example, you can use the Property Inspector to apply formatting to some text and Dreamweaver will automatically create a corresponding style, but you'll use the CSS Styles panel to edit that style later.

Create a Custom Style

Custom CSS styles are what people usually think of when they imagine a style sheet. With a custom style, you can create and modify a diverse set of attributes and apply them to any text selection or other object on your page.

For example, you might create a custom style to use for footnotes and other "fine print" that gives that text the following attributes: 10-pixel size, Verdana font, dark gray color. Then, whenever you want to apply the formatting, you just highlight some text and apply the style. If you later decide to change the color to dark blue, just change the custom style and all the "fine print" in your document will automatically change to reflect the updated style specification.

In CSS parlance, a custom style is referred to as a class. When you name a custom style, you can use pretty much any name you want, as long as it begins with a period. To create a custom style, follow these steps:

1. Click the New CSS Style button in the CSS Styles panel or select Text > CSS Styles > New from the menu. Dreamweaver opens the New CSS Rule dialog box shown in figure.
2. Select the Class radio button.

3. Enter a name for your style in the Name box. All class styles begin with a period, such as .boxytext or .copyright. If you forget to type the period yourself, Dreamweaver will add it for you.
4. Select the This Document Only radio button. This saves your style information in an internal style sheet in the current web document.
5. Click the OK button to add the style to the document's internal style sheet and to the list in the CSS Style panel. The CSS Rule Definition dialog box appears.
6. Click Type in the Category list. Adjust the Type settings in the CSS Rule Definition dialog box to define the text formatting attributes for your style:
   - Enter the name of the font you want to use for your style or select one from the Font pop - up menu.
   - Enter a font size in the Size box and select a measurement in the pop-up menu to the right of the Size box.
   - Select other options and attributes using the fields in the CSS Rule Definition dialog box. Click Help for description of each field and the available attributes.
7. Click OK to close the CSS Rule Definition dialog box and finish creating your style. The style is ready for use to format your web page.

Apply Your Style

After you create a custom style, you have several options for applying it to a text selection. First, you need to select the text to which you want to apply the style:

- To select a text range within a paragraph, drag across the text in the Document window to highlight it. The style will apply only to the selected text.
- To select a paragraph or other tag, click to place the insertion point within the paragraph or use the Tag Selector in the status bar to select the tag.

After you select the text, you can apply the style with any of the following techniques:

- Click All in the CSS Styles panel to display a list of styles, then right-click the desired style and choose Apply from the pop-up menu that appears.
- Choose the style from the Style list in the Property Inspector.
- Right-click the selection in the Document window and choose CSS Styles > Stylename from the pop-up menu that appears.

Redefine HTML Tags

In addition to defining custom styles from scratch, CSS enables you to redefine the attributes of the standard HTML tags. These tag selector styles allow you to change the way existing HTML tags are rendered by the viewer's browser. This feature can be very useful for making quick, global changes to a page or a web site. For example, you can instantly change the font for all normal text in your web page by redefining the font property of the <p> tag that marks all normal paragraphs.

To create a tag selector style, follow these steps:

1. Click the New CSS Rule button in the CSS Styles panel or choose Text > CSS Styles > New CSS Style to open the New CSS Rule dialog box.
2. Select the Tag radio button.
3. Select an HTML tag to redefine from the Tag list box. The list shows all the available HTML tags without the angle brackets that normally surround them.
4. Select the This Document Only radio button. This saves your style information in the internal style sheet for the current HTML document.
5. Click the OK button to open the CSS Rule Definition dialog box, where you define the attributes for your new style.

6. Click Type in the Category list. Then adjust the Type settings in the Rule Definition dialog box to define the text formatting attributes for your style:
   - Enter the name of the font you want to use for your style or select one from the Font pop-up menu.
   - Enter a font size in the Size box and select a measurement in the pop-up menu to the right of the Size box.
   - Select other options and attributes using the fields in the Rule Definition dialog box. Click Help for descriptions of each field and the available attributes.
7. Click OK to close the Rule Definition dialog box and finish creating your style. Dreamweaver adds the style definition to the internal style sheet for your document.

No further steps are necessary to apply the style; it will automatically apply to any text currently surrounded by the HTML tag you have redefined and to any text you mark with that tag in the future.

Advanced Selector Styles

The Advanced selector option in the New CSS Style dialog box enables you to create more sophisticated versions of tag selector styles that will apply to a tag only in certain circumstances. For example, you can create a style that will apply only to a tag with a specific ID attribute or only to a tag nested within another tag. The most common use of this kind of selector is to change the attributes of the various states (called pseudo-classes) of the <a> (hypertext anchor) tag. This enables you to control the appearance of hyperlinks when they are visited, clicked or under the mouse pointer.

To create Advanced selector styles to control link colors and rollover colors, follow these steps:

1. Open the New CSS Rule dialog box.
2. Select the Advanced radio button.
3. Select a click state from the Selector list box. For example, select a:active to set the appearance attributes for active links. These are the available states:
   - a:active The way the link appears when the user clicks it
   - a:hover The way the link appears when the pointer is hovering over it
   - a:link The way the link appears normally
   - a:visited The way the link appears after the user has already visited it
4. Select the This Document Only radio button to save the style in the document's internal style sheet.
5. Click the OK button to open the CSS Rule dialog box, where you define the formatting attributes for your link.
6. Click the Type category and enter the text attributes for the link text. Remember that you're setting the way a link should appear in a particular state – active, hover, normal or visited. Usually, you'll want to select different colors for each state.
7. Click OK to close the New Style dialog box and apply the style.

This procedure defines the attributes for one state of the <a> tag. Repeat the steps to create style definitions for the remaining link states to complete the effect.

As with tag styles, there's generally no need for a separate step to apply advanced styles to your text since the style selectors are usually built-in pseudo-classes or nested tags. Of course, if you're creating an ID selector, you'll need to make sure the page element you're targeting with the selector is tagged with the matching ID attribute.

In most cases, you can do that by selecting the page element (table, div or whatever) and entering the ID in the Property Inspector. If the Property Inspector for the selected page element doesn't include a place to enter the ID, you can always edit the code in Code view.

View and Edit Styles in the CSS Styles Panel

Creating a CSS style is a fairly straightforward process. You can use the technique described earlier in this chapter or you can apply formatting to a text selection by adjusting settings in the Property Inspector and let Dreamweaver create a style for you automatically. But formatting a web page isn't usually a matter of creating a few styles and applying them to your text. Instead, it's an iterative process that involves lots of revision and refinement of your styles.

As a result, you usually spend a lot more time studying how your styles affect a given page element and then editing the styles to achieve the desired effect. To make this process easier, Adobe made some major changes to the CSS Styles panel in Dreamweaver CS3. The CSS Styles panel is now your one-stop-shop for creating, viewing and editing styles.

I've already covered how to create styles, so now it's time to see how you view and edit those styles.

View a Style Summary

When you're working with CSS styles, it's important to remember that the style properties cascade-which means that formatting applied at a higher level "flows" down to all included lower levels unless it is overridden by a more specific style applied at one of those lower levels.

As a result, the formatting of a given page element, such as a paragraph, can be influenced by several styles. For example, a paragraph may be nested within a layer defining a column, which is nested within another layer defining the main content area of the page, which is nested within the body tag. The paragraph text may get its font from a style applied to the body tag, its size and color from a style applied to the main content layer, its alignment from a style applied to the column layer and its line height and margins from a style applied to the paragraph itself.

With all this cascading style stuff going on, it's important to know not only what formatting properties are being applied to a given page element, but also where those properties come from. That's what the new Summary For Selection list in the CSS Styles panel shows you. When you click the Current button at the top of the CSS Styles panel, the Summary for Selection list appears in the upper portion of the panel. It lists all the formatting properties that are defined for the currently selected page element, regardless of whether those properties are from a style applied directly to the selected object or inherited from other styles higher in the cascade.

When you select any property in the Summary For Selection list, Dreamweaver displays the properties defined in that style in the Properties list in the lower portion of the CSS Styles panel. The name of the style appears at the top of the Properties for... list and all of the properties are available for view and editing.

Another useful feature of the CSS Styles panel is the list that appears in the middle of the Current mode display, between the Summary For Selection list above and the Properties list below. You can use the two buttons on the right side of the list to change what Dreamweaver displays in this space-either the About (information) display or the Rules list. In Information mode, it simply helps identify what property is selected in the Summary For Selection list, which is helpful if the highlighted selection has scrolled out of view. When you click the Show Cascade... button, the list expands to show all the cascading styles that apply to the selected page element. You can click a style in that list to show the corresponding properties in the Properties list below. The Rules list makes it easy to select a style that may not have a property listed in the Summary For Selection list because all its properties are overridden by subsequent styles.

Edit a Style

One of the greatest advantages of style sheets is the ability they give you to quickly change the appearance of your pages by simply editing the styles. The CSS Styles panel gives you two ways to edit a style. The first technique is a variation on the same technique you use to create a style in the first place.

Here's how it goes:

1. Select the style you want to edit from the display in the CSS Styles panel. If the panel is in All styles mode, you click the style name in the All Rules list in the upper portion of the CSS Styles panel. If the panel is in Current mode, you can select a property in the Summary For Selection list to select the style from which that property is derived or you can select a style from the Rules list in the middle of the panel.
2. Click the Edit Style button at the bottom of the CSS Styles panel. Dreamweaver opens the CSS Rule Definition For dialog box.
3. Change the settings in the CSS Rule Definition For dialog box as needed.
4. Click OK to close the dialog box and record your changes to the style. Dreamweaver automatically updates the page in Design view to reflect the changes to any page elements affected by the style.

The second technique for editing a style uses the new Properties list in the lower portion of the CSS Styles panel. The Properties list isn't just a viewer that displays the properties for a given style. The list is also fully interactive, enabling you to edit existing properties of a style and define additional properties.

The Properties list appears in the lower portion of the CSS Styles panel in both All Styles mode and Current Selection mode. At first glance, the Properties list may look a little intimidating because of the high density of information it presents. But it's actually quite convenient and easy to use once you become accustomed to the property names that appear in the Properties list. For the most part, those names come straight from the HTML/XHTML and CSS standards so it helps to be familiar with that terminology.

The Properties list shows all the properties of the CSS style highlighted in the upper portion of the CSS Styles panel. The three buttons in the lower-left corner of the CSS Styles panel enable you to switch between different views in the Properties list. You can select a categorized list, a straight alphabetical listing of available properties or an abbreviated list showing only those properties that are defined for the selected style.

In category mode, you can click the + / - button beside a category name to expand/collapse the category. In alphabetical mode, any property with defined values floats to the top of the list, followed by undefined properties. The left column lists the possible properties for the selected tag. The right column lists the values of those properties. To change a property, click the right column beside the property you want to change and then type in the appropriate value or click the arrow button and select from the drop-down list box that appears.

Rename a Style

Dreamweaver tries to make things easy for you by automatically creating styles as needed to implement any formatting you apply from the Property Inspector. That way, you don't need to first create and define the properties of a style before you can apply that formatting to a text selection. Instead, you can just select some text and apply the desired formatting-Dreamweaver takes care of creating a style with those formatting properties and applying it to the text.

The problem is that these automatically created styles have arbitrary names such as style1 and style8, which make the styles hard to reuse. So, you'll probably want to rename the automatically generated styles to give them more meaningful names, such as .footnoteText and .sideText. Fortunately, renaming styles is easy to do. Just follow these steps:

1. Click the All button in the CSS Styles panel and scroll the All Rules list to show the style you want to rename.
2. Right-click the style in the All Rules list and choose Rename from the pop-up menu that appears. Dreamweaver opens the Rename class dialog box.
3. Enter the new style name in the New Name box.
4. Click OK. Dreamweaver closes the dialog box and changes the style name in the CSS Styles panel and also everywhere it appears in the code for the current page.

Duplicate a Style

Sometimes it's helpful to be able to make a duplicate copy of a style. You might want to make a backup copy before trying some formatting changes or you might want to create a new style that is based on an existing style by making a copy and then editing its properties. Whatever the reason, when you need to copy a style, follow these steps:

1. Click the All button in the CSS Styles panel and scroll the All rules list to show the style you want to copy.
2. Right - click the style in the All Rules list and choose Duplicate from the pop-up menu that appears. Dreamweaver opens the Duplicate CSS Rule dialog box.
3. Enter a new style name in the Name box.
4. Click OK. Dreamweaver closes the dialog box and creates a new style that contains all the same properties as the original.

Delete a Style

Sooner or later, you'll need to prune some unneeded styles from your style sheet. When that time comes, you can use either of the following techniques:

- Right – click a style name in the All Rules list in the CSS Styles panel and choose Delete from the pop - up menu that appears.
- Select a style name in the All Rules list in the CSS Styles panel and then click the Delete CSS Rule button at the bottom of the panel.

Create an External Style Sheet

The CSS style definition procedures covered earlier in this chapter describe how to create an internal style sheet that is saved within the current web document. But you can also save styles in an external style sheet. An external style sheet differs from an internal one only in that the code used to define the styles is saved as a separate text file instead of within the current document.

Saving style information this way provides one of the most powerful and compelling reasons to use Cascading Style Sheets: you can link to the external file from multiple pages, rather than having to include the style information on each page. This feature allows you to apply consistent styles to an entire site and update the entire site simply by making a few changes to the external style sheet. Many large web sites - such as Yahoo!, CNN and Microsoft - Use external style sheets to achieve consistent styling and formatting throughout their sites.

One of the easiest ways to create an external style sheet is to simply select the external style sheet option when you create a new style. Here's how:

1. Open the New CSS Rule dialog box.
2. Select the appropriate type of style: Class, Tag or Advanced.
3. Instead of selecting the This Document Only radio button, click the radio button next to Define In and then choose New Style Sheet File in the list box. Then click OK to open the Save Style Sheet File As dialog box.
4. Locate the folder where you want to save your new style sheet file and enter a name for the file. Dreamweaver automatically adds the extension .css to the end of the name when you enter it. Click Save to close that dialog box and open the CSS Rule Definition dialog box.
5. Set the attributes for your new style in the CSS Rule Definition dialog box. Then click OK to close the dialog box and create the style. Dreamweaver saves the style definition in the external style sheet file instead of embedding it in the header of the current document.

This procedure creates an external style sheet consisting of a single style and automatically links that style sheet to the current document. You can also use the same basic technique to add a style to the collection in an external style sheet. First, make sure the external style sheet is linked to the current document and then follow steps 1 and 2 just described. In step 3, select the linked style sheet name in the Define In list. Skip step 4 and then complete the style definition as instructed in step 5.

Link to an External Style Sheet

Since an external style sheet is a separate file, you need to create a link between your web document and the external style sheet to apply the formatting specified in the external .css file to the current document. When a browser accesses a web document that references an external style sheet, the browser retrieves the information from that style sheet to correctly render the page. The style sheet information can reside on the same server as the web document or anywhere else on the Web. To link the current web document to an external style sheet, follow these steps:

1. In the CSS Style panel, click the Attach Style Sheet button in the lower – right corner of the panel. This opens the Attach External Style Sheet dialog box.
2. Locate an existing style sheet (.css) or enter an external URL if the style sheet resides somewhere on the Internet.
3. Choose Link to establish a link between the current document and the external style sheet.
4. Click OK to close the dialog box and finish attaching the style sheet.

Export an External Style Sheet from Existing Internal Styles

If you've created CSS styles in an internal style sheet in the current document, you can easily export those styles to an external style sheet. In fact, it's a common approach to developing style sheets. You can create and test your styles in a single document where they won't affect other documents. Then, when you're ready to share the styles with other documents in your site, you export the styles to an external style and link to it from each of the other documents. Here's how:

1. Choose File > Export > CSS styles (this option is grayed out if the current document does not contain any style sheet information). The Export Styles As CSS File dialog box appears.
2. Enter a filename for the external style sheet and locate a folder in which to save it. Click Save to close the dialog box and save the style sheet.
3. Follow the instructions in the previous section for linking the current document to the external style sheet.

CSS Styles Are for More than Just Text

The focus of this chapter has been text formatting and the various text formatting properties. However, you can apply formatting to other page elements as well. You can use CSS styles to define background colors and background images, margins and padding, borders, list types and precise page position. You can apply these styles to paragraphs, images, tables, layers, divs and all sorts of other tags and page elements. The possibilities are endless. Fortunately, you don't have to deal with an endless variety of techniques for working with all the different applications of styles in Dreamweaver. If you know how to use the CSS panel to create a style that sets the font size in a text paragraphs, you can use that same technique to create a style that sets the thickness of the border around a layer or sets the background color of a table cell.

The only sets the thickness of the border around a layer or sets the background color of a table cell. The only difference is that you may need to select a different category in the CSS Style Definition dialog box or scroll a title farther down the Properties list in the CSS Styles panel to find the applicable settings. If you're interested in pursuing cutting – edge techniques that rely on CSS positioning of <div> tags to achieve tableless page layouts, you can do it with Dreamweaver. Of course, you'll need to have a solid understanding of XHTML and CSS concepts to pull it off successfully, but Dreamweaver gives you the tools you need to get the job done and to do it much quicker and easier than you could by hand-coding.

10 Integrating with Other Software

About Photoshop, Flash, and Fireworks integration

Photoshop, Fireworks, and Flash are powerful web-development tools for creating and managing graphics and SWF files. You can tightly integrate Dreamweaver with these tools to simplify your web design workflow.

Note: There is also limited integration with some other applications. For example, you can export an InDesign file as XHTML and continue working on it in Dreamweaver.

You can easily insert images and content created with Adobe Flash (SWF and FLV files) in a Dreamweaver document. You can also edit an image or SWF file in its original editor after you insert it in a Dreamweaver document.

To use Dreamweaver in conjunction with these Adobe applications, you must have these applications installed on your computer.

For Fireworks and Flash, product integration is achieved through roundtrip editing. Roundtrip editing ensures that code updates are transferred correctly between Dreamweaver and these other applications (for example, to preserve rollover behaviors or links to other files).

Dreamweaver also relies on Design Notes for product integration. Design Notes are small files that allow Dreamweaver to locate the source document for an exported image or SWF file. When you export files from Fireworks, Flash, or Photoshop directly to a Dreamweaver defined site, Design Notes containing references to the original PSD, PNG, or Flash authoring file (FLA) are automatically exported to the site along with the web-ready file (GIF, JPEG, PNG, or SWF).

In addition to location information, Design Notes contain other pertinent information about exported files. For example, when you export a Fireworks table, Fireworks writes a Design Note for each exported image file in the table. If the exported file contains hotspots or rollovers, the Design Notes include information about the scripts for them.

As part of the export operation, Dreamweaver creates a folder named _notes in the same folder as the exported asset. This folder contains the Design Notes that Dreamweaver needs to integrate with Photoshop, Flash, or Fireworks.

In order to use Design Notes, you must make sure they are not disabled for your Dreamweaver site. They are enabled by default. However, even if they are disabled, when you insert a Photoshop image file, Dreamweaver creates a Design Note to store the location of the source PSD file.

Fireworks

Insert a Fireworks image

Dreamweaver and Fireworks recognize and share many of the same file-editing procedures, including changes to links, image maps, table slices, and more. Together, the two applications provide a streamlined workflow for editing, optimizing, and placing web graphics files in HTML pages.

You can place a Fireworks exported graphic directly in a Dreamweaver document using the Insert Image command, or you can create a new Fireworks graphic from a Dreamweaver image placeholder.

In the Dreamweaver document, place the insertion point where you want the image to appear, then do one of the following:

- Select Insert > Image.
- In the Common category of the Insert panel, click the Image button or drag it to the document.

Navigate to the desired Fireworks exported file, and click Ok.

If the Fireworks file is not in the current Dreamweaver site, a message appears asking whether you want to copy the file to the root folder. Click Yes.

Edit a Fireworks image or table from Dreamweaver

When you open and edit an image or an image slice that is part of a Fireworks table, Dreamweaver starts Fireworks, which opens the PNG file from which the image or table was exported.

This assumes that Fireworks is set as the primary external image editor for PNG files. Fireworks is often also set as the default editor for JPEG and GIF files, although you may wish to set Photoshop as the default editor for these file types.

When the image is part of a Fireworks table, you can open the entire Fireworks table for edits, as long as the <!—fw table—> comment exists in the HTML code. If the source PNG file was exported from Fireworks to a Dreamweaver site using the Dreamweaver Style HTML And Images setting, the Fireworks table comment is automatically inserted in the HTML code.

1. In Dreamweaver, open the Property inspector (Window > Properties) if it isn't already open.
2. Click the image or image slice to select it.

When you select an image that was exported from Fireworks, the Property inspector identifies the selection as a Fireworks image or table and displays the name of the PNG source file.

To start Fireworks for editing, do one of the following:

- In the Property inspector, click Edit.
- Hold down Control (Windows) or Command (Macintosh) and double-click the selected image.
- Right-click (Windows) or Control-click (Macintosh) the selected image and select Edit With Fireworks from the context menu.

If Fireworks cannot locate the source file, you are prompted to locate the PNG source file. When you work with the Fireworks source file, changes are saved to both the source file and the exported file; otherwise, only the exported file is updated.

In Fireworks, edit the source PNG file and click Done.

Fireworks saves the changes in the PNG file, exports the updated image (or HTML and images), and returns focus to Dreamweaver. In Dreamweaver, the updated image or table appears.

Optimize a Fireworks image from Dreamweaver

You can use Dreamweaver to make quick changes to Fireworks images and animations. From within Dreamweaver, you can change optimization settings, animation settings, and the size and area of the exported image.

In Dreamweaver, select the desired image and do one of the following:

- Select Command > Optimize Image
- Click the Edit Image Settings button in the Property inspector.

Make your edits in the Image Preview dialog box:

- To edit optimization settings, click the Options tab.
- To edit the size and area of the exported image, click the File tab.

When you finish, click OK.

Use Fireworks to modify Dreamweaver image placeholders

You can create a placeholder image in a Dreamweaver document and then start Fireworks to design a graphic image or Fireworks table to replace it.

To create a new image from an image placeholder, you must have both Dreamweaver and Fireworks installed on your system.

1. Make sure you've already set Fireworks as the image editor for PNG files.
2. In the Document window, click the image placeholder to select it.
3. Start Fireworks in Editing From Dreamweaver mode by doing one of the following:
   - In the Property inspector, click Create.
   - Press Control (Windows) or Command (Macintosh) then double-click the image placeholder.
   - Right-click (Windows) or Control-click (Macintosh) the image placeholder, then select Create Image In Fireworks.
4. Use Fireworks options to design the image.

Fireworks recognizes the following image placeholder settings you may have set while working with the image placeholder in Dreamweaver: image size (which correlates to Fireworks canvas size), image ID (which Fireworks uses as the default document name for the source file and export file you create), and text alignment. Fireworks also recognizes links and certain behaviors (such as swap image, pop up menu, navigation bar, and set text) you attached to the image placeholder while working in Dreamweaver.

Note: Although Fireworks doesn't show links you've added to an image placeholder, they are preserved. If you draw a hotspot and add a link in Fireworks, it will not delete the link you added to the image placeholder in Dreamweaver; however, if you cut out a slice in Fireworks in the new image, Fireworks will delete the link in the Dreamweaver document when you replace the image placeholder.

Fireworks doesn't recognize the following image placeholder settings: image alignment, color, Vspace and Hspace, and maps. They are disabled in the image placeholder Property inspector.

1. When you finish, click Done to display the save prompt.
2. In the Save In text box, select the folder you defined as your Dreamweaver local site folder.
3. If you named the image placeholder when you inserted it in the Dreamweaver document, Fireworks populates the File Name box with that name. You can change the name.
4. Click Save to save the PNG file.
5. The Export dialog box appears. Use this dialog box to export the image as a GIF or JPEG file, or, in the case of sliced images, as HTML and images.
6. For Save In, select the Dreamweaver local site folder.
7. The Name box automatically displays the name you used for the PNG file. You can change the name.
8. For Save As Type, select the type of file or files you want to export; for example, Images Only or HTML And Images.
9. Click Save to save the exported file.

The file is saved, and focus returns to Dreamweaver. In the Dreamweaver document, the exported file or Fireworks table replaces the image placeholder.

About Fireworks pop up menus

Fireworks lets you quickly and easily create CSS-based pop up menus.

In addition to being extensible and fast to download, the pop up menus you create with Fireworks give you the following advantages:

- The menu items can be indexed by search engines.

- The menu items can be read by screen readers, making your pages more accessible.
- The code generated by Fireworks complies to standards and can be validated.

You can edit Fireworks pop up menus with Dreamweaver or with Fireworks, but not both. Changes made in Dreamweaver are not preserved in Fireworks

Edit Fireworks pop up menus in Dreamweaver

You can create a pop up menu in Fireworks 8 or later and then edit it with Dreamweaver or with Fireworks (using roundtrip editing), but not with both. If you edit your menus in Dreamweaver and then edit them in Fireworks, you will lose all your previous edits except for the text content.

1. If you prefer to edit your menus with Dreamweaver, you can use Fireworks to create the pop up menu and then use Dreamweaver exclusively to edit and customize the menu.
2. If you prefer to edit the menus in Fireworks, you can use the roundtrip editing feature in Dreamweaver, but you should not edit the menus directly in Dreamweaver.
3. In Dreamweaver, select the Fireworks table that contains the pop up menu, and then click Edit in the Property inspector.
4. The source PNG file opens in Fireworks.
5. In Fireworks, edit the menu with the Pop up Menu Editor, and then click Done on the Fireworks toolbar.
6. Fireworks sends the edited pop up menu back to Dreamweaver.

If you created a pop up menu in Fireworks MX 2004 or earlier, you can edit it in Dreamweaver using the Show Pop Up Menu dialog box, available from the Behaviors panel.

Edit a pop up menu created in Fireworks MX 2004 or earlier

1. In Dreamweaver, select the hotspot or image that triggers the pop up menu.
2. In the Behaviors panel (Shift+F3), double-click Show Pop Up Menu in the Actions list.
3. Make your changes in the Pop Up Menu dialog box and click OK.

Specify launch-and-edit preferences for Fireworks source files

When you use Fireworks to edit images, the images in your web pages are normally exported by Fireworks from a source PNG file. When you open an image file in Dreamweaver to edit it, Fireworks automatically opens the source PNG file, prompting you to locate the PNG file if it cannot be found. If you prefer, you can set preferences in Fireworks to have Dreamweaver open the inserted image, or you can have Fireworks give you the option of using the inserted image file or the Fireworks source file every time you open an image in Dreamweaver.

Dreamweaver recognizes the Fireworks launch-and-edit preferences only in certain cases. Specifically, you must be opening and optimizing an image that is not part of a Fireworks table and contains a correct Design Notes path to a source PNG file.

1. In Fireworks, select Edit > Preferences and then click the Launch And Edit tab.
2. Specify the preference options to use when editing or optimizing Fireworks images placed in an external application: Always Use Source PNG
3. Automatically opens the Fireworks PNG file that is defined in the Design Note as the source of the placed image. Updates are made to the source PNG file and its corresponding placed image.
4. Never Use Source PNG
5. Automatically opens the placed Fireworks image, whether or not a source PNG file exists. Updates are made to the placed image only.
6. Ask When Launching

Displays a message asking whether to open the source PNG file. You can also specify global launch-and-edit preferences from this message.

Insert Fireworks HTML code in a Dreamweaver document

From Fireworks, you can use the Export command to export and save optimized images and HTML files to a location inside a Dreamweaver site folder. You can then insert the file in Dreamweaver. Dreamweaver lets you insert Fireworks-generated HTML code, complete with associated images, slices, and JavaScript, into a document.

1. In Dreamweaver document, place the insertion point where you want to insert the Fireworks HTML code.
2. Do one of the following:
   - Select Insert > Image Objects > Fireworks HTML.
   - In the Common category of the Insert panel, click the Images button and choose Insert Fireworks HTML from the popup menu.
3. Click Browse to select a Fireworks HTML file.
4. If you will have no further use for the file, select Delete File After Insertion. Selecting this option has no effect on the source PNG file associated with the HTML file.

If the HTML file is on a network drive, it is permanently deleted—not moved to the Recycle Bin or Trash.

Click OK to insert the HTML code, along with its associated images, slices, and JavaScript, into the Dreamweaver document.

Paste Fireworks HTML code into Dreamweaver

A fast way to place Fireworks-generated images and tables in Dreamweaver is to copy and paste Fireworks HTML code directly into a Dreamweaver document.

Copy and paste Fireworks HTML code into Dreamweaver

- In Fireworks, select Edit > Copy HTML Code.
- Follow the wizard as it guides you through the settings for exporting your HTML and images. When prompted, specify your Dreamweaver site folder as the destination for the exported images.
- The wizard exports the images to the specified destination and copies the HTML code to the Clipboard.
- In Dreamweaver document, place the insertion point where you want to paste the HTML code, and select Edit > Paste Fireworks HTML.
- All HTML and JavaScript code associated with the Fireworks files you exported is copied into the Dreamweaver document, and all links to images are updated.

Export and paste Fireworks HTML code into Dreamweaver

- In Fireworks, select File > Export.
- Specify your Dreamweaver site folder as the destination for the exported images.
- In the Export pop up menu, select HTML And Images.
- In the HTML pop up menu, select Copy To Clipboard, and then click Export.
- In the Dreamweaver document, place the insertion point where you want to paste the exported HTML code, and select Edit > Paste Fireworks HTML.
- All HTML and JavaScript code associated with the Fireworks files you exported is copied into the Dreamweaver document, and all links to images are updated.

Update Fireworks HTML code placed in Dreamweaver

In Fireworks, the File > Update HTML command provides an alternative to the launch-and-edit technique for updating Fireworks files placed in Dreamweaver. With Update HTML, you can edit a source PNG image in Fireworks and then automatically update any exported HTML code and image files placed in a Dreamweaver document. This command lets you update Dreamweaver files even when Dreamweaver is not running.

1. In Fireworks, open the source PNG file and make your edits.
2. Select File > Save.
3. In Fireworks, select File > Update HTML.
4. Navigate to the Dreamweaver file containing the HTML you want to update, and click Open.
5. Navigate to the folder destination where you want to place the updated image files, and click Select.

Fireworks updates the HTML and JavaScript code in the Dreamweaver document. Fireworks also exports updated images associated with the HTML and places the images in the specified destination folder.

If Fireworks cannot find matching HTML code to update, it gives you the option of inserting new HTML code into the Dreamweaver document. Fireworks places the JavaScript section of the new code at the beginning of the document and places the HTML table or link to the image at the end.

Create a web photo album

You can automatically generate a website that displays a photo album of images located in a given folder. Dreamweaver uses Fireworks to create a thumbnail image and a larger image for each image in the folder. Dreamweaver then creates a web page containing all the thumbnails, as well as links to the larger images. To create a web photo album, you must have both Dreamweaver and Fireworks 4 or later installed on your system.

Before you begin, place all of the images for your photo album in a single folder. (The folder doesn't need to be in a site.) In addition, make sure that the image filenames have any of the following extensions: .gif, .jpg, .jpeg, .png, .psd, .tif, or .tiff. Images with unrecognized file extensions won't appear in the photo album.

1. In Dreamweaver, select Commands > Create Web Photo Album.
2. In the Photo Album Title text box, enter a title. The title will appear in a gray rectangle at the top of the page of thumbnails.

Fill in the Subheading Info and Other Info text boxes to enter up to two lines of additional text below the title.

Select the folder containing source images by clicking the Browse button next to the Source Images Folder text box. Then select (or create) a destination folder in which to place all the exported images and HTML files by clicking the Browse button next to the Destination Folder text box.

The destination folder should not already contain a photo album—if it does, and if any new images have the same names as previously used images, you may overwrite existing thumbnail and image files.

Specify display options for the thumbnail images:

- Select a size for the thumbnail images from the Thumbnail Size menu. Images are scaled proportionally so that the thumbnails fit within a square of the specified pixel dimensions.
- To display the filename of each original image below its thumbnail, select Show Filenames.
- Enter the number of columns for the table that displays the thumbnails.

From the Thumbnail Format menu, select one of the GIF (128 or 256 colors) or JPEG (better picture quality or smaller file size) formats.

From the Photo Format menu, select a GIF or JPEG format for the large images. It doesn't have to be the same as the format you specified for the thumbnails.

You can't use your original image files as the large images, because original image formats other than GIF and JPEG might not be displayed properly on all browsers. If your original images are JPEG files, the large images may have larger file sizes or be of lower quality than the original images.

1. Select a Scale percentage for the large-size images.

2. Setting Scale to 100% creates large-size images the same size as the originals. The scale percentage is applied to all the images; if your original images aren't all the same size, scaling them by the same percentage may not produce the desired results.
3. Select Create Navigation Page For Each Photo to create an individual web page for each source image, containing navigation links labeled Back, Home, and Next.
4. If you select this option, the thumbnails link to the navigation pages. If you don't select this option, the thumbnails link directly to the large images.
5. Click OK to create the HTML and image files for the web photo album.
6. Fireworks starts (if it's not already running) and creates the thumbnails and large images. This may take several minutes if you have many image files. When the processing is complete, Dreamweaver becomes active again and creates the page containing the thumbnails.

When you see the "Album Created" message, click OK.

You may have to wait a few seconds for your photo album page to appear. The thumbnails appear alphabetically by filename.

If you click Cancel while Dreamweaver is creating the album, you don't stop the process. Clicking Cancel merely prevents Dreamweaver from displaying the main photo album page.

About Photoshop Integration

You can insert Photoshop image files (PSD format) into web pages in Dreamweaver and let Dreamweaver optimize them as web ready images (GIF, JPEG, and PNG formats). When you do this, Dreamweaver inserts the image as a Smart Object and maintains a live connection to the original PSD file.

You can also paste all or part of a multi-layered or multi-sliced Photoshop image into a web page in Dreamweaver. When you copy and paste from Photoshop, however, no live connection to the original file is maintained. To update the image, make your changes in Photoshop, and copy and paste again.

If you use this integration feature often, you may want to store your Photoshop files in your Dreamweaver site for easier access. If you do, be sure to cloak them to avoid exposure of the original assets, as well as unnecessary transfers between the local site and the remote server.

About Smart Objects and Photoshop-Dreamweaver workflows

There are two main workflows for working with Photoshop files in Dreamweaver: the copy/paste workflow, and the Smart Objects workflow.

Copy/paste workflow

The copy/paste workflow lets you select slices or layers in a Photoshop file, and then use Dreamweaver to insert them as web-ready images. If you want to update the content later on, however, you must open the original Photoshop file, make your changes, copy your slice or layer to the clipboard again, and then paste the updated slice or layer into Dreamweaver. This workflow is only recommended when you want to insert part of a Photoshop file (for example, a section of a design comp) as an image on a web page.

Smart Objects workflow

When working with complete Photoshop files, Adobe recommends the Smart Objects workflow. A Smart Object in Dreamweaver is an image asset placed on a web page that has a live connection to an original Photoshop (PSD) file. In Dreamweaver Design view, a Smart Object is denoted by an icon in the upper left corner of the image.

Smart Object

When the web image (that is, the image on the Dreamweaver page) is out of sync with the original Photoshop file, Dreamweaver detects that the original file has been updated, and displays one of the Smart Object icon's

arrows in red. When you select the web image in Design view and click the Update from Original button in the Property inspector, the image updates automatically, reflecting any changes that you made to the original Photoshop file. When you use the Smart Objects workflow, you do not need to open Photoshop to update a web image. Additionally, any updates you make to a Smart Object in Dreamweaver are non-destructive. That is, you can change the web version of the image on your page while keeping the original Photoshop image intact. You can also update a Smart Object without selecting the web image in Design view. The Assets panel lets you update all Smart Objects, including images that might not be selectable in the Document window (for example, CSS background images).

Image optimization settings

For both the copy/paste and the Smart Object workflows, you can specify optimization settings in the Image Preview dialog box. This dialog box lets you set things like file format, image quality, and so on. If you are copying a slice or a layer for the first time, or inserting a Photoshop file as a Smart Object for the first time, Dreamweaver displays this dialog so that you can easily create the web image.

If you copy and paste an update to a particular slice or layer, Dreameaver remembers the original settings and re-creates the web image with those settings. Likewise, when you update a Smart Object using the Property inspector, Dreamweaver uses the same settings you used when you first inserted the image. You can change an image's settings at any time by selecting the web image in Design view, and then clicking the Edit Image Settings button in the Property inspector.

Storing Photoshop files

If you've inserted a web image, and have not stored the original Photoshop file in your Dreamweaver site, Dreamweaver recognizes the path to the original file as an absolute local file path. (This is true for both the copy/paste and Smart Object workflows.) For example, if the path to your Dreamweaver site is C:\Sites\mySite, and your Photoshop file is stored in C:\Images\Photoshop, Dreameaver will not recognize the original asset as part of the site called mySite. This will cause problems if you ever want to share the Photoshop file with other team members because Dreamweaver will only recognize the file as being available on a particular local hard drive.

If you store the Photoshop file inside your site, however, Dreamweaver establishes a site-relative path to the file. Any user with access to the site will also be able to establish the correct path to the file, assuming that you have also provided the original file for them to download.

Create a Smart Object

When you insert a Photoshop image (PSD file) into your page, Dreamweaver creates a Smart Object. A *Smart Object* is a web-ready image that maintains a live connection to the original Photoshop image. Whenever you update the original image in Photoshop, Dreamweaver gives you the option of updating the image in Dreamweaver with the click of a button.

1. In Dreamweaver (Design or Code view), place the insertion point on your page where you want the image inserted.
2. Select Insert > Image.
3. You can also drag the PSD file to the page from the Files panel if you're storing your Photoshop files in your website. If you do so, you'll skip the next step.
4. Locate your Photoshop PSD image file in the Select Image Source dialog box by clicking the Browse button and navigating to it.
5. In the Image Preview dialog box that appears, adjust optimization settings as needed and click OK.
6. Save the web ready image file to a location within your website's root folder.

Dreamweaver creates the Smart Object based on the selected optimization settings and places a web-ready version of the image on your page. The Smart Object maintains a live connection to the original image and lets you know when the two are out of synch.

Note: If you decide later that you want to change the optimization settings for an image placed in your pages, you can select the image, click the Edit Image Settings button in the Property inspector, and make changes in the Image Preview dialog box. Changes made in the Image Preview dialog box are applied non-destructively. Dreamweaver never modifies the original Photoshop file, and always re-creates the web image based on the original data.

Update a Smart Object

If you change the Photoshop file to which your Smart Object is linked, Dreamweaver notifies you that the web-ready image is out of sync with the original. In Dreamweaver, Smart Objects are denoted by an icon at the upper left corner of the image. When the web-ready image in Dreamweaver is in sync with the original Photoshop file, both of the arrows in the icon are green. When the web-ready image is out of sync with the original Photoshop file, one of the icon's arrows turns read.

To update a Smart Object with the current contents of the original Photoshop file, select the Smart Object in the Document window, and then click the Update from Original button in the Property inspector.

Note: You do not need Photoshop installed to make the update from Dreamweaver.

Update multiple Smart Objects

You can update multiple Smart Objects at once using the Assets panel. The Assets panel also lets you see Smart Objects that might not be selectable in the Document window (for example, CSS background images).

In the Files panel, click the Assets tab to view site assets.

1. Make sure that Images view is selected. If it isn't, click the Images button.

2. Select each image asset in the Assets panel. When you select a Smart Object, you'll see the Smart Object icon in the upper left corner of the image. Regular images do not have this icon.
3. For each Smart Object that you want to update, right-click the filename and select Update from Original. You can also Control-click to select multiple filenames and update them all at once.

You do not need Photoshop installed to make the update from Dreamweaver.

Resize a Smart Object

You can resize a Smart Object in the Document window just as you would any other image.

1. Select the Smart Object in the Document window and drag the resize handles to resize the image. You can maintain the width and height proportions by holding down the Shift key as you drag.
2. Click the Update from Original button in the Property inspector.
3. When you update the Smart Object, the web image non-destructively re-renders at the new size, based on the current contents of the original file, and the original optimization settings.

Edit a Smart Object's original Photoshop file

After you create a Smart Object on your Dreamweaver page, you can edit the original PSD file in Photoshop. After you make your changes in Photoshop, you can then easily update the web image in Dreamweaver.

1. Make sure that you have Photoshop set as your primary external image editor.
2. Select the Smart Object in the Document window.
3. Click the Edit button in the Property inspector.
4. Make your changes in Photoshop and save the new PSD file.

In Dreamweaver, select the Smart Object again and click the Update from Original button.

If you changed the size of your image in Photoshop, you need to reset the size of the web image in Dreamweaver. Dreamweaver updates a Smart Object based only on the contents of the original Photoshop file, and not its size. To sync the size of a web image with the size of the original Photoshop file, right-click the image and select Reset Size To Original.

Smart Object states

The following table lists the various states for Smart Objects.

SmartObject state	Description	Recommended action
Images synched	The web image is in sync with the current contents of the original Photoshop file. Width and height attributes in the HTML code match the dimensions of the web image.	None
Original asset modified	The original Photoshop file has been modified after the creation of the web image in Dreamweaver.	Use the Update From Original button in the Property inspector to sync the two images.
Dimensions of web image are different from selected HTML width and height	The width and height attributes in the HTML code are different from the width and height dimensions of the web image that Dreamweaver created upon insertion. If the web image's dimensions are smaller than the selected HTML width and height values, the web image can appear pixelated.	Use the Update From Original button in the Property inspector to re-create the web image from the original Photoshop file. Dreamweaver uses the currently specified HTML width and height dimensions when it re-creates the image.

Dimensions of original asset are too small for selected HTML width and height	The width and height attributes in the HTML code are larger than the width and height dimensions of the original Photoshop file. The web image can appear pixelated.	Don't create web images with dimensions larger than the dimensions of the original Photoshop file.
Original asset not found	Dreamweaver cannot find the original Photoshop file specified in the Original text box of the Property inspector.	Correct the file path in the Original text box of the Property inspector, or move the Photoshop file to the location that's currently specified.

Copy and paste a selection from Photoshop

You can copy all or some of a Photoshop image and paste the selection into your Dreamweaver page as a web-ready image. You can copy a single layer or a set of layers for a selected area of the image or you can copy a slice of the image. When you do this, however, Dreamweaver does not create a Smart Object.

While the Update from Original functionality is not available for pasted images, you can still open and edit the original Photoshop file by selecting the pasted image and clicking the Edit button in the Property inspector.

In Photoshop, do one of the following:

- Copy all or part of a single layer by using the Marquee tool to select the portion you want to copy, and then choose Edit > Copy. This copies only the active layer for the selected area into the clipboard. If you have layer-based effects, they are not copied.
- Copy and merge multiple layers by using the Marquee tool to select the portion you want to copy, and then choose Edit > Copy Merged. This flattens and copies all the selected area's active and lower layers into the clipboard. If you have layer-based effects associated with any of these layers, they are copied.
- Copy a slice by using the Slice Select tool to select the slice, and then choose Edit > Copy. This flattens and copies all the slice's active and lower layers into the clipboard.

You can choose Select > All to quickly select all of an image for copying.

In Dreamweaver (Design or Code view), place the insertion point on your page where you want the image inserted.

- Select Edit > Paste.
- In the Image Preview dialog box, adjust optimization settings as needed and click OK.
- Save the web ready image file to a location within your website's root folder.

Dreamweaver defines the image according to your optimization settings and places a web-ready version of your image in your page. Information about the image, such as the location of the original PSD source file, is saved in a Design Note, regardless of whether you have enabled Design Notes for your site. The Design Note allows you to return to edit the original Photoshop file from Dreamweaver.

Edit pasted images

After you paste Photoshop images in your Dreamweaver pages, you can edit the original PSD file in Photoshop. When using the copy/paste workflow, Adobe recommends that you always make your edits to the original PSD file (rather than the web-ready image itself), and then repaste to maintain single sourcing.

Make sure that you have Photoshop set as your primary external image editor for the file type you want to edit.

In Dreamweaver, select a web-ready image that was originally created in Photoshop and do one of the following:

- Click the Edit button in the image's Property inspector.
- Press Control as you double-click the file.

- Right-click an image, choose Edit Original With from the context menu, and then choose Photoshop.

This assumes that Photoshop is set as the primary external image editor for PSD image files. You may also want to set Photoshop as the default editor for JPEG, GIF, and PNG file types.

1. Edit the file in Photoshop.
2. Return to Dreamweaver and paste the updated image or selection into your page.
3. If you want to reoptimize the image at any time, you can select the image and click the Edit Image Settings button in the Property inspector

Setting Image Preview dialog box options

Image Preview dialog box options

- When you create a Smart Object or paste a selection from Photoshop, Dreamweaver displays the Image Preview dialog box. (Dreamweaver also displays this dialog box for any other kind of image if you select the image and click the Edit Image Settings button in the Property inspector.) This dialog box lets you define and preview settings for web-ready images using the right mix of color, compression, and quality.
- A web-ready image is one that can be displayed by all modern web browsers and looks the same no matter what system or browser the viewer is using. When you insert a Photoshop image, the Image Preview dialog box lets you adjust various settings for optimal web publication. In general, the settings result in a trade-off between quality and file size.
- Whatever settings you select only affect the exported version of the image file. The original Photoshop PSD or Fireworks PNG file always remains untouched.
- The Image Preview dialog box has three sections:
- The Options tab lets you define which file format to use and set preferences such as color.
- The File tab lets you set the scale factor and target file size of the image.
- The Preview panel lets you see a version of the image with your current settings.
- Many image options are available in the Options tab and they vary depending on the file format you choose. Several sets of GIF and JPEG image options are available for your convenience in the Saved Settings pop-up menu.

JPEG image options

- You can optimize a JPEG image by setting its compression and smoothing options. You cannot edit its color palette.
- Quality
- Use the slider to increase or decrease the quality of the image. Better quality results in a larger file.
- Smoothing
- Allows you to increase the smoothing as needed. Lower quality images may require a higher value.
- Progressive Browser Display
- Displays an image initially at low resolution and progressively increases the resolution during download. Not selected by default.
- Sharpen Color Edges
- Allows you to get a higher quality image.
- Matte
- Allows you to set the background of the image. You can maintain the transparency of a 32-bpc (bits per channel) PNG by clicking the transparency icon in the Matte dialog box. You can also use Matte to anti-alias soft-edged objects that lie directly above the canvas by matching the matte color to the target background.

View full size graphic

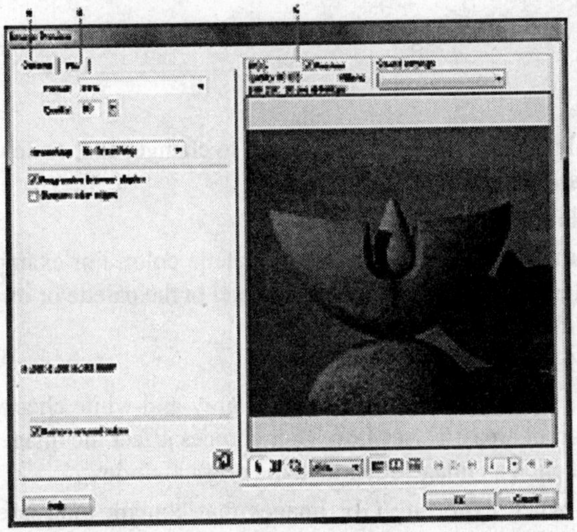

The Image Preview dialog box

A. Options tab **B.** File tab **C.** Preview panel

- Remove Unused Colors
- Reduces file size by removing colors not used in the image.
- Optimize to Size
- Specifies the image size, in kilobytes. For 8-bpc images, the wizard attempts to achieve the requested file size by adjusting the number of colors or dithering.

GIF and PNG image options

- In the Options tab, you can set a transparency value for individual colors in GIF and 8-bpc PNG images so that the background of the web page is visible through areas with those colors. Do this by adjusting the color palette on the left of the Options tab. PNG images that have 32-bpc format automatically contain transparency, though you won't see a transparency option for 32-bpc PNGs in the Optimize panel.
- Palette
- Set to Adaptive by default. Select one of the saved color palette settings from the pop-up menu if you want to use a preset set of options
- Loss
- Set to 0 by default. Not applicable to PNG images.
- Dither
- Approximates colors not in the current palette by alternating similar-colored pixels so that they appear to blend to the missing color. Dithering is especially helpful when exporting images with complex blends or gradients, or when exporting photographic images to an 8-bpc graphic format such as GIF. Not selected by default.
- Dithering can greatly increase file size.
- Number Of Colors List

- Set to 256 by default. The number of colors is dependent on the current behavior of the palette. For example, the "Web 216" palette only displays 216 colors.
- Color palette
- The display of colors varies depending on the selected palette behavior and maximum number of colors.
- Palette Tools
- Click any pixel in the palette and then click these icons to change, add, or delete color, or to make a color transparent, web safe, or locked.
- Select Transparency Color Icons
- These buttons allow you to select, add, or remove a palette color. For example, if you choose the Select Transparency Color option, you can click any pixel in the palette or on a point of color in the preview panel to render it transparent.
- Transparency Pop-Up Menu
- Allows you to set index, alpha, or no transparency. A gray-and-white checkerboard on document previews denotes transparent areas. To see how your choices affect the image, choose 2-up or 4-up in the image preview and click an image other than the original. Index
- Use index transparency when exporting GIF images that contain transparent areas. With index transparency, you set specific colors to be transparent upon export. Index transparency turns on or turns off pixels with specific color values.
- Alpha
- Use alpha transparency when exporting 8-bpc PNG images that contain transparent areas. Alpha transparency allows gradient transparency and semi-opaque pixels.
- Matte
- Lets you set the background of the image. You can maintain the transparency of a 32-bpc PNG by clicking the transparency icon in the Matte dialog box. You can also use Matte to anti-alias soft-edged objects that lie directly above the canvas by matching the matte color to the target background.
- Remove Unused Colors
- Reduces file size by removing colors not used in the image.
- Interlaced Browser Display
- Displays an interlaced image initially at low resolution and progressively increases to full resolution during download. Not selected by default.
- Optimize To Size
- Lets you specify a size, in kilobytes, for the image. For 8-bpc images, the wizard attempts to achieve the requested file size by adjusting the number of colors or dithering.

Saved settings

- Dreamweaver provides several option settings for your convenience. Depending on the saved settings you choose, the file-type-specific image options described above may change.
- GIF Web 216
- Forces all colors to web-safe colors. The color palette contains up to 216 colors.
- GIF Websnap 256
- Converts web-unsafe colors to their closest web-safe color. The color palette contains up to a maximum of 256 colors.
- GIF Websnap 128

- Converts web-unsafe colors to their closest web-safe color. The color palette contains up to 128 colors.
- GIF Adaptive 256
- A color palette that contains only the actual colors used in the graphic. The color palette contains up to a maximum of 256 colors.
- JPEG - Better Quality
- Sets quality to 80 and smoothing to 0, resulting in a high-quality but larger graphic.
- JPEG - Smaller File
- Sets quality to 60 and smoothing to 2, resulting in a graphic less than half the size of a Better Quality JPEG but with reduced quality.

Change the image's scale or export area options on the File tab

- Select the File tab.
- Shrink or expand the image in one of the following ways:
- Specify a scale percentage.
- Enter absolute pixel values for width or height.
- Select Constrain to maintain the image's original proportions as you rescale it.
- Change the shape of the placed image by choosing the Export Area option and doing one of the following:
- Drag the dotted border around the previewed image as needed. You can drag the image within the borders to move hidden areas into view.
- Enter pixel coordinates for the image's boundaries.

Preview and adjust images in the Preview panel

- In the Image Preview dialog box, select the Preview option if you want to see what the image looks like with your settings. If performance is an issue, you may want to deselect this option.
- Select one of the saved color palette settings from the Saved Settings pop-up menu if you want to use a preset set of options.
- If your image is larger than the preview area, use the pointer tool to grab the previewed image and pan it to see different parts.
- Use the crop tool to reduce the image's size. You may need to first zoom out to see the entire image.
- Choose a value from the Zoom pop-up menu to expand or reduce your view of the previewed image. You can also choose the Zoom tool and click to zoom in; Alt-click (Windows) or Option-click (Macintosh) to zoom out.
- You can preview two or four different optimizations by clicking the 2-up or 4-up button at the bottom of the preview panel and choosing different color palettes for each pane.
- The animation controls in the Image Preview dialog box are always disabled for Photoshop images.

Working with Flash

Edit a SWF file from Dreamweaver in Flash

If you have both Flash and Dreamweaver installed, you can select a SWF file in a Dreamweaver document and use Flash to edit it. Flash does not edit the SWF file directly; it edits the source document (FLA file) and re exports the SWF file.

1. In Dreamweaver, open the Property inspector (Window > Properties).
2. In the Dreamweaver document, do one of the following:

- Click the SWF file placeholder to select it; then in the Property inspector click Edit.
- Right-click the placeholder for the SWF file, and select Edit With Flash from the context menu.

3. Dreamweaver switches the focus to Flash, and Flash attempts to locate the Flash authoring file (FLA) for the selected SWF file. If Flash cannot locate the Flash authoring file, you are prompted to locate it.
4. If the FLA file or SWF file is locked, check out the file in Dreamweaver.
5. In Flash, edit the FLA file. The Flash Document window indicates that you are modifying the file from within Dreamweaver.
6. When you finish making edits, click Done.
7. Flash updates the FLA file, re exports it as a SWF file, closes, and then returns the focus to the Dreamweaver document.

To update the SWF file and keep Flash open, in Flash select File > Update for Dreamweaver.

To view the updated file in the document, click Play in the Dreamweaver Property inspector or press F12 to preview your page in a browser window.

Working with Bridge

About Adobe Bridge

Dreamweaver provides seamless integration with Adobe® Bridge, a stand-alone file-browsing application. Adobe Bridge is a cross-platform application included with Adobe® Creative Suite® 3 components that helps you locate, organize, and browse the assets you need to create print, web, video, and audio content. You can start Bridge from any Creative Suite component (except Acrobat 8), and use it to access both Adobe and non-Adobe asset types.

From Adobe Bridge, you can:

- Manage image files: Preview, search, sort, and process files in Bridge without opening individual applications. You can also edit metadata for files, and use Bridge to place files into your documents, projects, or compositions.
- Manage your photos: Import and edit photos from your digital camera card, group related photos in stacks, and open or import camera raw files and edit their settings without starting Photoshop. You can also search leading stock libraries and download royalty-free images by way of Adobe Stock Photos.
- Work with Adobe Version Cue®-managed assets.
- Perform automated tasks, such as batch commands.
- Synchronize color settings across color-managed Creative Suite components.

Start Bridge from Dreamweaver

You can start Bridge from Dreamweaver to view your files before placing them or dragging them in your page layout.

You can start Bridge in several different ways:

- Select File > Browse In Bridge.
- Click the Browse In Bridge button in the Standard toolbar.
- Press the Browse In Bridge shortcut from the keyboard: Control+Alt+O.

Bridge opens in File Browser mode, showing the contents of the last-opened folder in Dreamweaver. If Bridge was already open, it becomes the active window.

Placing files into Dreamweaver from Bridge

You can insert files into Dreamweaver pages by inserting them or by dragging them from Bridge into your page. The Dreamweaver document in which you want to insert the file must be open and in Design view to use this feature.

You can insert most file types into your pages, but Dreamweaver handles them differently:

- If you insert a web ready image (JPEG, GIF, or PNG), Dreamweaver inserts the image files directly into your page and places a copy in your website's default images folder.
- If you insert a Photoshop PSD file, you need to define its optimization settings before Dreamweaver can place it in your page.
- If you insert a non-image file, such as mp3, PDF, or a file with an unknown file type, Dreamweaver inserts a link to the source file.
- If you insert an HTML file, Dreamweaver inserts a link to the source file.
- If you have Microsoft Office installed and you are inserting a Microsoft Word or Excel file, you must specify if you want to insert the file itself or insert a link to the source file. If you want to insert the file, you can specify how much of the file's formatting you want to keep.

Place a Bridge file in your page

In Dreamweaver (Design view), place the insertion point on your page where you want the file inserted.

1. In Bridge, select the file and choose File > Place In Dreamweaver.
2. If the file is not in your site's root folder, you are prompted to copy it there.
3. If you have set Edit > Preferences > Accessibility to show attributes when inserting images, the Image Tag Accessibility Attributes dialog box is displayed when you insert web ready images such as JPEG and GIF.

If your insertion point is in Code view, Bridge starts as usual but cannot place the file. You can only place files in Design view.

Drag a file from Bridge into your page

In Dreamweaver (Design view), place the insertion point on your page where you want the image inserted.

1. Start Bridge if it isn't already open.
2. In Bridge, select one or more files and drag them into your Dreamweaver page.
3. If a file is not in your site's root folder, you are prompted to copy it there.
4. If you have set Edit > Preferences > Accessibility to show attributes when inserting images, the Image Tag Accessibility Attributes dialog box is displayed when you insert web safe images such as JPEG and GIF.

If your insertion point is in Code view, Bridge starts as usual but cannot place the file. You can only place files in Design view.

Working with Device Central

Using Adobe Device Central with Dreamweaver

Device Central enables Dreamweaver web designers and developers to preview how Dreamweaver files will look on a wide variety of mobile devices. Device Central uses Opera's Small Screen Rendering™ to give designers and developers an impression of how their web page looks on a small screen. It also enables designers and developers to test if their CSS behaves correctly. For example, a web developer may have a customer who wants to make a website available on mobile phones. The web developer can use Dreamweaver to create preliminary pages and use Device Central to test how those pages look on different devices.

Preview mobile content with Adobe Device Central and Dreamweaver

To preview pages created in Dreamweaver on various mobile devices, use Device Central with its built in Opera Small Screen Rendering feature. Different devices have different browsers installed, but the preview can give a good impression of how content will look and behave on a selected device.

1. Start Dreamweaver.
2. Open a file.
3. Do one of the following:
   - Select File > Preview in Browser > Device Central.
   - On the document window toolbar, click and hold the Preview/Debug In browser button and select Preview In Device Central.

The file is displayed in the Device Central Emulator tab. To continue testing, double-click the name of a different device in the Device Sets or Available Devices lists.

Tips for creating Dreamweaver web content for mobile devices

Device Central previews web pages created in Dreamweaver using Opera's Small-Screen Rendering. This preview can give you a good idea of what a web page looks like on a mobile device.

Note: Opera's Small-Screen Rendering may or may not be pre-installed on any individual emulated device. Device Central simply gives a preview of how the content would look if Opera's Small-Screen Rendering was installed.

Use the tips below to ensure that web pages created in Dreamweaver display well on mobile devices.

- If you use the Adobe® Spry framework to develop content, add the following line of HTML to your pages so they can render CSS and execute JavaScript™ correctly in Device Central:

```
<link href="SpryAccordion.css" media="screen" rel="stylesheet"
type="text/css"/>
<link href="SpryAccordion2.css" media="handheld" rel="stylesheet"
type="text/css"/>
```

- Opera's Small-Screen Rendering does not support frames, pop ups, underlining, strikethrough, overlining, blink, and marquee. Try to avoid these design elements.
- Keep web pages for mobile devices simple. In particular, use a minimum number of fonts, font sizes, and colors.
- Scaling down image sizes and reducing the number of colors required increase the chances that the images will appear as intended. Use CSS or HTML to specify an exact height and width for each image used. Provide alt text for all images.

The Opera software website is a good source of information about optimizing web pages for mobile devices.

Working with Dreamweaver sites

An Adobe® Dreamweaver® CS4 site is a collection of all of the files and assets in your website. You can create web pages on your computer, upload them to a web server, and maintain the site by transferring updated files whenever you save them. You can also edit and maintain websites that were created without Dreamweaver.

About Dreamweaver sites

A website is a set of linked documents and assets with shared attributes, such as related topics, a similar design, or a shared purpose. Dreamweaver is a site creation and management tool, so you can use it to create individual documents and complete websites.

In Dreamweaver the term "site" refers to a local or remote storage location for the documents that belong to a website. A Dreamweaver site provides a way to organize and manage all of your web documents, upload your site to a web server, track and maintain your links, and manage and share files. You should define a site to take full advantage of Dreamweaver features.

To define a Dreamweaver site, you only need to set up a local folder. To transfer files to a web server or to develop web applications, you must also add information for a remote site and testing server.

A Dreamweaver site consists of as many as three parts, or folders, depending on your development environment and the type of website you are developing:

Local root folder

Stores the files you're working on. Dreamweaver refers to this folder as your "local site." This folder can be on your local computer or it can be on a network server. If you work directly on the server, Dreamweaver uploads files to the server every time you save.

Remote folder

Stores your files for testing, production, collaboration, and so on. Dreamweaver refers to this folder as your "remote site" in the Files panel. Typically, your remote folder is on the computer where your web server is running.

Together, the local and remote folders enable you to transfer files between your local hard disk and web server, making it easy to manage files in your Dreamweaver sites.

Understanding local and remote folder structure

When you want to use Dreamweaver to connect to a remote folder, you specify the remote folder in the Remote Info category of the Site Definition dialog box. The remote folder that you specify (also referred to as the "host directory") should correspond to the local root folder of your Dreamweaver site. (The local root folder is the top-level folder of your Dreamweaver site.) Remote folders, like local folders, can have any title, but commonly, Internet Service Providers name the top-level remote folders for individual user accounts public_html, pub_html, or something similar. If you are in charge of your own remote server, and can name the remote folder anything you want, it is a good idea for your local root folder and remote folder to have the same name.

The following example shows a sample local root folder on the left and a sample remote folder on the right. The local root folder on the local machine maps directly to the remote folder on the web server, rather than to any of the remote folder's sub folders, or folders that exist above the remote folder in the directory structure.

Note: The above example illustrates one local root folder on the local machine, and one top-level remote folder on the remote web server. If, however, you are maintaining a number of Dreamweaver sites on your local machine, you would need an equal number of remote folders on the remote server. In such a case the above example would not apply, and you would instead create different remote folders within the public_html folder, and then map them to their corresponding local root folders on your local machine.When you first establish a remote connection, the remote folder on the web server is usually empty. Then, when you use Dreamweaver to upload all of the files in your local root folder, the remote folder populates with all of your web files. The directory structure of the remote folder and the local root folder should always be the same. (That is, there should always be a one-to-one correspondence between the files and folders in your local root folder, and the files and folders in your remote folder.) If the structure of the remote folder doesn't match the structure of the local root folder, Dreamweaver uploads files to the wrong place, where they might not be visible to site visitors. Additionally, image and link paths can easily break when folder and file structures are not in synch.

The remote folder must exist before Dreamweaver can connect to it. If you don't have a designated folder that acts as your remote folder on the web server, create one or ask the server's administrator to create one for you.

Using the Manage Sites dialog box

Use the Manage Sites dialog box to create a new site, edit a site, duplicate a site, remove a site, or import or export a site's settings.

1. Select Site > Manage Sites and select a site from the list on the left.
2. Click a button to select one of the options and click Done. New
3. Enables you to create a new site.

Edit

Enables you to edit an existing site.

Duplicate

Creates a copy of the site you selected. The copy appears in the site list window.

Remove

Deletes the selected site; you cannot undo this action.

Export

Enables you to export a site's settings as an XML file (*.ste).

Import

Enables you to select a site's settings file (*.ste) to import.

Set up and edit a local root folder

- After you plan your site structure, you set up (define) a site in Dreamweaver. You should also define a site in order to edit a website that wasn't created in Dreamweaver. Setting up a Dreamweaver site is a way to organize all of the documents associated with a website.
- The local root folder is your working directory for your Dreamweaver site. This folder can be on your local computer or on a network server.
- If you want to start editing files on your computer (without publishing them), set up only a local folder, and then add remote and testing information later.
- You can use Dreamweaver to edit an existing website on your local disk or to edit a remote site (or a branch of a remote site), even if you didn't use Dreamweaver to create the original site.
- You don't need to specify a remote folder if your local root folder is on the system running your web server. This implies the web server is running on your local computer.
- Select one of the following:
- To set up a new site, Select Site > New Site.
- To edit the setup of an existing site on your local disk or a remote site (or a branch of a remote site), whether it was created in Dreamweaver or not, select Site > Manage Sites and click Edit.
- If you haven't defined any Dreamweaver sites, the Site Definition dialog box appears and you don't need to click New.
- Enter the setup information:
- To set up a site using the site setup wizard, click the Basic tab and follow the prompts.
- To set up local, remote, and testing folders (for processing dynamic pages) directly, click the Advanced tab, select the Local Info category and set the options.
- Click OK and Done to create the site (displayed in the Files panel).

Local root folder setup options

- If you choose to set the local root folder options directly instead of by using the Basic tab of the Site Definition dialog box, click the Advanced tab and enter the information.
- Only the first two options are required to set up a working site on your computer. Site Name
- The name that appears in the Files panel and in the Manage Sites dialog box; it does not appear in the browser.
- Local Root Folder
- The name of the folder on your local disk where you store site files, templates, and library items. Create a folder on your hard disk or click the folder icon to browse to the folder. When Dreamweaver resolves root-relative links, it does so relative to this folder.
- Default Images Folder
- The path to the folder where the images you use in your site are kept. Enter the path or click the folder icon to browse to the folder.
- Links Relative To
- Changes the relative path of the links you create to other pages in the site. By default, Dreamweaver creates links using document-relative paths. Select the Site Root option to change the path setting and make sure that you specify the HTTP address in the HTTP Address option.
- Changing this setting does not convert the path of existing links; the setting will only apply to new links you create visually with Dreamweaver.
- Content linked with a site root-relative path does not appear when you preview documents in a local browser unless you specify a testing server, or select the Preview Using Temporary File option in Edit > Preferences > Preview In Browser. This is because browsers don't recognize site roots—servers do.
- HTTP Address
- The URL that your website will use. This enables Dreamweaver to verify links within the site that use absolute URLs or site root-relative paths. Dreamweaver also uses this address to make sure site root-relative links work on the remote server, which may have a different site root. For example, if you are linking to an image file located on your hard disk in the C:\Sales\images\ folder (where Sales is your local root folder), and the URL of your completed site is http://www.mysite.com/SalesApp/ (where SalesApp is your remote root folder), you should enter the URL in the HTTP Address text box to ensure that the path to the linked file on the remote server is /SalesApp/images/.
- Use Case-sensitive Link Checking
- Checks that the case of the links matches the case of the filenames when Dreamweaver checks links. This option is useful on UNIX systems where filenames are case-sensitive.
- Enable Cache
- Indicates whether to create a local cache to improve the speed of link and site management tasks. If you do not select this option, Dreamweaver asks you if you want to create a cache again before it creates the site. It is a good idea to select this option because the Assets panel (in the Files panel group) only works if a cache is created.

Set up a remote folder

- This folder is where you store files for production, collaboration, deployment, or a number of other scenarios. Typically, the remote folder is on the computer where your web server is running. You can set options for this folder by answering the wizard questions in the Basic tab or by clicking the Advanced tab and entering the information directly.

- In the Dreamweaver Files panel, the remote folder is referred to as your *remote site*. When you set up a remote folder, you must select an access method for Dreamweaver to upload and download files to your web server.
- Dreamweaver supports connections to IPv6-enabled servers. Supported connection types include FTP, SFTP, WebDav, and RDS.
- Select Site > Manage Sites.
- Click New and select Site to set up a new site, or select an existing Dreamweaver site and click Edit.
- Click the Advanced tab, select the Remote Info category and select the access method you want to use to transfer files between local and remote folders: None
- Keep this default setting if you do not plan to upload your site to a server.
- FTP
- Use this setting if you connect to your web server using FTP.
- Local/Network
- Use this setting to access a network folder, or if you are storing files or running your testing server on your local computer.
- RDS
- (Remote Development Services) Use this setting if you connect to your web server using RDS. For this access method, your remote folder must be on a computer running Adobe® ColdFusion®.
- Microsoft Visual SourceSafe
- Use this setting if you connect to your web server using Microsoft Visual SourceSafe. Support for this method is only available for Windows; to use it, you must have Microsoft Visual SourceSafe Client version 6 installed.
- WebDAV
- Use this setting if you connect to your web server using the WebDAV protocol.
- For this access method, you must have a server that supports this protocol, such as Microsoft Internet Information Server (IIS) 5.0 or an appropriately configured installation of Apache web server.
- If you select WebDAV as your access method, and you are using Dreamweaver in a multiuser environment, you should also make sure that all of your users select WebDAV as the access method. If some users select WebDAV, and other users select other access methods (FTP, for example), Dreamweaver's check-in/check-out feature will not work as expected, since WebDAV uses its own locking system.

Set options for FTP access

- Select Site > Manage Sites.
- Click New and select Site to set up a new site, or select an existing Dreamweaver site and click Edit.
- Select the Advanced tab and click the Remote Info category.
- Select FTP and enter the host name of the FTP host to which you upload files for your website.
- Your FTP host is the full Internet name of a computer system, such as ftp.mindspring.com. Enter the full host name without any additional text. In particular, don't add a protocol name in front of the host name.

- If you do not know your FTP host, contact your web hosting company.
- Enter the host directory (folder) at the remote site where you store documents that are visible to the public.
- If you're uncertain about what to enter as the host directory, contact the server's administrator or leave the text box blank. On some servers, your root directory is the same as the directory you first connect to with FTP. To find out, connect to the server. If a folder with a name like public_html, or www, or your login name, appears in the Remote File view in your Files panel, that's probably the directory you should enter in the Host Directory text box.
- Enter the login name and password that you use to connect to the FTP server.
- Click Test to test your login name and password.
- Dreamweaver saves your password by default. Deselect the Save option if you prefer that Dreamweaver prompt you for a password each time you connect to the remote server.
- Select Use Passive FTP if your firewall configuration requires use of passive FTP.
- Passive FTP enables your local software to set up the FTP connection rather than requesting the remote server to set it up. If you're not sure whether you use passive FTP, check with your system administrator.
- Select Use IPv6 Transfer Mode if you are using an IPv6-enabled FTP server.
- With the deployment of version 6 of the Internet Protocol (IPv6), EPRT and EPSV have replaced the FTP commands PORT and PASV, respectively. Thus, if you are trying to connect to an IPv6-enabled FTP server, you must use the extended passive (EPSV) and the extended active (EPRT) commands for your data connection.
- Select Use Firewall if you connect to the remote server from behind a firewall.
- Click Firewall Settings to edit your firewall host or port.
- Select Use Secure FTP (SFTP) if your firewall configurations requires use of secure FTP.
- Click the Server Compatibility button for more advanced options related to server connection.
- Select Maintain Synchronization Information if you want to automatically synchronize your local and remote files. (This option is selected by default.)
- Select Automatically Upload Files to Server on Save if you want Dreamweaver to upload your file to your remote site when you save the file.
- Select Enable File Check In and Check Out if you want to activate the Check In/Out system.
- Click OK.

Connect to or disconnect from a remote folder with FTP access

- In the Files panel:
- To connect, click Connects to Remote Host in the toolbar.
- To disconnect, click Disconnect in the toolbar.

Set options for local or network access

- Select Site > Manage Sites.
- Click New and select Site to set up a new site, or select an existing Dreamweaver site and click Edit.
- Select the Advanced tab, click the Remote Info category, and select Local/Network.
- Click the folder icon beside the Remote Folder text box to browse to and select the folder where you store your site files.

- Select Maintain Synchronization Information if you want to automatically synchronize your local and remote files. (This option is selected by default.)
- Select Automatically Upload Files To Server On Save if you want Dreamweaver to upload your file to your remote site when you save the file.
- Select Enable File Check In And Check Out if you want to activate the Check In/Out system.
- Click OK.

Set options for WebDAV access

- Select Site > Manage Sites.
- Click New and select Site to set up a new site, or select an existing Dreamweaver site and click Edit.
- Select the Advanced tab, click the Remote Info category, and select WebDAV.
- For the URL, enter the complete URL to the directory on the WebDAV server you want to connect to.
- This URL includes the protocol, port, and directory (if not the root directory). For example, http://webdav.mydomain.net/mysite.
- Enter your user name and password.
- This information is for server authentication and is not related to Dreamweaver. If you are not sure of your user name and password, check with your system administrator or webmaster.
- Click Test to test your connection settings.
- Click Save if you want Dreamweaver to remember your password each time you start a new session.
- Select Maintain Synchronization Information if you want Dreamweaver to automatically synchronize your local and remote files. (This option is selected by default.)
- Select Automatically Upload Files To Server On Save if you want Dreamweaver to upload your file to your remote site when you save the file.
- Select Enable File Check In And Check Out if you want to activate the Check In/Out system.

Connect to or disconnect from a remote folder with network access

- You don't need to connect to the remote folder; you're always connected. Click the Refresh button to see your remote files.

Set options for RDS access

- Select Site > Manage Sites.
- Click New and select Site to set up a new site, or select an existing Dreamweaver site and click Edit.
- Select the Advanced tab, click the Remote Info category, and select RDS.
- Click the Settings button and provide the following information in the Configure RDS Server dialog box:
- Enter the name of the host computer where your web server is installed.
- The host name is probably an IP address or a URL. If you are unsure, ask your administrator.
- Enter the port number that you connect to.
- Enter your root remote folder as the host directory.
- For example, c:\inetpub\wwwroot\myHostDir\.
- Enter your RDS user name and password.
- These options might not appear if you set your user name and password in the ColdFusion Administrator security settings.

- Select Save if you want Dreamweaver to remember your settings.
- Click OK to close the Configure RDS Server dialog box.
- Select the Automatically Upload Files To Server On Save if you want Dreamweaver to upload your file to your remote site when you save the file.
- Select Enable File Check In And Check Out if you want to activate the Check In/Out system and click OK.

Set up Microsoft Visual SourceSafe access

- Select Site > Manage Sites.
- Click New and select Site to set up a new site, or select an existing Dreamweaver site and click Edit.
- Select the Advanced tab, click the Remote Info category, and select Microsoft Visual SourceSafe.
- Click the Settings button and provide the following information in the Open Microsoft Visual SourceSafe Database dialog box:
- For the Database Path, click Browse to browse for the Visual SourceSafe database you want, or enter the full file path.
- The file you select becomes the srcsafe.ini file used to initialize Visual SourceSafe.
- For Project, enter the project within the Visual SourceSafe database you want to use as the remote site's root directory.
- For Username and Password, enter your login user name and password for the selected database.
- If you don't know your user name and password, check with your system administrator.
- Select the Save option if you want Dreamweaver to remember your settings.
- Click OK to return to the Site Definition dialog box.
- Select Automatically Upload Files To Server On Save if you want Dreamweaver to upload your file to your remote site when you save the file.
- Deselect Check Out Files When Opening if you do not want Dreamweaver to download your files from the server automatically when you open the local file.

Troubleshoot the remote folder setup

The following list provides information on common problems you may encounter in setting up a remote folder, and how to resolve them:

- The Dreamweaver FTP implementation might not work properly with certain proxy servers, multilevel firewalls, and other forms of indirect server access. If you encounter problems with FTP access, ask your local system administrator for help.
- For a Dreamweaver FTP implementation, you must connect to the remote system's root folder. Be sure to indicate the remote system's root folder as the host directory. If you've specified the host directory using a single slash (/), you might need to specify a relative path from the directory you are connecting to and the remote root folder. For example, if the remote root folder is a higher level directory, you may need to specify a ../../ for the host directory.
- Use underscores in place of spaces, and avoid special characters in file and folder names wherever possible. Colons, slashes, periods, and apostrophes in file or folder names can sometimes cause problems.
- If you encounter problems with long filenames, rename them with shorter names. On the Mac OS, filenames cannot be more than 31 characters long.

- Many servers use symbolic links (UNIX), shortcuts (Windows), or aliases (Macintosh) to connect a folder on one part of the server's disk with another folder elsewhere. Such aliases usually have no effect on your ability to connect to the appropriate folder or directory; however, if you can connect to one part of the server but not another, there might be an alias discrepancy.
- If you encounter an error message such as "cannot put file," your remote folder may be out of space.

Note: In general, when you encounter a problem with an FTP transfer, examine the FTP log by selecting Window > Results (Windows) or Site > FTP Log (Macintosh), then clicking the FTP Log tag.

11 Keyboard Shortcuts of Dreamweaver CS4

Description	*Keyboard command*
Add a keyframe	Shift+F9
Add a new frame to	Alt+Control-drag frame border frameset using push method
Add a new frame to frameset	Alt-drag frame border
Add a row at end of table	Tab in the last cell
Add object to timeline	Control+Alt+Shift+T
Add or remove layer from selection	Shift-click layer
Add selected items to library	Control+Shift+B
Align selected layers to the	Control+Up/Down/Left/Top/Bottom/Left/Right Right Arrow of the last selected layer
Alignment > Center	Control+Shift+Alt+C
Alignment > Left	Control+Shift+Alt+L
Alignment > Right	Control+Shift+Alt+R
Apply Headings 1 through 6 to a paragraph	Control+1 through 6
Balance Braces	Control+'
Change image source attribute	Double-click image
Change link	Control+L
Character select left	Shift+Left
Character select right	Shift+Right
Check in	Control+Shift+Alt+U
Check links in the entire site	Control+F8
Check links selected	Shift+F8
Check links	Shift + F8
Check out	Control+Shift+Alt+D
Check spelling	Shift+F7
Clear	Delete
Close	Control+W
Copy text or object to another place in the page to new location	Control-drag selected item
Copy	Control+C or Control+Ins

Description	*Keyboard command*
Create a new paragraph	Enter
Create hyperlink (select text)	Control+L
Create new editable region	Control+Alt+V
Create new file	Control+Shift+N
Create new folder	Control+Shift+Alt+N
Cut	Control+X or Shift+Del
Debug in primary browser	Alt+F12
Debug in secondary browser	Control+Alt+F12
Delete a column	Control+Shift+ - (hyphen)
Delete the current row	Control+Shift+M
Drag and drop to create a hyperlink from a object, then Shift-drag	Select the text, image, or document the selection to a file in the Site window
Drag and drop to create a hyperlink using the Property inspector	Select the text, image, or object, then drag the point-to-file icon in Property inspector to a file in the Site window
Dreamweaver Support Center	Control+F1
Edit image in external editor	Control—double-click image
Edit Style Sheet	Control+Shift+E
Exit/Quit	Control+Q
Find and Replace	Control+F
Find next	F3
Find Next/Find Again	F3
Find	Control+F
Format > None	Control+0 (zero)
Get selected files or folders	Control+Shift+D or drag from remote FTP site files from Remote to Local pane in Site window
Head content	Control+Shift+W
Indent Code	Control+Shift+]
Indent	Control+]
Insert a column	Control+Shift+A
Insert a line break 	Shift+Enter
Insert a nonbreaking space	Control+Shift+Spacebar
Insert a row (before current)	Control+M
Insert any object (image, Shockwave movie, and so on)	Drag file from the Explorer or Site window to the
Insert Flash movie	Control+Alt+F
Insert Image	Control+Alt+I

Description	Keyboard command
Insert Named anchor	Control+Alt+A
Insert Shockwave Director movie	Control+Alt+D
Insert Table	Control+Alt+T
Launch External Editor	Control+E
Layout view	Control+F6
Link to existing file	Control+Shift+K
Make root	Control+Shift+R
Make selected layers the same height	Control+Shift+]
Make selected layers the same width	Control+Shift+[
Make selected text bold	Control+B
Make selected text italic	Control+I
Merge selected table cells	Control+Alt+M
Minimize all windows	Shift+F4
Move selected layer by pixels	Arrow keys
Move selected layer by snapping increment	Shift+arrow keys
Move text or object to another place in the page	Drag selected item to new location
Move to end of code	Control+End
Move to end of line	End
Move to page down	Page Down
Move to page up	Page Up
Move to start of line	Home
Move to the next cell	Tab
Move to the previous cell	Shift+Tab
Move to top of code	Control+Home
New document	Control+N
Open an HTML file	Control+O, or drag the file from the Explorer or Site window to the Document window
Open and close the Property inspector	Control+Shift+J
Open in frame	Control+Shift+O
Open Quick Tag Editor	Control+T
Open selection	Control+Shift+Alt+O
Open the History panel	Shift F10
Open the linked-to document in Dreamweaver	Control-double-click link
Outdent Code	Control+Shift+[

Description	Keyboard command
Outdent	Control+[
Page properties	Control+Shift+J
Paragraph Format	Control+Shift+P
Paste	Control+V or Shift+Ins
Play all plugins	Control+Shift+Alt+P
Play plugin	Control+Alt+P
Play recorded command	Control+P
Preferences	Control+U
Preview in primary browser	F12
Preview in secondary browser	Control+F12
Put selected files or folders to remote FTP site	Control+Shift+U or drag files from Local to Remote pane in Site window
Redo	Control+Y or Control+Shift+Z
Reference	Shift+F1
Refresh Local pane	Shift+F5
Refresh remote site	Alt+F5
Remove a keyframe	Delete
Remove hyperlink	Control+Shift+L
Remove link	Delete
Rename file	F2
Replace	Control+H
Resize selected layer by pixels	Control+Arrow keys
Resize selected layer by snapping increment	Control+Shift+arrow keys
Restore all windows	Alt+Shift+F4
Rulers	Control+Alt+R
Save as	Control+Shift+S
Save	Control+S
Select a frame	Alt-click in frame
Select a layer	Control+Shift-click
Select a word	Double-click
Select All	Control+A
Select and move layer	Shift+Control-drag
Select child	Control+Shift+>
Select first child frame or frameset	Alt+Down Arrow
Select line down	Shift+Down

Description	*Keyboard command*
Select line up	Shift+Up
Select next frame or frameset	Alt+Right Arrow
Select parent frameset	Alt+Up Arrow
Select parent tag	Control+Shift+<
Select previous frame or frameset	Alt+Left Arrow
Select table (with cursor inside the table)	Control+A
Select to end of code	Control+Shift+End
Select to page down	Shift+Page Down
Select to page up	Shift+Page Up
Select to top of code	Control+Shift+Home
Select word left	Control+Shift+Left
Select word right	Control+Shift+Right
Show Grid	Control+Alt+G
Show page titles	Control+Shift+T
Show/Hide Floating panels	F4
Show/Hide link	Control+Shift+Y
Snap to Grid	Control+Alt+Shift+G
Split table cells	Control+Alt+S
Standard view	Control+Shift+F6
Start/stop recording command	Control+Shift+X
Stop all plugins	Control+Shift+Alt+X
Switch between design view and code editors	Control+Tab
Switch to design view	Control+Tab
Toggle Assets	F11
Toggle Behaviors	Shift+F3
Toggle objects	Control+F2
Toggle breakpoint	Control+Alt+B
Toggle Code inspector	F10
Toggle CSS Styles	Shift+F11
Toggle Frames	Shift+F2
Toggle History	Shift+F10
Toggle HTML Styles	Control+F11
Toggle Layers	F2
Toggle nesting preference on or off when creating a layer	Control-drag
Toggle Properties	Control+F3

Description	Keyboard command
Toggle Reference	Control+Shift+F1
Toggle Site Files	F5
Toggle Site Map	Control+F5
Toggle the display of the grid	Control+Shift+Alt+G
Toggle Timelines	Shift+F9
Toolbar	Control+Shift+T
Undo	Control+Z
Update table layout (forces a redraw when in "faster table editing" mode)	Control+Spacebar
Using Dreamweaver Help Topics	F1
View site files	F8
View site map	Alt+F8
Visual Aids	Control+Shift+I
Zoom in site map	Control+ + (plus)
Zoom out site map	Control+ - (hyphen)

12 Questions

Answer the Following Questions

Chapter 1 Introduction to Dreamweaver CS4

1. Describe the new additions to the version CS4 of Dreamweaver.
2. How would you start Dreamweaver CS4?
3. Describe the various options of toolbar.
4. Describe the various options of statusbar.
5. Describe the various options of Property Inspector.
6. Which are the buttons on the Object Panels?
7. Describe the various options of following panels:
   Common Objects
   Layout Objects
   Forms objects
   Text
   HTML
8. How would you customize Dreamweaver for you?

Chapter 2 Creating a New Page in Dreamweaver CS4

1. How would you create a new page?
2. What steps would you take to see your page in the browser?
3. How would add text to your page?
4. Describe the process of adding a line in the page.
5. How would you do the following:
   Create Unordered List
   Create Ordered List
   Change Font
   Add New Font
   Make Text Bold/Italics
   Change Colour of the Text
   Create a New CSS Style
   Change a New CSS Style

Chapter 3 Adding Graphics and Multimedia in DreamWeaver CS4

1. Describe the process of doing the following:

   Adding an Image

   Adding a Border to an Image

   Resizinng the Image

   Changing Dimensions by Dragging

   Wrapping Text around Image

   Adding Horizontal Rule

   Adding Background Image

   Adding Multimedia Files

   Add a Sound File

   Inserting a Plugin object

   Adding Looping to the Sound

   Creating Flash Text

   Creating a Flash Button

   Inserting a Java Applet

   Inserting applet into a Web page

   Downloading Plugins

   Adding Flash Files

Chapter 4 Working with Tables in Dreamweaver CS4

1. How would you insert a table in your web page?
2. Describe how would you do the following:

   Insert a Table within a Table

   Change Background Colour of a Table

   Insert Image in a Table

   Insert Rows or Columns in a Table

   Split a Table Cell

   Merge Cells of a Table

   Design Your Page Layout Using Tables

   Add a Layout Table and Layout cells

   Create a page layout

   Use Autostretch to Fit the Page

   Turn on Autostretch

   Align Table Cell Content

   Turn Your Table into Layers

Chapter 5 Working with Forms in Dreamweaver CS4

1. How would you do the following:

   Create a Form

   Add a Form

Add Text Fields
Apply Text Field Attributes
Add Labels
Add Radio Buttons
Add Check Boxes
Add a List of Menu
Create a list
Add Push Buttons and Picture Buttons
Add submit and Reset Buttons
Add an Image Field to Submit a Form
Add a generic Button
Create a Jump Menu
Validate the Form

Chapter 6 Working with Frames in Dreamweaver CS4

1. Describe how you would do the following?
Dividing a Page into Frames
Inserting a Frameset
Adding Contents to Frames
Adding New Content to a Frame
Saving Frames Pages
Saving the Frameset
Naming Frames
Deleting Frames
Hyperlinking to a Frame
Changing Frame Dimensions
Setting Frame Borders
Turning off the Borders
Adding Noframes Content
Nesting Page Frames
Viewing Library Items
Viewing Templates

Chapter 7 Working with Style Sheets and Layers in Dreamweaver CS4

1. Describe how would you do the following?
Create a HTML Tag
Create a Class
Apply a Class
Edit a Style Sheet Class
Use CSS selectors to Modify Links

Create an External Style Sheet

Create a Layer

Resize a Layer

Reposition a Layer

Add a Background Color to a Layer

Change the Stacking Order of Layers

Chapter 8 Creating and Applying Templates in Dreamweaver CS4

1. How would you do the following?

   Create a Template

   Use the Template Category of the Asset Panel

   Create a template from an Existing Web page

   Create a Template from Scratch

   Make an Existing Region Editable

   Make a New Editable Region

   Apply a Template to a Web Page

   Make Changes to a Template

   Update Pages That Contain the Template

   Use Behaviours, Styles and Timelines in Templates

Chapter 9 More Commands of Dreamweaver CS4

1. How would you create a Custom Snippet?
2. Describe the process of Editing the Keyboard Shortcuts.
3. Describe the process of Using Third Party Extensions.
4. How would you share searches in Dreamweaver CS4?
5. How would you make a menu command?